THE DISSOLUTION OF YUGOSLAVIA AND THE BADINTER ARBITRATION COMMISSION

This book is dedicated to my mother and in memory of my father

The Dissolution of Yugoslavia and the Badinter Arbitration Commission

A contextual study of peace-making efforts in the post-Cold War world

STEVE TERRETT, LLB, PhD
Lecturer in Law
British and European Law Centre, University of Warsaw

Routledge
Taylor & Francis Group
LONDON AND NEW YORK

First published 2000 by Dartmouth Publishing Company and Ashgate Publishing

Reissued 2018 by Routledge
2 Park Square, Milton Park, Abingdon, Oxon OX14 4RN
711 Third Avenue, New York, NY 10017, USA

Routledge is an imprint of the Taylor & Francis Group, an informa business

A Library of Congress record exists under LC control number: 00029954

ISBN 13: 978-1-138-72041-1 (hbk)
ISBN 13: 978-1-138-72039-8 (pbk)
ISBN 13: 978-1-315-19504-9 (ebk)

Contents

Preface

> "[The end of the Cold War offers]...the opportunity to forge for ourselves and for future generations a new world order, a world where the rule of law, not the law of the jungle, governs the conduct of nations".
> George Bush's Address to the Nation as American President, 16th January 1991.

The Yugoslav conflict developed at the same time as a New World Order was being proclaimed and when the rhetoric of international law's capabilities was at its highest for some time. Unfortunately, it also occurred at a time when the majority of the world's States were focusing largely on domestic, rather than international, issues and before the practicalities of greater international cooperation had been worked out.

From a narrow perspective, Yugoslavia is important because of the way it shocked the international community into realising that the rhetoric of New World Orders was some way ahead of the capacity for practical international intervention to prevent such conflicts. This realisation was enhanced by widespread atrocities and mass population movements, prompting comparisons with World War Two. Much has been written on various aspects of the conflict and its influence of international law will probably not be fully realised for some time. This study focuses on the reasons behind Yugoslavia's dissolution and the role of the Badinter Commission in seeking to assist peaceful resolution of the conflicts which developed during the dissolution process. From a wider perspective, Yugoslavia is an important case-study because it allows assessment of how the major international actors attempted to resolve a conflict in the immediate post-Cold War period. Yugoslavia shows the stark contrast between the rhetoric of a New World Order and the more somber reality. Furthermore, it evidences important international trends, such as the changing nature of threats to international peace and security and the emerging framework within attempts are made to restore peace.

The Badinter Commission is important for a number of reasons. First, it is significant because of its role as the first international judicial organ to become involved in the Yugoslav conflict. The Commission is unique in having provided a legal appraisal of events surrounding the dissolution of a sovereign State as they occurred. In this sense, Yugoslavia benefited from a greater level of contemporaneous international legal advice than any other conflict. The nature and validity of this advice forms an important part of this study. Second, the Commission's composition furthers its uniqueness, since it was composed for much of its working-life by constitutional lawyers with experience in domestic, rather than international matters. In light of what will be said about the increasing international focus on issues *within* States, rather than *between* them, this case-study evidences some of the problems involved in seeking peaceful dispute-resolution in intra-State conflicts. Furthermore, as sub-State actors and intra-State conflicts become the focus of an increasing amount of international law, the comments of constitutional judges may help to identify areas of common concern to both international and domestic law. Finally, the Commission's jurisprudence is interesting because it covered many important international law doctrines and international political issues, such as self-determination, State-succession and State-recognition which have rarely received judicial consideration either during or after previous conflicts. Although this book discusses all of the Commission's jurisprudence, practical considerations mitigate against an in-depth analysis of all aspects covered therein. Accordingly, since the book's primary focus is on Yugoslavia's *dissolution* and the lessons this may yield for other intra-State conflicts, we will only briefly touch upon issues of State-succession and war damages, which relate more to events *after* Yugoslavia's dissolution than the dissolution process itself.

As an inter-disciplinary evaluation of the Yugoslav conflict this book should prove relevant to students of international law, international relations, politics and those researching central/eastern European studies. The book will be divided into ten chapters. Chapter 1 outlines the methodology and describes the predominant techniques adopted throughout the research and subsequent chapters. Chapter 2 provides a brief historical analysis of Yugoslavia's history and describes the main events leading-up to its dissolution in 1990-1991. A knowledge of these events is a necessary pre-condition to a proper evaluation of the Badinter Commission. Chapter 3 places the Yugoslav conflict in its wider international context and highlights some of the more important features of the post-Cold War international scenario to show that Yugoslavia's dissolution was the result of international as well as internal factors. These international factors may affect other States similarly. Chapter 4 analyses the responses of the major international institutions involved in the conflict. Chapter 5 begins an analysis of the Commission's role in the dissolution process, focusing on its work under the EC's Conference on Yugoslavia. Chapter 6 continues this analysis, focusing on the Commission's role within the International Conference on the Former Yugoslavia, set up under the joint auspices of the EC and UN. Chapter 7 examines Yugoslavia's dissolution in light of the Commission's jurisprudence relating to self-determination and recognition of Statehood. Chapter 8 discusses how Yugoslavia may be seen as an example of the changing nature of contemporary threats to international peace and security, and argues for an appropriate international legal response. Chapter 9 continues arguments for international legal developments in respect of the peaceful dispute-resolution mechanisms. Chapter 10 appraises the foregoing chapters and recapitulates the main arguments.

Acknowledgements

Many people have played an important part in making it possible for me to complete this book. In particular, Professor Dominic McGoldrick has been a constant source of inspiration, support and friendship and I owe him more than I could ever hope to repay. The preparation of camera-ready copy would also not have been possible without the tremendous assistance of Gaye Harrison and Steve Cooper. My friends and family have shown faith in me throughout my studies and early academic career and I thank each and every one of them for their love and friendship. Finally, and most importantly, I wish to thank my mother for everything she has given me and remind her that she has always been, and continues to be, the single most influential person in my life.

Table of Treaties and International Agreements

1648	Peace of Westphalia
1794	US-UK Jay Treaty of Amity, Commerce and Navigation
1814	US-UK Treaty of Ghent
1864	Geneva Convention for the Amelioration of the Condition of the Wounded in Armies in the Field
1866	France-Spain Treaty of Bayonne
1868	St. Petersburg Declaration Renouncing the Use of Explosive Projectiles Under 400 Grammes in Weight
1899	Hague Convention on the Peaceful Settlement of International Disputes
1906	Geneva Convention on the Wounded and Sick
1907	Hague Convention on the Peaceful Settlement of Disputes
	Hague Convention on the Laws and Customs of War
1913-40	Bryan Treaties
1917	Declaration of Corfu
1918	Italy-Allies London Treaty
1919	Treaty of Versailles
	Covenant of the League of Nations
1920	Treaty of Rapallo
	Statute of the Permanent Court of International Justice
1928	Pact of Paris
1933	Montevideo Convention on the Rights and Duties of States
1945	Charter of the United Nations
	Statute of the International Court of Justice
	North Atlantic Treaty
1949	Geneva Conventions
1954	Hague Convention for the Protection of Cultural Property in the Event of Armed Conflict
1957	Treaty of Rome
1963	Constitution of the SFRY
1966	International Covenants

1968	Nuclear Non-Proliferation Treaty
1969	Vienna Convention on the Law of Treaties
1974	Constitution of the SFRY
1975	CSCE Helsinki Final Act
1976	Algiers Declaration on the Rights of Peoples
1977	Geneva Protocols Additional to the 1949 Conventions
	UNCITRAL Model Rules of Arbitration
1978	Vienna Convention on the Succession of States in Respect of Treaties
1981	African Charter on Human Rights and Peoples
	US-Iran Claim Tribunal Agreement
	Statute of the European Court of Justice
1983	Vienna Convention on Succession of States in respect of State Property, Archives and Debts
1986	Single European Act
1990	CSCE Charter of Paris
1991	Treaty on Succession to the Soviet Union's State Debts and Assets
1992	Permanent Court of Arbitration's Optional Rules for Arbitration Between Two States
	CSCE Helsinki Conference Documentation
	CSCE Court of Conciliation and Arbitration Convention
	Treaty on European Union
	UN Declaration on the Rights of Persons Belonging to National or Ethnic, Religious and Linguistic Minorities
1994	CSCE Budapest Conference Documents
	EC Pact on Stability in Europe
1995	General Framework Agreement for Peace in Bosnia-Hercegovina
1998	Statute of the Permanent International Criminal Court

Table of Cases

Aaland Islands Case (1920), LNOJ, Supp. 4
Admissions Case (1947), ICJ Rep, 57
Arbitral Award of 31st July 1989 Case (1991), ICJ Rep, 70
Barcelona Traction Case (1970), ICJ Rep, 32
Bosnia-Hercegovina v Yugoslavia (1996), ICJ Rep, 3
Burkino Faso/Mali (Frontier Dispute Case) (1986), ICJ Rep, 554
Caroline Case (1841), 29 Brit & For.St. Papers, 1137
Case re Military Activities in and Against Nicaragua (1986), ICJ Rep, 14
Certain Expenses Case (1962), ICJ Rep, 151
Certain German Interests in Upper Silesia (1926), PCIJ Series B, 3
East Timor Case (1995), ICJ Rep, 90
Eastern Carelia Case (1923), PCIJ Series B, 27
Fisheries (Jurisdiction) Case (1973), ICJ Rep, 3
German Settlers Case (1928), PCIJ Rep Series B, 29
ICI v EC Commission (re Dyestuffs) (1972) ECR, 619
ILO Administrative Tribunal Judgement Case (1956), ICJ Rep, 77
Interpretation of Greco-Turkish Agreement (1928), PCIJ Series B, 20
Interpretation of Peace Treaties Case (1950), ICJ Rep, 3
Interpretation of Neuilly Peace Treaty (1924), PCIJ Series A, 4
Legality of Secession of Quebec Case (1998), Can. Rep, 52
Legality of Threat or Use of Nuclear Weapons Case (1996), ICJ Rep, 1
Maritime Safety-Committee Constitution Case (1960), ICJ Rep, 160
Mavrommatis Palestinian Concessions Case (1924), PCIJ Series A, 11
Namibia (South-West Africa) Case (1971), ICJ Rep, 16
Nationality Decrees in Tunisia and Morocco (1923), PCIJ Series B, 24
North-Sea Continental Shelf Case (1969), ICJ Rep, 46
Nottebohm (Preliminary Objections) Case (1953), ICJ Rep, 119
Privileges and Immunities of the UN Case (1989), ICJ Rep, 9
Prosecutor of the ICTY v Tadic (1997), ICTY Rep, 32
R v Secretary of State for Transport (Factortame) (1989), CMLR, 46
Reparations Case (1949), ICJ Rep, 174
SS Wimbledon Case (1923), PCIJ Series A, 25
Western Sahara Case (1975), ICJ Rep, 12

Abbreviations

AC	Appeal Cases
AJIL	American Journal of International Law
ASIL	Proceedings of the American Society of International Law
AVNOJ	Anti-Fascist Liberation Council of Yugoslavia (*Anti-fašisticko Vijece Narodnog Oslobododenja Jugoslavije*)
AUP	Australian University Press
AbUP	Aberdeen University Press
BIICL/ILG	British Institute of International and Comparative Law/International Law Group
BYIL	British Yearbook of International Law
C&W	Chatto & Windus Publications
CFSP	Common Foreign and Security Policy
CLP	Current Legal Problems
CSCE	Conference on Security and Cooperation in Europe
COMINFORM	Communist Information Bureau
CUP	Cambridge University Press
EC	European Communities
ECCY	European Communities Conference on Yugoslavia
EJIL	European Journal of International Law
EPC	European Political Cooperation
EU	European Union
EUP	Essex University Press
FRY	Federal Republic of Yugoslavia
GATT	General Agreement on Tariffs and Trade
H&S	Hodder and Stoughton Publications
HDZ	Croatian Democratic Union (*Hrvatska Demokratska Zajednica*)
HILJ	Harvard International Law Journal
HMSO	Her Majesty's Stationery Office
ICRC	International Committee of the Red Cross
ICFY	International Conference on the Former Yugoslavia

ICJ	International Court of Justice
ICJ Rep.	International Court of Justice Law Reports
ICJur	International Commission of Jurists
ICLQ	International and Comparative Law Quarterly
ILM	International Legal Materials
IMF	International Monetary Fund
ISSJ	International Social Science Journal
IWPR	Institute for War and Peace Reporting
JHUP	Johns Hopkins University Press
JIRev	JANES Intelligence Review
JNA	Yugoslav Peoples Army (*Jugoslovenska Narodna Armija*)
KLA	Kosovo Liberation Army
MLRev	Modern Law Review
MichJIL	Michigan Journal of International Law
MUP	Manchester University Press
MinUP	Minnesota University Press
MRG	Minority-Rights Group Publications
NATO	North Atlantic Treaty Organisation
NBY	National Bank of Yugoslavia
Nijhoff	Martin Nijhoff Publications
NGO	Non-Governmental Organisation
NUP	Nebraska University Press
OIC	Organisation of the Islamic Conference
OIP	Oxford International Publications
OSCE	Organisation on Security and Cooperation in Europe
OUP	Oxford University Press
PCA	Permanent Court of Arbitration
PCIJ	Permanent Court of International Justice
PUP	Princeton University Press
RIIA	Royal Institute of International Affairs
S&M	Sweet and Maxwell Publications
SCCC	Steering-Committee Co-Chairmen
SDA	Party of Democratic Action (*Stranka Demokratske Akcije*)
SDS	Serbian Democratic Party (*Srpska Demokratska Stranka*)

SFRY	Socialist Federal Republic of Yugoslavia
SLR	Stanford Law Review
SRBH	Socialist Republic of Bosnia-Hercegovina
TDF	Territorial Defence Force
TEU	Treaty on European Union
TND	Total National Defence
UN	United Nations
UNDPI	UN Department of Public Information
UNGA Resn.	UN General Assembly Resolution
UNHCR	UN High Commissioner for Refugees
UNIDR	UN Institute for Disarmament Research
UNP	University of Nebraska Press
UNSC Resn.	United Nations Security Council Resolution
VCLT	Vienna Convention on the Law of Treaties
VJIL	Virginia Journal of International Law
WEU	Western European Union
WIP	Worldwatch Institute Press
YbkEL	Yearbook of European Law
YWA	Yearbook of World Affairs

Maps

Map 1: Yugoslavia's Geographical Location

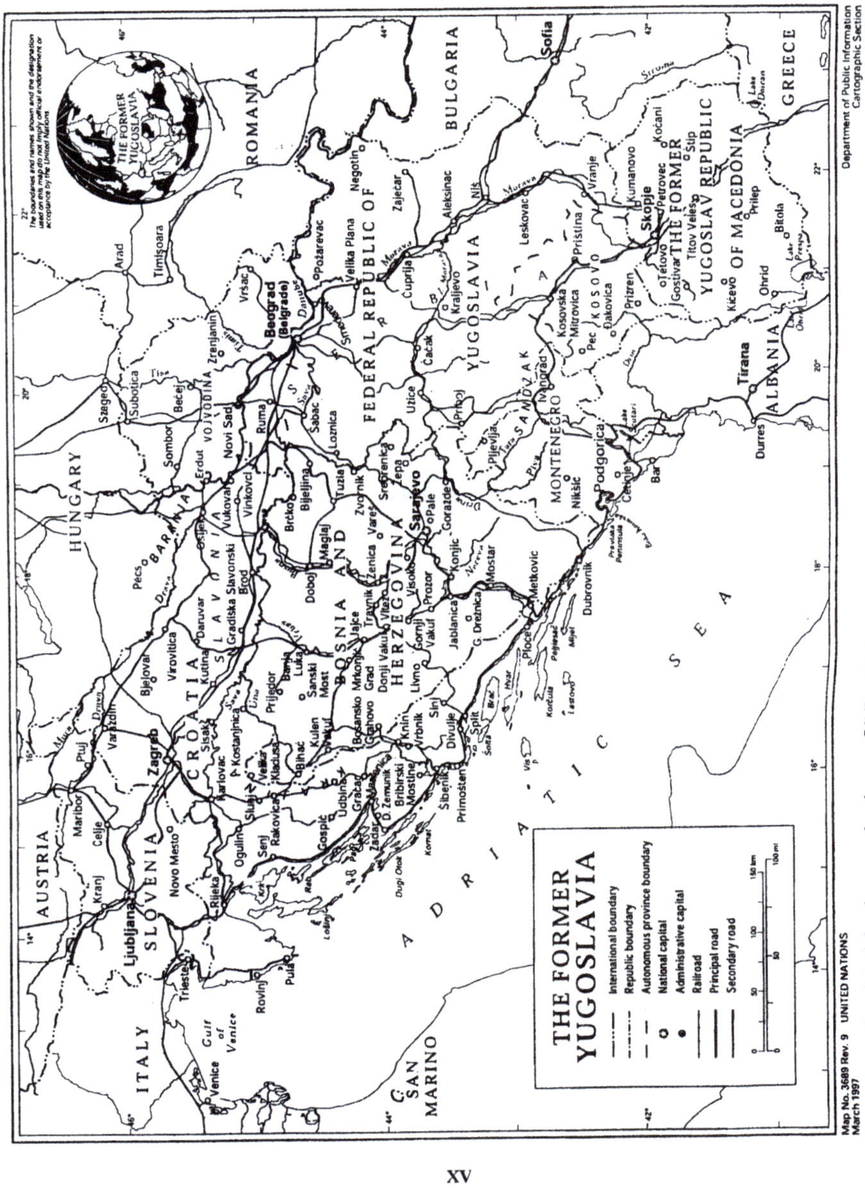

Reprinted with kind permission of UNDPI.

Map 2: Yugoslavia's Physical Geography

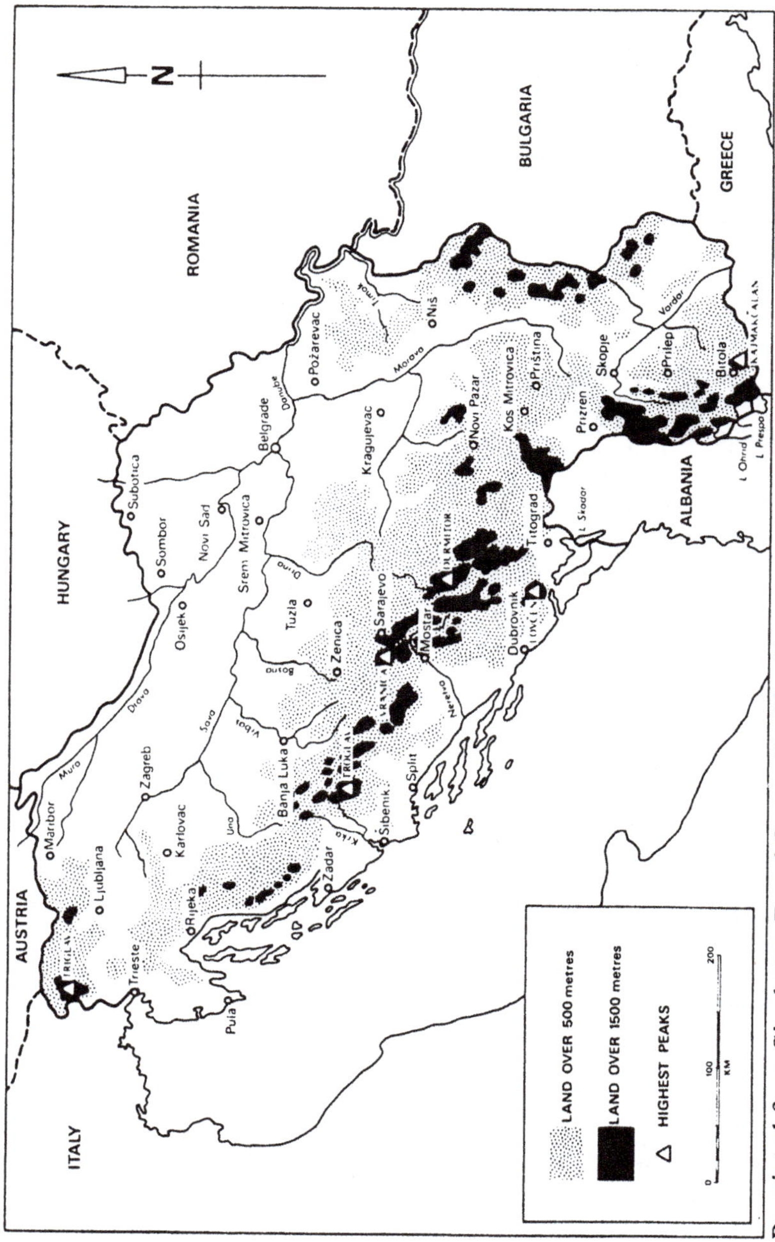

Reprinted from Singleton, F. and Carter, B., *The Economy of Yugoslavia*, (1982), with kind permission of Croom-Helm Publications.

Map 3: Yugoslavia's Ethnic Distribution

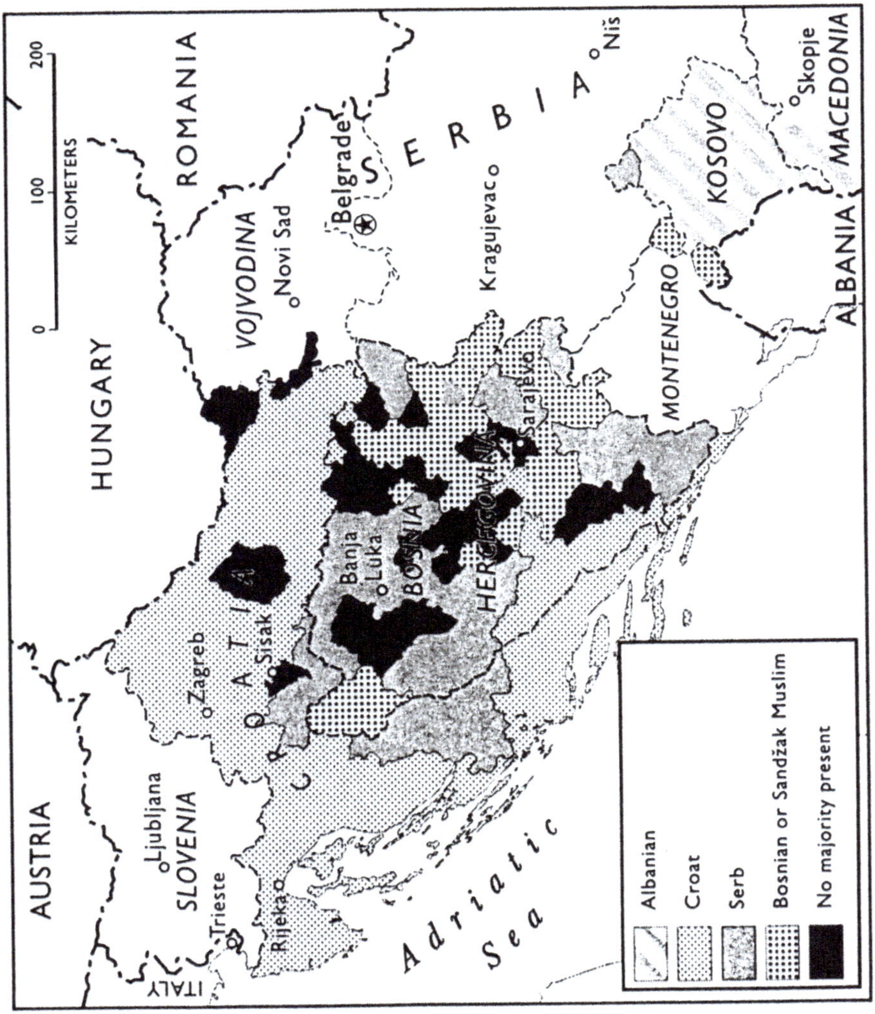

Reprinted from Lampe, J.R., *Yugoslavia as History*, (1996), with kind permission of Cambridge University Press.

Map 4: The Kingdom of the Serbs, Croats and Slovenes (1918-1929)

Map 5: The Partition of Yugoslavia During World War Two

Reprinted from Donia, R.J. and Fine, V.A., *Bosnia-Hercegovina: A Tradition Betrayed*, (1994), with kind permission of Hurst Publications.

Map 6: Yugoslavia's Regional Economic Inequalities

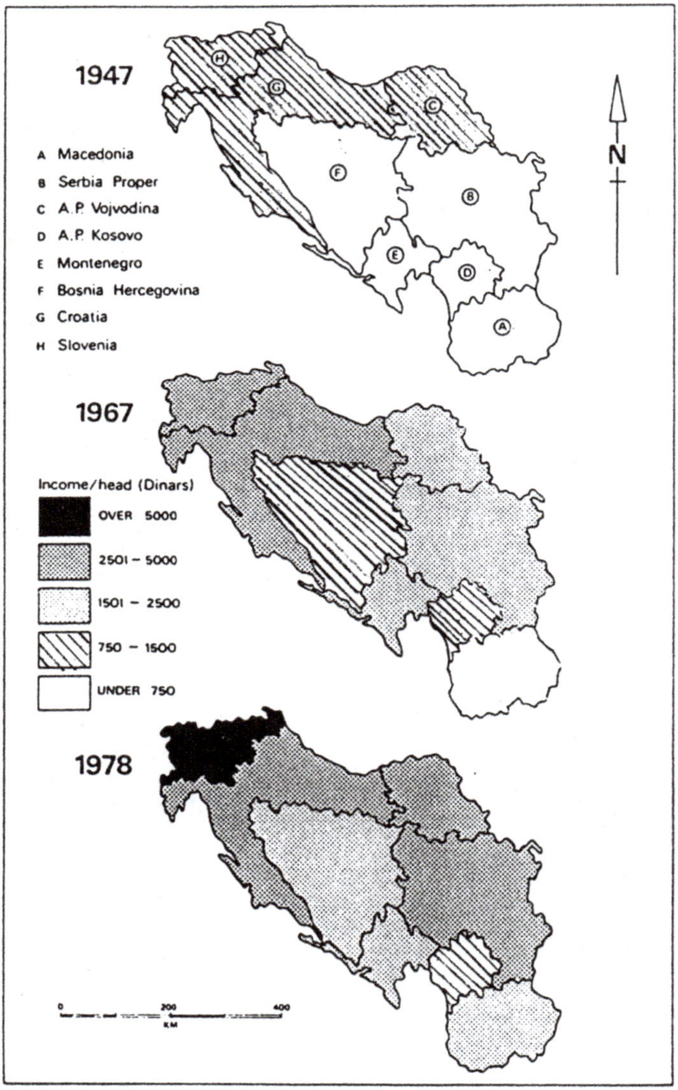

Reprinted from Singleton, F. and Carter, B., *The Economy of Yugoslavia*, (1982), with kind permission of Croom-Helm Publications.

Map 7: Ethnic Distribution in Bosnia-Hercegovina

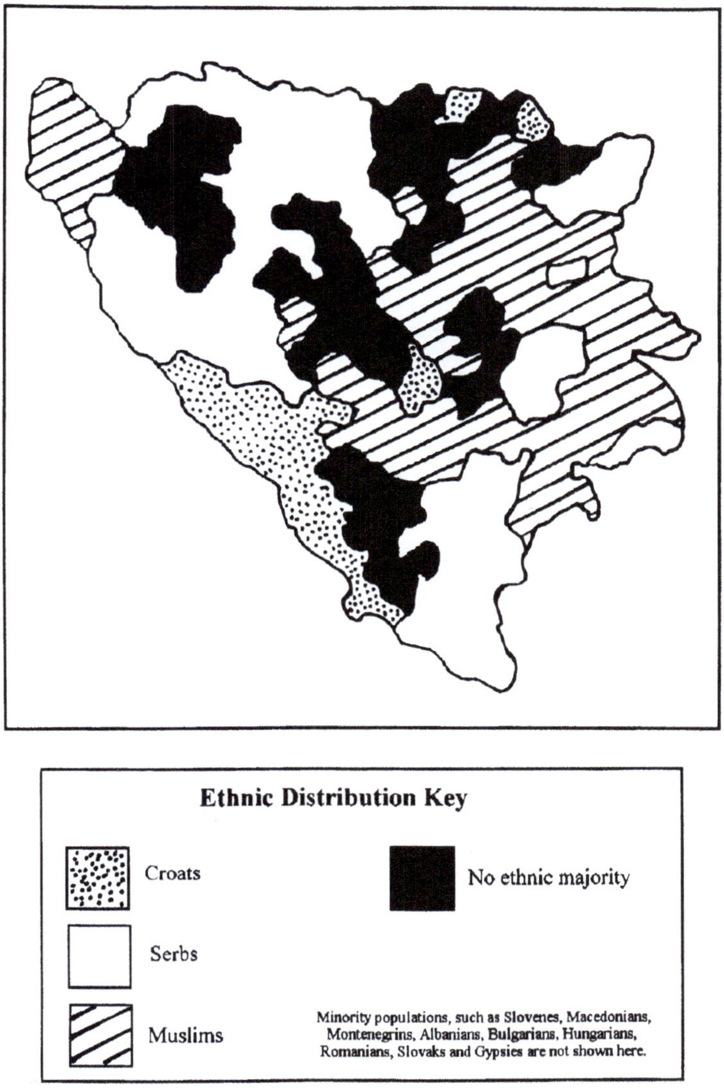

Map collated by S. Harris, using statistics from the 1991 Yugoslav census, cited in *The Role of the UN in the Former Yugoslavia*, (1994), UNDPI.

1 Methodology

"Clothes make the man"
Babylonian Talmud: Shabbath (c.450).
"Beware of all enterprises that require new clothes"
H.D. Thoreau (c.1856).
"Les habits trop chers et sumptueux monstrent, que l'homme a peu de sens qui les porte [Clothes too rich and sumptuous show that the man who wears them has little sense]"
Saint Bernard, Le Regisme de Mesnaige (c.1130).[1]

1.1 Introduction

Choosing a research methodology is comparable to choosing an outfit. Each item is chosen as a result of the consumer's ultimately subjective judgement, although fashion may affect his decisions. Rarely will one piece of clothing be sufficient and he is required to match various items to produce a compatible whole. This process of matching items, and methodologies, leaves the consumer at the mercy of those who disagree with his style as a whole or with the inclusion of one, or more, element(s) of the overall 'outfit'. He will undoubtedly have to explain, justify and defend his individual choices and the overall image he has created. Inevitably, some will disagree with those choices that differ from their own personal and subjective tastes. Fashion, or the consumer's changing tastes, may eventually persuade him to choose different styles in the future, but this is irrelevant to assessing those choices made at the present time.

The quotations cited above indicate the problems in adopting a methodology. On the one hand, the methodology may 'make' the research as clothes 'make' the man. On the other hand, many are suspicious of new fashions and methodological approaches and one must be careful not to give the impression that the approach taken is so lavish that it proffers too much while offering little in substance.

Whilst the choice of research styles is unlikely to convince every reader of its worth, and most unlikely to actually *convert* the critic, this does not invalidate the chosen approach(es) and merely highlights the inherently subjective process of methodological selection. The challenge is, therefore, to convince the reader that the writer has chosen not *the* correct methodology but *a* justifiable methodology.[2]

1.2 Methodological Techniques[3]

The chosen methodology involves an inter-disciplinary qualitative research paradigm incorporating normative-contextual, yet holistic, analysis, to achieve a neo-realist perspective. This may seem an indecipherable mixture of terms, designed to obscure rather than elucidate. Another intended approach, however, is the constant emphasis placed upon the need for *transparency*, both within international legal research and within international norms themselves.[4] It is, accordingly, proposed to separate and discuss each of the component elements of the overall research methodology. It is naturally difficult to isolate the elements of a methodological 'outfit', but an attempt must be made nevertheless.

1.2.1 *A Qualitative Research Paradigm*

Most international legal discourse is based on a qualitative research paradigm. This is defined as "…an inquiry process of understanding a social or human problem, based on building a complex, holistic picture, formed with words…"[5] This is distinguishable from quantitative paradigms, associated with physical sciences, involving tests on a standard set of variables that are analysed via statistical procedures to test the original hypothesis.

The qualitative research paradigm cannot hope to offer any objective 'truth'[6] because it involves inherently subjective interpretation of materials which are not susceptible to scientific tests and which yield no empirical data or incontrovertible information. As Koskenniemi notes, in any conflict analysis, "...there is no 'purely' factual account of the events at all".[7] When one studies a conflict scenario, one chooses the 'relevant' information, interprets their significance and evaluates the responses of the actors involved. The researcher adopts *inductive*, rather than *deductive*, interpretive techniques and works with few, if any, known variables. Such uncertainty, however, enhances the flexibility in the methodological approach. Creswell notes that "...the qualitative design [is one] in which the 'rules' are not fixed, but...are open and emerging. This design calls for an individual who is willing to take the risks inherent in an ambiguous procedure".[8] The study's subject matter is undeniably affected by the chosen methodology, and may be capable of yielding different conclusions under different methodological approaches. As Schreur notes, "...[i]n the social sciences, including law, theoretical models do not just explain reality. They also influence the facts under observation".[9]

The qualitative paradigm adopted herein is distinguishable from the relatively recent concept of 'ethno-methodology', where value-laden foundations are avoided by gathering mainly observational data, to which little interpretive analysis is applied. Within a qualitative paradigm, the researcher acknowledges that his conclusions are necessarily value-laden (the *axiological* assumption) and arrived at as a result of his physical involvement with the subject matter (the *epistemological* assumption), and are merely one subjective interpretation of 'reality' (the *ontological* assumption).[10]

1.2.2 *Normative Contextualism*

The dissolution of Yugoslavia has had an undeniable impact on international law. Whether one considers that the handling of this conflict may be seen as a success for international law, or that it merely highlights the impotence of the current international system and the need for change, one cannot deny the focus which has been placed upon international law as a result of this conflict.[11] Furthermore, the media, the world's political leaders and the general public are increasingly willing to categorise the success or failure of the international legal system based upon its response in individual conflicts. Witness, for example, the euphoria following the international community's response to the Gulf War in 1990-1991 and compare the perceptions of failure in Rwanda, Somalia and Yugoslavia.[12] Kahn notes the "...inherently controversial..." methodology of drawing lessons from individual conflicts but concedes that "...international legal analysis *must* look to single events...because particular incidents of State behaviour are an important source of innovation in international law. More importantly, only by looking to the operation of law in particular events are we able to discuss realistically the force and effect of the formal system of international law".[13]

This case study therefore adopts a contextualist approach, which investigates the processes leading to, and the results arising from,

Yugoslavia's dissolution. Contextualism seeks to "...work on international incidents as a new international epistemic unit..." and show how "...detailed analysis of international disputes highlight the inner workings of the international legal system".[14] In this respect, there is no contemporary case scenario worthier of study than Yugoslavia.

The dividing line between law and politics is often difficult to discern and nowhere more so than in international law. Speaking of Yugoslavia, Mullerson notes that "...the inseparability of politics and law in this case [...] necessitates the introduction of significant political elements into our analysis".[15] Law does not exist in a vacuum and it is vital that conflicts, and international laws aimed at resolving them, are discussed in light of the wider political contexts within which they arise. As "...a broad, dynamic, complex process of interactive decision-making that is constantly evolving and responding to changing circumstances..."[16] international law, and international legal study, must acknowledge the importance of contextualism. The end of the Cold War represents the political backdrop against which this case study will be conducted.

The most obvious criticism of contextualism is the possibility of adopting international legal responses relevant only to the individual case study. Fragmentation of international legal jurisprudence could create difficulties in assessing the universal applicability of international norms.[17] It is true that an approach which condoned the resolution of individual conflicts without recourse to any doctrinal foundations, or at the expense of consistency with other similar conflicts, would cause severe problems. As Franck notes, the need for coherence and legitimacy in conflict resolution implies that the apparent resolution of one conflict may be merely temporary unless it fits within a coherent framework free from perceptible bias and where norms are applied in a principled, if contextual, manner.[18] The objectives of individual, yet comparable, conflict resolution settlements must be consistent if a lasting peace is to be achieved.

Contextualism can only flourish within a principled framework and, without such, an *ad hoc* contextual approach becomes unpredictable and unworkable. Franck argues that inconsistent application of the self determination doctrine has undermined its legitimacy as a right under international law.[19] Similarly, Tomuschat, notes that "...[s]ecession is an explosive issue. It should not be dealt with in an *ad hoc* manner, when an actual need arises, but some formal planning should take place".[20] These powerful arguments against a purist form of contextualism have caused this writer to term the adopted approach *normative contextualism,* whereby contextualism's flexibility is built upon the consistency and predictability provided by identifying the normative foundations of individual norms. In essence, this may be described to the layman as principled pragmatism,[21] allowing universal norms to be given contextual nuance in specific conflicts without departing from the doctrinal foundations underlying them.

Although the inherently individuality of every conflict may make consistency difficult, it is striking how many conflicts arise from similar situations and involve similar disputes. Yugoslavia provides an example of such situations, where claims of self-determination provoke the use of force by governmental authorities and create bitter intra-State conflicts.[22] The growing frequency with which such situations threaten international peace and security strengthens, rather than weakens, the case for identifying normative objectives. Subsequent chapters show how normative rules may be applied contextually to maximise the benefits of both approaches. Chapter 7, discussing self-determination, suggests that it is possible to identify a common foundational basis from which various contextual solutions can be adapted to the individual needs of the conflict in question. Equally, the creation of the Badinter Commission, discussed in Chapters 5 and 6, provides an example of contextual dispute resolution based on established normative foundations.

Normative contextualism rejects Westlake's 1894 definition of international law as "...the *body of rules* prevailing between States [emphasis added]..."[23] and prefers Higgins' approach, which considers international law "...a *process*...[which]...entails harder work in identifying sources and applying norms, as nothing is mechanistic and context is always important".[24] This follows the approach of her predecessor at the ICJ, Judge Jennings, who considered it "...a besetting weakness of lawyers...to think of law...as if it consisted only of rules suitable to be applied by courts in adversarial proceedings...This distorted view...is singularly inapt for international law which, throughout its history, has been employed much more as an instrument of diplomacy than of formal forensic confrontation".[25] Since 'rules' are necessarily the accumulation of past decisions, any such definition of international law would render it unable to cope with changing political environments such as the post-Cold War world.

1.2.3 *A Holistic Approach*

A holistic approach complements normative contextualism by showing how international norms interact with each other and how developments in one area may impact on other areas. This is emphasised in the *Friendly Relations Declaration*, which outlines principles relating to the prohibition of force, peaceful settlement of disputes, territorial integrity, non-intervention, sovereign equality and self-determination and declares that "...the above principles are inter-related and each principle should be construed in the context of the other principles".[26]

It is impossible for one writer to specialise in every international dispute and every international legal norm, but holism does not seek this. What is required is merely an *appreciation* of the wider picture to complement the more detailed contextual case study. Cassesse believes that academics should "...stick to small fragments of reality..." rather than attempt to evaluate the whole "...espirit de system...".[27] It is submitted, however, that a holistic approach is required to assess how the case study fits into the wider subject area and ensure it has an *appreciation* of matters outside the limited scope of this book.

Disagreements over specific legal norms may involve more fundamental disagreements over the underlying policy paradigms underpinning them. Writers often seek to 'fill' legal lacunae with the espirit de system which Cassesse suggests should be rejected.[28] Koskenniemi describes how "...lawyers have recourse to 'deep structural' purposes or principles, economic laws, the needs of interdependence, moral necessities etc. But these are unable to sew the legal fabric together because they are themselves subject of legal controversy".[29] It is submitted, however, that resort to the prevailing paradigm underpinning the entire international system is controversial when there is little consensus on the nature of that paradigm.[30] Chapter 3 argues that tensions between two conflicting paradigms, namely State sovereignty and an emerging New World Order (NWO) paradigm, prevent the identification of an unchallengeable basis from which to 'fill' legal lacunae or encourage legal developments. In light of the need for transparency in legal research, it is necessary for this writer to identify his personal viewpoint. It is submitted that dynamic changes in contemporary international relations must be reflected in academic analysis if international law scholars are to play an active role in the ongoing debate over international legal developments.[31] Suggestions for legal development necessarily pre-date those developments and ideas must continue to precede changes if the system is to evolve.[32] International lawyers, discussing a system with no traditional sovereign authority or legislature, have a more creative role than their domestic counter-parts,[33] as reflected in *Article 38* of the *Statute of the International Court of Justice*, which refers to "...the teachings of the most highly-qualified publicists of the various nations as subsidiary means for the determination of rules of law…".

Watson notes the need for a paradigm to make way for a new one whenever it fails to account for available data, but suggests this cannot be done until the new paradigm is supportable by incontrovertible data itself.[34] In addition to the inapplicability of scientific nomenclature to international law, this approach fails to appreciate that, when a system finds itself *between* paradigms, the competing forces they exert on existing norms means that the paradigms themselves possess a normative function. The active role of the paradigm demands a reciprocal level of activity from scholars to argue the case for their preferred manner of development.

This writer prefers the human rights, as opposed to the traditional Westphalian, paradigm. It is submitted that international legal development will continue moving away from Westphalian conceptions of State sovereignty and towards greater concern for non-State actors. Sovereignty is not an immutable concept[35] and must adapt to new contextual circumstances. Whether one believes this will result in the concept of relative sovereignty[36] is less important than reflecting current contextual priorities and approaches in scholarly debate. The adoption of the NWO paradigm is, naturally, a policy decision, but no moreso than preference for the Westphalian paradigm, which traditionally provides apologetic acceptance of the unsatisfactory state of international law which results from over-emphasis of the State-sovereignty doctrine.[37] Whilst academic analysis must reflect existing realities it must also seek to develop them and this can only be done with reference to the future. A dichotomy clearly arises between an approach that strays beyond existing international realities in seeking to encourage legal development and one which better reflects existing realities but is hesitant to posit developments beyond current State practice. It is submitted that legal analysis as a whole requires both approaches and this book errs towards the former.

1.2.4 *Neo-Realism*

Realism became the dominant post-war methodology and dismissed international law as virtually irrelevant in 'high politics'. Scott notes that "...[f]or a realist who considers power the prime determinant of foreign policy, any correspondence between international law and political action is mere coincidence. Law is, at best, a disguise for policies based on power considerations".[38]

Realism has certain advantages as a methodological approach. It ensures that extra-legal factors, such as reasons for compliance with international norms, are taken into account. It also prevents academic discussion becoming 'utopian' and divorced from the *realpolitik* of international relations. Current legal debate is faced with the problem of taking account of important changes in the international system whilst maintaining a 'realist' approach. It is submitted that what often passes for 'realism' is, paradoxically, not realistic enough and "...tends to characterise politics in a traditional fashion, to disregard the movement of history, represented...by the ideological and structural changes that alter the nature of international relations".[39] Realism emphasised the importance of the *realpolitik* which engulfed the post-war system and often dominated it. It is not difficult to see how 'realism' may evolve into a culture of pessimism and cynicism. Franck describes how "...hard-nosed realism tends to generate dull, rather absurdly defensive, rule description and even more plodding prescription".[40] Similarly, Brownlie notes that traditional realism can "...lead not to healthy inquiry but to a neurotic nihilism".[41]

A more effective and 'realistic' approach is to acknowledge the importance of developments that have moved the international system on from the point at which 'realism' evolved and reflect them in analysis. This acknowledges the importance of comparing aspirational standards with existing practice, or rhetoric against reality, whilst being reflective of trends in *contemporary* international society. This will be termed *neo-realism*[42] and begins from the premise that traditional realism fails to explain the increasing tendency of States, including the most powerful States, to comply with international law, even to their detriment.[43] It also argues that there is an emerging paradigm of *legitimacy* which rivals the importance of power in international relations.[44] Neo-realism, therefore, looks forward to new international developments and new international problems just as 'realism' looks backwards.[45]

1.2.5 *An Inter-Disciplinary Approach*

The inter-disciplinary option is available because of the freedom provided by the qualitative research paradigm. As Cresswell notes, "...[t]hose who conduct qualitative research...are faced with many possibilities of design drawn from disciplinary fields of anthropology, psychology, social psychology, sociology, and education".[46] To this one may add historical studies, international relations, political science and many others. An interdisciplinary approach is useful for many reasons. First, in choosing a methodology, it is vital to be aware of the cognitive biases which affect all research and which, without identification, may render a project flawed from the outset. An appreciation of psychological studies has, therefore, helped to identify, if not remove, the potential for bias within the project. Second, a contextual approach requires appreciation of events outside the scope of a purely legal analysis. Contextualism and inter-disciplinarianism are thus intrinsically linked.[47] This point was made by the eminent historian, Professor Sir Michael Howard when he said that "...neither political action, nor culture, are fully explainable without an appreciation of both".[48] Third, in considering the institutional responses to Yugoslavia's dissolution, a 'functionalist' approach more commonly associated with traditional legal analysis will be adopted.[49] Fourth, in evaluating the Badinter Commission's role in the Yugoslav crisis a number of approaches will be required, since this was a legally created organ involved in an episode of political, constitutional and anthropological conflict, considering questions of international and constitutional law and attempting to resolve issues which have a social-scientific origin.

1.2.6 *Objectivity*[50]

> "We see things not as they are, but as we are".
> H. M. Tomlinson, novelist (1873-1958).[51]

Academic literature involves hypotheses which researchers seek to establish or refute. It is important to maintain academic integrity, highlighting flaws in original hypotheses and indicating the sustainability of any conclusions reached. Whether this may be described as objectivity, however, is doubtful.

It is impossible to dismiss all prejudices and opinions with which one begins to research. It may be assumed that academics come to a research project with either a history of research in this area, hence certain foundational assumptions from past work, or with a new interest in the area, often arising from strong opinions held on the topic or after having read others opinions. In a qualitative research study, such as this, Creswell notes that "...the only reality is that constructed by the individual involved in the research...".[52]

A more convincing approach makes these foundational assumptions transparent, allowing the critic to evaluate the research against them. The *axiological dilemma* is met with an acknowledgement of the qualitative, and interpretative, nature of the research. The need for transparency has also been recognised by other disciplines. Psychologists, for example, have noted that "... [t]he problem for methodology is not *whether* values are involved in inquiry, but *which*...".[53] Similarly, international relations and political analysts have noted that "...apolitical experts are...*never* apolitical...".[54] Psychological analysis shows that, in addition to *foundational bias,* human reasoning finds true objectivity almost impossible as a result of *confirmational bias*,[55] whereby we seek information consistent with our foundational beliefs and minimise the importance of, or even ignore, evidence which may prove these incorrect. This bleak picture is worsened by the difficulty of self awareness, or *meta-cognition*, caused because that such biases are sub-conscious and therefore out of reach. This writer is no more capable of changing his subjective sub-conscious than anyone else but an appreciation of these problems, combined with transparency in the policy decisions made, is a step towards improving the validity of the research.

1.2.7 *Rhetoric Versus Reality*

The declaration of a New World Order was accompanied by a "...global outbreak of nearly euphoric optimism..."[56] fostering a new kind of rhetoric regarding international law. Rhetoric is the art of persuasion, however,[57] and considerable divides may exist between rhetoric and reality. This book will argue that such divides were commonplace in the Yugoslav conflict, such as the declarations and actions of the politicians and international institutions involved in the conflict and in many of the Badinter Commission's *Opinions*. Chapters describing these divides will be 'neo-realistic' in providing an appraisal of State practice whilst also offering suggestions for developing ways to narrow this divide.

1.3 Conclusions

The various techniques described here cannot truly be compartmentalised or isolated. Once combined, they form an overall methodological 'outfit' which is effectively more than the sum of its parts. The approach differs from some traditional methodologies, but is becoming increasingly popular amongst international lawyers. A traditional legal positivist methodology was vital in ensuring the post-war development of the international system, since progress may have been prevented by wildly idealistic proclamations of world orders or global governance. The caution shown by post-war realists helped create an environment where States were willing to accept the international system's expansion. What has been suggested, however, is that such 'realism' may now prevent further development by constantly referring to the difficulties of the past.

Carty laments "...the failure of the profession to respond in a creative way to the developments which have affected the composition of the State in recent international history...".[58] In grander terms, Allot notes that "...the actual is not natural and inevitable. The actual was made by us and can be remade by us. *The actual is possible. The function of the international lawyer is to change the course of human history*".[59] Where legal norms appear to be hovering between conflicting paradigms, the contemporary international lawyer should feel no more constrained to support a progressive way out of this deadlock than the traditionalist international lawyer feels in justifying the continuation of this unsatisfactory situation with references to the past. The reluctance of the traditional international lawyer to suggest legal developments beyond existing State practice confines their role to description of the system's inadequacies. Cassesse epitomises such an approach when stating that "...[t]he scholar, however dissatisfied he may be...cannot but take note of the present legal condition - all he can do is delineate the existing legal regime with all its flaws and lacunae and pinpoint the emerging trends of the international community".[60] Suggesting new legal developments and approaches may leave the writer facing a wealth of contradictory State practice and methodological criticism and, as Warbrick notes, "...[i]t is uncomfortable to embark upon an enquiry which might have such far reaching consequences...".[61] Nevertheless, such a voyage of discovery is vital if international law is to adapt to the challenges of the modern world.

Notes

1 Quotations taken from Levinson, L.L. (ed.), *Bartlett's Unfamiliar Quotations*, (1972), Allen and Unwin.

2 Koskenniemi, M. 'Theory: Implications for the Practitioner', in Allot, P., Carty, T., Koskenniemi, M., Warbrick, C., *Theory and International Law: An Introduction*, (1991), BIICL/ILG, 3, at 44.

3 Carty, A., 'Why Theory: The Implications for International Law Teaching', ibid, 75, at 76, criticises the absence of methodological discussion in much international legal study except in "...doctoral dissertations...which, by and large, are not supposed to demonstrate something *about* the discipline, but rather to prove the competence of the candidate *in* the discipline".

4 Higgins, R., *Problems and Process: International Law and How We Use It*, (1994), Clarendon, at 5, considers transparency necessary to ensure that "...all factors are properly considered and weighed, instead of the decision-maker unconsciously narrowing or selecting what he will take into account...". See also Koskenniemi, M., *From Apology to Utopia - The Structure of International Legal Argument*, (1989), Finnish Lawyers, 487.

5 Creswell, J.W., *Research Design - Qualitative and Quantitative Approaches*, (1994), SAGE, 1-2.

6 See section 1.2.6.

7 Supra n.2, at 37. Carr, E.H., *What is History?*, (1961), Macmillan, 23, says "...facts are not like fish on a fishmonger's slab. They are like fish swimming about in a vast and sometimes inaccessible ocean and what is caught will depend...mainly on what part of the ocean one fishes in and what tackle one uses. These two factors being, of course, determined by the kind of fish one wants to catch".

8 Supra n.5, at 8-10.

9 Schreuer, C., 'The Waning of the Sovereign State: Towards a new Paradigm for International Law?', (1993), 4 *EJIL*, 447, at 470.

10 Cresswell, supra n.5, at 5. Note, however, the more recent development of 'critical ethnography', where the researcher complements observational data with his own value-judgements and expands beyond the role of narrator.

11 See Chapter 4, section 4.1. for academic opinion on international legal responses to the Yugoslav conflict.

12 On the Gulf War, see Rowe, P.J. (ed.), *The Gulf War 1990-91 in International and English Law*, (1993), Routledge; Kahn, P.W., 'Lessons for International Law from the Gulf War', (1993), 45 *SLR*, 425; Greenwood, C., 'New World Order or Old? The Invasion of Kuwait and the Rule of Law', (1992), 55 *MLRev*, 153. On the effect on American foreign policy which occurred after the killing of 17 US members of the UNOSOM mission in Somalia, see Dowden, R., 'Western Troops Leave Somalia', (1994), *Guardian*, 19th March.

13 Kahn, ibid, 426.

14 Chinkin, C.M. and Sadurska, R., 'Learning about International Law through Dispute Resolution', (1991), 40 *ICLQ*, 529. See also Forsythe, D.P. *Human*

Rights and Peace - International and National Dimensions, (1993), NUP, for a case study methodology.

15 Mullerson, R., *International Law, Rights and Politics: Developments in Eastern Europe and the CIS*, (1994), Routledge, 126. See also ibid, at 2, where he states "...it is especially important to put international law in the proper context at times of revolutionary change in the international system".

16 Carlsson, I. (ed.), *Our Global Neighbourhood: The Report of the Commission on Global Governance*, (1995), OUP, 4. See also Scott, S.V., International Law as Ideology: Theorising the Relationship between International Law and International Politics', (1994), 5 *EJIL*, 313.

17 Higgins alluded to the problems of fragmented international responses in the 20th F.A. Mann lecture of 26th November 1996, partly published as 'Time and the Law: International Perspectives on an Old Problem', (1997), 46 *ICLQ*, 501. See also Schreuer, supra n.9, 470.

18 Franck, T.M., *The Power of Legitimacy Among Nations*, (1990), OUP, 150-183.

19 Franck, T.M., 'The Emerging Right to Democratic Governance', (1992), 86 *AJIL*, 79. See also McCorquodale, R., 'Self-Determination: A Human Rights Approach', (1994), 43 *ICLQ*, 857.

20 Tomuschat, C., 'Self-Determination in a Post-Colonial World', in Tomuschat, C. (ed.), *Modern Law of Self-Determination*, (1993), Nijhoff, 18.

21 Koskenniemi, M., supra n.4, 498, calls this approach "...contextual equity...".

22 See Chapter 8.

23 Westlake, J., *Chapters on the Principles of International Law*, (1984), Grotius, 1.

24 Supra n.4, 8. See also Higgins, R., 'The Identity of International Law', in Cheng, B. (ed.), *International Law: Teaching and Practice*, (1982), Stevens, 37; Rosenne, S., *Practice and Methods of International Law*, (1984), Oceana, 3; Mullerson, supra, n.15, 196 and 53-7.

25 Quoted in Harris, D.J., *Cases and Materials on International Law - Fourth Edition*, (1991), S&M, 968.

26 *UNGA Resn. 2625(XXV)* (1970), *Article 2*. The *CSCE Helsinki Final Act, Principle X*, uses a comparable equation, stating that "All the principles...are of primary significance and, accordingly, they will be equally and unreservedly applied, each of them being interpreted taking into account the others". See also Sinclair, I., 'The Significance of the Friendly Relations Declaration', in Lowe, V. and Warbrick, W. (eds.), *The United Nations and the Principles of International Law*, (1994), Routledge, 1; Rosenstock, R., 'The Declaration of Principles of International Law Concerning Friendly Relations', (1971), 65 *AJIL*, 43.

27 Cassesse, A., *Self-Determination of Peoples - A Legal Reappraisal*, (1995), CUP, Preface.

28 Higgins, supra n.4, at 5, states that "...[r]eference to the 'correct legal view' or 'rules' can never avoid the element of choice (though it can seek to disguise it), nor can it provide guidance to the preferable decision. In making this choice one must inevitably have consideration for the humanitarian, moral and social purposes of the law". In the *Advisory Opinion on the Legality of the Threat or*

Use of Nuclear Weapons, (1996), ICJ Rep., 1, Judge Higgins, in paragraphs 31-41 of her dissenting opinion, lamented the fact that the ICJ had effectively pleaded a *non-liquet* on the question posed in this case. She rejected the assertion that any answer would require judicial legislation and argued that acknowledging international legal lacunae was no part of the ICJ's jurisprudence and considered international judge's obliged "...to resolve, in context, and on grounds that should be articulated, why the application of one particular norm rather than another is to be preferred in the particular case".

29 Supra n.4, at 495.

30 Simmonds, supra n.16, at 5, suggests that disagreements over specific legal norms may involve more fundamental disagreements over the underlying policy paradigms which underpin them.

31 See generally Allot, supra n.2.

32 Scott, supra n.16, 321-3. Badinter, R., 'Final Report', in Engel, N.P. (ed), *Universality of Human Rights in a Pluralistic World*, (1990), CEP, 168, considers it lamentable if legal scholars "...resemble neo-classical artists whose talent was restricted to indefinitely reproducing the models of their great ancestors".

33 Cf. Watson, J.S., 'A Realistic Jurisprudence of International Law', *YWA*, (1980), 265.

34 Ibid, 271.

35 Koskenniemi, supra n.2, at 39. See also Chapter 3, section 3.4., Chapter 9, section 9.3.

36 See Ferencz, B.B. (ed.), *World Security for the 21st Century*, (1991), Oceana, at 19-21; Koskennieni, M., 'The Wonderful Artificiality of States', (1994), 88 *ASIL*, 22.

37 On the apologetic nature of much international legal debate, and the 'utopian' alternative, see Koskenniemi, supra n.4.

38 Supra, n.16, at 323. For a more extreme interpretation see Mayall, J., *Nationalism and International Society*, (1990), CUP, 1. On the problem of applying realism to contemporary research, see Senarclens, P., 'The 'Realist' Paradigm and International Conflicts', (1991), 127 *ISSJ*, 5.

39 Senarclens, ibid, 7-8.

40 Supra n.18, at 7. Cf. Watson, supra n.39.

41 Brownlie, I., 'The Reality and Efficacy of International Law', (1981), 52 *BYIL*, 1.

42 Although this phrase has been used before, it was used to indicate a resurgence of realism after an intervening period of 'idealism' had been discredited. It was, thus, used to indicate its *proximity* to the traditional realism rather than, as here, its conceptual *distance* therefrom. See Hulsman, J.C., *A Paradigm for the New World Order*, (1997), Macmillan, 38-56.

43 Franck, supra n.18. See also Alvarez, J.E., 'Why Nations Behave', (1998), 19(2) *MichJIL*, 303.

44 Forsythe, supra n.14, at ix; Georgiev, D., 'Deconstruction and Legitimacy in International Law', (1993), 4 *EJIL*, 1.

45 Senarclens, supra n.38, at 17, says "...a conceptual framework...that has nothing to say about the challenges of development, of the environment, of refugees, of

population growth, or about new religious and cultural antagonisms, or that reduces these phenomena to traditional inter-state confrontations is necessarily incomplete, and therefore inadequate".

46 Supra n.5, 146-7. See also Koskenniemi, supra n 4, 485.

47 Allot, P., 'New International Law', supra n.2, 107, at 113; Allot, P., 'Reconstituting Humanity - New International Law', (1992), 3 *EJIL*, 219.

48 Extract from Leverhulme Memorial Lecture, Liverpool University, 29th April 1996.

49 See White, N., 'The Law of International Organisations', (1996), MUP, 2-7, on functionalism.

50 See generally Riley, G. (ed.), *Values, Objectivity and the Social Sciences*, (1974), Addison-Wesley.

51 Supra, n.1.

52 Supra n.5, at 4.

53 Kaplan, A., *Values in Inquiry*, in Riley, supra n.50, 101.

54 Denitch, B. (ed.), *Legitimation of Regimes: International Frameworks for Analysis,* (1979), SAGE, 17.

55 See Evans, J. (ed.), *Bias in Human Reasoning: Causes and Consequences,* (1990), Lawrence-Erlbaum, Chapter 3.

56 Franck, T.M., 'International Law After the Cold War', (1990), 84 *ASIL*, 156.

57 Stark, B., 'Postmodern Rhetoric, Economic Rights and an International Text: A Miracle for Breakfast', (1993), 33 *VJIL*, 433, at 434.

58 Carty, A., 'The Failed State and the Tradition of International Law - Towards a Renewal of Legal Humanism', (1995), inaugural lecture, Derby University, 6th December, at 9.

59 Supra n.47, 116. See also Onuf, N., 'The Constitution of International Society', (1994), 5 *EJIL*, 1, at 6.

60 Cassesse, supra n.27, 162. The majority opinion of the ICJ in the *Nuclear Weapons Advisory Opinion*, supra n.36, would appear to support this position.

61 Warbrick, C., 'The Theory of International Law: Is There an English Contribution?', in Allot, supra n.2, 47, at 64.

2 A Brief History of Yugoslavia

> "In facing up to the mixed legacy of the Cold War, the international community must be realistic. History cannot be denied or uprooted. The solving of problems which sometimes have their roots in centuries past is a slow, sometimes very frustrating, business".
> Douglas Hurd, former UK Foreign Secretary, addressing the UN General Assembly, 22nd September 1992.

> "The history of the peoples of the Balkans is a tangle of legend and myth, of claims and counter-claims over who did what to whom and when".
> Gutman, R., *A Witness To Genocide*, (1993), Macmillan, at xviii.

2.1 Introduction

A historical study of Yugoslavia is necessary for a number of reasons. First, in light of the contextual approach adopted,[1] an intimate knowledge of the Yugoslav case study is required. One must consider the factors which divided communities along lines explainable only in historical terms. Second, the international community's responses, and the Badinter Commission's jurisprudence, can only be evaluated if one fully appreciates the nature of the problems to be faced. Hart's comment that "...if you want peace, understand war..."[2] is as relevant to individual conflicts as to war in general. Third, one must assess whether international norms applied in the Yugoslav case address the underlying causes behind its dissolution and explain, if not, why this is. Fourth, Yugoslavia evidences trends which are relevant to other conflicts and provides a classic example of how intra-State conflicts are posing threats to international peace and security.[3] It cannot be considered unique or *sui generis* if these lessons are to be learned.

2.2 Ancient History

To limit a historical study to the creation of the first Yugoslav State in 1918 would ignore many of the problems which preceded this and which made Yugoslavia's survival in the post-Cold War world less likely.

2.2.1 *Geographical Features*

Yugoslavia's history has been greatly affected by its geographical location. On the political map at the end of the Cold War, it was situated in eastern Europe and bordered by Italy, Austria, Hungary, Romania, Bulgaria, Greece and Albania.[4] Apart from its western border, surrounded by the Adriatic, Yugoslavia's frontiers have always been vulnerable to attack from eastern and western Europe and the Middle East

The mountainous nature of much of the terrain reduced arable land to around 25% and, in later years, created economic inequalities between areas which remained dependent on agriculture and those which had moved into more profitable industrialised labour.[5] The mountainous topography and natural river and forest boundaries also divided Yugoslavia into distinct geographical communities, providing physical barriers between inter-community relations.[6]

During periods of external occupation, large population movements were common, such as the many Serbs who fled to Bosnia following the Ottoman invasions or the converted Bogomils and Albanians who moved into the evacuated parts of southern Montenegro. The areas in which these new arrivals gathered created 'ethnic' pockets wherein they represented a majority of the population.[7] These cultural mini-States, including the Military Frontier, or Krajina, region of Croatia and the Kosovo and Vojvodina areas of Serbia, played an important role in Yugoslavia's 'minorities problem'.

2.2.2 *Sociological Differences*[8]

Slight sociological differences existed between the Southern-Slav communities which were exaggerated and exploited by competing external powers to such an extent that each community eventually perceived itself as entirely distinct from their neighbours. The group now known as Slovenes, whose language differed from the Serbo-Croat spoken by the other communities, moved into the western areas along with the Croats, while the Serbs moved into the East.[9]

Almost immediately upon arrival, religious divides developed which created tensions between the communities. Those in the West came under the influence of the Roman Catholic church while Serbs in the East became loyal to the Orthodox church in Constantinople. In Bosnia, competing attentions of both East and West churches left the confused Bosnians vulnerable to conversion by the Bogomils, a Muslim group who introduced a third religion to the area. Persecution of religious minorities drove a wedge between the communities which proved disastrous in later years but, although this was feared most from the Turkish invaders, it was more common at the hands of over-zealous Bogomil converts against Catholics in Bosnia and by the Orthodox areas in Catholic Austria and Croatia.

These initial divides became self-perpetuating, since internal unrest among the areas many zupans or chieftains allowed various expansionist imperial powers to influence, exploit and often annex different portions of the territory without encountering any united defence.

2.2.3 *External Political Involvement*

External involvement in the area pre-dated its occupation by the Southern-Slavs, in approximately AD 650. Even before its annexation by the Roman Empire in AD 9, there were trading colonies from Greece and Celtic Europe. The division of the Roman Empire provided the opportunity for the Southern Slavs to move into the area following their displacement by the Avars from the Carpathian mountains to the North.[10]

When the Magyars occupied what is now Hungary, the physical separation of the Southern Slavs, in what became Yugoslavia, from their Slav brethren in Russia, Poland and Czechoslovakia provided the first indication of the distinct historical development which followed. It also made the isolated Southern Slavs easier to divide and rule in accordance with standard expansionist practice of the period.

During the relatively short period from the tenth century to the thirteenth century, Slovenia defeated Rome's renewed attempt to annex the area only to be transferred to Austria's Habsburg Empire which, along with Italy, was engaged in numerous wars against Hungary in an attempt to gain control of Croatia and coastline-Dalmatia. Hungary sought territory in Bosnia and was engaged against the Byzantine Empire, which in turn was in conflict with the Avars of Bulgaria for influence in Serbia and Macedonia.

Throughout the fourteenth century, although Slovenia remained under Austrian control, many of the other areas expanded territorially. Bosnia acquired Hum, or Hercegovina, parts of Serbia and areas of Dalmatia, whilst Serbia expanded southeastwards into Macedonia, Albania and Greece until the combined efforts of the Byzantine and Ottoman Empires defeated the fledgling Serbian Empire at Kosovo on 28th June 1389,[11] before destroying it in 1459 Bosnia fell in 1463 when failed attempts by the Catholic and Orthodox Churches to eradicate the Bogomils led the "...heretics..."[12] to assist a Turkish invasion and convert to the Moslem religion. Croatia-Slavonia had expanded into areas of Bosnia and Dalmatia during this period, albeit as a Hungarian vassal, until the Monarch's death in 1526 when the area passed to Ferdinand of Austria. Zeta, or Montenegro, gained independence from Serbia in 1355 but Turkish attacks soon left its southern areas depopulated.

The seventeenth-century defeat of the Ottoman Empire saw Austria advance South into Serbia only as far as Kosovo, causing more northwards migrations by Serbs who feared violent reprisals for having risen against the Turks, which left the area deserted until populated by Moslems from Albania. Meanwhile, the Napoleonic Campaigns had forced Italy to cede its areas of Dalmatia to Austria, which in turn was defeated and compelled to let them join other areas controlled by Vienna, including Slovenia, Croatia and Dalmatia. These 'Illyrian Provinces' became the first Slav union since their seventh-century arrival, despite only lasting from 1809-1812. These events coincided with a wave of self-identity across Europe which had already resulted in Montenegro's independence and Serbia's autonomy within the Ottoman Empire. Thus, when the 'Provinces' were returned to Austria following Napoleon's defeat in the Russian Campaigns and centralised control was shared only with Hungary, enormous resentment was aroused since the regions were calling for independence or, at least, an autonomous Slav union. Tensions worsened when the Provinces helped the Habsburgs crush the 1848 Hungarian Revolution but were kept within the Austro-Hungarian Dual Monarchy.

During 1875-1876, Russia and Serbia defeated the Ottoman Empire in Serbia and Montenegro,[13] both of which achieved independence, and in Bosnia, which was occupied by the Dual-Monarchy despite Austrian agreement to the contrary. At the Congress of Berlin, Bosnia-Hercegovina had been assigned to the Dual-Monarchy "...under nominal Turkish suzerainty..."[14] but its annexation in 1908 contributed to the tensions which led to the First World War. Serbia's expansionist plans were thwarted by Bosnia's annexation so a Balkan League coalition of Serbia, Montenegro, Greece and Bulgaria fought the Turks in Macedonia to allow eastward access to the Aegean. The Ottomans had been greatly weakened in the Italian War and were easily defeated, but Austro-Italian demands for an independent Albania within this captured territory caused disagreement between Bulgaria and the other League members over the distribution of the remaining lands.[15] The second Balkan War saw Bulgaria defeated by the other League allies[16] and the creation of a single territorial unit comprising Serbia and Montenegro which was to prove the strongest link in the chain of Yugoslavia. These Serb victories heightened calls for a Slav union from

Croatia, Dalmatia, Bosnia, Hercegovina and Vojvodina, but the Dual-Monarchy sought to prevent this. When the heir to the Austrian throne, Archduke Francis Ferdinand was assassinated on a visit to Sarajevo by a member of a Bosnian-Serb terrorist group protesting at their unfavourable treatment in the Empire, Austria demanded a policing presence within Serbia, which it accused of being a terrorist training ground.[17] Having only recently freed itself from Turkish occupation and fought in the two Balkan Wars to expand its regional influence, Serbia naturally refused to contemplate this and war was declared by the Dual-Monarchy on 28th July 1914.[18]

2.3 The Formation of Yugoslavia

The political will for a Slav union at the outbreak of World War One was greater than ever before, although account must be taken of the alternatives. Maintenance of the status quo was strongly opposed by areas under Dual-Monarchy control but disagreement existed over the relative advantages of forming two smaller unions, between Catholic and Orthodox areas, or creating one united Southern-Slav State. In all likelihood, the removal of Austro-Hungarian control from the territories currently held would require a united Slav movement which would be weakened if disagreement existed over contested areas of land, such as Bosnia. Accordingly, the creation of a single union became the favoured option. Since they were still under Dual-Monarchy control, political shrewdness required Croatia and Slovenia to exclude Serbia and Montenegro from this proposal and to request merely union under Habsburg rule. The Yugoslav Committee in London, however, consisting of exiles from the Monarchy's various Slav provinces, was more representative of general opinion when it proclaimed the intention to create a united and independent Slav State, in the *Declaration of Corfu 1917*.[19]

Even before it was established, however, the Slav movement was divided by a discovery that the Allies - England, France and Russia - had promised areas of Slovenia and Croatia to Italy in return for assistance in defeating Austria, Germany and Bulgaria.[20] Furthermore, rumours began that Serbia and Russia were only interested in expanding Orthodox areas and were prepared to abandon other territories if this were achieved. Whether true or not, these encouraged Croatia and Slovenia to join Austria against the Serbs. Interestingly, Josip Broz, or Tito as he later came to be known, fought with the Croatian armies against the Serbs until he was captured and sent to Russia, where he first became acquainted with Communism.[21] The fall of Belgrade in 1915 quelled whatever thoughts may have existed of a Greater Serbia, however, and led to renewed proposals for a Southern-Slav union.

Italy continued pressuring the Allies to fulfill their promises under the *1919 London Treaty* and this was partly achieved by the *Treaty of Rapallo 1920*,[22] which transferred Istria and some of the surrounding coastline to Venetian control, despite the largely Slav population. This arbitrary allocation of land, combined with the insistence of America's President Wilson on the exercise of national self-determination,[23] produced an "...ethnic and cultural mosaic..."[24] in Yugoslavia due to the highly dissipated nature of its communities. Thus, areas of Austria[25] and Hungary[26] joined Serbia and Montenegro in the formation of the 'Kingdom of the Serbs, Croats and Slovenes' on 1st December, 1918.[27] This union was "...the work of long-term factors and the consequence of immediate causes..."[28] and had been entered "...without any very clear idea of the lines on which it was to be worked out, and without any generally recognised bargain or contract...".[29] It is unsurprising, therefore, to find that this new State encountered political difficulties.

Serbian hard-liners of the Radical Party felt that, having fought for the creation of the State within which their Croatian former enemies were also to live, Serbs deserved a dominant political role. Croats argued for a federal solution but Serbs were unwilling to compromise and, when the Croatian opposition boycotted the Constituent Assembly, the Radical Party passed the founding constitution of 1921, centralising political power in Belgrade. Slovenia and Croatia perceived this as renewed attempts to create Greater Serbia.[30] When the Croatian opposition leader was shot and killed in the Assembly by a Serbian member in 1928, the political system collapsed entirely and a Counter-Parliament was created in Zagreb which maintained the federalist stance.[31] The Kingdom's western areas were aware that secession would leave them open to renewed interest from Austria, Italy and Hungary. With neither camp willing to compromise King Alexander established Monarchy Rule[32] and, ironically, prevented any immediate conflict by annoying both the Serbs, in limiting the role of Serbian customs in union affairs, and the Croats, in continuing to centralise power rather than devolving it to the provinces.

Alexander ordered the Kingdom's name to be changed to

Yugoslavia, meaning a union of Slavs, in 1929 and gave his three sons Serbian, Croatian and Slovenian names.[33] Nevertheless, he appeared capable of generating agreement amongst the various opponents only in a negative manner. The Serbian Radical Party and Croatian opposition united for the first time to reject his 1931 draft constitution.[34] The Communist Party, declared illegal under the 1921 constitution,[35] sought to abolish the Monarchy and attempted to assassinate Alexander. A Croat separatist movement, the Ustashe, pursued similar policies from Italy and Hungary, but more moderate opinion in Serbia and Croatia agreed on peacefully replacing Monarchy-Rule with a return of political power to Parliament. When Alexander was assassinated by Croatian extremists in 1934, attempts to restore Parliamentary rule failed initially but, after a brief return to the Counter-Parliament, discussions began on possible federal solutions. Again, however, acrimonious disagreement arose from competing territorial claims to areas such as Bosnia and Vojvodina. Whilst Serbia, Croatia-Slavonia, Slovenia, Bosnia-Hercegovina, Dalmatia, Montenegro, Macedonia and Vojvodina argued their respective claims for independence, the political situation in central Europe provoked fears of conflict at a worldwide level which overshadowed such domestic disputes.

2.4 Yugoslavia during World War Two

By 1939 Russia had annexed East Poland, Italy had occupied Albania and called for German assistance to defeat Greece, and Germany had occupied Czechoslovakia, annexed Austria and begun fighting against the British. Yugoslavia, fearful of invasion from every direction, opted for neutrality and signed a treaty allowing German advancement southwards to aid Italy in Greece.[36] A *coup d' état* in March 1941 overthrew the Yugoslavian Government and Monarchy[37] and attempted to prevent Germany's passage. In response, Hitler invaded and partitioned Yugoslavia between Italy,[38] Germany,[39] Albania,[40] Bulgaria,[41] and Hungary.[42]

Croatia, including Bosnia-Hercegovina, was declared an independent country controlled by the Ustashe, who claimed Muslims were their bewildered brethren and denounced Serbs and Orthodox religion. The Ustashe pursued a policy of "...kill a third, convert a third, expel a third..."[43] to solve the 'problem' of having 1.9 million Serbs in Croatia's 6.3 million population.[44] Cultural diversity became an instrument of hate. Opposition movements soon formed in Croatia, where 'Chetniks'[45] grouped in the mountains, and in Serbia, where Tito's Communist 'Partisans' resisted German occupation and forged close relations with Russia.[46]

A combination of personality clashes and divergent tactics between Tito and the Chetnik leader General Draza Mihailovic soon ended their temporary collaboration and led to a Nazi-Chetnik agreement to crush the Partisans. Allied assistance was almost entirely directed towards the Chetniks, who did not espouse the Partisans' Communist revolution, and most Yugoslavs were equally disinterested in replacing the Monarchy and Government with a Communist regime. Not even Russia provided assistance to Tito's rebels, believing control of post-war Yugoslavia would pass to the Chetniks and needing weapons themselves to defend against German invasion.[47] In the face of such isolation, it is incredible that the Partisans survived the combined military aggression against them in Serbia, Bosnia and Montenegro, before recovering land in Bosnia where the Anti-Fascist Liberation Council Of Yugoslavia (AVNOJ) was established in November 1942. The Partisans finally took control of Yugoslavia in 1945.

2.5 Yugoslavia under Tito - 1945-1980

The period of isolated Partisan resistance during World War Two encouraged Tito to place his independent political objectives above any external allegiances. In one of his first speeches after the war, he declared that "We [Yugoslavs] will not be dependent on anyone ever again...".[48] In gaining control of wartime Yugoslavia, Tito engaged in pacts and received assistance from Germany, Britain and Russia, whilst ensuring that his own objectives were not compromised. This approach became synonymous with Yugoslavia's international relations after the war and was responsible for limiting foreign influence over the area more successfully than at any previous time. Yugoslavia's political isolation was confirmed when the Allies forced it to cede areas of southern Austria, gained from the Ustashe, and the Dalmatian region of Trieste, to Italy. The Allies had forced the Slav Kingdom to cede Trieste to Italy after World War One and Tito seemed prepared to fight against identical demands during the "...forty days confrontation..."[49] which nearly restarted the war. When the Soviet Union, aware of America's nuclear capacity, refused to support Tito's territorial claims, he distanced Yugoslavia from both East and West.

Internal unrest remained in the guise of the Chetniks and their substantial Serbian supporters whom Tito enraged when he, ironically, executed General Mihailovic for collaborating with the Germans. The Communist constitution adopted on 29th November 1945 abolished the Monarchy and created the Federal Republic of Yugoslavia, which had provincial governments in Serbia,[50] Croatia, Bosnia-Hercegovina, Macedonia, Montenegro and Slovenia. These constitutional arrangements remained fundamentally unchanged until Yugoslavia's dissolution.

Tito's initial politics caused many in the West to view him as a Soviet puppet. Enforced collectivisation of resources, centralisation of economic, legal and security affairs, eradication of political opposition and persecution of dissidents were all policies familiar to Communist Russia. Nevertheless, Tito failed to surrender to Soviet control, as had been expected by both East and West, and pursued a number of non-aligned ventures, such as demanding a Yugoslav 'policing' role in Albania, purportedly to defend against the civil war in Greece though also to prevent unity between Albania and Kosovo. Yugoslavia became the leader of the Non-Aligned Movement, which sought political independence from the Capitalist and Communist blocs formed after World War Two.[51]

A crucial split with Russia came in 1948 when Stalin proposed two unions incorporating, on the one hand, Yugoslavia, Albania and Bulgaria and, on the other hand, Poland, Hungary, Czechoslovakia and Rumania in order to facilitate Soviet influence. Yugoslav-USSR relations were never as comfortable as many in the West imagined, due to the absence of Russian support for the Partisans and the Trieste affair, so this proposal made a break appear imminent. Tito's refusal to send a delegation to a Communist Information Bureau (COMINFORM) meeting resulted in Yugoslavia's expulsion and a political and economic blockade removing over 50% of Yugoslavia's trade,[52] which was worsened by a serious drought in that year.[53]

Tito worked hard to rise above ethnic politics and to unite the Southern Slavs in a positive manner, effectively for the first time.[54] Ironically, while ensuring Tito's legendary status, such decentralisation and iconoclasm also played a significant part in the dissolution of the State.[55] 'Titoism', as this period came to be known, resulted from the unlikely combination of Communist political philosophy and Capitalist economic aid. Whilst maintaining a party political monopoly akin to Communism, Tito reversed many Soviet-orientated economic structures and implemented his own policies. He established Worker's Councils and introduced the concepts of 'social ownership' and 'self-management',[56] whereby these Councils and the republics in which they were situated could own their own property and exercise greater economic autonomy. The "...de-Stalinisation..."[57] of Yugoslavia was epitomised by the introduction of tourism and western culture, the reduction of taxes, the implementation of the 1953 and 1963 constitutions and the change of its name, in 1963, to the Socialist Federal Republic of Yugoslavia (SFRY).

In 1953 Trieste was divided between Yugoslavia and Italy, with whom relations improved.[58] Political relations with the West strengthened when Austria became an ally and trading partner. Stalin's death improved Yugoslav-USSR relations which generally remained stable despite faltering during the Hungarian and Czechoslovakian uprisings.[59] Yugoslavia's fragile international relations environment which had existed to various degrees since 1945 dissipated, allowing Tito to explore other Non-Aligned countries, mainly in Third-World Africa and South America. Inter-community tensions also declined for a period.

At this point, opinion is divided over the wisdom of maintaining a centralised political monopoly rather than following the pattern of economic liberalisation and implementing democracy into this unusually stable environment. No political opposition existed and no direct elections existed for any of the regional or federal assemblies. People were compelled to vote for candidates selected by the trade unions, who were in turn controlled by the Communist Party.[60] Tito believed that Serbo-Croat divisions could destroy a union before it was fully functional and that improved economic conditions were a pre-requisite to democratic reform. Even amongst Tito's closest allies, however, this approach was criticised. Milovan Djilas, one of Yugoslavia's three Vice-Presidents and a former Partisan, believed economic improvements from industrialisation and the absence of international tensions made the timing perfect to implement democracy.[61]

Although the full consequences of Yugoslavia's political infancy remained unappreciated until the 1990s, there were signs of a return of the "...nationalities problem..."[62] before Tito died in 1980. Greater economic freedom and connections with western business had improved the average standard of living but this was unevenly distributed, with Slovenia and Croatia receiving most of the benefits because of their geographical location and industrialised economies. This led to demands for greater economic autonomy and a reduction of their relative tax burdens. It was argued that

Yugoslav economic policy and institutions such as the National Bank of Yugoslavia (NBY) discriminated against them and in favour of Serbia and the poorer southeastern economies.[63] Such demands were later joined by linguistic and cultural arguments for greater autonomy as "...regional economic and political rivalries turned for support to existing national feelings, which flowed into these new moulds...".[64] An Albanian uprising in Kosovo in 1968 demanded republican status for the area and improvements in its economic situation. Union with Albania was spoken of.[65] Attempting to diffuse these tensions, Tito granted more autonomy to the republics and moved Yugoslavia towards a confederal State.[66] Kosovo-Albanians were enraged at the differential treatment of republics as well as Tito's decision not to extradite known Ustashe members from Europe to face trial, which appeared to legitimise their independence struggle and led to Serbo-Croat clashes in Croatia and Serbia.

The 1974 constitution[67] granted autonomous-region status to the regions of Kosovo and Vojvodina, which aggravated Serb nationalists. 'Self-management' was expanded to allow greater autonomy to the republics and hopefully diffuse the tensions which had historically accompanied threats of centralised authoritarianism. A "...peripheralised federalism..."[68] resulted, strengthening regional governments at the expense of federal institutions by giving each republic and autonomous-region a veto in federal legislative actions. This obstructed most federal legislation and resulted in divergent regional approaches or compelled reliance on federal 'temporary measures' which depended on Tito's personal popularity to avoid being vetoed. Neither situation was desirable - the former aggravated differences between regions exhibiting secessionist tendencies and the latter perpetuated Tito's role as a "...centrifugal force..."[69] without whom the political system faltered. Some considered that the creation of a rotating-Presidency and Federal Council in the 1974 constitution prepared the way for a post-Tito Yugoslavia,[70] but with little experience in anything other than an autocratic Tito-centred political system this later caused considerable problems.

If Tito's constitutional changes indicated that inter-community tensions were threatening Yugoslavia's unity, one must question his decision to declare himself Catholic on his deathbed, despite his lifelong profession of atheism, and arranging the "...administrative absorption..."[71] of his Serbian wife.

2.6 Post-Tito Yugoslavia[72]

Tito's death left a vacuum in Yugoslavia's political system. This section concentrates on economic, political and military developments after Tito's death and discusses the rise of nationalism.

2.6.1 *Economic Divisions*[73]

Liberalisation of Yugoslavia's economy after the split from COMINFORM improved the economic situation throughout the 1950s and 1960s,[74] whilst showing how inter-regional economic differences could aggravate inter-community tensions. A 1970 EEC-Yugoslavia commercial agreement strengthened Yugoslavia's links with the powerful western economies but these benefits fell largely on Croatia and Slovenia's industrialised markets at the expense of the more agricultural South-East.[75] This led to a process of "...ethnogenesis..."[76] with economic issues taking on ethnic characteristics.

Throughout the 1970s, declining levels of western aid combined with growing inflation, unemployment and balance-of-payments deficits which worsened Yugoslavia's general prosperity. By 1981, a global recession and oil crisis left Yugoslavia owing over $21 billion and national living standards had fallen to below their 1967 levels.[77] Reactions differed to this situation. An uprising in Kosovo in 1981 demanded greater subsidisation of the SFRY's poorest regions[78] whilst Croatia and Slovenia demanded an end to their subsidisation of Yugoslavia's inefficient regions.[79] Croatia and Slovenia had strengthened trade links with the West, particularly Italy and Germany, whilst the southeastern areas maintained most trade with the declining USSR economy.

The average inflation rate between 1980-1990 was 122.9% and had reached 583% by the time Slovenia and Croatia began to debate independence. Strikes, a phenomena hitherto unknown in Yugoslavia,[80] became increasingly common and by the time a wage-freeze was introduced in 1987 numbered 1570.[81]

In 1988, the International Monetary Fund (IMF) made the provision of $2.2 million loan capital conditional upon centralised control of the economy, infuriating Croatia and Slovenia.[82] When Ante Markovic's Federal Government attempted to implement significant reforms in 1989,[83] such opposition caused them to fail.

Yugoslavia's declining geo-strategic importance was matched by a reduction in economic aid at precisely the point it may have played a constructive role in relieving economic tensions which contributed to Yugoslavia's dissolution.[84] Whether economic aid would have been sufficient to prevent Yugoslavia unravelling remains debatable.[85] What is clearer is that Yugoslavia's destruction caused massive human losses and did little to improve the economies of most successor States.[86]

2.6.2 *Nationalism*

After Tito's death, it was made illegal to criticise his memory, but the political void left in his wake required politicians to mobilise popular support in a country devoid of democratic debate, plagued by inter-community differences and deprived of their unifying leader. The most effective means of mobilising such support is to create a readily identifiable group to support a political agenda. 'Group-building' requires criteria to identify that group and prohibition of political dissent in Yugoslavia made 'political' groups difficult to identify and political agendas necessarily simplistic. Accordingly, groups were constructed on a territorial basis, corresponding largely with the 'ethnic' composition of their majority populations. Whilst acts of ethnic or cultural self-identification are not inherently dangerous, 'group-building' requires the exclusion of non-group members and this exclusionary aspect can mutate into aggressive nationalism where 'ethnic' groupings are concerned.[87] Creating the 'us' required exclusion of 'them' and this was rationalised by demonising 'them'.

Nationalist politicians justified this demonisation with references to historical betrayals and 'ethnic' hatreds, real or imagined, and populations were subjected to a "...consciously fostered paranoia..." through the media.[88] Croatian news referred to Serbs as 'Chetnik terrorists', Serbs denounced the 'Ustashe' in Croatia and 'Fundamentalists' in Bosnia, whose Muslim populations became the subject of arguments that they were initially Croats or Serbs.[89] Nationalism became a short-term alternative to secular democratic mobilisation.

By the 1990 elections, many renounced their 'Yugoslav' nationality and identified themselves 'ethnically'.[90] Nationalists won these elections overwhelmingly on the basis that they would protect their ethnic groups interests. Political compromise, portrayed as capitulation to 'them', became a threat to popular support.[91] Serbia's leaders were as unable to contemplate relaxation of centralised control as Croatia and Slovenia were unable to back down on their claims for greater autonomy or independence. Ironically, whilst each group condemned 'their' nationalism they were incapable of acknowledging their own. Milosevic dismissed "...all nationalism and discrimination, and any division along those lines..."[92] at the same time as pursuing a Greater Serbia. Nationalist rhetoric contrasted starkly with reality.

The rise of nationalism lessened the likelihood of political compromise and had a direct impact on the conduct of ethnically based military forces once conflict arose.[93]

2.6.3 *Political Developments*

In May 1984 Veselin Djuranovic[94] became the first post-Tito President under the rotating-Presidency system. He was followed in successive years by Radovan Vlajkovic,[95] Sinan Hisani,[96] Lazar Mojsov,[97] Raif Disdarevic,[98] and, in May 1990, by Borisav Jovic.[99] When the latter assumed the Presidency, the potential for its political abuse became obvious and he used the platform to call for stronger federal powers to prevent Croatia and Slovenia's demands of greater autonomy and Kosovo's claim for republican status.

It was Slobodan Milosevic's handling of the Kosovo situation which enabled him to take over the Serbian Presidency in 1987.[100] On 28th June 1989, the 600th anniversary of the battle of Kosovo, Milosevic gave a speech in which he reacted to alleged mistreatment of the Serbian minority in Kosovo. In a fiercely nationalistic speech which enraged his mentor, Serbian President Ivan Stambolic, Milosevic informed the Serbs that he would ensure they were not mistreated again and would take whatever measures were necessary to achieve this aim. Over subsequent months Milosevic challenged, and beat, Stambolic for the Serbian Presidency whilst ousting political leaders from Kosovo, Vojvodina and Montenegro via carefully staged 'rallies of truth' which attacked existing leaders and called for the installation of people known to be loyal to Milosevic. Fearing that Kosovo's political demands could have destabilising effects, Milosevic began repressing the Kosovo-Albanian's existing political and cultural rights. Albanians were dismissed from public positions, Albanian-speaking schools were closed down, street signs were changed into the Serbian Cyrillic alphabet and ultimately Kosovo's autonomous status was abolished alongside that of Vojvodina.[101] This gave Milosevic control of half the Federal Presidency's eight votes and generated fear of a "...Serboslavia...".[102] Slovenia reacted by proposing unilateral constitutional amendments to secure greater autonomy, including the right to secede from a Serb-dominated SFRY, and Prime-Minister Markovic resigned, claiming civil war was imminent. Slovenia's proposals included the holding of multi-party elections and Croatia, following suit, legalised previously prohibited political parties such as Franjo Tudjman's Croatian Democratic Union (HDZ).[103] Slovenia and Croatia campaigned to hold a referendum on independence and reverse Serb domination. Tudjman's electoral victory in Croatia and Milan Kucan's victory in Slovenia united these republics against Serbia's centralist agenda. Tudjman's nationalist rhetoric was entrenched in the 1990 Croatian Constitution, which relegated Serbs from the 'constituent nation' status they enjoyed in Yugoslavia.[104] Croatian-Serb areas such as Knin, in the Krajina, were incensed and organised their own referendum which overwhelmingly supported plans for Krajina to remain in Yugoslavia.[105] The Yugoslav National Army (JNA) intervened to prevent Tudjman blocking the referendum and began a military link between the JNA Serbs in other republics.

Fearing civil conflict, the JNA disarmed Slovenian and Croatian Territorial Defence Forces (TDF's),[106] which nevertheless smuggled arms from abroad. Croatia replaced its TDF with an armed police force, the Croatian National Guard, organised in every local village. The Serb-dominated Federal Presidency ordered the disarming of all local militias and Serbian media filmed secret evidence of Croatia's arms smuggling operations. Nevertheless, with only four votes under Milosevic's control he was unable to authorise JNA-intervention in Croatia or a national state of emergency when other republican leaders vetoed these. Jovic resigned, arguing that he refused to preside over a Presidency unprepared to take measures necessary to save Yugoslavia and was joined by allies from Montenegro, Kosovo and Vojvodina. This created a power vacuum and, when Serbia threatened unilateral military action, cast the next political move into the hands of the JNA, whom Milosevic declared "...had the constitutional authorisation and obligation to defend Yugoslavia's constitution...".[107] On the same day, Knin declared its independence from Croatia.

If Milosevic could not control a united Yugoslavia, he was prepared to accept war to create an enlarged 'Greater Serbia'. Although Slovenia contained few Serbs, and therefore fell outside this aim, Croatia and Bosnia were different. Milosevic realised the benefits of removing Croatian opposition whilst maintaining Serb-occupied territories. Speaking of possible Croatian secession from Yugoslavia, he stated that "...it should not occur to anyone that a part of the Serbian nation will be allowed to go with them...".[108] Milosevic's rhetoric of Yugoslav unity was plausible only insofar that existing structures entrenched Serbia's domination of federal institutions and he was clearly willing to sacrifice Yugoslavia for Greater Serbia. His rhetoric of the right to self-determination for Serbs in other republics did not extend to Muslims in the Sandzac region of Serbia or the Kosovo-Albanians. Equally, Tudjman's insistence on the indivisibility of republican borders did not extend to Bosnia, which he and Milosevic contemplated dividing.

The Knin rebellion was replicated in Croatia-Slavonia in early 1991. Tudjman's National Guard successfully recaptured Pakrac, the first non-Krajina Serb area to claim autonomy, but Serbian news reports falsified the death toll and other facts.[109] Other Croatian-Serb areas began to arm themselves, declaring autonomy and unity with Serbia. Jovic, returning as President, unilaterally authorised JNA intervention into Croatia, which interposed itself between Croats and Serb-occupied areas, preventing Croatia from recapturing them. "Under a cloak of impartiality, the JNA was another step closer to becoming the army of Greater Serbia".[110] Slovenia saw JNA-intervention as Serbia's attempt to implement *coups* similar to those in Kosovo, Vojvodina and Montenegro. A Slovenian declaration of *Sovereignty Within Yugoslavia* on 2nd July 1990 was followed by a referendum in December supporting such action. A similar Croatian declaration a day later was equally endorsed in a referendum on 19th May.[111]

From May-June 1991, a series of Federal-Presidency meetings discussed Yugoslavia's future. These meetings appeared to accept the inevitability of Slovenian and Croatian independence and concentrated on whether this would require the redrawing of republican borders. Caught "...between the hammer and the anvil of Serbian and Croat nationalism..."[112] Bosnia and Macedonia proposed an 'asymmetrical federation', with differing levels of autonomy in a continuing Yugoslavia.[113] Each of the other republics had already gone too far in their opposite directions to consider such a plan, however. Compromise represented political suicide because of their nationalist power base. Instead, Slovenia and Croatia shifted from demanding greater autonomy within Yugoslavia's existing borders to preparing for independence. The only real results of these meetings was the formation of a Croatia-Slovenia joint defence agreement, contemplating JNA intervention, which was later reneged upon by Croatia.[114]

Slovenian readiness for independence was assisted by the absence of Serb minorities but this did not prevent Croatia attempting to keep pace with Slovenia. Both republics issued declarations of independence on 25th June 1991 which the Federal Parliament declared unconstitutional.[115] When Jovic's Presidential term expired his allies prevented the succession of Croatia's Stipe Mesic, leaving Yugoslavia without a President. Prime Minister Markovic, having returned, issued a decree giving the Defence Minister, JNA General Veljko Kadijevic, control over Yugoslavia's security. This redressed Kadijevic's previous concerns about the constitutional legitimacy of JNA action.

On 27th June 1991, JNA operations began in Slovenia but met with opposition from a well prepared Slovenian TDF.[116] Under EC pressure, and Milosevic's desire to 'lose' Slovenian disruption to his plans, Jovic was ordered to allow Mesic's succession to the Presidency, which then ordered a JNA withdrawal after just ten days.[117] Elements of the JNA, including the Chief-of-Staff General Adzic, refused to cooperate initially, saying the JNA would fight until it had regained control of Slovenia.[118] Serbia then recognised Slovenia's right to secede whilst denying Croatia the same right.

In Croatia, the 'Serb Republic of Krajina' demanded Croatian withdrawal from its borders and Milan Martic, leader of a paramilitary group known as the 'Marticevci', declared that they were part of the Yugoslavian defence force. Acting together with the JNA military chief in Knin, Ratko Mladic, the Marticevci 'cleansed' a Croatian village in Krajina of all Croats. Similar assaults, and 'ethnic-cleansing', of towns of Vukovar, Pakrac, Ocucani and Karlovac followed, with local Croatian-Serb militias, such as 'Arkan's Tigers', given JNA support.[119] Tudjman's right wing opposition considered him to be failing to protect Croatia and formed their own militias. Those loyal to Dobrosav Paraga are one of many examples.[120] JNA barracks were attacked and weapons placed into the hands of numerous military factions. Fighting continued until November 1991, when Milosevic and Tudjman agreed to the United Nations Protection Force (UNPROFOR) of peacekeepers, by which time Serbs had gained almost a third of Croatia. Milosevic then turned his attentions to Bosnia.

In September 1991, a EC Conference on Yugoslavia (ECCY) was convened and Croatia and Slovenia were recognised as independent States in January 1992. Fearing Serb domination of a residual Yugoslavia, Bosnia and Macedonia also applied for recognition, though were initially refused.[121]

Bosnia's application started a war which proved more ferocious than those in Slovenia and Croatia combined.

The 1990 election results reflected Bosnia's ethnic composition.[122] The Muslim Party of Democratic Action (SDA) led by Alija Izetbegovic won the majority of votes with the Bosnian-Serb leader of Milosevic's Serbian Democratic Party (SDS), Radovan Karadzic, coming second and the Croatian-HDZ party third. Izetbegovic became head of a rotating Bosnian Presidency which allowed Croatian and Serbian representatives to share political power and was joint author of a plan with Macedonia to save Yugoslavia by confederalising its constitution.[123] After JNA operations in Slovenia and Croatia Karadzic called for a united Serb army throughout Yugoslavia before boycotting the Bosnian Parliament, creating a Serb Parliament in Pale, organising a referendum which indicated Bosnian-Serbs desire to remain in Yugoslavia or to secede from an independent Bosnia and erecting barricades around the newly proclaimed Serb Republic of Bosnia, Republika Srpska.[124] Due to lack of progress in constitutional negotiations, remaining Bosnian Assembly representatives declared Bosnia's willingness to abide by EC conditions for recognition and produced a *Memorandum* and *Platform* to this effect before declaring sovereignty on 15th October 1991.[125]

Macedonia organised a referendum which voted in favour of "...an independent Macedonia within an association of Yugoslav States..."[126] but again political stalemate resulted in a decision to choose independence. By December 1991 every republic except Serbia and Montenegro had applied for EC recognition. Macedonia largely escaped federal attack due to the absence of significant Serb minorities, the concentration of JNA forces elsewhere and the stationing of UN troops in a preventative role within the republic.[127] Bosnia was not so fortunate.

As the most ethnically mixed republic with different ethnic majorities in its numerous villages and towns, Bosnia became the subject of expansionist plans from both Serbia and Croatia. JNA withdrawal from Croatia resulted in large numbers of troops and weapons moving to Bosnia and Bosnian-Serb JNA members were transferred to Bosnia.[128] When EC recognition was granted on 6th April 1992 conflict erupted immediately. The pattern of conflict was similar to that in Slovenia and Croatia. Local and regional militia, supported by the JNA,[129] attacked and ethnically-cleansed areas such as Zvornik, Banja Luka, Bijelina, Brcko, Doboj and the capital, Sarajevo, to secure a corridor between Serb-occupied areas in Croatia, Bosnia and Serbia.[130] When Milosevic ordered the JNA's withdrawal in May

1992, Bosnian-Serbs held almost two-thirds of Bosnian territory and over 80,000 Bosnian-Serb JNA members remained to form a Bosnian-Serb army, under the control of General Ratko Mladic, which inherited weaponry left by the JNA. Both Karadzic and Mladic have twice been indicted by the ICTY for atrocities allegedly committed during the Bosnian conflict.[131] Various sieges prompted the creation of 'safe areas' but this still did not prevent them falling to the Bosnian-Serb army.[132] During 1992, a Muslim-Croat war developed in the remaining third of Bosnia, despite a Tudjman-Izetbegovic military pact of June 1992.[133] Tudjman's Bosnian-HDZ representative, Mate Boban, created a Croatian mini-State called 'Herzeg-Bosna' in western Hercegovina and Bosnian-Croat militias, supported by Croatia's National Guard,[134] fought for territories in Prozor, Vitez, Travnik, Zenica and Mostar. Bosnian-Muslims, lacking a strong TDF and fighting militias backed by political and military patronage from Croatia and Serbia, were thus most adversely affected by a UN arms embargo imposed in September 1991.[135] Bosnian-Muslim territory was reduced to "...a leopard spot smattering of isolated enclaves...".[136] This led to the formation of Muslim-fundamentalist militias such as the Seventh Muslim Brigade, who emulated policies of ethnic-cleansing which had been used so effectively against them by Bosnian-Croats and Bosnian-Serbs. Ironically, it also led to an inter-Muslim war around Bihac, with Fikret Abdic declaring an 'Autonomous Province of Western Bosnia'.[137]

During the period of time discussed here, both Serbia and Montenegro avoided conflict within their own borders. Nevertheless the Kosovo question remained unresolved. Kosovo-Albanian demands for restoration of autonomous status within Serbia were never formally addressed by the various peace-initiatives proposed by the international community, despite the fact that Kosovo had clearly acted as the catalyst for Yugoslavia's dissolution. Throughout the EC's conference on Yugoslavia and the later EC-UN conference, negotiations were limited to republican and federal representatives, thus excluding representatives from Kosovo and Vojvodina. Frustration with Serbian recalcitrance over the restoration of autonomy caused growing support amongst Kosovo-Albanians for full Yugoslav-republic status and, following the declarations of independence from Slovenia, Croatia, Macedonia and Bosnia, for independence and union with Albania.

Kosovo had not taken up arms against Serbia-Montenegro but a small military force known as the Kosovo Liberation Army (KLA) increasingly began to exact reprisals against Serbs living in the region. The KLA's activities and membership were relatively small-scale until 1997 when, following the pyramid banking disaster, imports from Albania's arms manufacturers were drastically cheaper than before. Equally, having viewed the independence of Slovenia, Croatia and Bosnia and the conflicts which achieved such independence, many Kosovo-Albanians were convinced by the KLA's position that armed rebellion was the only way to evade Serbian domination. The international community's failure to discuss Kosovo's future whilst negotiating the *Dayton Peace Agreement* in 1995 indicated to many Albanians that their path of non-violent opposition to Serbia's actions had failed to arouse the same level of international interest or support as the bloody conflicts in Croatia and Bosnia. Accordingly, the KLA launched a series of operations which saw them take military control of much of the Kosovo region. Inevitably, this provoked a fierce response from the JNA and Serb forces which destroyed many Kosovo-Albanian houses before ethnically-cleansing the region and creating nearly a million refugees and internally-displaced persons.[138] These events succeeded in creating sufficient interest for the international community to devote a series of governmental meetings solely to the Kosovo question for the first time. After a series of diplomatic failures and 11 weeks of NATO bombing in Serbia, an uneasy peace was agreed in June 1999 and an international peace-keeping force deployed to police the agreement. At the time of writing it is too early to say whether the UN Mission in Kosovo (UNMIK) and the Kosovo-Force (K-FOR) will succeed in stabilising the region but it is clear that there remains much rebuilding, physically and psychologically, to be done before it is possible to speak of a long-term peace with any real confidence.

In addition to the problematic status of Kosovo, questions remain about the future of Vojvodina, in northern Serbia, and Montenegro. The situation in Vojvodina is, in some senses, incomparable to that in Kosovo. The 1991 Yugoslav demographic census indicated that Hungarians constituted only 18% of the population of Vojvodina in contrast with the 90% Albanian population in Kosovo. This would severely limit attempts to form a liberation army capable of challenging the military power of the JNA and other Serb militias who would oppose any attempt to challenge the current political situation. Furthermore, Vojvodina does not possess the symbolic historical importance of Kosovo for the Serbs which caused them to react so swiftly to the KLA's actions. Nevertheless, the potential for destabilisation clearly still exists. Although the current peace-plan fails to indicate Kosovo's future status and whether it will have its autonomy restored or even be allowed to unite with Albania, an earlier plan, known as the Rambouillet Accords, planned for an international conference with a 'mechanism' for resolving this issue. Those in Vojvodina seeking to ensure that their future is not separated from Kosovo's, and more specifically that Kosovo does not benefit from some form of greater autonomy which is denied to Vojvodina, may pursue a path of violent opposition such as in Kosovo. The Vojvodina League of Social Democrats was amongst the first political groups to call for Milosevic's resignation in the wake of NATO's bombings and behaviour such as this may encourage an aggressive response from Serbia's President, who has always acted swiftly to previous threats to his power. Much will depend on developments in Kosovo following the June 1999 peace-plan and on the future of Milosevic and his allies in light of their recent indictment by the International War Crimes Tribunal for Yugoslavia.[139]

Finally, further conflict may arise as a result of recent indications that Montenegro is considering seeking independence and leaving the residual 'Yugoslavia' with only Serbia as a constituent unit. The Serbia-Montenegro link has proved the strongest bond so far in the former Yugoslavia but signs are now beginning to show that Montenegro desires to lose the international pariah status which accompanies its association with Serbia under Milosevic's rule.[140] Miodrag Vokovic, of the leading Montenegro Democratic Socialists party, has said that Milosevic is directly to blame for the poor economic and political conditions now faced by Serbia and has expressed his desire to extract Montenegro from the detrimental aid, trade and diplomatic conditions imposed against the Federal Republic of Yugoslavia. Such a development would leave Milosevic totally isolated in the Balkans and may cause him to attempt to prevent such a move, perhaps igniting another bitter war.

2.6.4 *Military Factors*

The JNA was the only Yugoslav federal institution not operating under the carefully crafted ethnic balance in other areas of public life and Serbs were grossly over-represented therein.[141] "The degree of military participation in Yugoslavia's political life is greater than that in any other socialist country..."[142] and it was felt that the JNA would be one of the main forces capable of preventing Yugoslavia's dissolution.[143] Nevertheless, entrenched positions of power under existing Yugoslav structures caused the JNA to adopt a political position broadly aligned with Serbia and Montenegro.[144]

The JNA's active political role in Yugoslavia's dissolution does not compare with its military role. Military support given to Serb militias in other republics, pursuing Milosevic's Greater Serbia dream, has already been described. Non-Serbs within the JNA were largely reluctant to fight against their own ethnic communities and often deserted and joined republican militias rather than face prosecution as 'traitors'.[145] The JNA's dissolution, and the confused chains of command which resulted, mirrored events in Yugoslavia's other federal institutions.[146]

The JNA was not the only armed force in Yugoslavia, however. The military situation was complicated by the creation of Territorial Defence Forces (TDF's) under Tito's 1969 defence review, which sought to avoid a replica of the USSR's intervention in Czechoslovakia a year earlier by spreading Yugoslavia's military capacity throughout the various republics, equipping each with its own mini-army. The Total National Defence policy created a 'hedgehog' structure of military forces, where "…every commune, every town, every major factory [could] roll-up an invading force of some two million men…".[147] Republics seeking independence rapidly expanded their TDF's to counter any JNA attack, especially in Croatia where "…the influx of so many young Croats, promoted to positions of authority which their age did not warrant…weakened chains of command and accountability".[148] Discipline in many TDF's was poor and diverse chains of command reduced political and military control over newly-recruited troops fuelled by nationalist rhetoric.[149] Widespread use of ill-disciplined local militias, such as Arkan's Tigers, the White Eagles and those loyal to Milan Martic, Vojislav Šešelj, Dobrosav Paraga and Fikret Abdic, made the Yugoslav wars distinctive for their barbarity.

2.7 Conclusions

Just as the creation of Yugoslavia was "...the work of long-term factors and the consequence of immediate causes..."[150] so was its dissolution. Yugoslavia's vulnerable geographical location allowed successive foreign forces to foment, exaggerate and manipulate 'ethnic' differences of the Southern-Slav communities. Once divided, foreign interference was rationalised because of their inability to unite. This has been compared to

"...hitting a dog and then accusing it of limping".[151] Historically cultivated differences were later used by career-minded nationalists for their own political agendas, renewing 'ethnic' divisions. Yugoslavia did not dissolve because of intractable 'ethnic' hatreds. The possibility of peaceful union amongst the Yugoslav communities is evidenced by the high percentage of inter-community marriages shortly before its dissolution.[152]

Yugoslavia's problems were political and required political solutions. In a country without any democratic history, deprived of Tito's charismatic ability to resolve inter-community tensions and controlled by politicians whose nationalist power base made them unwilling, and unable, to accept political compromise, political solutions were unlikely to come from within. History shows that the Southern-Slavs have always been forced to fight for their political ambitions, either for their own territorial expansion or to resist political centralisation. In 1991, the conflicts were not conducted against colonial rulers or external invaders but against other Yugoslav communities. Serbs sought to preserve their disproportionate influence within Yugoslavia or realise the historical dream of a Greater-Serbia whilst other republics sought to dilute centralised control within Yugoslavia before fighting to achieve their independence. To label these events as irreconcilable 'ethnic' hatreds ignores the political foundations of the Yugoslav conflict and accepts the inevitability of it's violent disintegration. It also discounts the possibility that these events could be repeated in other States.

When Tito died, Yugoslavia's dissolution was by no means inevitable, though it increasingly became so as the situation worsened. The challenges it faced were ultimately incapable of being resolved by the Yugoslav communities and international intervention arrived only when those communities were divided by conflicts which had been predicted by international intelligence agencies long before they occurred.[153] Serbia has generally been deemed the most culpable Yugoslav party[154] and, whilst this writer would not disagree with this assessment, factors other than the Yugoslav parties behaviour affected the evolution of the conflict. Chapter 3 highlights how the changing international environment may have impacted on Yugoslavia's troubles and *vice versa*. Chapter 4 analyses the international community's response to the conflict. Chapters 7-9 suggest that the Yugoslav conflict evidences wider changes in threats to international peace and security and discuss an alternative international approach to those currently adopted.

Notes

1 See chapter 1, section 1.2.1.

2 Cited in Howard, M. (ed.), *The Causes of War and Other Essays: Second Edition*, (1983), Temple-Smith, 24.

3 See chapters 7-8. Denitch, B., *Ethnic Nationalism: The Tragic Death of Yugoslavia*, (1994), MinUP, 1, describes Yugoslavia as "...a prism through which to examine several far wider sets of problems". Cf. Cassesse, A., *Self-Determination of Peoples: A Legal Reappraisal*, (1996), CUP, 361.

4 See Map 1.

5 See section 2.6.1.

6 Burg, S.L., *Conflict and Cohesion in Socialist Yugoslavia: Political Decision-Making Since 1966*, (1983), *PUP*, 3. See Map 2.

7 See Maps 3 and 7. See also Phillips, A (ed.), *Minorities in the Balkans*, (1989), MRG.

8 West, R.W., *Tito and the Rise and Fall of Yugoslavia*, (1994), Sinclair-Stevenson, at 2, refutes the categorisation of the Southern Slavs along 'ethnic' lines, despite these differences. See also Stanovcic, V., 'History and Status of Ethnic Conflicts', in Rusinow, D. (ed.), *Yugoslavia: A Fractured Federalism*, (1988), Wilson, 23.

9 See Map 3.

10 West, supra n.8., 3.

11 Saint Vitus, or Vidovdan Day, is sacred to Serbs and has been an important date in Yugoslavia's history. Archduke Ferdinand's assassination, German recognition of the Slav Kingdom, the massacre of hundreds of Serbs in Croatia during World War II and the introduction of the founding Yugoslav Constitution all occurred on anniversaries of the Battle of Kosovo.

12 Darby, H.C., *A Short History of Yugoslavia from Early Times to 1966*, (1966), CUP, 62.

13 Montenegro had been retaken by the Ottomans in 1853 after Russia withdrew its support which had helped the seventeenth-century defeat of Turks in Montenegro and Serbia. Russia had been annoyed at the neutrality of Serbia and Montenegro during the Crimean War.

14 Hunter, B. (ed.), *The Statesman's Yearbook*, (1992-3), Macmillan, 1616. Suzerainty originated as a constitutional law term to describe the relationship between a feudal lord and his vassal. With the disappearance of the feudal system, suzerainty developed into an international law concept to indicate the rights of one State over another State. Suzerainty implied a kind of international guardianship which, nevertheless, fell short of absolute sovereignty over the vassal State. It is now of purely historical interest, since no such vassal States exist in the modern international system. See Parry, C. and Grant, J.P. (eds.), *Encyclopaedic Dictionary of International Law*, (1986), Oceana, 385.

15 The Dual-Monarchy feared that a united Slav presence in the area with access to the Adriatic coastline would reduce its own influence, and demanded an independent Albania in the hope that this would prevent the situation arising.

16 Rumania had also joined the League at this stage.

17 Trifunovska, S. (ed.), *Yugoslavia Through Documents: From its Creation to its Dissolution*, (1994), Nijhoff, 125-34.

18 Ibid, 137.

19 Dragnich, A.N. *The First Yugoslavia: Search for a Viable Political System*, (1983), Hoover, 7-9.

20 Most of Dalmatia was to pass to Italy under the *Treaty of London*. See Map 4.

21 West, supra n.8., chapter 3.

22 See Trifunovska, supra n.17, 71, for the text.

23 See chapter 7, section 7.2.2.

24 Darby, supra n.12, 3.

25 Dalmatia, Carniola, Styria and Carinthia.

26 Croatia-Slavonia, Bosnia, Hercegovina, Vojvodina, Baranja and Banat.

27 Trifunovska, supra n.17, 157. See Map 4.

28 Pavlowich, S.K., *The Improbable Survivor: Yugoslavia and its Problems 1918-1988*, (1988), Hurst, 65.

29 Darby, supra n.12, 164.

30 This was not helped by the fact that Germany's signing of the *Versailles Treaty*, in 1919, recognising the 'Kingdom' and the introduction of the 1921 constitution were done on 28th June, anniversary of St. Vitus Day.

31 Despite roughly equal numbers of votes obtained in the federal elections, the opposition parties, mainly Croatian federalists, were allocated only 67 seats in comparison with the Governments 301 seats. See Dragnich, supra n.19, 147.

32 Alexander had been regent of Serbs since 1914 and became King of the Slav Kingdom in August 1921.

33 Dragnich, supra n.19, 150.

34 Darby, supra n.12, chapter 9.

35 Hunter, supra n.14, 1615.

36 Mercer, D. (ed.), *Chronicle of the Second World War*, (1994), Chronicles, 4.

37 Prince Paul, who succeeded Alexander, had since been replaced with King Peter.

38 Southern Slovenia, Dalmatia and Montenegro. See Map 5.

39 Northern Slovenia.

40 Kosovo and western-Macedonia.

41 Eastern Macedonia and southern-Serbia.

42 Areas surrounding the Danube and northern-Serbia.

43 West, supra n.8., chapter 5 for details.

44 Malcolm, N., *A Short History of Bosnia*, (1994), Macmillan, 176.

45 See Milazzo, M.J., *The Chetnik Movement and Yugoslav Resistance*, (1975), JHUP.

46 Tito had been the head of the illegal Communist Party since 1937.

47 Grun, B. (ed.), *Timetables of History, Third Edition*, (1991), S&S, 518.

48 West, supra n.8., 221.

49 Ibid, 193.

50 Including Kosovo and Vojvodina.

51 On Yugoslavia's post-war foreign affairs, see Wilson, D., *Tito's Yugoslavia*, (1979), CUP, 225-34; Remington, R.A., 'Foreign Policy', in Rusinow, supra n.8, 156; Rubinstein, A.Z., *Yugoslavia and the Non-Aligned World*, (1970), PUP.

52 Darby, supra n.12, 247.

53 Lydall, H., *Yugoslavia in Crisis*, (1989), Clarendon, 2.

54 Simonovcic, I, 'Socialism, Federalism and Ethnic Identity', in Rusinow, supra n.8, 41.

55 See section 2.6.3.

56 Wilson, supra n.51, 122-36. See also 137-80 for details of Tito's economic reforms.

57 Lydall, supra n.53, 236. On the break with Stalin, see Wilson, ibid, 49-59.

58 In 1975, Trieste Zone A was formally recognised as Italian, whilst Zone B, the Free Territory of Trieste, passed to Yugoslavia. See Hunter, supra n.14, 1667. For the text of the agreement, see *Materials on Succession of States in Respect of Matters Other Than Treaties*, (1978), UNDPI, 65-75.

59 Tito condemned both of these as illegal interventions, in addition to the Soviet involvement in Cambodia and Afghanistan. See Miller, R.F., *Tito as Political Leader and External Factors in Yugoslav Political Development*, (1977), AUP, 25-9. On post-Stalin relations between the SFRY and USSR, see Wilson, supra n.51, 95-106.

60 See Lydall, supra n.53, 3 and 18-19 for details.

61 Stankovic, S., *The End of an Era: Yugoslavia's Dilemmas*, (1981), Hoover, chapter 1.

62 West, supra n.8., chapter 15.

63 Wilson, supra n.51, at 214, notes that the three largest banks in Yugoslavia were Serb-controlled and accounted for 66% of the total economy, in comparison with 17% under Croatian control. See chapter 6, section 6.10.2. for discussion of State-succession problems relating to the NBY.

64 Lydall, supra n.53, 21.

65 Burg, S.L., supra n.6, 83-187, for details.

66 Malcolm, supra n.44, chapter 15, for details.

67 Trifunovska, supra n.17, 224. Mullerson, R., *International Law, Rights and Politics*, (1994), Routledge, 127, describes it as "...a clever piece of work..." which attempted to accommodate conflicting ethnic and political interests. Wilson, supra n.51, 216, considers it "...perhaps the longest and most complicated Constitution in the world...".

68 Kostunica, V., 'The Constitution and the Federal States', in Rusinow, supra n.8, 78-9.

69 Ibid, 80.

70 Lydall, supra n.53, chapter 11; Wilson, supra n.51, 260, prophesied that, even after Tito's death, "...there is little cause for immediate concern about the stability of Yugoslavia".

71 West, supra n.8., 312.

72 See Woodward, S., *Balkan Tragedy*, (1995), Brookings; Bordon, A. (ed.), *Breakdown, War and Reconstruction in Yugoslavia*, (1992), IWPR; Thompson,

M., *A Paper House: The Ending of Yugoslavia*, (1992), Pantheon; Cohen, L.J., *Broken Bonds*, (1995), Westview.

73 For figures on the Yugoslav economy in the post-Tito era, see generally Dyker, D.A., *Yugoslavia: Socialism, Development and Debt*, (1990), Routledge; Simmie, J. and Dekleva, J. (eds.) *Yugoslavia in Turmoil: After Self-Management*, (1991), Pinter; McFarlane, B., *Yugoslavia: Politics, Economy and Society*, (1988), Pinter, Bicanic, I., *Fractured Economy* and Burkett, J. and Skegro, B., 'Are Economic Fractures Widening?', in Rusinow, supra n.8, 120. For a study of the economy during 1989-90, see *OECD Economic Surveys: Yugoslavia*, (1990), OECD Publications. For a review of economic conditions from Yugoslavia's creation to the initial post-Tito era see Singleton, F., and Carter, B., *The Economy of Yugoslavia*, (1982), Croom-Helm.

74 Lydall, supra n.53, 236.

75 Bicanic, supra n.73, 120. See Map 6. See also Fink-Hafner, D and Robbins, J.R. (eds.), *Making a New Nation: The Formation of Slovenia*, (1997), Dartmouth, 308, for statistics on the Slovenian economy.

76 Pavlowich, supra n.28, 73.

77 Ibid, 143.

78 Silber, L. and Little, A., *The Death of Yugoslavia*, (1995), Penguin, 33.

79 Dyker, supra n.73, at 114-127, for details. See also Mencinger, J., 'Costs and Benefits of Secession', in Fink-Hafner, supra n.75, 204.

80 Pavlowich, supra n.28, 175.

81 Edwards, S. (ed.) *European World Yearbook*, (1993), 3225.

82 Dyker, supra n.73, at 122-5, for details. This was at the time the biggest ever IMF loan and "...represented a milestone in Yugoslavia's relations with the international financial community...". At 184 *et seq*, Dyker suggests that the IMF must bear some responsibility in aggravating Yugoslavia's economic and political situation.

83 See Donia, R.J., and Fine, V.A., *Bosnia-Hercegovina: A Tradition Betrayed*, (1994), Hurst, 203-6.

84 Chapter 3, section 3.5.2. See Borowiec, A., *Yugoslavia After Tito*, (1977), Praeger, 94, for statistics of declining international aid to Yugoslavia.

85 Denitch, supra n.3., at 12, argues that this would have worked. Borowiec, id, notes that aid from the USA alone during 1951-9 amounted to $700 million, which casts the IMF's loan into perspective.

86 Denitch, ibid, at 192-3. See also Silber, supra n.78, 386. Slovenia is the only exception to this statement. See Mencinger, supra n.79, 213.

87 See Mayall, J., *Nationalism and International Society*, (1990), CUP; Anderson, K., 'Illiberal Tolerance and the Fall of Yugoslavia', (1993), 33 *VJIL*, 385; MacCormack, N., 'Is Nationalism Philosophically Credible?', in Twining, W. (ed.), *Issues of Self-Determination*, AbUP, 8; Bengoetxea, J., 'Nationalism and Self-Determination', ibid, 133. Carr, E.H., *What is History?*, (1961), Macmillan, at 145, suggests that "...study of mass psychology shows that the most rapid way to secure acceptance of their views is through an appeal to the irrational element in the make-up of the elector...".

88 Silber, supra n.78, 98. See also Hampson, F., *Incitement and the Media: Responsibility of and for the Media in the Conflicts in the Former Yugoslavia*, (1992), EUP; Ramet, P., 'The Yugoslav Press in Flux', in Ramet, P. (ed.), *Yugoslavia In The 1980s*, (1985), Westview, 100; Hrvatin, S.B., 'The Role of the Media in the Transition', in Fink-Hafner, supra n.75, 276; Woodward, S.L., *Balkan Tragedy: Chaos and Dissolution After the Cold War*, (1995), Brookings, 352; *Report of the CSCE Human-Rights Rapporteur Mission to Yugoslavia*, (1992) CSCE Communication 41, paragraph 8.

89 Silber, ibid, 155; Malcolm, supra n.44, chapter 15.

90 Simonovcic, supra n.54, 49, cites statistical proof linking this phenomenon with periods of economic hardship.

91 Rogoff, M.A., 'The Obligation to Negotiate in International Law: Rules and Realities', (1994), 16 *Mich. JIL*, 141, at 153, notes that "...the principal inhibition to undertaking the search for common solutions to international problems is domestic pressure militating against co-operation and compromise, particularly with respect to issues that are emotionally charged".

92 Silber, supra n.78, 142.

93 See chapter 8, section 8.3.

94 A Montenegrin.

95 A Vojvodinan.

96 A Kosovar.

97 A Macedonian.

98 A Slovenian.

99 A Serbian.

100 Glenny, M., *The Fall of Yugoslavia, Second Edition*, (1993), Penguin, at 15-16, cites evidence of over 50,000 Kosovo-Serb refugees caused by allegations of their mistreatment by Kosovo-Albanians. For interviews with the politicians involved in the events discussed herein see the excellent television series *Death of Yugoslavia*, (1995), BBC TV.

101 Karaosmanoglu, A.L, *Crisis in the Balkans*, (1993), UNIDR, 6-7.

102 Silber, supra n.78, at 66. West, supra n.8., 343-5.

103 Tudjman had, under Tito, been expelled from the Communist Party for his nationalist beliefs.

104 Trifunovska, supra n.17, at 252; Denitch, supra n.3, at 14-15; Silber, supra n.78, 96.

105 Silber, ibid, 98-112.

106 See section 2.6.4.

107 Silber, supra n.78, 141.

108 Ibid, 142.

109 Silber, ibid, 147, describes how a Serbian tabloid described the killing of an Orthodox priest on its cover-page, the mere wounding of the same priest on page two and a statement from the surviving priest on page three.

110 Id.

111 This is unsurprising, since the referendum was held shortly after the JNA interventions into Croatia. A referendum in favour of autonomy within Croatia, or union with Serbia, was held in Croatian-Serb territories on 19th August 1990.

112 Malcolm, supra n.44, 218.

113 Silber, supra n.78, 162, for details of the Izetbegovic-Gligorov Plan.

114 Ibid, 163.

115 Trifunovska, supra n.17, 286-301, and 353.

116 Silber, supra n.78, 169-185.

117 Only Mesic voted against JNA withdrawal from Slovenia, realising that this effected Slovenian independence without resolving Croatia's situation. After this, Mesic left the Presidency, returning it to Milosevic's control, under the nominal Presidency of Montenegro's Branko Kostic.

118 Silber, supra n.78, 179.

119 Ibid, 206.

120 Ibid, 205.

121 See chapter 5, section 5.10.12.

122 Silber, supra n.78, 232, for details of election results. See Map 7 for Bosnia's ethnic composition.

123 Supra n.112.

124 Silber, supra n.78, 149. See also Badinter Commission *Opinion 4*, in chapter 5, section 5.10.8.

125 See chapter 4, section 4.3.8. Weller, M., 'The International Response to the Dissolution of the SFRY', (1992), 86 *AJIL*, 569, notes that Bosnia also felt compelled to claim independence because of the legal requirement that only a sovereign State can declare neutrality between combatants in the manner sought by Bosnia after JNA-intervention in Slovenia and Croatia.

126 See Badinter Commission *Opinion 1*, in chapter 5, section 5.7.7. The Carrington plan built upon this approach. See chapter 4, section 4.3.7.

127 See chapter 4, section 4.5.5.

128 Silber, supra n.78, 240.

129 The Trial-Chamber of the Yugoslav War-Crimes Tribunal found that the Bosnian-Serbs enjoyed significant political support and received training, finance, logistical and military support from the JNA, even to the point of having dictated the military objectives of paramilitary leaders such as Vojislav Šešelj. See *Prosecutor of the International Criminal Tribunal for the Prosecution of Persons Responsible for Serious Violations of International Humanitarian Law Committed in the Territory of the Former Yugoslavia Since 1991 v Dusko Tadic,* (1997), Case IT-94-1-T, paragraphs 577-608 and the dissent of Presiding Judge Kirk-McDonald, paragraphs 5-33.

130 Silber, supra n.78, 154, notes that ethnic cleansing, or "...*etnicko ciscenje*... became the defining characteristic of the [Bosnian] conflict. [Refugees]...were not the tragic by-product of a civil war; their expulsion was *the whole point of the war*".

131 See ICTY Prosecutor's Press Releases CC/PIO/013-E (25th July 1995) and CC/PIO/026-E (16th November 1995). Karadzic has also been indicted in America for alleged war crimes and acts of genocide and torture. See *Kadic v Karadzic*, reprinted (1995), 34 *ILM*, 1592; Turns, D., 'War Crimes In Non-International Conflict', (1995), 7(4), *ASICL*, 804, at 828.

132 Silber, supra n.78, 293-305. See chapter 4, section 4.5.6.

133 Ibid, 326. Even during this alliance, Croatia and Bosnian-Croats maintained discussion with Serbia and Bosnian-Serbs over possible division of Bosnia between them. See 339-42.

134 Ibid, 355. Around 30,000 National guard personnel were engaged in Bosnia. See Vego, M., 'The Croatian Forces in Bosnia-Hercegovina', (1993), *JIRev*, 99; UNSC Presidential Statement S/PRST/1994/6, 3rd February 1994. For suggestions that the UN was uneven in its treatment of Croatian and Serbian military support to groups in Bosnia see Gray, C., 'Bosnia-Herzegovina: Civil War or Inter-State Conflict? Characterization and Consequences', (1996), 47 *BYIL*, 155.

135 See chapter 4, section 4.5.2.

136 Silber, supra n.78, 330.

137 Ibid, 339.

138 See Carr-Brown, J. and Scott, C., *Refugees Inherit a Wasteland*, (1999), 13th July, *Sunday Times* for UN figures cited therein. On the history of the Kosovo region see generally Malcolm, N., *A Short History of Kosovo*, (1998), Macmillan. On details of the early stages of the conflict see 'OSCE Reports on Events in Kosovo', (1998), 5(4) *OSCE Newsletter*, 1; Kurin, M., *Kosovo's Attempted Liberation Crushed*, (1998), 14th August, bosnet. On the June 1999 peace-plan and the earlier Rambouillet Accords see Steele, J., *Serbs Forced to Settle for Less*, (1999), 4th June, *Guardian*.

139 Milosevic has been indicted for orchestrating the Kosovo conflict and ordering the commission of war crimes and crimes against humanity. Zeljko Raznatovic, better known as Arkan, has sought legal information on his position in the event that he surrender to the ICTY's jurisdiction and provide information for the tribunal. See Khan, H., *Milosevic Indicted by War Crimes Tribunal*, (1999), 1st July, bosnet; Castle, S., *Arkan May Surrender to Extradition*, (1999), 15th July, *Independent*. See also Trueheart, C., *Hague Indictment Names Serb Chiefs*, (1999), 28th May, *Herald Tribune*. President Milan Milutinovic of Serbia, the Serbian Interior Minister Vlajko Stojilkovic, the deputy PM of the FRY Nikola Sainovic and the FRY's ranking General Dragoljub Ojdanic were indicted alongside Milosevic. More charges are possible in respect of Milosevic's role in the Bosnian conflict.

140 See Prentice, E.A., *One Man Opens Floodgates for Wave of Serbian Protest*, (1999), 7th July, *Times* and Thorpe, N., *Montenegro Hopes for Amicable Divorce*, (1999), *Guardian*.

141 Denitch, supra n.3, 40-41; Gow, J., 'Belgrade and Bosnia: An Assessment of the Yugoslav Military', (1993), *JIRev*, 243; Isby, D.C., 'Yugoslavia 1991: Armed Forces in Conflict', (1991), *JIRev*, 394.

142 Ibid, 92.

143 Borowiec, supra n.84, 91.

144 See generally Gow, J., *Legitimacy and the Military: The Yugoslav Crisis*, (1992), Pinter; Vego, M., 'Yugoslavia's Ground Forces', (1993), *JIRev*, 247.

145 Silber, supra n.78, 195.

146 See chapter 8, section 8.3.1. The *CSCE Human-Rights Report*, supra n.88, 7, considered the JNA "...out of constitutional control..." by late 1991.

147 Borowiec, supra n.84, 95. See 90 *et seq* on the General People's Defence Programme.

148 Silber, supra n.78, 154.

149 Remington, R.A., 'Political-Military Relations in Post-Tito Yugoslavia', in Ramet, supra n.88, 56.

150 Pavlowitch, supra n.34.

151 Dragnich, supra n.19, 2.

152 Simonovcic, supra n.54, 52.

153 Rusinow, D., 'Yugoslavia: Balkan Breakup?', in Forsyth, D.P., *Foreign Policy*, (1992), UNP, 140.

154 See Gray, supra n.134 for various UNGA and UNSC resolutions condemning Serbia; chapter 4, section 4.3. for the EC's approach; CSCE CSO *Declaration on Bosnia*, (1992), Helsinki conference 12th May, reprinted in Trifunovska, supra n.17, 572; and Silber, supra n.78; Glenny, supra n.100, for academic opinion.

3 The Yugoslav Conflict in its International Context

> "To understand law is to understand a community...To understand international law requires an appreciation of the influence of predominant world conditions. These conditions will affect, directly and indirectly, the operation of the international legal system. Certain key factors may be reflected in the scope and nature of international legal rules. Likewise they may prove crucial in law creation and application".
> Holder, W.E. and Brennan, G.A. (eds.), *The International Legal System*, (1972), Butterworths, at 1.

3.1 Introduction

Chapter 2 considered domestic events which led to Yugoslavia's dissolution. This chapter argues that developments in the international community also played a part in this process. Conversely, the Yugoslav conflict may be argued to have had an impact on the international system itself. It will examine the international legal environment during the time the events in chapter 2, and the international responses thereto, took place.

3.2 The Relevance of the International System[1]

Every legal system is part of a wider social system within which the legal sub-system functions. At a macro-level, social values will impact on legal developments and *vice versa*. At a micro-level, the resolution of individual cases will be affected by the nature of legal and societal values at any given time. Any legal lacunae will be 'filled' by a judicial organ in accordance with the prevailing social and legal values.[2] Societal development and legal development are thus intrinsically linked and may be argued to have a parasitic relationship.[3] Whilst this is also true of the international system, international society is far more diffuse and diverse than any single State's municipal system. There is no international equivalent to a State's central government and States, the primary subjects of international law,[4] participate in that system, at least in theory, on an equal basis. International legal developments require a element of consent and enforcement mechanisms are incomparable to domestic models.[5] Sea-changes in society's approaches to prevailing problems are likely to be less frequent, since there are no international political parties with competing agendas to be elected as a world government. Changes in international society's values require political developments of a far grander scale. Many international legal developments occurred after the World Wars, indicating the magnitude of events often required to alter the collective values of the world's States.[6] This chapter discusses whether the contemporary international system has undergone such developments and whether, and how, these may affect the resolution of conflicts within that system.

3.3 Setting the Scene - A New International Scenario?

3.3.1 *The Cold War*[7]

The Cold War began even before the signing of the United Nations Charter in 1945. The political divisions which existed in the run-up to and during the Yalta Conference, held as the Allies poised to celebrate their victory over Hitler's Germany, prophesied the divisions which were to mark the forthcoming fifty years of East-West relations. Ideological, political, economic and military opposition followed the end of World War Two and these divisions were epitomised within the UN. The Security Council operated in an environment of East-West non-cooperation and was often prevented from acting during the Cold War as a result of the veto available to each Permanent Member of the Council.[8] The Cold War, much more global in its effect than either of the World Wars which preceded it, created an international environment which hindered legal development and paralysed many attempts to deal with many conflicts during its forty-four year duration.

3.3.2 *End of the Cold War*

The end of the Cold War arrived in 1989, almost as suddenly as it began. Communism was 'defeated' and the USSR 'lost' the battle of the super-powers. No longer able to match American expenditure on military escalation and financially limited by its rejection of the growing global free-market, the USSR dissolved in a manner comparable with Yugoslavia.[9] A growing realisation that the former Communist countries would have to reassess their international relations with the West reduced much of the non-cooperation of Cold War relations. Such changes global circumstances were said to force the Old World Order to yield to a New World Order (NWO).[10]

An increasingly inter-dependent world, where borders are less relevant in economic and political life, where technological advances ensure free flow of information within and between States and where international co-operation has reached unprecedented levels on an informal and institutionalised basis, marks the contemporary international environment as unique.[11] These developments challenged many assumptions underpinning the international system since World War Two and forced analysts to "...rethink conceptual structures that have become comfortable lenses for our view of world politics".[12] It is now common to hear references to the "...global neighbourhood..."[13] and for writers to acknowledge the reality of inter-dependence often overshadowing the theoretical position of sovereign independence. The expectations of the NWO were tremendous.

The notion of a NWO is not a new one, however. Many periods have claimed to witness unprecedented international legal order, from the development of the traditional international system in Westphalia (1648) through the French Revolution (1789), Russian Revolution (1917), the creation of the League of Nations (1918) and UN (1945), the decolonisation period (1950s-1990s) and the growth of human rights concerns since the Second World War.[14] Each of these periods began with a flurry of rhetoric similar to that which greeted the end of the Cold War, yet each developed into more pessimistic realities and, in some way, failed to live up to this rhetoric.[15] Nevertheless, developments in international legal order need not, and should not, be disparaged simply because they fail to resolve every drawback of previous international-relations periods. Developments need not be faultless to be acknowledged as progression.

The post-Cold War period has been considered the international system's greatest development since the Peace of Westphalia.[16] Increasing interdependence has forced States to "...water their sovereign wine..."[17] by accepting international involvement in a number of areas which would once have fallen solely within their domestic jurisdiction. State sovereignty is an "...essentially relative question..."[18] and contemporary developments have forced many changes on its scope and, perhaps, its meaning. Whereas previous NWO's remained fundamentally State-centric, the post-Cold War world had been transformed so far by technological advances and new threats to international peace and security that the problems faced by the new international order are no longer solely those between States, and the solutions to these problems are often sought by utilising actors other than States. In other words, the nation State is now too small for the world's large problems, and too big for the small problems.[19] These developments have an impact on a number of levels. This chapter will focus on the effects at inter-State, intra-State, institutional and international-constitutional levels.

The thawing of East-West relations, the end of Super-Power confrontation and expansion of political freedom and democracy promised the removal of one of the biggest threats to international peace and security.[20] At an intra-State level, radical political changes were evident in many areas of the globe. Gorbachev's Glasnost and Perestroika programmes during 1988 were followed by the European 'Year of Miracles',[21] witnessing the growth of political liberalism in much of Eastern Europe. Independence for Lithuania, Latvia and Estonia signalled the end of the USSR and the birth of numerous States which accepted international obligations to guarantee democratic government, rule of law and human rights.[22] The "...velvet revolution..."[23] surrounding Czechoslovakia's dissolution in 1989 and the collapse of the Berlin Wall, compared with the fall of the Bastille during the French Revolution,[24] provided further evidence of change. Equally, the release and subsequent election of Nelson Mandela as South Africa's first black president evidenced massive political changes in one of Africa's most notorious States. Intra-State affairs throughout the world were affected directly by the end of the Cold War and the end of the long-running civil war in Cambodia in 1992 shows how the removal of super-power activity in a State on the other side of the globe can have an immediate impact on the future of that region. At an institutional level, the dissolution of States in the former Eastern bloc was mirrored by the institutional dissolution of the Warsaw Pact in March 1991. Eastern bloc States sought economic and political alliances with their former ideological enemies. NATO and the EC both received requests for membership from many of the Warsaw Pact

States.[25] In the UN, super-power co-operation over the Iran-Iraq war and the decisive response by the Security Council to the Iraqi invasion of Kuwait, including the notable absence of the veto, appeared to provide solid evidence of the new political environment.[26]

In addition to such political changes, it has been contended that the NWO may have changed the constitutive principles and underlying norms of international law itself.[27] In addition to new conceptions of State-sovereignty, increased emphasis on human rights,[28] legitimacy,[29] sustainable development[30] and democracy[31] has been suggested to evidence fundamental changes to the international system's 'constitution'. Subsequent chapters dealing with specific international legal norms will examine whether, and how, they have been modified to take account of the current international context.

3.3.3 *The Problems of a New World Order*

The end of any system of order inevitably creates societal uncertainties regarding the future, which can lead to legal uncertainties. When these problems relate to a system of global order, they are vastly more complicated.

The Cold War's numerous faults nevertheless provided a "...warped stability..."[32] which may have prevented a Third World War. With this imperfect, yet familiar, system gone, one must ask what has replaced it. It is submitted that, whereas the post-Cold War world is substantially different from the previous international environment, it's realities are far from the rhetorical levels of revolution proclaimed during the early 1990s. The current international system is in a paradigmatic limbo, having shifted from the Old World Order without fully establishing a New World Order.

3.4 A Shifting Paradigmatic Basis in International Law

> "We are wandering between two worlds...one dead, the other unable to be born". Ohmae, K., *The End of the Nation-State*, (1996), Harper-Collins, at 10.

A paradigm is "...a basic concept, model or approach, that is widely accepted - and rarely seriously examined - in a particular field of study".[33]

This section argues that international law is undergoing a paradigm shift which leaves many of its founding principles open to debate.[34]

When the nation-State international system was created with the *Treaty of Westphalia* in 1648 State sovereign equality formed the dominant paradigm.[35] As time progressed, however, international society and international law altered. In the nineteenth century "...international law further expanded. This was due to a number of factors...[such as]...the further rise of powerful new States both within and outside Europe, the expansion of European civilisation overseas, the modernisation of world transport, the greater destructiveness of modern warfare, and the influence of new inventions".[36] International law became more complex, more structured and more institutionalised throughout the nineteenth and twentieth centuries, epitomised by the creation of the League of Nations[37] and its successor, the United Nations.[38]

Modern international relations are unrecognisable from the Westphalian system of nearly four centuries ago. Increasing inter-dependence caused by a vast network of international obligations and facilitated by the globality of modern communications, trade and tourism, have greatly altered international society. One may imagine that the Westphalian system's values and objectives have disappeared alongside slavery and other out-dated concepts.[39] In one respect, this is true and international law has expanded its sphere of competencies both quantitatively and qualitatively.[40] Institutionalisation has strengthened the arguments that an international legal system is more of a reality than ever before,[41] as have improvements in the law-making process itself, such as the recognition of customary law and the possibilities of regional and 'instant' custom.[42] States have seen major areas of policy removed from their sole competence and either prohibited, restricted or subjected to judicial review. *Article 2(4)* of the *UN Charter*, prohibiting the use of force in international relations, is a perfect example. The increasing importance of human rights also evidences this. These developments challenge the unquestionable supremacy which the State enjoyed under the Westphalian system and, collectively, symbolise a paradigmatic shift in the international system. They are no longer explainable as anomalies and, holistically, they "...provide the contours of an emerging new picture, if only we are prepared to see it. [...] Once a theory has become punctuated with exceptions and inconsistencies the time has arrived to rethink it and build a new one".[43]

General reluctance to modify long-standing paradigms is even greater in the international system, however, where the initial paradigm has taken many centuries to form and where prominent elements of the traditional paradigm remain clearly visible in the contemporary international legal system. State sovereignty, territorial integrity and non-intervention into State's domestic jurisdiction were *Gründnorms* of the original international system and remain fundamental principles.[44] Each of them features in *Article 2* of the *UN Charter*, outlining the UN's Principles and visions of international order. They represent a backbone running through international law and often conflict with the application of more recent norms. *Article 2(7)* specifically protects States competencies to deal with "...matters which are essentially within [their] domestic jurisdiction..." and a number of other UN resolutions have reinforced this principle.[45] Universal human rights concerns transcend the Westphalian system's understandable preoccupation with State sovereignty, however, and self-determination claims present constant challenges to Westphalia's static conception of international relations. Whilst it is possible, therefore, to highlight long-term movements away from the Westphalian paradigm, it is not possible to say that it has been fully superseded. The rhetorical New World Order may be closer than ever before but it has still not yet arrived. The entire international system is thus caught between paradigms, rendering specific international norms unclear and making it impossible to clearly ascertain the paradigmatic basis from which to 'fill' legal lacunae that arise.[46] It is extremely difficult to assess the relative strength of the Westphalian and NWO paradigms,[47] and essentially scholarly commentary must choose whether to suggest developments in international norms which, perhaps prematurely, follow the NWO paradigm or to maintain a preference for the Westphalian elements of the international system. A choice has already been made, in respect of this book, for the former.[48]

3.5 New International Problems

Just as the contemporary international scenario challenges borders at a practical level, new international problems facing the post-Cold War world challenge borders at a legal level. Whilst breaking down barriers which prevent trade and information flowing between States, increasing interdependence also breaks down barriers preventing one State's problems affecting another. These problems are not necessarily of a military nature.

Global repercussions may now be caused by economic, environmental or political developments in individual States.[49] Thus, as the new international environment creates opportunities for greater legal development, it also unleashes new international problems which had been stifled by the Cold War. Yugoslavia is used as the main example here but this phenomenon is equally applicable to all States.

3.5.1 *Political Lacunae*

Inter-State political lacunae. The maintenance of a negative confrontational attitude between super-powers was far easier to maintain than the co-operation required to build a new international order.[50] The ending of the latest period of détente effectively left a *political vacuum* in international relations. Western States, having previously based their foreign policies on opposing Communism were faced with the dilemma of identifying and implementing new agendas when the Communist threat dissipated. Conversely, ex-Communist countries were required to realign themselves economically, politically and militarily when the USSR dissolved. Whilst the threat of a Third World War appeared to have subsided, there existed many areas on which the mutual suspicions created during the Cold War would hinder a fully cooperative inter-State alliance. Such difficulties caused disagreements amongst the international actors responding to the Yugoslav conflict, as will be seen in chapter 4. In addition to East-West political realignments, many non-European States were affected by the new political scenario. The extensive political and economic patronage given by the Super-Powers during the Cold War diminished once Communism began to crumble. The USSR could no longer afford to buy loyalty from its satellite States and the West no longer needed to bribe Non-Aligned countries to disavow Communism. Equally, political intervention became less likely as the Non-Aligned States declined in geo-strategic importance. Yugoslavia was merely one of many States to suffer from these events.

Intra-State political lacunae. Perhaps the most direct effect of the reduction in international tensions was the tendency of States to adopt a more introspective approach to their political concerns. For almost fifty years intra-State problems had been contained because of the greater threat posed by the possibility of an East-West war. With these threats largely vanquished, internal problems were 'promoted'. 'Problem promotion' has occurred in Yugoslavia throughout history and chapter 2 describes how unity amongst the various Southern-Slav communities appeared possible only during the presence of a greater 'external' threat, such as invasion or political subjugation, and disappeared once those threats disappeared and internal problems resurfaced. The 'promotion' of internal problems during Yugoslavia's latter years evidences the effects of the Cold War's disappearance but other States also encountered the same phenomenon.[51] One consequence of contemporary interdependence is that intra-State problems are becoming increasingly similar in all States.[52]

Constitutional disagreements are perhaps the most visible example of 'promoted' intra-State problems. Grievances about inequalities in constitutional structures or the repression of human rights, often subverted during the Cold War as a result of unification against 'external' threats, grew more common. Many States were faced with domestic, as well as international, identity crises. Internal conflicts and 'ethnic' separatism have grown since the end of the Cold War, as sub-State groups question the artificiality of borders and political organisations which were taken for granted during the enforced stability of the Cold War period.[53] The growth of nationalism in the post-Cold War world may also be attributed to the political vacuum left in its wake. Sub-State groups seeking a greater role in national affairs turn political issues into ethnic issues which can prevent political compromise and result in conflict.[54] A similar phenomenon occurred in many African States after they were decolonised. Yugoslavia's problems have been discussed but other States, such as Canada, Italy, Spain, Georgia, Russia, Czechoslovakia, Algeria and many others also experienced an increased focus on their constitutional structure. The absence of armed conflict in many of these examples indicates that it is by no means inevitable that demands for greater political, cultural or economic autonomy, protection of human rights and democratisation are inherently dangerous. Nevertheless, the fact that such factors led to the conflict in the former Yugoslavia cannot be overlooked, nor can the existence of similar conflicts in other States. In fact, the bulk of force in the international system now occurs within, rather than between, States and it will be suggested that international law must 'promote' intra-State conflicts to the top of the international agenda in response to their 'promotion' to the top of the post-Cold War political agenda, especially since interdependence tends to internationalise the effects of turbulence within one State.[55] The international significance of domestic disputes has led to such disputes being called

"...inter-mestic...".[56]

Smith notes an increasing tendency for international institutions to consider internal conflicts as within their competence, despite the importance of domestic jurisdiction. He notes that "...[s]ince the Gulf War...the Security Council has treated several internal conflicts as within its jurisdiction. It specifically designated Iraqi suppression of Kurds as a source of refugee flows that threatened international peace and security. Peacekeeping missions in both Cambodia and former Yugoslavia have attempted to remedy internal ethnic or political conflicts. The relief mission in Somalia is a response to internal armed conflict caused by clan rivalry. In each instance, the activity undertaken by the UN has moved beyond the traditional notions of response to threats to international peace and security".[57] Recent involvement in Kosovo equally illustrates this point. Even following the June 1999 peace-plan,[58] it is clear that Kosovo currently remains a part of Serbia and this creates certain legal difficulties in respect of international intervention. Kosovo's lack of legal independence means that the World Bank faces difficulties in authorising credit in the absence of a governmental guarantor for such loans. The international community is faced with the desire to provide humanitarian aid and reconstruction assistance to part of a country which is still subject to an international trade-sanctions regime and lawyers are currently pondering whether it would be legal for the UN to establish a new legal tender for such assistance in order to avoid economic problems associated with the Yugoslav dinar which is now almost worthless.[59]

A corollary of the 'promotion' of internal conflicts, however, has been an increasing tendency for States to focus attention on their own problems, rather than international issues. One manifestation of this is a reallocation of expenditure towards domestic economic difficulties, but a similar reallocation of political priorities may also be discerned. In America, for example, Clinton's election in November 1992 signalled a victory for politicians who stated their intentions to place domestic politics at the top of their agenda, at the expense of foreign affairs or defence.[60] International intervention in civil conflicts has, it is submitted, been limited largely to instances where the most powerful States considered themselves to have a direct strategic interest in the existence or outcome of a specific conflict. This will make *a priori* identification of issues which prompt international intervention a complex analytical task which resembles an art more than a science.[61] Such isolationism conflicts with the increasingly global effects of many domestic disputes and causes a tension which must be resolved if international law in the NWO is to operate consistently.

Institutional political lacunae. In addition to confusion within and between States lay confusion within and between institutions. International institutions are not truly autonomous actors, in the sense that they are composed of States and their representatives who control the institution's agendas. To the extent that the end of the Cold War altered the political agendas of most States, these changes were reflected in the actions of institutions within which they are members. When the foreign policies of those member States are uncertain or contradictory, it is most difficult for collective institutions to act in a consistent and decisive manner. This was shown to be abundantly true throughout the Cold War years, especially in the United Nations.[62]

The post-Cold War foreign policy agendas of many States were pulled in contradictory directions because of the tension between the global effects of intra-State conflicts and the political preference for concentrating on domestic issues. The role of the global media has had an important influence on foreign policy agendas, since television "...makes it harder to sustain indifference or ignorance".[63] The point must be made, however, that the media can not only play a part in shaping governmental agendas but can also be driven by those agendas. States perceived to be 'friendly' to a powerful government's political stance may not incur the criticism of that government's national press, whereas States adopting a more independent, or even confrontational, stance are more likely to be found denounced in our newspapers for their 'extremist', 'terrorist' or 'threatening' positions. Witness, for example, a general failure of the western media to publish or discuss *Amnesty International* reports from 1984 and 1985 which described Saddam Hussein's widespread torture of Iraqi children to obtain information about their parents' political views. Contrast this with the coverage given to the famous scene in which Hussein patted a kidnapped British child on the head as he sat on Hussein's knee, which was accompanied in the *New York Post* with the headline 'Child Abuser'. The organisation known as FAIR - Fairness and Accuracy in Reporting - attribute this to the fact that Hussein was supported, politically, economically and militarily, by the West during the earlier period as a stalwart against the 'fundamentalism' of Iran, whereas the latter period saw Hussein out of favour as he attempted to ensure Iraqi control of oil supplies in the region and thereby threatened western industrial interests. This is not to argue that Hussein's subsequent vilification was not justified but rather that the reporting of such events appears to be inconsistent, to say the least. Political leaders are publicly supported, despite their terrible human-rights records, whilst they support the foreign-policy interests of the world's most powerful States only to be condemned once they attempt to pursue an alternative agenda. Such condemnations generally involve accusations of human-rights abuses and internal political repression which are neither new, in a temporal sense, nor unique, in the sense that they are committed by many other political leaders who escape similar condemnation for reasons which are unknown to those newspapers' readers.[64]

Since consistency is a prime factor in the legitimacy of international intervention, it is submitted that much current intervention is rightly criticised for its inconsistency and partiality. After excessive interventionism during the Cold War, powerful States became increasingly unwilling to finance international intervention unilaterally or through international institutions. As Grenville notes, "...without the Cold War, the policemen's role diminished. A conflict in a country or region not vitally affecting the interests of the West or East was likely to be allowed to find its own bloody solution. Diplomacy, good-offices, sincere attempts at mediation...and humanitarian aid might well be offered, but there would be reluctance to intervene militarily".[65] The high expectations placed on international institutions to enforce the rhetorical NWO were, therefore, in excess of the political will needed to allow them to do so. This situation created an *institutional vacuum* wherein no identifiable framework existed to assess whether, and to what extent, institutions would intervene in new threats to international peace and security and no coherent strategy for inter-institutional cooperation had been agreed. Although the Warsaw Pact had been dissolved, this still left the North Atlantic Treaty Organisation (NATO), the European Community (EC), the Conference on Security and Co-Operation in Europe (CSCE), the Western European Union (WEU) and, of course, the United Nations (UN) with individual identity crises.[66]

From an intra-State perspective, this is problematical because States which encounter the kind of 'inter-mestic' problems outlined above can no longer rely on the intervention of the international community, or powerful individual members thereof, to assist in their resolution. During the Cold War era, States such as Yugoslavia could guarantee that the international community's major powers would intervene to protect wider geo-political interests but this was no longer guaranteed. The impact of these uncertainties on the institutional responses to the Yugoslav conflict are discussed further in chapter 4.

3.5.2 *Economic Difficulties*

Inter-State economic difficulties. The demise of Communism was as much an economic victory for the West as a political victory. It was the inability to finance the Cold War which eventually defeated Communism and free-market economics was not only a primary factor in this process but also a chief beneficiary thereof. Accordingly, inter-State relations in the NWO had to take account of the fact that the world economy was now essentially a free-market one.[67]

These developments had a number of effects. First, many eastern States became heavily indebted to the West's economies and were saddled with large amounts of interest for any loans they had taken out, forcing them to contemplate closer political and economic relations with their financiers and causing further interdependence. Second, inter-State economic problems were 'promoted' to replace the diminishing likelihood of an East-West military conflict. Focus also grew on the under-developed nature of many African economies and tensions increased between the relatively affluent North of the globe and the poorer South. Third, with focus recast on internal problems, inter-State relations were affected by the declining levels of economic aid given to Non-Aligned States by super-powers seeking to ensure their loyalty.[68] Fourth, promotion of internal concerns led to a growth in economic protectionism which largely contradicted free-market philosophies. Such protectionism was also seen at a supra-State level and institutions such as the EU were accused of growing increasingly hostile to trade from outside their borders and immigration from non-Member States.

Intra-State economic difficulties. The Cold War drained resources from non-military issues from most of the countries in the world. Many writers spoke of a 'peace dividend'[69] having arisen as the Cold War ended which would allow funds to be diverted to more positive, non-military, expenditure. Nevertheless, adopting an introspective outlook, many States viewed this 'peace dividend' as an opportunity to focus spending on domestic problems, rather than international concerns. Clinton's electoral victory in 1992 evidenced the political reality that the electorate was more concerned about issues such as unemployment, inflation and health than it was about the resolution of a civil conflict in Africa or an economic crisis in Asia. Internal affairs are increasingly becoming the barometer by which the success or failure of a government is measured and George Bush's defeat seemed to contain the message that success on the foreign affairs front was insufficient to command electoral loyalty.

As mentioned above, many States which benefited from the economic dividends of the Cold War foreign aid budgets found themselves facing economic instability at the same time as encountering constitutional divides. The international economy no longer provided handsome rewards for remaining politically independent and, just as many States required economic support to prevent their fragile political situations from worsening, such long-standing support largely disappeared. Yugoslavia encountered massive financial difficulties during the period considered here, the effects of which are considered in chapter 2.[70] Economic aid had always been an important source of Yugoslav income and was greater than international loans. During 1951-1959, for example, aid from the USA alone amounted to $700m in comparison with the 1988 IMF conditional loan of $2.2m.[71] Other States were affected likewise. Thus, "...attempts in Africa and Latin America to escape poverty through modernisation and industrialisation created huge debts whose interest payments outstripped international aid".[72] It appears incontrovertible that economic hardship is a corrosive force which may assist the dissolution of sovereign States in the existing precarious global climate.

Institutional economic difficulties. The end of the Cold War saw the Warsaw Pact dissolve, NATO drastically reduce its troop deployments across Europe and the UN seeking to devolve primary dispute resolution responsibility of intra-State conflicts to regional organisations because its inadequate budget had not expanded to meet the rhetorical expectations placed on it. Pressures to refocus the 'peace dividend' internally had a direct impact on the perceptions of international security institutions by the States funding them. In addition to the political recalcitrance to commit ones own troops to participate in a foreign conflict came economic arguments against committing ones own resources to resolve such conflicts. Chief proponents of the argument that it could not act as the world's policeman was the US, which pushed for financial cuts in both NATO and the UN, the latter of which suffered from the non-payment of America's 25% contribution towards UN funds.[73]

The UN's financially-driven desire to curtail its role in international intervention arose at the same time that a number of international organisations were seeking to expand their competencies into security and foreign policy areas. The EC and CSCE had both made moves in this direction during the latter years of the Cold War and Yugoslavia provided the first opportunity to put these into practice.

3.5.3 *Ideological Lacunae*

The global effects of 'inter-mestic' issues and the increasing interdependence of global relations would tend to suggest that international law must become more interventionist in its outlook, making legal inroads into State sovereignty to match political and economic inroads. Nevertheless, States jealously guard this sovereignty and are reluctant to cede control over important issues to any other entity. International institutions, composed largely of State representatives, are thus caught between conflicting tensions which are not easily resolved. Such tensions were discussed by two former UN Secretary-Generals during their terms of office. Javier Perez de Cuellar noted that the increasing demand for international intervention could "...call into question one of the cardinal principles of international law, one diametrically opposed to it, namely the obligation of non-interference in the internal affairs of a State...". Boutros Boutros-Ghali also stated that "...[r]espect for [a State's] fundamental sovereignty and integrity is crucial to any common international progress..." but that "...the time of absolute and exclusive sovereignty...has passed. Its theory was never matched by reality".[74] These contradictions are built into the *UN Charter* itself and are not easily overcome.[75] Again, one must choose between the Westphalian and NWO paradigms.

It is submitted that, since 'inter-mestic' and intra-State problems have come to represent a growing threat to international peace and security, international law must develop accordingly. Instances in which international intervention is necessary do not generally involve States with a stable economic and political situation and intervention is not undertaken lightly. Where it is necessary, however, it should not be prevented on the basis of over-exaggerated fears of a neo-imperialism and hegemonic international agendas which would purportedly destroy the very essence of State sovereignty. In many cases intervention may preserve a State, which must surely be the most obvious manifestation of respecting such sovereignty. In cases where intervention is delayed and limited because of fears over international law's legitimate domain, such as in Yugoslavia, far greater threats to sovereignty may arise. Those who seek to constrain international law must accept the realities of non-intervention and balance them against the rhetorical value of respecting State sovereignty. To limit international law's remit to inter-State conflicts is defensible only whilst such conflicts represent the sole, or primary, threat to international peace and security. Of course, such intervention must be seen to operate within a consistent and impartial legal framework, free from political bias and selective application, before it can be acknowledged as legitimate and this clearly represents one of the major obstacles in encouraging support for a more interventionist approach. International institutions and international law will undoubtedly lose support if they are used as shields to hide political decisions taken by a handful of powerful States according to their own foreign-policy agendas. Nevertheless, this writer is convinced that only by adopting a twin-track approach which aims to increase both the legitimacy and scope of international law will it be possible to deal with future intra-State conflicts similar to those arising from Yugoslavia's dissolution. More will be said on this in subsequent chapters.

3.6 Conclusions

This chapter has described the turbulent political environment which followed the end of the Cold War and discussed how problems created by the new international environment may impact on an inter-State, intra-State and institutional level. These problems may also affect the international system at a constitutional level. New international problems are, however, matched by the possibility for greater international cooperation and new legal developments. It has been suggested that international law must develop beyond its traditional fixation with inter-State conflicts if it is to address the needs of the contemporary world. It is not suggested that the State's claim to be the primary international legal actor will be undermined by these developments, but merely that changing societal conditions necessitate changing legal regulation. The lines between a State's domestic jurisdiction and legitimate international concerns, vital to the Westphalian notion of international law, have become increasingly blurred by the modern world to the extent that they now often overlap.

Yugoslavia's domestic difficulties were the result of, or aggravated by, prevailing conditions in international society but the factors described in chapter 2 and herein cannot be confined to the SFRY. To dismiss the dissolution of Yugoslavia as a *sui generis* example of the collapse of an unstable and artificial State is to ignore many of these valuable lessons. As the first internal conflict to provoke international intervention in the post-Cold War world, Yugoslavia represents a highly useful case study. Yugoslavia epitomises the impact of the international system on individual States. The disappearance of 'external' threats which existed during the Cold War allowed internal problems to be 'promoted'. Constitutional issues developed aggressive nationalist characteristics and its declining geo-strategic importance resulted in economic aid being greatly reduced, aggravating inter-community tensions, and a deferment of international intervention until armed conflict had begun and Yugoslavia's sovereignty appeared beyond salvation. The Yugoslav conflict permits examination of the effects of the international environment on conflicts within a sovereign State and the effects of such conflicts in causing, or encouraging, changes in the system itself.

Notes

1 See also chapter 8, section 8.2. and chapter 9, section 9.2.

2 See chapter 1, section 1.2.3.

3 Simmonds, N.E., *Central Issues in Jurisprudence: Justice, Law and Rights*, (1986), S&M, 3-5

4 See Allot, P., 'New International Law', in Allot *et al*, *Theory and International Law: An Introduction*, (1991), BIICL/ILG, 107, at 112; Mullerson, R., *International Law, Rights and Politics*, (1994), Routledge, 10; Shreuer, C., 'The Waning of the Sovereign State: Towards a New Paradigm for International Law?', (1993), 4 *EJIL*, 447, at 453.

5 Touzmohammad, R.A., participating in discussion in Ferencz, B.B. (ed.), *World Security for the 21st Century: Challenges and Solutions*, (1991), Oceana, at 2, suggests that analysts of the international system should talk of "...*implementation* rather than enforcement..." because of these problems.

6 See chapters 8-9 for examples.

7 See generally Walker, M., *The Cold War*, (1993), Fourth-Estate; Smith, J., *The Cold War: 1945-1991*, (1997), OUP; Cronin, J.E., *The World the Cold War Made*; Fleming, D.F., *The Cold War and its Origins*, (1961), Doubleday.

8 Former UN Secretary-General, Boutros Boutros-Ghali, noted the existence of 279 Security Council vetoes between 1945-1990. Interestingly, empirical evidence disproves the popular misconception that the USSR and China have consistently been the States to exercise the veto. Whilst this was true of the USSR during the immediate post-Charter years, the period of 1965-1990 shows the veto to have been used only 13 times by the USSR in comparison with 69 vetoes by the USA, 27 from the UK and 14 from France. China, another common scapegoat for UN Cold-War inactivity, used the veto on only 3 occasions during 1945-1990. See *FCO Table of Vetoed Draft Resolutions in the UN Security Council*, (1994), Foreign Policy Doc. 249. For critical commentary surrounding the use of the veto see Curtis, M., *The Great Deception*, (1998), Pluto 173-81. See also Boutros-Ghali, B., *An Agenda for Peace: Report of the Secretary-General Pursuant to the Statement Adopted by the Summit Meeting of the Security Council On 31st January 1992*, reprinted in Roberts, A. and Kingsbury, B. (eds.), *United Nations, Divided World*, (1993), Clarendon, 470. See also Patil, A.V., *The UN in World Affairs 1946-1990: A Complete Record and Case-Histories of the Security Council's Veto*, (1992), Mansell.

9 Lukic, R. and Lynch, A., *Europe from the Balkans to the Urals: The Disintegration of Yugoslavia and the Soviet Union*, (1996), OUP; Jeffer, J., *Shockwaves: Eastern Europe After the Revolution*, (1992), Southend; Gray, C., 'Self-Determination and the Breakup of the Soviet Union', (1992), *YEL*, 465.

10 See section 0.6. The features of the NWO are subject to fierce debate and are beyond the scope of this work. Some common suggestions include democracy, human-rights (both individual and collective), sustainable-development, economic liberalisation and international trade as cornerstones of the new international environment. See, for example, Boutros Ghali's *Agenda for Peace*, supra n.8., and *An Agenda for Development*, (1995), UNDPI; CSCE *Budapest Summit Declaration: Towards a Genuine Partnership in a New Europe*, (1994), CSCE Publications, sections 767(4), 769(14-15), 779(4), 793(2) and 801(36); Sellers, M. (ed.), *The New World Order: Sovereignty, Human Rights and the Self-Determination of Peoples*, (1996), OIP.

11 Rosenau, J.N., 'Sovereignty In A Turbulent World', in Lyons, G.M. and Mastanduno, M., *Beyond Westphalia? State Sovereignty and International Intervention*, (1995), JHUP, 191; Ferencz, B.B., *New Legal Foundations for Global Survival*, (1994), Oceana.

12 Smith, E.M., 'The UN: Meeting the Challenges of the Post-Cold War World', (1993), 87 *ASIL*, 268.

13 Carlsson, I., *et al*, *Our Global Neighbourhood: The Report of the Commission on Global Governance*, (1995), OUP; Horsman, M. and Marshall, A., *After the Nation-State*, (1994), Harper-Collins. Cf. Ignatieff, M., *The Warrior's Honor - Ethnic War and Modern Conscience*, (1998), C&W, 88 e*t seq*, who considers the 'international-community' "...an exalted fiction".

14 See generally Lyons, G.M. and Mastanduno, M., 'International Intervention, State Sovereignty and the Future of International Society', in Lyons, supra n.11.

15 Warbrick, C., 'The Theory of International Law: Is There an English Contribution?', in Allot., supra n.4, 70.

16 Wolfrum, R.*et al*, *The International Legal System Following the Bipolar World*, (1993), ASIL, 153. See also Sellers, supra n.10; Lyons and Mastanduno, supra n.14.

17 Schermers, H.G. and Blokker, N.M. (eds.), *International Institutional Law - Unity Within Diversity: Third Edition*, (1995), Nijhoff, 136. See also Wood, D.P. *et al*, *The Internationalization of Domestic Law: The Shrinking Domaine Réservé*, (1993), 87 ASIL, 553.

18 *Nationality Decrees in Tunis and Morocco*, (1923), PCIJ Series B, 24.

19 *UN Human Development Report*, (1993), UNDPI, 25.

20 Franck, T.M., *International Law After the Cold War*, (1990), 84 ASIL, 156. Parsons, A., *The UN and the National Interests of States*, in Roberts, supra n.8, 104.

21 Walker, supra n.7, 309.

22 Chapter 4, section 4.3.8.

23 For discussion of the events which surrounded the dissolution of Czechoslovakia, see Grenville, J.A.S., *The Collins History of the World in the Twentieth Century*, (1994), Collins, 891-909.

24 Mullerson, supra n.4, at 1.

25 See *House of Commons Defence Committee Report: The Future of NATO*, (1995), HMSO, for details.

26 Urquhart, B., 'The UN and International Security After the Cold War', in Roberts, supra n.8, 81. Cf. Grenville, supra n.23, 925, who cites the "...unusual combination of circumstances..." creating such a consensus. See also Evans, K., *Reasons for Intervention are the Same: Kuwait's Oil*, (1994), 12th October, *Guardian*. See chapter 1, n.12, for references to the Gulf-War.

27 Krause, K.R., 'The United Nations in the Post-Cold War World: Adaptation, Transformation, Openness or Obsolescence?', (1993), 87 *ASIL*, 272.

28 Cassesse, A., *International Law in a Divided World*, (1986), Clarendon; Mahoney, K.E. and Mahoney, P. (eds.), *Human Rights in the 21st Century: A Global Challenge*, (1993), Nijhoff; Claude, R.P. and Weston, B.H., *Human Rights in a World Community*, (1989), Princeton; Henkins, L. and Hargrove, J.L., *Human Rights: An Agenda for the Next Century*, (1994), ASIL; Reisman, W.M., 'Sovereignty and Human Rights in Contemporary International Law', (1990), 84 *AJIL*, 866.

29 Legitimacy may refer to the legitimacy of States themselves, based on some international-validation criteria, or the legitimacy of Statehood as the basis for international legal order. On the former question, see Franck, T.M., *The Power of Legitimacy Among Nations*, (1990), OUP. On the latter, see Koskenniemi, M., 'The Future of Statehood', (1991), *HILJ*, 397.

30 McGoldrick, D., 'Sustainable Development and Human Rights: An Integrated Concept', (1996), 45 *ICLQ*, 796; Sands, P., 'International Law in the Field of Sustainable Development', (1994), 65 *BYIL*, 303.

31 Boutros-Ghali, B., *Agenda for Development*, supra n.10, 121, notes that "...democracy is the only long-term means of both arbitrating and regulating the many political, social, economic and ethnic tensions that constantly threaten to tear apart our societies and destroy States. In the absence of democracy as a forum for competition and a vehicle for change, development will remain fragile and be perpetually at risk". See chapter 7 for further references to democracy in international law.

32 Walker, supra n.7, 1; Brands, H.W., *The Devil We Knew: The Cold War*, (1993), OUP. Cf. Mullerson, supra n.4, 15.

33 Kuhn, T. S., *The Structure of Scientific Revolutions: Second Edition*, (1970), Chicago, 35.

34 See also chapter 1, section 1.2.3.

35 See Shearer, I.A., *Starke's International Law: Eleventh Edition*, (1994), Butterworths, 1-27; Shaw, M.N., *International Law: Fourth Edition*, (1997), CUP, 12-26; Jennings, R. and Watts, A., *Oppenheim's International Law: Ninth Edition, Volume I*, (1992), Longmans, 339-79.

36 Shearer, ibid, 12.

37 See Fry, C.B. and Ranjitsinhji, K. (eds.), *Key Book of the League of Nations*, (1923), H&S; Walters, F.P. *A History of the League of Nations*, (1960), RIIA.

38 See chapter 4, section 4.5. for references.

39 Carty, A., *The Failed State and the Tradition of International Law - Towards a Renewal of Legal Humanism*, inaugural lecture at the University of Derby, 6th December 1995, 1-12.

40 Shaw, *op cit*, speaks instead of *horizontal* and *vertical* growth, the former relating to expansion of the content of international law, the latter relating to its growing application to non-State actors. On this latter point, see also Broms, B., 'Subjects: Entitlement in the International Legal System', in MacDonald, R.St.J. and Johnston, D.M. (eds.), *The Structure and Process of International Law*, (1983), Nijhoff, 383; Shreur, supra n.4.

41 Schermers, supra n.17, 1188.

42 Shaw, supra n.35, 56-73.

43 Schreuer, supra n.4, at 469.

44 Onuf, N., 'The Constitution of International Society', (1994), 5 *EJIL*, 1, considers the relationship between State sovereignty and the *UN Charter*. See also Warbrick, supra n.15, 63; Koskenniemi, M., *From Apology to Utopia: The Structure of International Legal Argument*, (1989), Finnish Lawyers, 192-263; Ferencz, supra n.5, 163-77. See also *Case Concerning Military and Paramilitary Activities in and against Nicaragua*, (1986), ICJ Rep, paragraph 202.

45 See GA Resn. 2131 (XX) (1965), *Declaration on the Inadmissability of Intervention in the Domestic Affairs of a State and the Protection of their Independence and Sovereignty*; GA Resn. 2625 (XXV) (1970), *Declaration on the Principles of International Law Concerning Friendly Relations and Cooperation Among States in Accordance with the UN Charter.*

46 See chapter 1, section 1.2.3.

47 Kuhn, supra n.35, 37-9.

48 See above, chapter 1, section 1.2.3.

49 Kennedy, P., *Preparing for the Twenty-First Century*, (1993), Harper-Collins, 3-21; Horsman, supra n.13, 91-103; Carlsson, supra n.13, 42. See also chapter 8, section 8.2.

50 Higgins, R., *Problems and Process: International Law and How We Use It*, (1995), Clarendon, 239; Grenville, supra n.23, 931.

51 South Africa and Iraq provide examples of inter-community fighting once 'external' enemies of differing kinds have subsided. See Mallaby, S., *After Apartheid*, (1992), Faber; Rugman, J., *Kurds Find Enemy Within is Themselves*, (1994), 12th June, *Sunday Times*.

52 Giddens, A., *The Consequences of Modernity*, (1990), Polity, 63.

53 See Sandoz, Y., *View of the ICRC on the Law of Armed Conflict in a New Strategic Environment*, available from http://www.icrc.ch/ icrcnews/4312.htm, 1. The views are those of the Director of International Law and Policy of the ICRC.

54 See chapter 2, section 2.6.2.

55 See below, chapter 8, section 8.2.

56 Mullerson, supra n.4, 7. See also Forsythe, D.P., *Human Rights and Peace: International and National Dimensions*, (1993), NUP, 162.

57 Smith, supra n.12, 269.

58 See above chapter 2, section 2.6.3. and chapter 4, section 4.5.8.

59 Castle, S., *Kosovo Rebuild Starts from Scratch*, (1999), 13th July, *Independent*.

60 Grenville, supra n.23, 840 *et seq*.

61 Ignatieff, supra n.13, 4.

62 See supra, n.8.

63 Ignatieff, supra n.13, 8 *et seq*; Horsman, supra n.15, 45-53.

64 On the issue of bias in reporting, and for many contextual examples, see generally Edwards, D., *Free to be Human*, (1998), Green Books Ltd; Herman, E.S. and Chomsky, N., *Manufacturing Consent: The Political Economy of the Mass Media*, (1988), Pantheon; Chomsky, N., *Deterring Democracy*, (1991), Verso.

65 Grenville, supra n.23, 926.

66 Other international organisations exist but, since these were the chief actors in the Yugoslav conflict, they deserve special attention.

67 Borowiec, A., *Yugoslavia After Tito*, (1977), Praeger, 104, notes that the economies of East and West were tied for some time before the end of the Cold War. In 1976, for example, Soviet importation of Western goods had reached the $5 billion level. These levels are incomparable with the current economic links, however.

68 For figures on Yugoslavia's declining foreign-aid receipts see Dyker, D.A., *Yugoslavia: Socialism, Development and Debt*, (1990), Routledge, 122 *et seq*.

69 Boutros-Ghali, supra n.10, paragraph 31, cites a "...peace-dividend of $500 billion..." between 1987-1992. See also Renner, M., *Budgeting For Disarmament*, (1995), WIP, 5 *et seq*; Connors, D. (ed.), *The True Cost of Conflict*, (1995), Saferworld.

70 Section 2.6.1.

71 Borowiec, supra n.64, 94.

72 Grenville, supra n.23, 927.

73 See Roberts, supra n.8, 530-6 for a table of contributions to the UN budget. For discussion of the problems caused by American arrears, see Tran, M., *Annan Acts to Curb UN Bureaucracy*, (1997), 17th July, *Guardian*; Bone, J., *UN Chief to Appeal for Reform Backing*, (1997), 22nd September, *Times*.

74 Quoted in Lyons, supra n.11, 2.

75 See section 3.4.

4 The Institutional Responses to the Dissolution of the SFRY

4.1 Introduction

Having examined the dissolution of Yugoslavia in its domestic and international contexts, it remains to examine the international responses to these events. This chapter adopts an institution-specific examination, highlighting the major policy approaches of the chief institutions which became involved in the Yugoslav conflict. The proliferation of international institutions and Non-Governmental Organisations throughout the twentieth-century makes it impossible to examine every organ which became involved in the Yugoslav crisis and this chapter is limited in a number of ways. First, it discusses only the approaches of the major actors in the crisis, these being the European Communities, the Conference for Security and Co-Operation in Europe, the United Nations, the North Atlantic Treaty Alliance and the Western European Union. Second, it deals only with the major policy initiatives of these institutions and does not attempt to analyse every resolution or statement made during the course of the conflict. Third, since the book is concerned the period of Yugoslavia's dissolution, the institutional analysis focuses specifically on this period and only briefly mentions involvement thereafter. Fourth, the analysis excludes the role played by the Badinter Commission, which is considered in chapters 5 and 6.

Some tentative conclusions will be offered on the ways in which the responses to the Yugoslav conflict may exhibit a need for new approaches to conflicts of this kind. A hypothesis will be introduced, which will be developed further in subsequent chapters, that, in light of changing threats to peace and security in the contemporary international arena, the major institutional actors must focus on new ways to address these conflicts.

Other writers have commented upon the overall international responses to the Yugoslav conflict as well as those of specific institutions or States and it is instructive to note the division of opinion on the effectiveness of such intervention. McGoldrick rightly notes that the Yugoslav crisis was widely viewed as the "...litmus test..." of the post Cold-War security order, and that "...[t]he responses of the international community and of international law have been condemned as inadequate".[1] He concludes, nevertheless, that "...it is clear that the international community made massive attempts to end the conflict and alleviate the suffering. Tens of thousands of lives have been saved. The financial costs have run into billions of dollars and reconstruction costs will add many more. Almost every known diplomatic and economic strategies have been employed and many military ones. Personal responsibility for war crimes has at least some possibility of effective enforcement".[2] Szasz, who became involved with the Badinter Commission under the ICFY,[3] considered the international community's responses "...marked more by haphazard improvisation and ingenuity than by steadfast determination and willingness to take or risk some sacrifices. The result has been the involvement of an unprecedented number of international organs, which in turn have spawned a variety of sometimes elaborate *ad hoc* organs, with complex inter-actions".[4] Weller considered intervention to have been undertaken in "...a confused and inconsistent manner".[5] Cohen bluntly refers to the EC and UN having "...exacerbated [the conflict]...by incompetent international meddling".[6] Lauterpacht considers the responses to have evidenced "...on the one hand, an impoverished display of procrastination, tergiversation, contradiction, feebleness and hypocrisy; on the other, well-intention and at times energetic, even imaginative, endeavours, both individual and collective, to resolve the manifold problems of the area".[7] It is suggested herein that the main fault with international intervention lay not with the policies adopted but in delaying intervention until Yugoslavia's dissolution was virtually inevitable.

4.2 Pre-Institutional Involvement

Even before any of the major international institutions became involved in the crisis, representatives from certain individual States had been sent to Yugoslavia to voice concerns over political developments. In January 1991, as Slovenia and Croatia armed themselves in preparation for conflict with Serbia, Warren Zimmerman, the US Ambassador to Yugoslavia, met the SFRY's then President, Borisav Jovic, and told him that America would not accept a forceful outcome of the political crisis.[8] In June, shortly before Croatia and Slovenia's declarations of independence, US Secretary of State James Baker met with republican representatives and gave a message which greatly confused the Yugoslav parties.

On the one hand, he told Slovenia and Croatia that America supported their claims for self-determination but would not recognise their unilateral independence. On the other hand, he told Serbia and the federal government that America would not accept the legitimacy of the use of force to resolve the crisis.[9] This message convinced all parties that they enjoyed a degree of international support for their opposing political agendas and was to repeated by various institutions, as will be seen below. Similarly, Douglas Hurd, the UK's incumbent Foreign Secretary, denounced the "...illegal use of forces under [Federal Presidency] command..." and spoke of the illegitimacy of "...territorial conquests..." which were taking place in Yugoslavia once the wars in Slovenia and Croatia erupted. Both of these concepts are traditionally applicable only in international conflicts, yet the conflicts at this stage were not of this nature. These latter comments took place once the EC had become involved in the crisis.

4.3 The European Community and European Union (EC/EU)

> "The age of Europe has dawned"
> "This is the hour of Europe...not the hour of the United States"
> Jacques Poos, Luxembourg's Foreign-Minister.[10]

4.3.1 *Introduction*

Chief amongst the institutions demonstrating confidence in its post-Cold War role was the European Community. The EC's agenda in the NWO was different to many other international organisations. The Cold War's economic costs which had fallen on existing security organisations such as the Warsaw Pact, NATO and the UN had not been encountered by the EC since it was not involved with security issues at the time. Whereas those latter institutions were financially-pressured into curtailing international intervention in the NWO, therefore, the EC was preparing for a greater role in international society.

During 1991, the EC was in the final stages of negotiations on a new Treaty which marked an important period of the Community's evolution. The *Treaty on European Union* (TEU) aimed to build on the EC's economic successes by creating two new 'pillars' of competence within the framework of a European Union. One of these pillars, on Common Foreign and Security Policy (CFSP), stated that one of the EU's new objectives was to "...assert its identity on the international scene, in particular through the implementation of a common foreign and security policy, which might in time lead to a common defence".[11] The pillar was to extend to all areas of foreign and security policy of the Union and its Member States[12] and was aimed, *inter alia*, at preserving peace, strengthening international peace and security, and developing and consolidating democracy, the rule of law and respect for human rights and fundamental freedoms.[13] Although the TEU had not been ratified by all Member States at the time that the EC first became involved in the Yugoslav crisis, it is submitted that the crisis presented the EC Member States with an opportunity to test political commitment to the forthcoming CFSP pillar and that the nature of the EC's involvement may indicate the difficulties of this new area of competence. Yugoslavia essentially became an experimental test-case.[14]

The EC had been instrumental in introducing the Yugoslav crisis to the CSCE agenda and made clear its intentions to take the primary role in attempting to resolve the crisis, despite the fact that Yugoslavia was not a member of the EC.[15] The EC's desire to prove the viability of its CFSP objectives was matched by the desire of other institutions to take a lesser role in conflicts which could be resolved at a regional level. America's desire to reduce its financial commitment to foreign policy and similar financial concerns within the UN meant that the EC was practically left alone to police its own 'backyard'.[16]

4.3.2 *Initial Diplomacy*

The EC's first real actions came after fighting began in Slovenia on 27th June 1991. A troika of EC foreign-ministers was sent to Yugoslavia within three days of the outbreak of fighting, in order to negotiate the withdrawal of Slovenia's declaration of independence, a cease-fire between the warring factions and Stipe Mesic's accession to the Yugoslav Presidency.[17] Preservation of the SFRY was the chief aim of the EC, as agreed in a European Political Co-operation (EPC) meeting of 26th March 1991, although in pursuing this aim it was also made clear that the EC would not accept the legitimacy of force by any of the parties to the crisis.[18] This initial dilemma would persist throughout the EC's attempts to resolve the crisis.

It appears clear that the EC's intended manner of resolving this dilemma was to assist in the re-negotiation of the SFRY constitution, with which little success had been made in meetings of the republican leaders.[19] A European Parliamentary Resolution of 15th March 1991 called for the creation of a constitution which would "...by respecting the rights of all the peoples in Yugoslavia...enable the State of Yugoslavia to continue. It accepted that the constituent republics and autonomous provinces of Yugoslavia must have the right freely to determine their own political future in a peaceful and democratic manner and on the basis of recognised international and internal borders. It condemned the violent conduct of the army in maintaining public order and the continuing violations of the human rights of the ethnic Albanians population in Kosovo".[20] Whilst it will be suggested that internal constitutional arrangements are the most viable way of resolving conflicts such as those in Yugoslavia,[21] a number of problems arise from the approach adopted here. First, the timing of the EC's involvement left much to be desired. By March 1991, the factors which led to calls for independence from Slovenia and Croatia had existed for a number of years and had created a political situation replete with suspicion and mistrust. Constitutional negotiations between republican leaders had failed to break the political deadlock which had arisen and yet, even at this time, the EC refrained from seeking an active role within that negotiation process. Second, the wording of the resolution creates much confusion about the international legal rights with which it deals. To speak of the rights of the "...peoples..." of Yugoslavia is to use the language of self-determination, which was being used as the legal base for the independence movements within Slovenia and Croatia.[22] Assuming that the relevant peoples possessed the right to self-determination, the resolution provides no justification for its suggestion that Yugoslavia should continue as a unified State and on the basis of recognised internal and international borders. In the event that the territorial integrity of Yugoslavia was a valid aim, one must question the condemnation of the JNA and their role in preserving such unity. The confused messages within this resolution typified the EC's approach to the conflict and served only to convince each Yugoslav republic that they received the implicit support of the international community for their juxtaposed political aims. At a time when the future of Yugoslavia hung in the balance, such influences may be argued to have played an active role in the dissolution of the SFRY.[23]

Having secured Mesic's election to the Presidency, the EC provided him with its full support for the economic programme which had been agreed between Yugoslavia and the IMF.[24] The EC also supported Yugoslavia's moves towards democracy.[25] Ironically, both of developments were aggravating the separatist conflict which was evolving in the SFRY.

Numerous EPC statements referred to the EC's commitment to a "...united and democratic Yugoslavia..."[26] as well as the need to ensure "...respect for [Yugoslavia's] territorial integrity".[27] This preference for the status quo reflects not only a general premise in international relations that stability is preferable to territorial disruption, but also more specific concerns that Yugoslavia should not be allowed to set a precedent which would encourage the USSR to fragment.[28]

4.3.3 *The Brioni Accord*

The EC troika's first perceived achievement during this initial stage was the conclusion of the Brioni Accord on 8th July 1991.[29] This was the first real instance of institutional cooperation, since the EC-troika had concluded the agreement alongside a CSCE 'good offices' delegation. The Accord secured a cease-fire in Slovenia and a three-month moratorium on the declarations of independence from Slovenia and Croatia, pending negotiations on their future relations. Despite the claims that this represented a beginning to the resolution of the conflict, the reality was that this effectively allowed Slovenia to consolidate its *de facto* independence from Yugoslavia whilst allowing the JNA to regroup and concentrate their attentions on Serb-populated areas within Croatia and Bosnia. When violence escalated in Croatia shortly after the Brioni Accord, it became clear that the EC was far from resolving the conflict, or indeed understanding its aims.

The Brioni Accord followed an EPC statement of 5th July in which the EC accepted that "...a new situation has arisen..." in the SFRY.[30] This new situation required a more forceful EC involvement in the negotiations process and, accordingly, it was announced that the troika would make preparations for EC participation therein. The statement noted that such negotiations should be "...based on the principles enshrined in the CSCE's *Helsinki Final Act* and the *Charter of Paris for a New Europe*, in particular respect for human rights, including the rights of minorities, and the rights of peoples to self-determination in conformity with the *Charter of the United Nations* and with the relevant norms of international law, including those relating to the territorial integrity of States...".

The EC's phyrric victories at Brioni were marred by the growth of violence in Croatia. An EPC statement of 28th August 1991 condemned such violence and specifically directed such condemnation towards Serbian irregulars and "...elements of the Yugoslav National Army [JNA]...lending their active support to the Serbian side".[31] The statement called on the Federal Presidency to "...put an immediate end to the *illegal use* of the forces under its command...[emphasis added]". This repeats the confusion inherent in the views of Douglas Hurd[32] and it is not clear what is meant by the reference to illegality. On the one hand, it may refer to the *domestic* illegality of the JNA deployment, based on the fact that its initial deployment had been authorised at a time when the Federal Presidency was not functioning and military control had been handed over to JNA-General Kadijevic, as Defence Minister.[33] Furthermore, this decision had been possible only as a result of Serbia's control of four of the eight votes in the Presidency, after revocation of Kosovo's and Vojvodina's autonomy.[34] On the other hand, it may be a reference to an emerging *international* norm which limits the means by which a sovereign State's government may protect its territorial integrity. Douglas Hurd had told the House of Commons that the existing international environment was one in which it was no longer legal to "...keep a State together by shooting its citizens...",[35] which may provide some support for this latter position. Furthermore, all of the previous EC statements and resolutions dealing with the issue of Yugoslavia's territorial integrity made it clear that it was unacceptable to resolve the crisis by military force.[36] Nevertheless, given the territorial integrity is one of the most fundamental norms in international law[37] and the fact that the reference to illegality is not explained in any detailed way, it is not possible to draw firm conclusions on this question.

The statement went on to say that the EC and its Members would "...never accept a policy of *fait accompli*..." and that "...territorial conquests not recognised by the international community will never produce the kind of legitimate protection sought by all in Yugoslavia". Again, the statement appears to apply an international legal term - "...territorial conquests..." - to a non-international scenario, without providing any explicit justification for doing so. Any legitimate solution to the crisis would require "...negotiations based on the principle of the fullest protection of the rights of all, wherever they may live in Yugoslavia". The Community then announced the creation of a peace conference, within which an "...arbitration procedure..." would seek to help the disputing parties resolve their differences. This conference became known as the European Communities Conference on Yugoslavia (ECCY).

4.3.4 *Sanctions*

The EC attempted to use its economic power to encourage a settlement of the conflict, by suggesting that future economic relations with the Community would be conditional upon a peaceful and united SFRY. A Parliamentary resolution of 15th March 1991 thus spoke of "...seriously detrimental effects..." on EC-SFRY relations in the event that the Yugoslav parties sought to resolve their differences by force and concluded that "...a positive solution to the present crisis and absolute respect for human rights would allow the adoption of the third protocol by Parliament and the opening of negotiations on an association agreement". In the nationalistic environment within Yugoslavia during this period, however, such matters were incomparable with the primary desire to protect ones community from the 'others' who threatened from within.[38] Accordingly, agreements made by the EC negotiators with the federal and republican representatives were often breached soon after their adoption. Commenting on his work with the same people, Lord Owen said that he had never before negotiated "...in such a climate of dishonour, propaganda and dissembling".[39]

When the initial euphoria about the Brioni agreement gave way to renewed intransigence and unwillingness of the parties to engage in meaningful negotiations, the EC announced its decision to suspend its financial protocols with Yugoslavia and to implement an arms embargo against the SFRY.[40] Neither of these measures was particularly effective however since, in the former case, it left the JNA with a disproportionate stockpile of weapons to use against the other republics and, in the latter case, economic sanctions were of little concern to the politicians involved in the talks.[41] With no military capacity, however, the EC was left with only diplomatic and economic tools at its disposal.

When Serbia and Montenegro refused key principles of Lord Carrington's peace plan, discussed below, the EC suspended all trade agreements and favourable tariff schemes and prevented Yugoslav delegates attending the next meeting of the G-24 countries. America also suspended economic assistance to Yugoslavia in December 1991. These economic and political sanctions were soon removed from all of the republics except Serbia and Montenegro.[42] Such sanctions removed over $1 billion of economic aid to Yugoslavia at a time when the economic situation was already creating pressure towards its disintegration.[43]

4.3.5 *The EC Monitoring Mission*

The EC-CSCE 'good-offices' delegations secured agreement on the creation of a 50-man EC Monitoring Mission (ECMM) whose mandate was to monitor the implementation of the terms of the Brioni Accord.[44] EC-CSCE cooperation was strengthened when the ECMM later included CSCE-representatives from States outside the EC.[45] When Serbia objected to an extension of the ECMM mandate in Croatia, the EC threatened to take "...additional measures, including international action..." if no progress was made by 1st September 1991. Whilst this statement is vague, it specifically notes that the EC's Member States occupying positions on the UN Security Council would bring this statement to the attention of the Security Council, and it may thus be thought that the intended "...international action..." would involve the United Nations in some way.

As violence escalated in Croatia, the role of the ECMM became increasingly untenable and the EC announced the decision to contemplate inclusion of representatives from the Western European Union (WEU), which would nevertheless not involve any military intervention.[46] This expansion of institutional cooperation also led the EC to announce that it intended to seek the support of the UN Security Council, the CSCE Member States and "...the international community as a whole..." in resolving the crisis.

Despite the considerable difficulties placed before them in undertaking their task, the ECMM is perceived as having performed a valuable service in respect of its monitoring functions as well as in its collaborative work with NGO's such as Medicin sans Frontiers and the International Red Cross.[47]

4.3.6 *The EC Conference on Yugoslavia*

The creation of the European Conference on Yugoslavia (ECCY) in August 1991, two months after fighting broke out in Slovenia and Croatia, heralded a new approach to the growing conflict in the Balkans. One possible reason for creating a peace conference may have been to avoid the possibility of contradictory messages arising from the consideration of the same issues by both the European Parliament and foreign ministers within the EPC framework. An alternative, and more cynical possibility, is that the use of an international conference enabled the European countries to exclude direct influence from the USA and Russia in a manner which would not be possible if organisations such as the CSCE or UN were involved. Lord Owen, who later became Co-Chairman of the ICFY,[48] believes that one of the major factors affecting EC activity during this early period was a desire to avoid American policy input into what was seen as a European problem. Nevertheless, joint statements by the EC-USA-USSR indicate that support for the peace conference was solicited from non-EC States. A more convincing possibility is that the ECCY allowed the diplomatic efforts of the EC to be intensified and maintained on a permanent basis, unhindered by other subjects. It should not be forgotten that this was not only the first internal conflict to challenge the institutional order of the post-Cold War world but also the first attempt of the EC to rehearse the CFSP provisions of the TEU. As such, it is to be expected that a concerted effort would be made to demonstrate the ability of the EC to take a leading role in such affairs, and the use of a permanent negotiating forum would seem an obvious way of achieving this.[49]

Since the declarations of independence from Croatia and Slovenia in June 1991 fighting had escalated to the point where an internally negotiated settlement seemed most unlikely. The Peace Conference was, therefore, to fulfill the role of an impartial negotiating forum, involving, "...on the part of Yugoslavia..". the Federal President,[50] the Federal Government[51] and the Presidents of the various Republics[52] and, on behalf of the European Community, the President of the European Council of Ministers[53] and various representatives of the Member States and European Commission. The ECCY also included an Arbitration Commission which was to assist in the resolution of the differences between the Yugoslav parties. The role of the Badinter Commission within the ECCY is considered in greater detail in chapter 5 below.

The ECCY was convened in the Hague on 7th September 1991 under the Chairmanship of Lord Peter Carrington, the EC's special-envoy to Yugoslavia.[54] Its mandate was to "...ensure the peaceful accommodation of the conflicting aspirations of the Yugoslav peoples on the basis of the following principles: no unilateral change of borders by force, protection of the rights of all in Yugoslavia and full account to be taken of all legitimate concerns and aspirations".[55] An EPC statement of 19th September acknowledged that the new situation in Yugoslavia called for "...new relationships and structures..." and that, although the ECCY was intended to facilitate negotiations on this basis, the EC was willing to "...accept any outcome that is the result of negotiations conducted in good faith".[56] Lord Carrington was instrumental in securing agreement on a number of cease-fires and extensions to the ECMM mandate at the same time as fulfilling his role within the ECCY negotiations and proposing a peace-plan to resolve the crisis.

The European Parliament fully supported the creation of the ECCY and expressed their desire to allow participation by Kosovo and Vojvodina, who had been excluded from the EPC statement's list of participants. Parliament explicitly endorsed the claim that the republics and the autonomous provinces enjoyed the right of "...democratic self-determination..." which it considered could only be negotiated within "...new processes of voluntary cooperation".[57] It appears clear, therefore, that the ECCY and the arbitration procedure therein were somehow intended to assist in the implementation of self-determination in Yugoslavia. The composition of the Commission, discussed in chapter 5, lends support to the hypothesis that the EC still aimed at achieving self-determination peacefully and within existing boundaries, unless the Yugoslav parties unanimously agreed otherwise.

A unique joint statement between the EC-USA-USSR was published on 18th October which sought to evidence widespread international support for the EC's initiatives and the ECCY in particular. The statement also provides further support for the idea that an emerging international norm may extend the applicability of international legal rules to intra-State conflicts such as Yugoslavia. It rejected the legitimacy of force to resolve political disputes or change boundaries, "...whether internal or external...".[58] The CSCE-principles dealing with the inviolability of borders, respect for minority rights and the importance of political pluralism were said to guide international policies relating to Yugoslavia.

A crucial change of direction was evident from an EPC statement of 6th October, which acknowledged that any realistic political solution would be "...in the perspective of recognition of the independence of those republics wishing it, at the end of a negotiation process conducted in good faith and involving all parties".[59] The role of the ECCY was then explained in terms of ensuring that the rights of ethnic minorities within the republics were respected in this negotiation process. This conflicted with the major policies underlying the Carrington Plan, however.

4.3.7 *Lord Carrington's Peace-Plan*

Lord Carrington's role in the ECCY's task was complicated by two factors. First, Yugoslavia as a sovereign State appeared beyond repair. Second, he was aware that recognition of either Croatia and Slovenia, the only two republics thus far to have declared themselves independent, would be disastrous for Bosnia in the absence of an overall peace-deal. His Draft Convention followed the principles of the Izetbegovic-Gligorov Plan,[60] in the sense that it aimed at providing greater autonomy to sovereign republics who would nevertheless continue to cooperate at a federal level on issues such as common-currency, defence and foreign policy.[61] The Draft Convention was essentially "...a looser version of the EC's own constitution...".[62] It proposed a "...free association...[amongst] sovereign and independent republics with international personality for those that wish it...[and] comprehensive arrangements, including supervisory mechanisms, for the protection of human rights and special status for certain groups and areas...". The plan also mentions the creation of mixed commissions to assist in the resolution of disputes concerning human rights, minority rights and questions involving the areas having special status, as well as a requirement that the republics refer any disputes arising out of the implementation of the Plan to a binding arbitration procedure. It is not made clear whether the Badinter Commission was intended to play any role in these respects, but, since the plan was not adopted, it is impossible to say if this would have occurred. European involvement, where appropriate, was outlined and the whole process would take place "...in the framework of a *general settlement* [involving] recognition of the independence, *within existing borders*, unless otherwise agreed, of those republics wishing it...[emphasis added]".[63] The primary aim of the Carrington plan was to ensure that the resolution of the Yugoslav crisis did not focus on specific republics within which fighting was currently occurring but acknowledged the need for an overall settlement on the basis of existing borders.

The plan faced opposition from Serbia, on the basis that it sanctioned the end of the SFRY and obstructed Milosevic's political ambitions to rule a centralised Yugoslavia or create a Greater Serbia, and from the other republics, on the basis that the requirement for consensus gave Serbia a veto over the negotiations.[64] Nevertheless, only Serbia formally opposed the adoption of the Plan and thereby effectively ended the possibility of Yugoslavia surviving as a nominal sovereign State or a collection of States enjoying cooperation on significant issues of joint concern This strengthened the opinions of States such as Germany who believed that recognition was the key to solving the conflict.

4.3.8 *Recognition*

The growing pressure to consider recognising the Yugoslav republics, subject to "...adequate guarantees for the protection of human rights and the rights of national or ethnic groups..."[65] was given EC backing with two Declarations that were published on 16th and 17th of December.[66] As mentioned earlier, the dissolution of the SFRY coincided with that of the USSR, and many of the same issues were raised in relation to both cases. Accordingly, the EC produced a set of guidelines to coordinate EC-recognition of the new States resulting from the fragmentation of these two countries. The first, entitled *Guidelines for the Recognition of New States in Eastern Europe and in The Soviet Union*, detailed a number of political demands which must be satisfied before EC recognition would be forthcoming. The importance of self-determination as the legal basis for such independence is implicit in the first paragraph of this Declaration which states that recognition is based on the EC's "..attachment to the principles of the *Helsinki Final Act* and the *Charter of Paris*, in particular the principle of self-determination". Recognition, and the establishment of diplomatic relations with the EC, would be conditional upon "...the normal standards of international practice and the political realities in each case..." and would be limited to "...new States...which have constituted themselves on a democratic basis...accepted the appropriate international obligations and...committed themselves in good faith to a peaceful process and negotiations". The principles enshrined in the *UN Charter*, the *Helsinki Final Act* and the *Charter of Paris* must be respected, "...especially with regard to the rule of law, democracy and human rights...[and in particular]...respect for the rights of ethnic and national groups and minorities...". The inviolability of "...all frontiers..." must be acknowledged and change to those frontiers could only be implemented by peaceful means and common agreement. All new States were required to accept commitments on nuclear non-proliferation and disarmament and to accept regional and security obligations.[67] All questions of State succession and regional disputes must be settled by pacific means "...including, where appropriate, recourse to arbitration".[68] The Declaration finally emphasised the EC's refusal to recognise entities which were the result of aggression and noted that account would be taken of the effect of recognition on neighbouring States. The *Guidelines* have been described as "...profoundly innovative...[even] revolutionary..."[69] in that they explicitly link the fulfillment of criteria associated with 'internal' self-determination, including minority rights, with acceptance of the legitimacy of 'external' self-determination.[70]

A separate *Declaration on Yugoslavia* made further demands of the Yugoslav republics seeking recognition, which was to be granted to the appropriate "...republics..." on 15th January 1992. Kosovo and Vojvodina would thus be left to resolve their political differences within Serbia and would be required to endure the same political repression and domination which the other republics sought to avoid by seeking independence. First, it demanded support for the ECCY and peace-efforts of the UN Secretary-General. Second, it required acceptance of the principles in the *Guidelines* and the Carrington Draft Convention, especially those in Chapter II thereof, relating to the human rights of ethnic and national groups and minorities. Third, it required the republics to adopt constitutional and political guarantees "...ensuring that it has no territorial claims towards a neighbouring Community State and that it will conduct no hostile propaganda activities versus a neighbouring Community State, including the use of a denomination which implies territorial claims".[71] Applications for recognition were required to be submitted to the Arbitration Commission before 23rd December 1991, a mere week after the adoption of the Declarations. The Commission would consider the applications and provide advice on whether the republics had fulfilled the requirements of the *Guidelines* and *Declaration*. The Commission's role in the recognition procedure is discussed below in chapter 5.

Slovenia and Croatia were officially recognised by the EC on 15th January 1992, but Germany had made it clear as the *Guidelines* were announced that it had already decided to recognise Slovenia and Croatia, even before the Commission had considered their applications.[72] Germany said it intended to delay "...implementation..." of this decision until the 15th January, as stipulated by the *Guidelines* and *Declaration*, but it made it clear that this decision to recognise had already been made in principle. This fatally undermined the EC's initial objectives of maintaining a united Yugoslavia, but, with the political imperative of consensus within the EC appearing to outweigh the consequences of such action, the other Member States acquiesced to Germany's demands on this issue. One may question whether the UK's position was influenced by Germany's sudden turn-about in acepting the UK's demands for opt-outs from the provisions of the Social Chapter and Economic and Monetary Union.[73]

4.3.9 *Post-Recognition*

Lord Carrington resigned his position as ECCY Chairman once recognition of Croatia and Slovenia was announced on 15th January 1992,[74] believing recognition to be premature and likely to escalate the conflict. The offer of recognition had forced Bosnia and Macedonia to seek independence or risk absorption into a Greater-Serbia, and plebiscites which were held in Bosnia resulted in an outbreak of fighting fiercer than that in Slovenia and Croatia combined. Parliament called for the intervention of a UN force and Croatia requested emergency aid from the Community to cope with the 200,000 refugees from Bosnia.[75] Again, the EC stated that it was in no doubt that "...the greatest share of the blame falls on the JNA and the authorities in Belgrade which are in control of the army, both directly and indirectly by supporting Serbian irregulars".[76] and requested the prevention of the delegates of the Federal Republic of Yugoslavia (Serbia and Montenegro) attending international forums such as the CSCE and the Organisation for Economic Cooperation and Development (OECD).

An EC-USA joint statement of 10th March 1992 declared the intention of these nations to coordinate their approaches towards recognition of the republics seeking independence, although the timing of this declaration makes such cooperation seem illusory, arriving as it did following recognition of Slovenia and Croatia and the positive indications given to Bosnia-Hercegovina and Macedonia.[77]

As the hostilities continued to escalate in Bosnia, the limitations of the EC's influence became increasingly evident and the involvement of the United Nations was gradually increased. From this point, the role of the EC as the chief institutional actor in the Yugoslav crisis was greatly reduced. Although Parliamentary resolutions and EPC statements continued to identify and condemn atrocities occurring in the former republics,[78] action to be taken was urged upon the UN rather than being assumed by the EC, which returned to a role more in line with its economic *raison d'etre*.[79] Nevertheless, the creation of the EC-UN International Conference on the Former Yugoslavia in August 1992 left the EC with an important role in the negotiations process and the EC later assumed responsibility for the administration of Mostar in Bosnia, under the Dayton Peace Agreement.[80] These non-economic functions were, however, more in support of UN peace efforts than autonomous policies of the EC.

4.4 The Conference of Security and Cooperation in Europe and the Organisation of Security and Cooperation in Europe (CSCE/OSCE)

4.4.1 *Introduction*

The Conference for Security and Cooperation in Europe (CSCE) was created by the *Helsinki Final Act* (HFA) of 1st August 1975.[81] Unlike the other organisations to be considered in this section, the HFA is famous for its non-binding nature and the CSCE was clearly not an international institution in the traditional sense of the word but a political forum in which a range of European issues were discussed.[82]

The end of the Cold War saw the adoption of the *Charter of Paris for a New Europe* on 21st November 1990 and the expansion of the CSCE's mandate into security issues more reminiscent of a genuine collective security organisation. The *Helsinki Document* of 1992, the *Budapest Summit Declaration* of 1994 and the *Lisbon Summit Declaration on a Common and Comprehensive Security Model for Europe* of 1996 created institutional structures which were to implement this wider mandate and symbolised the transformation of the CSCE into the *Organisation* for Security and Cooperation in Europe (OSCE).[83] Such structures included the creation of an Office for Democratic Institutions and Human Rights (ODIHR), a Conflict Prevention Centre (CPC) and a High Commissioner on National Minorities (HCNM).

Although the OSCE specifically excludes the possibility of engaging in enforcement action, in the sense of *Chapter VII* of the *UN Charter*, it has developed the capacity to perform a wide range of tasks in relation to threats to international security resulting either from conflict between or within its Member States and has been recognised as a regional agency in accordance with *Chapter VIII* of the Charter.[84] Such activities have included peace-keeping missions, observer missions, fact-finding missions and election-monitoring and have seen the OSCE involved in Estonia, Latvia, Chechnya, Tajikistan, Georgia, Nagorno-Karabakh, Moldova, the Ukraine and the former Yugoslavia.[85] All of these activities require the consent of the parties engaged in the conflict and such missions are created on an *ad hoc* basis from voluntary contributions from willing Member States, reflecting the fact that the organisation "...has no significant capabilities of its own".[86]

Although there is no established hierarchy amongst the numerous regional institutions and organisations in the NWO,[87] Weller notes that the OSCE has been treated as "...the first post of call with respect to intra-European issues".[88] Such an approach was reflected in the decision of the EC Member's heads of State, acting within the European Council, to request an emergency meeting of the CSCE to consider the events in Yugoslavia.[89] One of the primary differences between the CSCE and the EC in respect of Yugoslavia was that the SFRY was a member of the CSCE.

4.4.2 *Diplomatic Resolutions*

The CSCE was compelled to act under the potentially-conflicting norms of its founding instruments and, more specifically, between the norm of territorial integrity and the right of self-determination.[90] The latter was being used by Slovenia and Croatia to justify their attempts at independence from the SFRY, while the former was being used by Serbia, Montenegro and the JNA to justify the forceful maintenance of a united Yugoslavia. The CSCE did not wish to encourage secessionism and territorial fragmentation, yet was not willing to accept the legitimacy of the use of force by the JNA to retain a unified Yugoslavia. Accordingly, a statement on Yugoslavia noted that the Council of Ministers of the CSCE "...expressed their friendly concern [regarding the Yugoslav situation] and their support for democratic development, unity and territorial integrity of Yugoslavia, based on economic reforms, full application of human rights...including the rights of minorities, and the peaceful solution of the current crisis". Equally, they stressed that "...it is only for the *peoples* of Yugoslavia to decide on the country's future [emphasis added]".[91]

The Conflict Prevention Centre (CPC) issued a statement on 1st July 1991 calling for a complete and immediate cease-fire between the JNA and Slovenian forces, pending negotiations on Yugoslavia's political problems.[92] The Committee of Senior Officials (CSO) then issued a statement which noted that "...*any* recourse to the use of force...continues to be absolutely inadmissible".[93]

On April 9th 1992, three days after EC-recognition of Bosnia, Hungary and Austria had activated the CSCE's provisions for *Consultation and Cooperation With Regard to Emergency Situations* because of JNA activities in the newly-independent State.[94] Following a similar line of argument as the EC, the CSCE stated that all JNA and Serbian irregular forces should refrain from threatening the territorial integrity of Bosnia and that all neighbouring States should not interfere with Bosnia's independence. Any action to the contrary would constitute "...a pattern of clear, gross and uncorrected violation of CSCE commitments".[95]

4.4.3 *Human-Rights Rapporteur Missions*

A Human-Rights Rapporteur Mission was established and sent to Yugoslavia on behalf of the CSO in December 1991 and January 1992, shortly before Slovenia and Croatia were recognised by the EC.[96] Delegates, composed of representatives from the CSCE, EC and the ECCY, met representatives from all republics and the two former autonomous regions of Serbia. They also spoke to ethnic-group representatives, journalists and Non-Governmental Organisations (NGO's) including human-rights NGO's. The Report concluded that, although the ongoing conflict in Croatia and growing tensions in Bosnia had limited the enforceability of human-rights, there was also no culture of individual human-rights in the Yugoslav communist legal tradition. They noted that "...there is a considerable discrepancy between legal rules and norms on the one hand and the actual implementation of such rules and norms on the other hand. Despite official declarations at various levels, human-rights are frequently violated in many respects, in some places even systematically".[97] Again, the divide between rhetoric and reality pervades the Yugoslav case-study. The Report recommended the Carrington Draft-Convention as the most viable way of ensuring human-rights protection in a united Yugoslavia.

A follow-up Human-Rights Mission was dispatched in May 1992 and confirmed the findings of the original Mission whilst noting that the federal, Serbian and Montenegrin authorities criticised many of the same findings.[98] The Report concluded that little progress had been made on the human-rights situation in the republics and formerly-autonomous regions.

Other CSCE missions were dispatched by the CSO to Kosovo, Vojvodina and Sandjak during May-June 1992. The aim of such missions was to "...promote peace, avert violence and restore respect for human rights and fundamental freedoms...".[99] The Report produced alleged that the human-rights situation in these areas was "...alarming..." and that, specifically, the situation in Kosovo was "...grave...".[100] Failure of the ECCY and ICFY to pay sufficient attention to the status of Kosovo and Vojvodina in subsequent negotiations is, therefore, subject to criticism. The Report suggested the creation of longer-term Missions for these areas to assist in the resolution of ethnically-orientated problems. Although these missions were initially deployed, the FRY authorities refused a request to prolong their initial six-month mandate.[101]

CSCE Rapporteurs were dispatched to Croatia in September-October 1992 following a similar mission in Bosnia in August-September 1992. The Report indicated that 'ethnic-cleansing' was being committed by all sides to the conflict in those republics but that the activities of the JNA and Serb-irregulars supported by Belgrade were "...by far the most serious".[102] The Report also recommended that an *ad hoc* international criminal tribunal be established for the prosecution of such practices and other war-crimes, together with the creation of a Committee of Experts (COE) to collect information on war crimes.[103]

4.4.4 *High Commissioner on National Minorities*

The High-Commissioner on National Minorities (HCNM) also played a role in Croatia and the Former Yugoslav Republic of Macedonia (FYROM) and produced recommendations on issues such as the return of refugees from areas which had been ethnically-cleansed and the re-establishment of inter-ethnic dialogue and cooperation.[104] The aim of the HCNM is to "...provide 'early warning' and, as appropriate, 'early action' at the earliest possible stage in regard to tensions involving national minorities which have not yet developed beyond an early warning stage but...have the potential to develop into a conflict within the CSCE area...".[105] The post was created at the Helsinki Follow-Up Meeting of March-July 1992 and the first HCNM appointed in December 1992. This explains his limited role in the Yugoslav conflict, which had long since developed beyond an 'early-warning' stage, but the fact that the HCNM felt able to become involved in Croatia, where conflict had already occurred between Croats and Serbs, may indicate a broad interpretation of this mandate.

Under the Dayton Peace Agreement, the OSCE assumed a number of responsibilities in Bosnia-Hercegovina. Provision was made for an OSCE-appointed Human-Rights Ombudsperson,[106] elections were to be monitored by OSCE representatives and negotiations on issues such as regional arms control were to be conducted under OSCE auspices.[107]

4.4.5 *Suspension of Yugoslavia from the CSCE*

On 1st May, by which time Bosnia, Croatia and Slovenia had been admitted to the CSCE, the continuance of Yugoslavia's membership by Serbia-Montenegro was challenged by the USA.[108] Utilising the consensus-minus-one principle which had been developed in the *Prague Document on Further Development of CSCE Institutions and Structures* of January 1992, the CSCE's Committee of Senior Officials decided on 8th July 1992 to suspend the SFRY from participation in CSCE meetings until 15th October of that year, at which time the claim to continuance of Yugoslavia's legal title would be reassessed in light of the action taken by Serbia-Montenegro to implement CSCE commitments.[109] It was also noted that, by this time, "...the CSO will have available...information on deliberations within the UN and the legal opinion of the [Badinter] Arbitration Commission of the ECCY".[110] The CSCE later suspended deliveries of weapons and military equipment to Yugoslavia.[111]

4.4.6 *Participation with other Organisation's Peace-Efforts*[112]

The CSO initially sent representatives to join the EC-Troika and to form a joint EC-CSCE 'good-offices' mission which successfully facilitated the acceptance of the Brioni Accord of 8th July.[113] As a result of the CSCE's insufficient operational capacity, it decided to mandate an EC Monitoring Mission (ECMM) to monitor the provisions of the Accord, but the ECMM nevertheless included CSCE representatives from non-EC States such as Poland, Canada, Sweden and Czechoslovakia.[114]

The CSCE did not enjoy any formal participation rights in the ECCY, but the EC made it clear that the outcomes of the conference and the later recognition of the republics were to be conditional upon acceptance of CSCE obligations.[115] The OSCE participated in the London Conference and the resultant ICFY.[116]

The OSCE also assisted in the implementation of the Dayton Accords by supervising elections in Bosnia-Hercegovina alongside the monitoring of human-rights and facilitating arms control and security and confidence-building measures.[117] Equally, the OSCE assisted in the supervision of elections in Serbia,[118] and Montenegro[119]

4.5 The United Nations (UN)[120]

4.5.1 *Introduction*

As mentioned earlier, the political, economic and ideological lacunae which marked the birth of the New World Order meant that the UN, as the world's largest collective security institution, inherited the confused foreign-policy stances of its Members.[121] The institutional vacuum would create major problems in deciding the way in which the UN would respond to the growing categories of threats to international peace and security. In his *Agenda for Peace*, the newly-elected Secretary-General Boutros Boutros-Ghali spoke of a need to "...refashion...the instruments bequeathed to us by the Charter of the UN, to help us construct a new system of international relations..." and also of the need to utilise regional security organisations to "...lighten the burden of the Security Council...".[122] This desire to see regional conflicts such as that in Yugoslavia resolved at a regional level explained the UN's inaction during the early stages of the conflict but by the time the ECCY had been established hostilities had worsened in Croatia and the looming crisis in Bosnia-Hercegovina meant that the UN could no longer justify its decision to delegate total responsibility for the resolution of the conflict to the EC-CSCE peace-efforts. The UN was faced with the political imperative to intervene at the same time as it faced confusion about the manner in which such UN intervention should occur. The main policies adopted by the UN will be examined below.

4.5.2 *Arms Embargo*[123]

On September 25th 1991, only a few weeks into the ECCY process, the UN Security Council passed *Resolution 713* which imposed a "...general and complete embargo on all deliveries of weapons and military equipment to Yugoslavia".[124] This followed similar measures taken by the EC States in July 1991 and represented the kind of "...international action..." which the EC had threatened.[125] The arms embargo was monitored by a Sanctions Committee and applied to the whole of the former SFRY territory and served to ensure the military superiority of the JNA, which possessed the bulk of weapons. Bosnia challenged the UN's refusal to lift the embargo against it,[126] on the basis that it infringed the "...inherent right of self defence..." guaranteed by the *UN Charter*. The unilateral American initiative to stop enforcing the arms embargo can be seen to be a further example of the divisions of policy that prevented the unified approach which was sought to the conflict.[127] The General Assembly voted by 109 votes to 57 to request the Security Council to lift the arms embargo against Bosnia[128] but in the Security Council the requisite majority could not be found.[129]

The imposition of the arms embargo against Yugoslavia may reinforce earlier suggestions that the use of force to settle internal political disputes is increasingly being deemed illegitimate by international law. Weller notes, however, that the precedential value of the Yugoslav case is undermined by the fact that the embargo was requested by the SFRY government but is forced to concede that, in the light of a similar embargo against Somalia, the Yugoslav example is "...consistent with emerging practice...".[130]

4.5.3 *Economic Sanctions*[131]

In addition to military sanctions, economic sanctions were established against Yugoslavia, in line with existing EC sanctions.[132] Sanctions were supervised by a number of groups, including the UN Sanctions Committee, the ECMM and WEU personnel.

After all other republics had been admitted to the UN, the Security Council established sanctions against Serbia and Montenegro under *Chapter VII* of the Charter.[133] When Bosnian-Serbs defied the UN's call for a cease-fire and launched attacks on the 'safe-areas' which had been created in Bosnia-Hercegovina,[134] this led to the imposition of "…the most comprehensive set of mandatory sanctions…in UN history".[135] Commentators have noted that the sanctions package against Serbia and Montenegro "...had a powerful impact…"[136] and encouraged Milosevic to accept the defeat of his Greater-Serbia ideal and to withdraw support from previous allies in Croatia and Bosnia.

4.5.4 *Humanitarian Assistance*[137]

The hardships which were caused by the imposition of economic sanctions were to some extent redressed by the provision of large-scale humanitarian assistance to various areas throughout the former SFRY. Security Council *Resolution 770* endorsed the use of "...all measures necessary..." to ensure delivery of humanitarian aid to besieged cities such as Sarajevo and the eastern parts of the country such as Srebrenica, Cerska, Gorazde and Zepa but military deployments were insufficient to contemplate the use of force to guarantee humanitarian deliveries as a rule.

4.5.5 *The UN Protection Force (UNPROFOR)*

The EC States who occupied a seat on the Security Council during this period[138] requested the then UN Secretary-General, Javier Perez de Cuellar, to produce a report on the situation in Yugoslavia.[139] In October, Cyrus Vance was appointed as the Secretary-General's personal-envoy for Yugoslavia and sent to liaise with the ECCY participants and discuss the feasibility of a peace-keeping force. In November, Security Council *Resolution 721* approved in principle the suggested creation of a UN Peace-keeping force to operate in the SFRY.[140]

The first UN deployment involved 50 military-liaison officers whose aim was to prepare for a possible deployment but, despite rhetorical support from all parties for a UN peace-keeping force,[141] cease-fire breaches were commonplace and the UN refrained from authorising a deployment. Despite recurring breaches of the cease-fires negotiated by Lord Carrington and Cyrus Vance, the UN Secretary-General recommended the deployment of a UN force in February 1992, in order to prevent the conflict worsening and spreading to other areas of Yugoslavia.[142] The 'Vance Plan' was strengthened by an Implementing Accord signed on 3rd January 1992,[143] which permitted the creation of a UN Protection Force (UNPROFOR) for deployment in a number of United Nations Protected Areas (UNPA's) in Croatia.

Hesitant of breaching *Article 2(7)* of the *UN Charter*[144] to which a number of countries alluded during discussions of the Yugoslav conflict,[145] the Security Council had justified its consideration of the conflict by referring to "...strong international dimensions..." of the conflict and the threat to international peace and security which would result from "...the *continuation* of this situation...[emphasis added]", [146] rather than declaring it a threat to the peace *per se*. The request from Yugoslavia's federal government for the UN to consider the situation largely assisted in overcoming any ideological difficulties in authorising international intervention.

UN peace-keeping forces were deployed in Croatia, Bosnia and Macedonia and are considered individually below.

Croatia. UNPROFOR's initial deployment was limited to three UNPA's in Croatia which corresponded to those areas where Serbs constituted a significant minority, or indeed majority, of the population. They also corresponded with those areas which had been militarily wrested from the Croatian government's control. The UN forces in Eastern Slavonia, Western Slavonia and Krajina were sub-divided into sectors and UNPROFOR's mandate rested on the withdrawal of JNA troops and general demilitarisation of these areas, the maintenance of a cease-fire and the possibility for displaced persons to return to their homes. The initial UNPA's were extended to cover certain 'pink zones'[147] and UNPROFOR's mandate was repeatedly strengthened in a number of subsequent resolutions.[148] Hostilities were renewed in Croatia in early 1993 as the Croatian Army advanced on a number of 'pink zones' and Serbs responded by retrieving many of the weapons they had handed over to UN forces as part of the UNPA agreement.[149] This fighting continued until a cease-fire of 15th September 1993, following which an UNPROFOR force was deployed in the area and helped stabilise conditions to allow for the signing of a Christmas Truce Agreement on 17th December which was extended after the original expiry date of 15th January 1994 and has "...generally held since then".[150] The status of Serb-held areas remains outstanding however.

Bosnia. UNPROFOR's mandate was later extended to Bosnia, where fighting intensified after its independence was recognised by the EC.[151] The withdrawal of JNA troops from Croatia had also meant that they could re-deploy in Bosnia and the existence of substantial Serb and Croat populations throughout the region meant that the battle for territory would be much more widespread than that in Slovenia or Croatia. Such inter-ethnic fighting worsened when the initial

Muslim-Croat alliance faltered during 1993.[152]

Resolution 752 demanded the disarming, withdrawal or submission to Bosnia's government of the Croatian and JNA forces operating therein and extended this obligation to "...all irregular forces, whatever their origin...". It also demanded the immediate cessation of interference from other former-Yugoslav republics. *Resolution 836* condemned "...military attacks, and actions that do not respect the sovereignty, territorial integrity and political independence of...[Bosnia]...which, as a member State of the United Nations, enjoys the rights provided for in the Charter...". It is not immediately clear from this whether the attacks referred to are those from the factions within Bosnia itself or whether they include the assistance from Serbia and Croatia proper, which had both been criticised in previous resolutions. If the former were to be the case, it may be that the Security Council has effectively extended the notion of "...armed attack..." in *Article 51* of the Charter to include the internal fighting happening at the time, which would appear to be inconsistent with the traditional international legal approach to this question.

The Bosnian conflict was finally resolved upon the signing of the Dayton Peace Agreement, discussed below, albeit with numerous problems relating to the implementation of this peace-plan.

Macedonia. In November 1992, President Gligorov of Macedonia asked the Security Council to deploy a peace-keeping force in that republic. This was supported by the UN Secretary-General and was authorised in *Resolution 795*.[153] This 'trip-wire' force assumed a largely preventative role and greatly assisted in preventing conflict spreading to this region.[154]

4.5.6 *Safe Areas*

In March 1993, fighting in Bosnia had led to massive population flows in that republic and a number of areas within which Muslims collected after having been displaced from areas that had been taken by Serbs or Croats. UNHCR reports noted that many were starving and in desperate need of medical equipment and the International Red Cross had been calling for the establishment of safe areas since November 1992.[155] In *Resolution 819* of 16th April 1993, Srebrenica was declared a "...safe area which should be free from any armed attack or any other hostile act..." and this was later joined by Tuzla, Zepa, Gorazde, Bihac and Sarajevo, the latter of which was recognised as a "...multi-cultural, multi-ethnic and pluri-religious centre which exemplifies the viability of coexistence and interrelations between all the communities of the Republic of Bosnia and Hercegovina...".[156]

UNPROFOR's mandate in Bosnia was enlarged to allow measures including the use of force to deter attacks on the safe areas and promote the removal of belligerent forces whilst guaranteeing the safe delivery of humanitarian aid.[157] The crux of the problems in relation to the safe-areas was that, in order to ensure their safety, the UN would have had to protect them from attacks from one of the belligerents and, in doing so, would be forced to abandon the neutrality which is central to the legitimacy of any peace-keeping mission. Furthermore, given the lack of resources to perform anything like a peace-enforcement function, UNPROFOR was unable to demand the demilitarisation of the safe-areas because the Muslim populations therein refused to rely on UNPROFOR to protect them. Whilst military estimates of the required number of troops were placed at 35,000, the Security Council, composed of States who were unwilling to finance such a large operation, opted for a 'light-option' of only 7,500 troops, which Lord Owen called "...the worst single decision taken by the Security Council during [his] tenure as Co-Chairman of the ICFY...".[158]

The rhetoric of the safe-areas policy soon gave way to the harsh reality that they were far from safe. Bosnian Serbs assaults on Srebrenica, Gorazde, Sarajevo, Banja Luka and Bihac intensified and a number of those safe-areas fell, leaving the UN and the international community humiliated.[159]

4.5.7 *The International Conference on the Former Yugoslavia*

In July 1992, the Security Council expressed its desire for greater UN involvement in the ECCY and called upon the EC to involve the UN Secretary-General in any further negotiations as well as suggesting "...broadening and intensifying the present [ECCY] Conference with a view to providing a new momentum in the search for negotiated settlements...".[160]

Accordingly, the EC requested the new UN Secretary-General, Boutros Boutros-Ghali to co-chair a joint EC-UN Conference with the President of the European Council of Ministers.[161] The London Conference of 26th-28th August 1992 saw the creation of the EC-UN International Conference on the Former Yugoslavia (ICFY), which effectively subsumed the work of the ECCY whilst continuing to make use of much of the machinery which formed the initial Peace Conference, including the Arbitration Commission.[162] Since the London Conference meetings were held in private,[163] it is impossible to be entirely sure of the reasons behind the transfer of responsibilities from the ECCY to the ICFY, but it must be presumed that the EC's evident inability to cope with the Yugoslav conflict alone was chief amongst such reasons.

The ICFY was described by Boutros-Ghali as "...an innovative exercise..."[164] and, as with the ECCY, allowed negotiations to take place in a forum specifically created for those purposes. The London Conference adopted a number of important documents which formed the constitution and mandate of the ICFY. First, a Statement of Principles emphasised the policy of non-recognition of territorial changes brought about by non-peaceful means, as well as the need for negotiations to ensure the respect of human rights[165] and international humanitarian law.[166] The statement also spoke of the need to ensure the implementation of constitutional guarantees on human rights of ethnic and national communities and minorities. In the same paragraph, the statement speaks of the need to promote tolerance and the right of self-determination, in accordance with the commitments entered into in the ECCY. The physical proximity of, on the one hand, the clause dealing with constitutional guarantees to protect the human rights of minorities and ethnic communities and, on the other hand, respect for the right of self-determination, may not be accidental.[167] On the question of borders, the statement noted the duty to respect the "...inviolability of all frontiers in accordance with the *UN Charter*, the *CSCE Final Act* and the *Charter of Paris*". This may be viewed either as an endorsement of the Arbitration Commission's findings on the question of *uti possidetis* in the dissolution of Yugoslavia or as nothing more than an endorsement of the traditional prohibition on the modification of international borders by force.[168] The second major document outlining the function of the ICFY was its Work Programme. This specified that the ICFY would remain in being "...until a final settlement of the problems of the former Yugoslavia has been reached..." and went on to outline the functions of the Steering Committee and the various Working Groups of the ICFY. The London Conference also secured agreement on a statement on Bosnia and a list of specific decisions relating to matters such as humanitarian issues, sanctions and detention camps.

The Steering Committee orchestrated the multifarious tasks which were coordinated within the ICFY, first under the Co-Chairmanship of Lord Owen and Cyrus Vance and then after their replacement by Thorvald Stoltenberg, on behalf of the UN, and Carl Bildt, on behalf of the EC.

4.5.8 *Peace-Plans*

Under the auspices of the ICFY, the Steering Committee chaired by Lord

David Owen, on behalf of the EC, and Cyrus Vance, on behalf of the UN, attempted to negotiate a diplomatic solution to the worsening Bosnian crisis. The Vance-Owen Peace Plan (VOPP), published on 28th October 1992, proposed the creation of between seven and ten cantons, which reflected their ethnic composition, within a decentralised Bosnia.[169] Although the map was revised over subsequent months, to take account of the shifting territorial situation amongst the warring parties, the principles remained the same. The ICFY reserved the right to appoint its own representatives to key positions of power in the new Bosnian constitution, such as the Constitutional and Human-Rights Courts, the International Commission of Human Rights for Bosnia-Hercegovina and the Bosnian Ombudsmen. The plan also required international supervision of certain activities, such as the integration of the military and the creation of an ethnically-balanced armed force.[170]

The VOPP had the effect of splitting the Muslim-Croat alliance which had existed since the outbreak of the war. Soon after its announcement, Bosnian-Croat leaders declared the independence of a Croatian 'Herceg-Bosna' Republic and sought to maximise the Croatian share of land in Bosnia. Although sanctions against Serbia and Montenegro had secured their endorsement of the Plan, the Bosnian Serb Parliament in Pale rejected it and sparked fresh discussions about the Plan's viability. America effectively withdrew its support for the Plan in 1993 and began to support a move towards an inter-governmental process for designing a blue-print for Bosnia, incorporating the USA, Russia, France, UK and Spain.[171]

The Joint-Action Plan (JAP) represented not only a step-down from the VOPP principles of a unified, albeit decentralised, Bosnia but also represented a move away from the inclusive political process of the ICFY and towards a smaller collection of powerful States who would decide policy according to their own vital interests.[172] The JAP and successive plans failed to require as much territory to be yielded by the Serbs as did the VOPP. Owen notes how the American rhetorical position of demanding a reversal of ethnic cleansing was not matched by the reality of their decision to withdraw support for the VOPP. Equally, American support for the 'lift-and-strike' option, which would increase air-attacks in defence of the safe-areas whilst removing the arms embargo against Bosnia, took no account of the reality that America had no troops on the ground at this stage and did not contemplate the risks to UNPROFOR members in the event of such action.

The JAP proposed the division of Bosnia into three ethnically-organised mini-States which would cooperate within a nominal Bosnian confederacy.[173] Sarajevo would be placed under UN administration while Mostar would be administered by the EC. The plan was rejected by the Bosnian government on the same grounds that the VOPP had been opposed by the USA; namely that it failed to give enough territory to the Muslims of Bosnia.[174]

An EU Action Plan aimed to increase the territory given to the Muslims of Bosnia.[175] Again, however, specific territorial disputes prevented the plan being adopted. The next major peace-initiative was the Washington Agreement of February 1994, which aimed at securing renewed Croatian support for the Muslim-Croat alliance which had dissolved in the wake of the VOPP. America implicitly threatened to withdraw its support for Croatia's territorial claims over the Serb-held areas in Croatia and called upon Tudjman to pressure Bosnian-Croats to accept the plan. A statement by the President of the Security Council made it clear that the UN was willing to "...consider other serious measures if the Republic of Croatia fails to put an immediate end to all forms of interference in the Republic of Bosnia and Hercegovina..."[176] which clearly implied the prospective use of sanctions similar to those in effect against Serbia and Montenegro. This policy worked and on 18th March 1994 President Clinton presided over a signing ceremony in Washington. After this small but important victory, a Contact Group was established, comprising USA, UK, France, Germany and Russia, whose aim was to coordinate the aims of the international community at a time when disunity was commonplace.[177] The Group's plan was to ensure a 51% portion of Bosnia to the Muslim-Croat Federation created under the Washington Agreement which would require Bosnian-Serbs to return almost a third of the 70% of Bosnia they currently held. Despite pressure from Belgrade and Moscow, the Bosnian-Serbs rejected the Plan, causing Serbia to invoke sanctions against the Republika-Srpska which split the Milosevic-Karadzic political alliance. The final peace-initiative took place at the Wright-Patterson Air Force Base in Dayton, Ohio. The *Dayton General Framework Agreement for Peace in Bosnia-Hercegovina* was agreed on 22nd November 1995.[178] Under this agreement, there are two recognised 'entities' within a sovereign Bosnian State, whose new constitution was negotiated as part of the peace-plan and which involves much international supervision and administration. The Bosnian-Serb territories within the 'Republika Srpska' represent one entity while the other is constituted of the Muslim-Croat Federation. A Constitutional Court includes three members who are appointed by the European Court of Human Rights and the Council of Europe is responsible for appointing eight of fourteen members of a new Human Rights Chamber. An Ombudsman is also to be appointed by the OSCE.

4.5.9 *International Criminal Tribunal for Yugoslavia*[179]

The conflicts which arose out of the dissolution of Yugoslavia were characterised most by their barbarity and the extent of 'ethnic-cleansing' and war crimes which were committed to varying degrees by all warring factions. Individual liability for such actions and the possibility of "...serious consequences..." for the parties pursuing such a deliberate policy was threatened throughout the Bosnian conflict.[180] As mentioned above, the CSCE human-rights missions and the High Commissioner on National Minorities had both recommended the creation of an *ad hoc* international court to deal with the war crimes committed in the former Yugoslavia and this was taken up by the UN when it became involved.

The documents resulting from the London Conference announced that the Co-Chairmen of the ICFY would carry out a study on the creation of an international criminal court.[181] The eventual establishment of the International Criminal Tribunal for Yugoslavia (ICTY) was possible only as a result of the popular support for such an organ amongst UN members and was established by Security *Resolution 808* of 22nd February 1993. A Commission of Experts (COE) was also created to gather information on the extent and nature of war crimes.[182] A similar *ad hoc* criminal tribunal was created to deal with war crimes committed in the Rwandan civil war.[183] Both of these played an important role in achieving support for the creation of a permanent international criminal court, whose statute was adopted in July 1998.[184]

4.5.10 *No-Fly Zone*

A no-fly zone was established in Bosnia under Security *Resolution 781* in October 1992, although UN estimates show the number of breaches of this to have been extensive.[185] These infringements were largely ignored until they involved the use of combat aircraft in military operations around Srebrenica in March 1993, following which the Security Council decided to enforce the zone and authorised the use of "...all necessary measures..."[186] to deter attacks against the regions. NATO forces were used to enforce 'Operation Deny Flight'.[187]

4.5.11 *The UN Commission on Human Rights*

The first ever special meeting of the UNCHR appointed a Special-Rapporteur, former Polish Premier Tadeusz Mazowiecki, to report on the human-rights situation in the former Yugoslavia.[188] Acting in coordination with human-rights monitors from both the EC and CSCE, Mr Mazowiecki produced a number of periodic reports detailing the extent of war crimes and grave breaches of the Geneva Conventions during the various Yugoslav conflicts.[189] He resigned in protest against the policies of the international community after the fall of Srebrenica and Zepa, saying that "…one cannot speak about the protection of human-rights with credibility when one is confronted with the lack of consistency and courage displayed by the international community and its leaders. […] The international community should abandon its hypocrisy towards Bosnia. For we are claiming that we are defending it, while we are in fact abandoning it".[190] Mazowiecki's replacement, Elizabeth Rehn endorsed his findings and issued further damning reports.

4.5.12 *The UN High-Commissioner for Refugees*

The UNHCR, Sadako Ogata of Japan, and her staff were active in attempting to relieve the plight of refugees and internally-displaced persons who suffered because of the wide-scale 'ethnic-cleansing' in the Yugoslav wars.[191] The UNHCR attempted to coordinate an inter-agency programme of action on humanitarian issues in Yugoslavia and played an active role on the Humanitarian Issues Working Group within the ICFY.

4.5.13 *The UN Implementation Force and Stabilisation Force*

Under the terms of the Dayton Peace Agreement, an Implementation Force (I-FOR) was created to ensure that the provisions of the peace-plan were adhered to by all sides.[192] This was later transformed into a Stabilisation Force (S-FOR). S-FOR was also mandated to arrest those suspected of war-crimes if it encountered them during the course of its other duties.[193] The fact that the peace-deal negotiations were being conducted with the same people however, combined with the fact that they were provided with a much greater level of military protection than the UN were capable of challenging, meant that meetings with Karadzic and Mladic were commonplace and little was done by way of attempting to implement this mandate.

4.5.14 *The UN Educational, Scientific and Cultural Organisation (UNESCO)*

UNESCO dispatched a permanent observer to monitor the protection, or more correctly the destruction, of cultural treasures during the various conflicts.[194]

4.5.15 *Suspension of Yugoslavia from the UN General Assembly*

The Badinter Commission recommended in *Opinion 9* that "...the SFRY's membership of international organisations must be terminated according to their statutes..." following the SFRY's dissolution.[195] With regard to the UN, Yugoslavia did not occupy a non-permanent seat in the Security Council during this period and its participation was thus limited to the General Assembly. *UNSC Resolution 777* suspended the participation of the Federal Republic of Yugoslavia (FRY) in the General Assembly as of September 1992 but fell short of fully implementing the Commission's advice to terminate membership.[196] The International Monetary Fund (IMF) and World Bank concurred with the finding in *Resolution 757* that "...the State formerly known as the Socialist Federal Republic of Yugoslavia has ceased to exist".[197]

4.6 The North Atlantic Treaty Organisation (NATO)[198]

4.6.1 *Introduction*

NATO was a collective security alliance which developed as a result of the Cold War. In this sense, its *raison d'etre* disappeared with the end of the Cold War and the dissolution of the Warsaw Pact. Nevertheless, it is clear from the *London Declaration on a Transformed Alliance* that NATO Members perceived the organisation as having a positive role in shaping the NWO beyond the purely military dimension. NATO declared itself part of a new 'European security architecture' which also incorporated the EC, CSCE and WEU and which sought to take account of the expanding categories of threats to international peace and security in the new international environment.[199] NATO developed the capacity to act in concert with other institutions in areas outside its own Members' borders, effectively acting as a sub-contractor of the UN or CSCE in peace-keeping or peace-enforcement missions. It was on this basis that NATO activities in the former Yugoslavia were conducted.[200]

4.6.2 *Sanctions*

NATO assisted in the supervision of sanctions imposed by the EC and UN, working in conjunction with EC, WEU and UN monitors.

4.6.3 *Humanitarian Assistance*

UN-SC *Resolution 770*, mentioned above, authorised the use of "...all measures necessary..." to ensure the delivery of humanitarian assistance to Sarajevo and other parts of Bosnia. NATO enforcement action would clearly have been permissible under this resolution, on the authorisation of the Security Council.

4.6.4 *No-Fly Zone*

NATO's military capacity was used to monitor and enforce the no-fly zone established in Bosnia by UN Security Council 816. On 28th February 1994, after serious violations of the no-fly zone, NATO was called upon to perform its first military action and shot down four Bosnian-Serb planes.

4.6.5 *Safe Areas*

The resolutions authorising all necessary measures to support UNPROFOR in the performance of its role in the safe-areas and the ability to "...reply to bombardments against the safe areas..."[201] also envisaged NATO's assistance in implementing any such military measures. When a mortar round killed 68 civilians in Sarajevo market-square in February 1994, military air-strikes were threatened unless the heavy-weapons surrounding Sarajevo were withdrawn or placed under UN supervision. After considerable political brinkmanship, the weapons were finally withdrawn within the given deadline.

4.6.6 *Dayton Peace Agreement Functions*

Under the terms of the Dayton Agreement, NATO assumed a more autonomous role in policing the military aspects of the Agreement. Until Dayton, the UN had insisted on a 'dual-key' system for authorising NATO enforcement action, requiring civilian approval from the UN as well as military approval from NATO leaders, in order to take account of the safety of UN troops on the ground. Under the Dayton Agreement, discretion to use enforcement action was vested solely in the NATO high-command. Sixty thousand NATO troops were deployed as part of I-FOR to implement the terms of the Dayton Agreement, including representatives from non-NATO members such as Russia.[202]

4.7 The Western European Union (WEU)

4.7.1 *Introduction*

The WEU was a European collective-security alliance of the Cold War which had never really functioned in an active way as the signatory States had imagined. The moribund status of the WEU was to some extent redressed by developments within the EC, which planned to develop the WEU as its defence-wing alongside the development of the CFSP provisions. Similarly, the WEU declared its willingness to support CSCE activities in respect of humanitarian missions, peace-keeping missions and peace-enforcement missions.[203] Later declarations made it clear that institutional links with NATO were also to be expected and that the WEU may wish to utilise NATO assets and equipment in order to perform these missions.[204]

The WEU's activities in Yugoslavia were generally performed at the request of another institution and not with the WEU acting autonomously. A possible WEU mission in support of the ECMM was requested by the EC itself, WEU monitoring of sanctions was subordinate to NATO control of the operation and WEU deployment in Mostar was done at the request of the UN. Nevertheless, a WEU Working Group on Yugoslavia produced a report which outlines the approach and perspectives adopted by the organisation during its various roles.[205]

4.7.2 *WEU Missions in Yugoslavia*

In September 1991, an initial plan to send a WEU mission to protect the ECMM fell through because of the deteriorating political situation in the SFRY. Nevertheless, by July 1992, the WEU was active in monitoring sanctions against Yugoslavia and in providing surveillance of military activities by the various parties. The only WEU mission coming close to the functions of a peace-keeping force was the one dispatched to Mostar in 1994, incorporating 150 military and civilian personnel.

4.8 Other International Institutions and Organisations

Many other bodies produced reports and participated in various activities within the former Yugoslavia. The G-7 economic group, which became the G-8 after membership of Russia was secured, issued a declaration in June 1992 suspending Yugoslavia's economic assistance and participation as an observer in the Group's activities. The Organisation of the Islamic Conference (OIC) also made a declaration, arguing against the continuance of the arms embargo against the newly-independent Bosnia-Hercegovina. The Non-Aligned Movement, within which Yugoslavia had been a key member,[206] also produced a declaration in August 1992 expressing its desire to see a peaceful outcome to the developments on the SFRY.

On a more involved level, the International Committee of the Red Cross (ICRC) and Medicin sans Frontiers were instrumental in providing humanitarian assistance to civilians at risk during the various conflicts, especially in Bosnia. The ICRC also created a Commission to trace missing persons and mortal remains as well as assisting in the evacuation of refugees in areas which had been 'ethnically-cleansed'.

4.9 Conclusions

Having outlined the major policy approaches of the international institutions most heavily involved with the Yugoslav crisis, a number of interesting points arise. First, it is noticeable that, despite the rhetorical determination of all of these institutions to maintain a united and democratic Yugoslavia, this outcome was not achieved and Yugoslavia, as such, no longer exists.[207]

Whilst it must be acknowledged that primary responsibility for the Yugoslav crisis rests squarely on the shoulders of those who created a nationalistic political situation within which they could best pursue their personal political aggrandisement, the role of the international community may also have been a factor in the dissolution of the SFRY. It is submitted that the primary faults of the international community were the misallocation of responsibilities amongst international institutions and the tardy nature of international intervention at the outset of the crisis. The CIA and many political analysts had predicted the dissolution of Yugoslavia to be "...highly likely...most probably in the next 18 months..." as early as autumn 1990, yet international institutions were not ready to intervene in the crisis at an early stage, when it was most resolvable.[208] Hampered by the institutional identity crises of the NWO and basking in the glory of the international community's united response to the Gulf crisis, major international institutions left the Yugoslav conflict to develop into one where intervention would have little impact.

When institutional activity began, it limited itself to the diplomatic option and abortively attempted to negotiate cease-fires and peace-plans to preserve Yugoslavia in its present form with those politicians whose vested interests required the structure to be changed, either by centralisation or by liberalisation of the existing State structure. Confusing messages contained in these initial diplomatic responses served to convince these opposing parties that they enjoyed international support and reduced the likelihood of compromise. Little explanation of the relevant legal norms underpinning the institutional approach was provided by the institutions, particularly in respect of self-determination and the illegitimacy of armed conflict to resolve an internal political dispute. When such diplomacy failed, the instruments of persuasion were inadequate to resolve the conflict in light of its stage of development.

Economic sanctions were largely ineffective in achieving their desired effect, despite some later successes in encouraging a more compromisory Serbian attitude towards the peace-process. On the other hand, offers of economic assistance encouraged Montenegro to accept the Carrington Draft Convention and one wonders whether economic assistance to Yugoslavia at a stage before the crisis erupted may have removed many of the tensions which made dissolution more likely.[209] Military sanctions failed to appreciate that the dissolution of Yugoslavia would pit Serbia and Montenegro against the other republics and that an arms-embargo would provide the former with an unchallengeable military superiority by virtue of their control of the JNA.[210] Recognition of Croatia and Slovenia undermined Lord Carrington's attempts to hold Yugoslavia together, albeit nominally, and precipitated the carnage which followed in Bosnia.

Ultimately, it may be said that the capacities of the EC and CSCE to resolve internal conflicts once they have reached the level of actual violence appear questionable. Deployment of Monitoring Missions, human-rights rapporteurs and high-commissioners on minorities may have a preventive effect on the development of such conflicts but do little to resolve them once they have arisen. The EC's desire to demonstrate its capabilities in this area and the UN's desire to delegate such responsibility to relieve the burden on its own resources indicate that internal political factors within the institutions considered here undermined the potential for a unified international response such as was seen in the Gulf War. The EC's fatal acceptance of German and Greek pressure to form a common position on recognition, or non-recognition, of certain Yugoslav republics also evidences this.

UN involvement came disastrously late in the day to prevent the escalation of the conflict and again highlighted the misjudged and ill-timed nature of international intervention. UNPROFOR served only to consolidate Serb gains in Croatia and allowed the JNA to focus on Bosnia. Any peace-keeping force must, by definition, follow the conclusion of a satisfactory peace, which was clearly not the case in Yugoslavia. At times, UNPROFOR was forced to assist in ethnic-cleansing of areas in order to prevent lives being lost at the same time as UN resolutions condemned these practices. The troops representing the international community were ill-equipped to perform their rhetorical role in respect of peace-keeping and protection of the safe-areas.

Conclusion of the Dayton Peace Agreement achieved an uneasy peace in Bosnia but was only possible after decisive American intervention which had been lacking during the early stages of the Yugoslav crisis. Croatia's situation is currently frozen by the presence of UNPROFOR but questions remain as to the future relationship between the Croatian-Serbs and Croatia-proper. The Kosovo question, so vital to the outbreak of war, also remains unresolved in any long-term sense, as does the situation regarding Albanians in Macedonia and Hungarians in Vojvodina. Recent developments indicate that these areas remains a potential powder-keg for renewed fighting in the Balkan region.[211] Ironically, similar predictions were made in respect of violence in Kosovo and Macedonia as a result of growing Albanian nationalism, but again the international response has been reactive rather than proactive and, compared with the Yugoslav conflict, the Kosovo conflict received scant international attention.[212]

On a more positive note, it will be suggested that the desire to maintain a united Yugoslavia was a defensible one, albeit one rendered less viable in the face of such late intervention. A constitutional settlement within the SFRY's existing borders may have preserved the sovereignty of Yugoslavia if encouraged at a time before aggressive nationalism controlled the political situation. The creation of the ECCY and the Arbitration Commission, whose role it will be suggested was to assist in the redrafting of the SFRY 1974 constitution, offers some useful insights into possible ways of coordinating diplomatic efforts in relation to internal conflicts, but again failed to have the desired effect because of the late arrival of these initiatives. By the time the Commission was active, Slovenia and Croatia had already declared their independence and Germany had begun to seek EC support for recognising them as independent. This is not the environment in which efforts to preserve a State will have any great effect.

Humanitarian assistance undoubtedly saved many lives and the role of the ICRC and other humanitarian organisations is beyond reproof. To say the same of the major institutions is not possible, however, given what has been said above. To argue that humanitarian assistance is worthy of praise when previous reluctance to intervene may have assisted the dissolution of the SFRY is akin to someone watching a neighbour's house burn to the ground and then expecting thanks for having saved the garden-shed. When international institutions assume responsibility for the preservation of international peace and security, their performance must be judged against whether peace and security are preserved and not against their ability to provide food to those who suffer during the horrible conflicts which followed the dissolution of Yugoslavia.

On an intra-State level, the Yugoslav crisis also provided the backdrop for the first post-war deployment of German forces outside Germany's own borders.[213] The first ever preemptive deployment of UN troops, in Macedonia, may have prevented the outbreak of fighting in that republic but remains the exception rather than the rule of institutional intervention in the Yugoslav case. The work of the ICTY, together with the Rwandan tribunal, also clearly renewed international interest in the creation of a permanent international criminal court, whose statute was adopted in

July 1998. Nevertheless, despite the recent indictment of Milosevic and other Serbian leaders for crimes committed during the Kosovo conflict there has, as yet, been little progress on ensuring liability for similar activities which occurred during the Bosnian conflict. There have been leaked reports from those currently working at the ICTY that there is a feeling of despondency at the Tribunal, where many feel that they are not only struggling financially to fulfill their mandate but are also lacking the requisite political support for the same. The rhetorical wishes of the international community to see those responsible for war crimes arrested and charged are severely tested when those same people may be essential to the negotiation of a peace-deal to prevent further conflict.[214]

The end of the Cold War presented many challenges to the world international institutions and, as McGoldrick notes,[215] one may argue that the timing of the Yugoslav conflict was bad. This does not excuse, however, the misjudged and ill-timed responses of the same institutions. How then should the Yugoslav crisis have been addressed by the world's institutional actors? It is submitted that the paralytic tension which exists between the global effects of contemporary internal conflicts and the traditional reluctance to intervene in the domestic affairs of a sovereign State must be resolved with a shift towards intervention at an earlier stage. For international law, and the actors who aim to enforce it, to limit their role to one of conflict-management and containment after conflict has broken-out is to create a self-fulfilling prophesy of international law's failure to prevent such conflicts. If a domestic health-service limited its intervention until the patient was critically-ill and probably beyond saving, one would refuse to justify the death of the patient on the basis that they were already too ill to prevent this event. One would seek ways to prevent the patient ever reaching such a critical stage of illness. Equally, ways must be sought to allow international law to intervene at a stage when such intervention is likely to be most effective. A number of problems present themselves when this aim is sought, however.

First, traditional State concerns about the illegitimacy of intervention into a sovereign State's domestic affairs are bound to arise. The sovereignty of Statehood is one of the fundamental pillars of international society and is not easily side-stepped. Nevertheless, one must ask in respect of the Yugoslav case, whose sovereignty was respected by the approach adopted? Was the sovereignty of Yugoslavia preserved by adopting a cautious approach to intervention which saw the same State dissolve within months of institutional involvement? Was the sovereignty of Bosnia respected in the deterioration of the political situation, the maintenance of an arms embargo against a recognised independent government seeking to maintain territorial integrity in the face of massive internal, and external, threats thereto or the Dayton Agreement which carved-up Bosnia into two 'entities' which make effective governmental control extremely difficult? The point is that an over-cautious approach may destroy the sovereignty of the State it seeks to protect, perhaps the most ironic, yet tragic, aspects of rhetoric versus reality in the Yugoslav case-study.

Second, in light of concerns about the cost of intervention,[216] one must contrast the costs of intervention at an early stage with those at a later stage. One can only speculate at the levels of economic and diplomatic persuasion which may have been required to coerce Yugoslavia's politicians into a more compromisory position on Yugoslavia's future in the wake of Tito's death and during the early period of the NWO. Nevertheless, even a generous estimation would not approach the costs associated with the policies discussed above. UNPROFOR's annual costs approach $1.2 billion,[217] the rebuilding of Bosnia's destroyed infrastructure will run into many billions more and these greater costs are deployed in a far more negative fashion than may otherwise have been the case. They cannot hope to undo the massive loss of human life nor to begin the process of reconciliation if the newly-independent Balkan States are to begin a new era of inter-relations.

International cooperation was limited once responsibility for Yugoslavia was devolved to the EC-CSCE. The European organisations' desire to establish their credibility as fledgling security-collectives and the UN's desire to minimise its involvement in such local conflicts obscured the need for a coordinated and integrated approach to the complex problems faced by internal political conflicts. This writer would have preferred to see a UN contingent to advise on the approach to be adopted by the EC Members, in their first attempt at dispute resolution within the institutions auspices. Equally, the deployment of a peace-enforcement mission under UN auspices at an earlier stage may have prevented the scale of atrocities witnessed in Bosnia. As Karadzic himself noted, "...I knew that the international community needed only 100,000 troops in Zvornik and the Posavina corridor to neutralise the Serbs".[218] Nevertheless, the UN's Member States were unwilling to risk domestic political support in the event of casualties or deaths which are unavoidable in such situations.

The current institutional approach to internal conflicts appears inadequate. Whilst it is beyond the scope of this work to consider in detail how new approaches could be developed, some indications of the source of the problems associated with existing strategies have been indicated. Reflections, both formal and informal, have begun within some of the organisations involved in the Yugoslav conflict on the ways in which institutional cooperation could be improved.[219]

Having briefly examined the major policy initiatives of the international community during the dissolution of Yugoslavia, the next two chapters will analyse the role of the Badinter Arbitration Commission under the two international conferences mentioned above. Chapter 5 will focus on the role of the Commission under the ECCY and chapter 6 will deal with the Commission under the ICFY.

Notes

1 McGoldrick, D., 'Yugoslavia - The Responses of the International Community and of International Law', (1996), 49 *CLP*, 375.

2 Id, 393.

3 See section 4.5.7. and chapter 5, section 5.4.3.

4 Szasz, P.C., 'Documents Regarding the Conflict in Yugoslavia', (1992), 31 *ILM*, 1421.

5 Weller, M., 'The International Response to the Dissolution of the SFRY', (1992), 86 *AJIL*, 569, at 606.

6 Cohen, P.J., 'Ending the War and Securing Peace in Former Yugoslavia', (1994), 6 *PILRev*, 19, at 38.

7 Lauterpacht, E., foreword to Bethlehem, D. and Weller, M. (eds.), *The Yugoslav Crisis in International Law: General Issues, Part I*, (1997), CUP, xv.

8 Silber, L. and Little, A., *The Death of Yugoslavia*, (1995), Penguin, 121.

9 Ibid, 164-5.

10 Quoted in Lukic, R. and Lynch, A., *Europe From the Balkans to the Urals: The Disintegration of Yugoslavia and the Soviet Union*, (1996), OUP, 260.

11 *TEU, Article B.*

12 *TEU, Article J.1(1).*

13 *TEU, Article J.1(2).* See chapter 3, section 3.3.2. for discussion of the role of such values in the current international legal paradigm.

14 Prior to CFSP, *Article 30(1)* of the *Single European Act* (SEA) stated only that EC Member States shall "...*endeavour* jointly to formulate and implement a European foreign policy...", whereas the later provisions of *Article J.1* in the *TEU* state that "...the Union and its Member States *shall* define and implement a

common foreign and security policy... [and] *shall* refrain from any action which is contrary to the interests of the Union or likely to impair its effectiveness as a cohesive force in international relations...". See (1986), 25 *ILM*, 503. For information on EPC, see Bermann, G.A., Goebel, R.J., Davey, W.J. and Fox, E.M, *Cases and Materials on EC Law*, (1993), West, 922-27. For discussion on the progression from EPC to CFSP see McGoldrick, D., *International Relations Law of the European Union*, (1997), Longmans, 138-73; Bruckner, P., 'The EC and the UN', (1990), 1 *EJIL*, 174. For an overview of EPC practice during this period, see Dehousse, R., 'The International Practice of the EC: European Political Cooperation in 1991', (1993), 4 *EJIL*, 141.

15 Weller, supra n.5, 571. Yugoslavia had, however, entered a number of important economic agreements with the EC. See chapter 2, section 2.6.1.

16 See chapter 3, section 3.5.2.

17 The troika system involves representatives from the foreign ministries of the EC's Member States who are the previous, current and future Presidents of the Community. This initial troika was composed of Jacques Poos, Hans van den Broek and Gianni de Michelis, respectively from Luxembourg, the Netherlands and Italy.

18 EC Bulletin 3-1991, 71. See also Silber, supra n.8, 175.

19 See chapter 2, section 2.6.3.

20 Supra n.18, 70.

21 See below, chapter 7, section 7.5.

22 An EPC statement of 26th March was more cautious and referred only to the rights of the "...parties..." concerned. Supra n.18, 71.

23 Weller, supra n.5, 604.

24 See above, chapter 2, section 2.6.1. See also EC Bulletin 5-1991, 62.

25 Ibid.

26 See, for example, EPC statements on 26th March, 8th May and 12th June, reprinted in EC Bulletins for those months.

27 EPC Bulletin 5-1991, 63.

28 See generally Lukic, supra n.10.

29 For the full text of the Accord, see Trifunovska, S., *Yugoslavia Through Documents from its Creation to its Dissolution*, (1994), Nijhoff, 311-5.

30 EC Bulletin 7/8-1991, 107.

31 Ibid, 116. See also the European Parliament resolution of 10th October 1991, which "...deplored the failure of the parties involved in the conflict, and the federal army in particular, to observe cease-fires". EC Bulletin 10-1991, 71. An EPC statement of 6th October noted the use of "...disproportionate and indiscriminate use of force..." by the JNA, which had shown itself to be "...no longer a neutral and disciplined force". EC Bulletin 10-1991, 86.

32 See above, section 4.2.

33 See chapter 2, section 2.6.3.

34 An EPC statement of 5th October 1991 later condemned this action as "...illegal action contrary to the constitution of Yugoslavia and the *Charter of Paris*". EC Bulletin 10-1991, 86. The same statement noted that the EC States were no

longer willing to accept any decisions taken by "...a body which can no longer pretend to speak for the whole of Yugoslavia".

35 Quoted in Silber, supra n.8, 177.

36 See, for example, Parliament's Resolution of 15th March, supra n.18.

37 On this, see for example Cassese, A., 'The Fundamental Principles Governing International Relations', in Cassese, A. (ed.), *International Law in a Divided World*, (1986), CUP, 126.

38 Chapter 2, section 2.6.2.

39 Owen, D., *Balkan Odyssey*, (1995), Victor-Gollancz, 1.

40 EC Bulletin 7/8-91, at 108. See Bohr, S., 'Sanctions by the UN Security Council and the EC', (1993), 1 *EJIL*, 35.

41 Buchan, D., *Europe: The Strange Superpower*, (1993), Dartmouth, 68, notes that such sanctions were nothing more than "...a slap on the wrist to republican leaders, who were far more inflamed by atavistic nationalism than worried about the price of bread for their people".

42 EPC statements of 5th November and EC Council Regulation 3567/91, cited in EC Bulletins 11-1991, 91-2, and 12-1991, 99-100.

43 Weller, supra n.5, 573.

44 The ECMM was suggested by the CSCE Committee of Senior Officials on 4th July and confirmed by the EC the following day. See Morphet, S., 'UN Peacekeeping and Election Monitoring', in Roberts, A. and Kingsbury, B. (eds.), *United Nations, Divided World: Second Edition*, (1993), Clarendon, 183, at 225.

45 EPC statement, 3rd September 1991, in EC Bulletin 9-91, 63-5.

46 Ibid. The WEU mission was never actually deployed. See below, section 4.7.

47 Buchan, supra n.41, 79.

48 See below, section 4.5.7.

49 See Perez de Cuellar, J., 'The Role of the UN Secretary-General', in Roberts, supra n.44, 125, at 133 on the benefits of a multilateral diplomatic approach as opposed to a more limited diplomatic mission such as the EC-troika.

50 Stipe Mesic.

51 Ante Markovic.

52 President Alija Izetbegovic of Bosnia-Hercegovina, President Franjo Tudjman of Croatia, President Kiro Gligorov of Macedonia, President Momir Bulatovic of Montenegro, President Slobodan Milosevic of Serbia and President Milan Kucan of Slovenia.

53 Mr. R. Lubbers of the Netherlands. See EC Bulletin 9-91, 48.

54 Peter Carrington had been the UK's Foreign Minister under Mrs Thatcher and had been instrumental in resolving the Rhodesia crisis, which resulted in the independence of Zimbabwe in 1980. He had then become Secretary-General of NATO and had retired from political office when he was asked to become the EC's special-envoy for Yugoslavia. Information from 'Installation of Lord David Owen as Chancellor of the University of Liverpool', *Liverpool University Recorder* (1996).

55 EPC statement 3rd September, EC Bulletin 9-91, 63.

56 EC Bulletin 9-91, 65.

57 EP-Resn. 11th September 1991, EC Bulletin 9-1991, 48.

58 EC-USA-USSR joint statement of 18th October 1991, EC Bulletin 10-1991, 87.

59 EC-Bulletin 10-91, 86.

60 See chapter 2, section 2.6.3.

61 For the full text of the Draft Convention, see Trifunovska, supra n.29, 357-65.

62 Buchan, supra n.41, 75

63 Supra n.61, paragraph 1.1.

64 Weller, supra n.5, 587. For the text of Serbia's rejection, see Trifunovska, supra n.29, 363-5.

65 Parliamentary Resolution of 22nd November 1991, EC Bulletin 11-1991, 71.

66 Both Declarations are reprinted in (1992) 31 *ILM*, 1485-7.

67 These concerns were more related to the spread of nuclear weapons throughout the USSR than to circumstances in Yugoslavia.

68 It is not clear whether this was intended to require the Yugoslav republics referring such issues to the arbitration procedure within the ECCY or another forum of their choosing. As will be seen in chapters 5 and 6 below, the Badinter Commission was required to consider issues of State-succession.

69 Cassese, A., *Self-Determination of Peoples: A Legal Reappraisal*, (1995), CUP, 268.

70 See chapter 7, section 7.2.3. for description of these concepts and further discussion.

71 The clause was inserted at Greece's insistence, claiming that 'Macedonia' related to an area of Greece and that the Yugoslav republic should not be allowed to use this name. In subsequent EC statements which referred to the Yugoslav republic of 'Macedonia', a clause was inserted which stated that "...the terminology used to define the various geographical entities involved is purely geographical and in no way prejudices the future political status or names of these entities". See Council Regulation 545/92, EC Bulletin 1/2 (1992), 85.

72 Silber, supra n.8, 219; Weller, supra n.5, 588.

73 Perhaps it would be more accurate to describe these as opt-ins rather than opt-outs and the current Labour government has since reversed Conservative policy and joined the Social Chapter provisions whilst remaining outside the EMU provisions.

74 EC Bulletin 1/2 (1992), 108.

75 EC Bulletin 4 (1992), 67.

76 EPC statement 11th May 1992, EC Bulletin 5 (1992), 104.

77 EPC statement 10th March 1992, EC Bulletin 3 (1992), 101.

78 See, for example, EPC statement 7th January 1992, on the death of 5 members of the ECMM. EC Bulletin 1/2 (1992), 106.

79 See, for example, Council Regulation 1432/92 which strengthened the sanctions regime against Serbia and Montenegro, EC Bulletin 6 (1992), 90. See also Council Regulation 3953/92, on economic relations between the EC and other former-Yugoslav republics, EC Bulletin 12 (1992), 128.

80 See below, section 4.5.7.

81 Reprinted in McGoldrick, D., *Documents on the Human Dimension of the OSCE*, (1995), Warsaw, 1.

82 See Weller, M., 'The EU Within the 'European Security Architecture', in Koskenniemi, M. (ed.), *International Law Aspects of the European Union*, (1998), Kluwer, 57, at 78.

83 See McGoldrick, D., 'The Development of the CSCE After the Helsinki 1992 Conference', (1993), 42 *ICLQ*, 411; McGoldrick, D., 'The CSCE: From Process to Institution', in McGoldrick, D. and Jackson, B.S. (eds.), *Legal Visions of a New Europe*, (1993), LUP, 135.

84 *Chapter VII* deals with "...regional agencies or arrangements for dealing with such matters relating to the maintenance of international peace and security as are appropriate for regional action..." *UN Charter, Article 52(1).*

85 Rosas, A., 'Internal Conflicts and the CSCE Process', (1992), 3(2) *Helsinki Monitor*, 5.

86 Weller, supra n.82, at 81.

87 The *OSCE Seminar Within the Framework for the Common and Comprehensive Security Model for Europe for the Twenty-First Century: Regional Security and Cooperation*, (1997), OSCE, 1, suggests that the development of such a security model should be "...non-hierarchical and of a mutually-reinforcing nature...".

88 Ibid, 84.

89 The decision took place on 30th June 1991, at the initiation of Luxembourg. See EC-Bulletin 6 (1991), 13.

90 *Charter of Paris for a New Europe, Principles I* and *VIII*, supra n.83, 34.

91 *First Meeting of the Council: Summary of Conclusions and Statement on the Situation in Yugoslavia, Annex IV,* paragraphs 3-4. See section 4.3.2. for problems with this phraseology.

92 Decision of the Consultative Committee of the CPC, 1st July 1991.

93 Weller, supra n.5, 573.

94 Supra n.87, *Annex II.*

95 CSCE statement of 15th April 1992, cited in Weller, supra n.5, 598.

96 See generally, *Report of the CSCE Human-Rights Rapporteur Mission to Yugoslavia: 12-20th December 1991 and 7-10th January 1992.*

97 Ibid, 4.

98 *Report of the CSCE Follow-Up Human-Rights Mission to Yugoslavia: 3-9th May 1992.*

99 See *Report of the CSCE Exploratory Mission to Kosovo, Vojvodina and Sandjak*, CSCE Communication 236, 13th August 1992.

100 Ibid, 9.

101 *Survey of OSCE Long-Term Missions and Other Field Activities*, (1996), OSCE, 2.

102 *Report of the CSCE Mission to Croatia Established Under the Human-Dimension Mechanism According to Paragraph 12 of the Moscow Document*, (1992), CSCE Communication 342, 1.

103 Ibid, 17-24, for discussion of atrocities against unarmed civilians, mass-killings, arbitrary executions, forced deportations, detention camps, ethnic-cleansing, destruction and confiscation of property, discriminatory dismissal from employment, arbitrary arrests and harassment. See also chapter 8, section 8.4.2.

104 See Foundation on Inter-Ethnic Relations, *The Role of the High-Commissioner on National Minorities in OSCE Conflict Prevention*, (1997) OSCE, 48-52 and 56-9 for recommendations regarding Croatia and FYROM. See also *Bibliography on the OSCE HCNM,* (1997) and Van Der Stoel, M., *Reports of the OSCE HCNM*, (1996) and (1997), OSCE.

105 *The Role of the HCNM*, ibid, 18.

106 Dr. Gret Haller was appointed for a period of five years in March 1996. See *ODIHR Background Reports*, (1997), OSCE, 5-7 for details.

107 *Dayton Peace Agreement*, section 4.5.7. below, *Annex 1-B, Articles IV-V* and *Annex 3, Article II.*

108 Weller, supra n.5, 590.

109 CSO decision of 8th July 1992. See *Prague Document*, paragraph 16.

110 Supra n.9, paragraph 5.

111 Weller, supra n.5, 577.

112 See generally *OSCE Report on Cooperation Among International Institutions: Experiences in Bosnia-Hercegovina*, (1997), CSCE.

113 See above, section 4.3.3.

114 See above, section 4.3.5. See also Buchan, supra n.41, 72.

115 See above, section 4.3.8.

116 McGoldrick, supra n.1, 389.

117 For details, see *ODIHR Annual Report 1996*, (1996), OSCE Publications; *Bosnia-Hercegovina Municipal Elections Report 13-14th September 1997*, (1997), OSCE; *Republika Srpska National Assembly Elections 22-23rd November 1997*, (1997), OSCE. See OSCE Newsletters of 1996 and 1997 for political developments surrounding the Bosnian elections.

118 *Serbian Parliamentary Elections 21st September 1997 and Presidential Elections of 21st September and 5th October 1997*, (1997), OSCE; *Re-Run of the Presidential Election, 7th and 21st December 1997*, (1997), OSCE.

119 *Montenegro's Presidential Election of 5th and 19th October 1997*, (1997), OSCE.

120 For discussion of the changing role of the UN in the NWO, see *A Vision of Hope: The 50th Anniversary of the United Nations*, (1996), UNDPI; White, N.D. *Keeping the Peace - The United Nations and the Maintenance of International Peace and Security*, (1993), MUP; Lowe, V., and Warbrick, C. (eds.), *The United Nations and the Principles of International Law*, (1994), Routledge; Blum, Y., *Eroding the United Nations Charter*, (1993), Nijhoff; Luard, E., *The United Nations: What It Is and What It Does: Second Edition*, (1994), Macmillan; Bourantonis, D and Evriviades, M. (eds.), *A United Nations for the Twenty-First Century*, (1996), Kluwer; Weiss, T.G., Coate, R.A. and Forsythe, *The UN and Changing World Politics: Second Edition*, (1997), CUP; Lorenz, J.P.P., *The UN After the Cold War*, (1997), Stopford, M., 'The UN and the New World Disorder', (1994), 34 *VJIL*, 685; Gassama, I.J., 'World Order in the Post-Cold War Era: The Relevance and Role of the UN After Fifty Years', (1994), *Brooklyn JIL*, 255; Reisman, M., 'The Constitutional Crisis in the UN', (1993), 87 *AJIL*, 83; Boutros-Ghali, B. *et al*, 'Great Expectations: The UN at 50', (1995), 20 *MULRev*, 1-55. For the UN's role in Yugoslavia see 'The Role of the

United Nations in the Former Yugoslavia', (1994), *UNDPI*; Gowlland-Debbas, V., 'Security Council Enforcement and Issues of State-Responsibility', (1994) 43 *ICLQ*, 55.

121 Chapter 3, section 3.5.1.

122 Boutros-Ghali, B., 'Agenda for Peace: Preventive Diplomacy, Peace-Making and Peace-Keeping', reprinted in Roberts, supra n.44, 471.

123 McGoldrick, supra n.1, 390, calls this "...one of the most legally and politically controversial of the military measures..." pursued by the UN. See also Scott, C. *et al*, 'A Memorial for Bosnia: Framework of Legal Arguments Concerning the Lawfulness of the Maintenance of the UN Security Council's Arms Embargo on Bosnia-Hercegovina', (1994), 16 *MichJIL*, 1; Herring, E., 'The Manufacture of Consent for the Arms Embargo on Bosnia-Hercegovina', (1995), 6 *OIRev*, 32; Conlon, P., 'Legal Problems at the Centre of UN Sanctions', (1996), *NordJIL*, 73; Nagan, W.P., 'Rethinking Bosnia's Right of Self-Defence', (1994), 52 *ICJur*, 34; Bohr, supra n.40.

124 UNSC Resn. 713/91, 25th September 1991. These sanctions were supervised by a Committee established by UNSC Resn. 724/91, of 15th December 1991. Both Resolutions were passed under *Chapter VII* of the Charter which allows the Security Council to determine the existence of "...any threat to the peace, breach of the peace, or act of aggression..." and authorises it to "...make recommendations, or decide what measures shall be taken...to maintain or restore international peace and security". *UN Charter, Article 39*. See also UNSC Resolutions 757, 787, 820 and 943 for further details of economic sanctions during this initial period of UN involvement.

125 See above, section 4.3.5.

126 *Case Concerning Application of the Convention on the Prevention and Punishment of the Crime of Genocide (Bosnia-Hercegovina v Yugoslavia), Judgment on Preliminary Objections*, (1996), ICJ Rep, 3. See also Gray, C., 'Bosnia-Hercegovina v Yugoslavia: Case Comment', (1994), 43 *ICLQ*, 704.

127 Owen, supra n.39, 141-2.

128 GA-Resn. 48/88 (1993).

129 Six States voted in favour of lifting the embargo, none voted against, but nine abstentions prevented the resolution being adopted. See SC Draft Resn. S/25997, 29th June 1993 and SC Verbatim Record S/PV.3247, 29th June, cited in Bethlehem, supra n.7, 307.

130 Weller, supra n.5, 580-1.

131 See generally Conlon, supra n.123.

132 See supra n.124. for details of resolutions dealing with the sanctions committee.

133 See UNSC Resn. 757/92, of 30th May 1992, paragraph 4.

134 See below, section 4.5.6.

135 Silber, supra n.8, 306.

136 Ibid, 308.

137 For details, see Boutros-Ghali, B., *Confronting New Challenges - The Secretary-General's Annual Report on the Work of the UN Organisation,* (1995), UNDPI, 896; Petrovic, D., 'International Humanitarian Assistance to the Civilian

Population of Sarajevo', in Biserko, S. (ed.), *Yugoslavia: Collapse, War, Crimes*, (1993), BCAWA, 267.

138 France and the UK occupied seats as permanent members, whilst Belgium occupied a non-permanent seat during 1991-2.

139 See Franck, T.M. and Nolte, G., 'The Good Offices Function of the UN Secretary-General', in Roberts, supra n.44, 143, at 169-72 for the role of the UN Secretary-General in the Yugoslav conflict.

140 UNSC Resn. 721/91, 27th November 1991; *Concept for a Peacekeeping Operation in Yugoslavia*, reprinted in (1991), 31 *ILM*, 1442.

141 Silber, supra n.8, 222, notes that Croatia wanted a UN presence to allow it to prepare for conflict with Serbia, whilst Milosevic wanted the force to consolidate the territorial gains Serbs had already made.

142 UNSC Resns. 743/92, of 21st February, and 749/92, of 7th April, authorised the "...earliest possible full deployment..." of such a force.

143 See *UN: Security Resolutions Regarding the Situation in the Former Yugoslavia*, (1992), 31 *ILM*, 1425 *et seq* for the text of the 'Vance Plan' and implementing accord.

144 See chapter 3, section 3.4.

145 See Weller, supra n.5, 578-81.

146 UNSC Resn. 713, supra n.119.

147 UNSC Resn. 762/92, of 30th June 1992, paragraph 7.

148 See for example UNSC Resn. 769/92, of 7th August 1992, which increased the size of UNPROFOR and expanded its mandate to certain administrative functions, such as the creation of multinational police forces and measures to ensure the protection of local national minorities as well as immigration and customs functions.

149 UNSC Resn. 802, 25th January 1993.

150 *The United Nations and the Situation in the Former Yugoslavia*, (1994), UNDPI, 19.

151 See chapter 2, section 2.6.3. and chapter 5, section 5.10.8.

152 See above, chapter 2, section 2.6.3.

153 UNSC Resn. 795/92, of 11th December 1992.

154 Bennet-Jones, O., 'Macedonia and the UN', (1994), *www.writenet.co*; Urquhart, B., 'The UN and International Security After the Cold War', in Roberts, supra n.44, 100.

155 Owen, supra n.39, 66.

156 UNSC Resn. 824.

157 UNSC Resn 836, paragraph 5.

158 Owen, D., 'The Limits of Enforcement', (1995), *NethILR*, 249, at 255; Higgins, R., 'Peace and Security: Achievements and Failures', (1995), 6 *EJIL*, 445.

159 For details of the fall of Srebrenica, see Silber, supra n.8, 301-4.

160 UN-SC Presidential statement S/24346.

161 John Major, Prime Minister of the UK was the then President of the Council.

162 See below, chapter 6.

163 *London Conference: Rules of Procedure*, Rule 9, cited in (1992), 31 ILM, at 1532.

164 *Report of the UN Secretary-General on the ICFY*, (1992), 31 ILM, at 1552.

165 "...as embodied in the International Covenants of the UN, the European Convention on Human Rights and its Protocols and other instruments of the UN, the CSCE and the Council of Europe". *London Conference: Statement of Principles, Principles (i)-(xiii),* cited in (1992), 31 *ILM*, 1533.

166 "...in particular, the Geneva Conventions of 12th August 1949 and the personal responsibility of those who commit or order grave breaches of the Conventions". Ibid.

167 See below, chapter 7, section 7.4.

168 The statement may mean that "...*all* frontiers..." are inviolable, which would appear to extend the notion of *uti possidetis* to internal borders or may simply mean that only the borders referred to in "...the *UN Charter*, the *CSCE Final Act* and the *Charter of Paris*..." are inviolable, in which case the statement would be limited to the *international* borders of sovereign States. It will be seen that the latter was the approach adopted by the Commission. For the Commission's advice on *uti possidetis*, see below, chapter 5.9.2. and chapter 7, sections 7.4.-7.5.

169 For details of the VOPP see Owen, supra n.39, 89-149.

170 Ibid, *Article D*.

171 Silber, supra n.8, 319, suggests that the most likely reason for America's rejection of the VOPP was that it would have required over 50,000 troops to implement the Plan, of which USA had already committed itself to providing half.

172 Owen, supra n.39, 177, quotes the German Ambassador's opinion that the JAP was "...aimed more at bridging differences between western governments than at bringing peace to Bosnia". Equally, America had been active in criticising Germany's premature recognition of Slovenia and Croatia. Ibid, 192.

173 See generally ICFY Co-Chairmen's Reports S/26260 of August 6th 1993 and S/26922 of 29th December 1993 for an in-depth discussion of the political problems behind the development of the JAP.

174 The JAP gave 53% of Bosnia's contiguous territory to the Bosnian-Serbs, 17% to the Bosnian-Croats and 30% to the Muslims. Silber, supra n.8, 338, notes that the JAP would have created "...a bizarrely shaped and geographically disjointed [Muslim] State [which] would have only a slim chance of survival".

175 See Owen, supra n.39, 223-54, and 237 for details of the territorial division under this plan.

176 UNSC Presidential statement S/PRST/1994/6, of 3rd February 1994.

177 Silber, supra n.8, 375.

178 For the text of this Agreement, see (1996), 35 ILM, 75. See also Gaeta, P., 'The Dayton Agreement and International Law', (1996), 2 *EJIL*, 147; Yee, S., 'The New Constitution of Bosnia-Hercegovina', ibid, 164; Ramcharan, B.G., 'The Bosnian Peace-Accord', (1996), 9 *LJIL*, 131.

179 See Morris, V. and Scharf, M., *An Insider's Guide to the ICTY*, (1996), Transnational Publications; Greenwood, C., 'The Prosecution of War Criminals in the Former Yugoslavia', (1994), *Bracton LJ*, 13; O'Brien, J.C.O., 'The International Criminal Tribunal for Yugoslavia', (1993), 87 *AJIL*, 639; Shraga,

D. and Zacklin, R., 'The ICTY', (1994), 5(3) *EJIL*, 360; Warbrick, C., 'International Criminal Law', (1995), 44 *ICLQ*, 466; *UN Secretary-General's Report on Aspects of Establishing An International Tribunal for the Prosecution of Persons Responsible for Serious Violations of International Humanitarian Law Committed in the Former Yugoslavia*, reprinted at (1993), 32 *ILM*, 1159.

180 See, for example, UNSC Presidential statement S/25162, of 25th January 1993.

181 (1992) 31 ILM, 1541.

182 UNSC Resn. 780, 6th October 1992. For an overview of the work of the COE, see the *Final Report of the COE*, S/1994/674. See chapter 8, sections 8.4.1.-8.4.2., for other COE Reports.

183 See UNSC Resn. 955/94, including the Statute of the Rwandan Tribunal as an Annex; Lee, R.S., 'The Rwanda Tribunal', (1996), 9 *LJIL*; Turns, D., 'War-Crimes in Non-International Armed Conflict', (1995), 7(4) *ASICL*, 804.

184 *Rome Statute of the International Criminal* Court, available, together with background information, from *http://www.un.org/icc*.

185 UN Reference Paper, supra n.149, 14, shows that, within six-months of the no-fly zone having been established, there had already been an estimated 465 violations by JNA aircraft.

186 UNSC Resn. 816, of 31st March 1993.

187 See below, section 4.6.4.

188 See Weissbrodt, D., 'The 44th Session of the UNHCR and the Special Session on the Situation in the Former Yugoslavia', (1993), 15 *HRQ*, 410; Glenny, M., *The Fall of Yugoslavia*, (1993), Penguin, 224, calls this "...one of [the UN's] least inspired appointments...".

189 For details of his appointment, mandate and reports, see *Final Report on the Situation of Human Rights in the Territory of the Former Yugoslavia* and Annexes thereto, E/CN.4/1997/S-1/9:28/8-1992, available from the web-site *gopher.un.org:70/00/esc/cn4/1996*.

190 Resignation letter and Press Release, Geneva, 27th July 1995.

191 See UNHCR *Information Notes on Yugoslavia*, 8/94 for details of the UNHC mandate and operations.

192 See Dayton Peace Accord, supra n.178, *Article VI*; UNSC Resn. 1031, reprinted in (1996), 35 ILM, 97.

193 See Williams, D., 'S-FOR's Mandate Makes Life Uncomfortable for War-Crimes Suspects', *bosnews*, 26th June 1997; Coleman, K., 'SAS Kills War-Crimes Suspect in Bosnian Raid', (1997), 11th July, *Guardian*.

194 See chapter 8, section 8.4.2. on the extent of cultural destruction in the Yugoslav wars.

195 See chapter 5, section 5.14.2.

196 For discussion of this peculiar resolution, see the ICJ's discussion in the *Case Concerning Application of the Convention on the Prevention and Punishment of the Crime of Genocide [Bosnia and Hercegovina v Yugoslavia] - Preliminary Objections*, (1996), ICJ Rep, 3, at 13-14; See Rich, R., 'Recognition of States: The Collapse of Yugoslavia and the USSR', (1993), 4 *EJIL*, 36; Hille, S.,

'Mutual Recognition of Croatia and Serbia (+Montenegro)', (1995), 6 *EJIL*, 598, at 610.

197 See Williams, P.R., 'State Succession and International Financial Institutions: Political Criteria Versus Protection of Outstanding Financial Obligations', (1994), 43 *ICLQ*, 777.

198 See generally *NATO Review*, (1998), NATO OIP; Rolfes, D. (ed.), *NATO Handbook*, (1992), NATO OIP; Scherwen, N. (ed.), *Prague Conference on the Future of European Security*, (1991), NATO OIP; Codevilla, A.M., *NATO Today: Curing Self-Inflicted Wounds*, (1982), IEDSS.

199 See Weller, supra n.82, 69-78.

200 For further details, see Leurdijk, D., 'The UN and NATO in the Former Yugoslavia', (1994), *NIIR*; Solana, J., 'NATO's Role in Bosnia: Charting a New Course for the Alliance', (1993), 44 *NATO Review*, 3; White, N., 'The Legitimacy of NATO Action in Bosnia', (1994), *NLJ*, 649.

201 UNSC Resn. 836, supra n.149.

202 See Fairhill, D., 'NATO-Russia Deal on Bosnia Force', (1995), 29th November, *Guardian*; Figa-Talamance, N., 'The Role of NATO in the Peace Agreement for Bosnia-Hercegovina', (1996), 2 *EJIL*, 164.

203 *Petersberg Declaration 1992*, cited in Weller, supra n.82, 64.

204 *Kirchberg Declaration, 1994*.

205 Reprinted at (1992), 31 *ILM*, 1423.

206 Chapter 2, section 2.5.

207 See below, chapter 5, section 5.7.1. on the attempts of Serbia-Montenegro to continue the legal personality of the SFRY with the Federal Republic of Yugoslavia (FRY).

208 Rusinow, D., 'Yugoslavia: Balkan Breakup?', (1990), *Foreign Policy*, 143.

209 For arguments against such use of foreign aid, see generally Lal, D. *et al*, 'Foreign Aid: Who Needs It?', (1996), 16(5) *JIEA*.

210 For an overview of the military superiority of the JNA, see Gow, J., 'An Assessment of the Yugoslav Military', (1993), *JANES Intelligence Review*, 243.

211 See chapter 2, section 2.6.3.

212 *CSCE Report on its Exploratory Mission to Kosovo, Vojvodina and Sandjak*, (1992) CSCE Communication 236; supra n.99.

213 *Germany's Role in Europe and the World in the 1990s*, CDU Publications, 13.

214 See for example Mufson, S., 'NATO Quandary: Can an Accused War Criminal Deal for Peace?', (1999), 28th May, *Herald Tribune*.

215 Supra n.1, at 377.

216 See above, chapter 3, section 3.5.2.

217 Supra n.180, 27.

218 Extract from Karadzic interview, *Death of Yugoslavia*, (1995), BBC TV.

219 See, for example, *OSCE Seminar Within the Framework for the Common and Comprehensive Security Model for Europe for the Twenty-First Century: Regional Security and Cooperation*, (1997), OSCE, 13-15; *OSCE Seminar on Cooperation Between International Institutions: Experiences in Bosnia-Hercegovina*, (1997), OSCE.

5 The Badinter Commission and the European Communities Conference on Yugoslavia

5.1 Introduction

As a case study, the Badinter Commission is interesting for a number of reasons. First, the Commission enjoyed unique legal foundations and a peculiar role in providing legal advice on issues relating to Yugoslavia's dissolution whilst those events were actually taking place.[1] Second, the Commission's role in the international community's attempts to resolve an intra-State conflict allows one to assess the viability of current approaches to such conflicts and the efficacy of existing dispute resolution procedures. Third, since the Commission was not composed of international law experts but constitutional lawyers, its jurisprudence provides insights of experts from another discipline and shows how their perspectives on the problems presented by Yugoslavia's dissolution may differ from a traditional international law approach.

This chapter examines the practice and procedure of the Commission under the European Communities Conference on Yugoslavia (ECCY). There are two predominant methodological approaches in such analysis - reductionist techniques and holistic techniques.[2] The first focuses in depth on a particular organ or institution to gain a comprehensive knowledge thereof. This approach, by virtue of its extensive research into the source of inquiry, is a popular one. It has been conducted in respect of various UN organs[3] and organs outside the UN framework.[4] Since the Badinter Commission is a primary focus of this thesis, a reductionist approach forms the basis of this section. Nevertheless, to facilitate a contextual and holistic analysis,[5] this chapter also utilises comparative techniques which are equally popular in institutional analyses.[6] For the sake of brevity, however, comparisons with other institutions will be made as succinctly as possible and only insofar as they facilitate analysis of the Commission's own procedure. Whereas comparative techniques often refer to evaluating organs other than the primary source of inquiry, they may also refer to an analysis of the same organ over different time periods. In this sense, a comparative approach is taken in comparing the Commission's procedural changes between the ECCY and the ICFY, discussed in chapter 6. Although the analysis conducted here differs from an institutional analysis *per se*, since institutions implicitly enjoy a degree of permanence not found in the Badinter Commission,[7] the methodological techniques involved are equally suitable to non-permanent and *ad hoc* organs.

It is submitted that the most important feature in assessing the practice and procedure of an organ is the function it is intended to perform. Organs such as the Commission are created for specific purposes and their performance must be judged against those purposes.[8] It will be argued that the Commission's functions were drastically altered from those originally envisaged. This resulted in the Commission's unique legal role which may offer some lessons for dispute resolution in future intra-State conflicts.

5.2 The Creation of the ECCY[9]

When conflict erupted in Croatia, the EC declared that it could not "...stand idly by as the bloodshed...increases day by day..."[10] and, with this short justification, announced the creation of the ECCY. Equally short was the reference to "...an arbitration procedure..." to operate within the Conference, which later became known as the Badinter Commission.[11]

The procedural issues dealt with in the EPC *Declaration* of 28th August 1991 were understandably minimal since the arbitration procedure did not yet exist and its intended function would presumably depend on the success of diplomatic negotiations within the ECCY. At this stage in the crisis, the EC was insisting that Serbia cease supporting Croatian-Serb attempts to prevent Croatia's independence, lift its objection to an extended ECMM mandate in Croatia[12] and agree on the monitoring of a cease-fire agreement. The issues to be dealt with by the arbitration procedure could be expected to be conditional on the level of progress made in these negotiations. Since the various methods of peaceful dispute resolution are complementary and not exclusive, what is resolved through negotiation and diplomatic means may not be required to be submitted to arbitration or other legal procedures.[13]

The EC's motives for creating an arbitration procedure highlight the unusual situation it faced in Yugoslavia. Since Yugoslavia had not accepted the *Optional Protocol* to the *Statute of the International Court of Justice*,[14] the ICJ was not an option for resolving the differences at hand. Furthermore, the ICJ can only hear disputes *between* States and not disputes between a State and sub-State actors such as the Yugoslav republics.[15] The European Court of Justice (ECJ) is only competent to hear cases brought by EC institutions, Member States or EC citizens, again leaving the SFRY conflict outside its jurisdiction. Furthermore, the ECJ is only competent to hear cases concerning the "...interpretation and application of this [EC] Treaty..."[16] which was clearly not the case in Yugoslavia's crisis. The CSCE 'Valetta Mechanism' whereby CSCE Member States, including Yugoslavia, agreed to refer disputes to one of the various methods of pacific dispute resolution, again applies only to inter-State disputes and does not apply if those disputes concern "...territorial integrity, or national defence, title to sovereignty over land territory, or competing claims with regard to the jurisdiction over other areas...".[17] In the absence of established mechanisms for dealing with such intra-State conflicts, the EC was therefore compelled to create an *ad hoc* organ for these purposes. More will be said on the need to develop appropriate mechanisms for resolving intra-State disputes in chapter 9 below.

5.2.1 *The Commission's Original Mandate*

The EPC *Declaration* of 28th August stated that the "...relevant authorities..." were to "...submit their differences to an Arbitration Commission..." which was to "...give its decision within two months". The ECCY was thus envisaged as the primary political vehicle through which the disputing parties would meet whilst the Arbitration Commission was the primary legal organ within this framework.

These basic rules are far from what one would expect to be the sum total of an arbitration commission's procedural mandate. Ragazzi thus states that "...just a few indications can be drawn from the written texts, while a more complete picture emerges from the practice of the peace conference and the Arbitration Commission...".[18] Similarly, Pellet notes their extreme terseness and the fact that they provide no indication of the applicable law or other vitally important questions.[19] Craven concludes that these initial terms of reference would not satisfy the minimum requirements of an arbitration *compromis* under the International Law Commission's *Model Rules on Arbitral Procedure*.[20] These Rules require a *compromis* to identify the disputing parties consent to the arbitration procedure, the subject matter of the dispute and, if possible, any specific points of disagreement, the composition of the tribunal, the applicable law, the procedural organisation of proceedings, the decision-making process, time limits for decision-making and the language of the proceedings. The EPC *Declaration* dealt only with the time limits for decision-making and the composition of the Commission, discussed next.

5.2.2 *The Commission's Composition*

The *Declaration* stated that the Commission would consist of five members chosen from the Presidents of the constitutional courts of the EC Member States. The method of selection is specified thus:

> "(i) two members [will be] appointed unanimously by the [Yugoslav] Federal Presidency;
> (ii) three members [will be] appointed by the Community and its Member States".

In the event that the Yugoslav Federal Presidency failed to agree on its two selected members, this selection would be made by the three EC-nominated arbitrators. It is common for appointments procedures to include default selectors in the event that the parties cannot agree on this *inter se*.[21] Given the intransigent positions of the Yugoslav parties on other issues, it is submitted that it was prudent of the EC to have catered for the eventuality that they may not be able to agree on their appointees. The method of EC-appointment is discussed below.

Since an arbitral tribunal is, in many ways, similar to a judicial tribunal and must arrive at a binding decision, it is usual for such organs to have an odd number of members, in order that a split-decision may not prevent the tribunal delivering a majority judgment.[22] Naturally, however, this does not apply if the decision making process demands unanimity since, in that case, it would not matter if the numbers were odd or even because a single member could obstruct a decision. Consensus is a most unusual requirement in judicial organs, however, especially where the parties have nominated their own representatives. The manner in which the Commission adopted its decisions will be discussed further below.[23]

Perhaps the most noticeable issue surrounding the selection of the Commission's members is that they were to be "...chosen from the Presidents of the constitutional courts existing in the Community countries". This requirement reinforces what is said below about the "...differences..." to be referred - i.e. given that these differences were of a *constitutional* nature, it seems reasonable to compose the Commission with members experienced in constitutional issues. Nevertheless, this requirement heavily circumscribed the Yugoslav parties ability to freely select members of their own choosing. Such selection must be made unanimously and is limited to candidates from a pool of European, and essentially *western* European, judges whose constitutional experiences are far removed from the Yugoslavian model. Furthermore, reference to the Presidents of European constitutional courts prevents participation in the Commission's work by States such as the UK, who have no constitutional court *per se*.[24] Naturally, there was no guarantee that a UK representative would have been appointed even if such a selection was possible, but it may have been preferable to have referred to *a European judge with experience in constitutional matters, emanating from the highest national court* rather than the arbitrary criteria used in the *Declaration*.[25] It may be argued that Yugoslavia's constitutional difficulties were best resolved by States experienced in federalism and that, despite their distance from the Yugoslavian-model of federalism, most EC States could demonstrate a wider experience of *federal* constitutional difficulties than the UK. Ironically, perhaps, such considerations may not have applied if the issues at hand were deemed international legal questions, rather than constitutional ones, as will be seen below.[26] Aside from the absence of British participation, limiting the composition to European judges prevented participation of Yugoslavian constitutional judges and denied the Commission the practical experience they offered. However, given the Yugoslav parties inability to unanimously select any European judges for the Commission,[27] it may be thought extremely unlikely that they could have agreed on a selection from Yugoslav judges. Yugoslavia's Federal constitutional court had already played an active role in the conflict by ruling that Slovenia and Croatia's declarations of independence were illegal whilst Serbia's retaliatory economic blockades were legal.[28] Clearly, the court suffered the same loss of faith as Yugoslavia's other federal institutions and, if Yugoslavian judicial participation had been required by the Commission's procedures, the EC may have been left with the unenviable task of choosing those two Yugoslav judges. One possibility would have been to allow the Yugoslav parties to select their appointees *either* from the SFRY or from the European constitutional courts. It may have been a greater incentive to reach unanimity to know that this would ensure national representation on the Commission, and it would have allowed the EC to have chosen European judges in default of such unanimity. A final possibility for the decision to limit the choice to European constitutional judges is that the EC's ultimate aims were to transform Yugoslavia's constitutional structures into something more akin to the western European model and that Yugoslavian participation on the tribunal may have hindered this objective. Ultimately, one is left only to speculate at the reasons for this criterion and to examine the identities of those who were actually appointed. This is done in section 5.4.

5.2.3 *What Issues was the Commission Intended to Rule Upon?*

The *Declaration* stated that the Commission would hear the parties "...differences..." without defining what this meant. Nevertheless, one must assume that these differences would be those which had prompted the ECCY's creation and would reflect factual events occurring in Yugoslavia at this time. By August 1991, federal-government reforms had failed to prevent growing dissatisfaction regarding the distribution of Yugoslavia's economic and political power, constitutional negotiations had collapsed and armed conflict had resulted when Slovenia and Croatia declared themselves independent as a result.[29] It is clear that the primary "...differences..." existing at this time were *constitutional* ones regarding Yugoslavia's internal political structuring. It is suggested that the "...differences..." referred to in the *Declaration* must be understood as referring to these constitutional differences and the composition of the Commission tends to affirm this suggestion. Given that these differences would involve some constitutional reorganisation and would probably involve consideration of Serbia's absorption of Kosovo and Vojvodina, these would be questions of a *legal* nature.[30] Reference to an "...*arbitration* procedure..." confirms the legal nature of the Commission's work, since it is widely accepted that "...arbitration commissions concentrate on the legal side of disputes".[31] Although Craven correctly notes that denomination alone cannot be determinative of the legal character of an organ,[32] it is nevertheless indicative of the way in which its creators envisaged its function. Although these legal questions were originally envisaged to be of an internal constitutional nature, it may be argued that "...it cannot have been far from the minds of those involved in the creation of the Commission that at least some of the Republics were likely to acquire independent Statehood in the foreseeable future and that questions of international law were therefore likely to arise".[33] The extent to which the nature of the questions changed as events proceeded is discussed below.

5.2.4 *Who was Entitled to Refer Differences to the Commission?*

The *Declaration* fails to define the "...relevant authorities..." who were authorised to submit "...their differences..." to the Commission. Since these differences were constitutional, it may be thought that any entity affected by the outcome of the Commission's findings would be allowed access to the Commission to ascertain its legal rights in any constitutional resettlement. Accordingly, a case may be made for including Kosovo and Vojvodina as such "...relevant authorities..." since the revocation of their constitutional autonomy was of tremendous significance in provoking Yugoslavia's dissolution. As a vital ingredient in the events which led to the ECCY's creation, it may be thought logical that they take part in the negotiation process to resolve these problems. Craven argues that authorities from the Serbian Autonomous Republic of Krajina (Republika Srpska) may also have had a case for inclusion but it is submitted that, since this entity was not a constitutionally recognised area of the SFRY and did not exist until it was unilaterally declared independent during the Bosnian conflict, there is a much weaker case for its inclusion.[34] The ECCY was intended to assist the EC's stated policy of maintaining a united Yugoslavia and to legitimise the creation of ethnically-based sub-State regions by granting them access to the Commission on the same terms as republican leaders would have sent the wrong message to numerous separatist factions. Nevertheless, as will be seen below, the Republika Srpska enjoyed a greater level of participation with the Commission's work than either of the former autonomous regions. The European Parliament had urged the ECCY to allow Kosovo and Vojvodina to participate therein,[35] but the *Declaration* failed to include them in its list of participants. It specified that the ECCY itself would be composed of:

"(i) on the part of Yugoslavia, the Federal Presidency, the Federal Government and the Presidents of the Republics;
(ii) [on the part of the EC] the President of the Council, representatives of the Member States and the Commission".

Since the Commission was described as operating "...within the framework of this peace conference..."[36] it is arguable that only those entities enjoying membership of the ECCY may be capable of utilising the Commission. This would argue against classifying Kosovo and Vojvodina as "...relevant authorities..." since Serbia controlled their votes within the Federal Presidency and the provinces were not republics.

The *Declaration* appears exhaustive in regard to whom may refer issues to the Commission. One notable omission, however, is the ECCY Chairman, Lord Carrington. The role played by Lord Carrington vis-à-vis the Commission is discussed further below, but at this point it appears that his ability to refer issues to the Commission was not envisaged.[37] It may be argued that, in failing to adequately define the "...relevant authorities...", inclusion of the ECCY Chairman is a logical and necessary interpretation of this phrase. Since the Commission operated within the ECCY framework, its Chairman may require access to the primary legal organ for achieving a peaceful dispute resolution. Furthermore, since the ECCY's composition explicitly refers to "...the President of the Council, representatives of the Member States and the Commission...", it may be argued that Lord Carrington, by virtue of his role as EC special envoy and ECCY Chairman, qualified as one of the "...relevant authorities..." in acting as a representative of the EC Member States. Nevertheless, although non-participation in the ECCY may argue against Kosovo and Vojvodina having direct access to the Commission, the reverse may not necessarily be true - i.e. membership of the Conference may not *per se* be sufficient to justify such access. Even assuming it possible to define Lord Carrington as a 'relevant authority', the *Declaration* specified that these authorities were entitled to submit "...*their* differences...[emphasis added]" to the Commission. Given that the only parties truly capable of claiming that the constitutional differences in question were "...*theirs*..." were the Yugoslav parties, it is unlikely that the *Declaration* creates authority for any other party to submit questions to the Commission. This logic relies on the fact that the disputed issues are essentially *intra-State* and outside the scope of international law *per se*. In the event that the issues may develop into questions of international law as opposed to domestic law, however, a stronger case may be made for the ability of the international institution to ask questions itself, via Lord Carrington.

5.2.5 *What Would be the Nature of the Commission's Responses?*

The *Declaration* stated that the Commission "...will give its *decision* within two months [emphasis added]". Given that arbitration is a method of peaceful dispute resolution which results in an award binding upon the arbitrating parties,[38] reference to a "...decision..." is not out of line with traditional practice.[39] What does not appear to be envisaged at this stage is an organ with *advisory* capacities to render *opinions* rather than decisions.

5.2.6 *Time-Limits*

Time-limits for making awards are common features of arbitral practice.[40] Whether the two-month period specified is adequate is debatable. Ultimately, the length of time required to properly consider an issue is related to the complexity of that issue and the familiarity of the decision-making organ with the subject matter. Whilst it initially appeared that the subject matter would be constitutional differences which would be heard by a Commission composed of constitutional lawyers, a two month limit may appear adequate. When the nature of the referred questions changed, however, and the subject matter had potential ramification beyond Yugoslavia and outside the scope of professional experience of the arbitrators, the same period may be inadequate. In referring to the extraordinary brevity of the time-limits, therefore, Pellet is probably addressing the situation after the subject matter changed and strayed from the Commission's area of expertise, rather than the position as was envisaged when the statement of the 28th August was made.[41] A case for extending the time-limit on the basis that the subject matter had changed would, of course, have raised questions about the wisdom of retaining the Commission in its current form.

5.3 The Convening of the ECCY

The ECCY convened in the Hague on 7th September 1991 and was opened by Hans van den Broek, the Dutch Foreign Minister and member of the EC-troika which had already been active in seeking to resolve the Yugoslav crisis.[42] Speeches were also given by the Yugoslav President, Stipe Mesic, the Federal Prime-Minister, Ante Markovic, Presidents of the six republics, the President of the EC Commission, Jacques Delors, and Lord Carrington. It was noted that Lord Carrington had agreed to act as ECCY Chairman and that his role would be to conduct the proceedings of the Conference on behalf of the EC and on the basis of an EC mandate.[43] Although that mandate was not made public, it must be thought that it would be in accordance with the overall mandate of the ECCY itself. The Conference principles were made public and were specified as being "... to ensure peaceful accommodation of the conflicting aspirations of the Yugoslav peoples, on the basis of the following principles:

> "(i) no unilateral change of borders by force;
> (ii) protection of the rights of all in Yugoslavia and;
> (iii) full account to be taken of all legitimate concerns and aspirations".[44]

5.3.1 *EPC Statement of 3rd September 1991*

An EPC statement of 3rd September shed further light on the nature of the envisaged "...arbitration procedure...". It was specified that the ECCY Chairman would "...transmit to the Arbitration Commission the issues submitted for arbitration, and the results of the Commission's deliberations will be put back to the Conference through the Chairman". In referring to the applicable rules of procedure to be employed by the Commission, the statement said only that "...rules of procedure for the arbitration will be established by the Arbitrators, after taking into account existing organisations in that field". This brief statement raises some further points of interest which may be evaluated in the light of the Commission's subsequent practice.

5.3.2 *Who was Entitled to Refer Differences to the Commission?*

The omission of the ECCY Chairman from the original list of authorities allowed to submit issues to the Commission is clearly modified by this statement, and the Chairman's role in the arbitration process is enlarged. Nevertheless, it is possible to argue that only a minor alteration of the original position of the "...relevant authorities...". In the EPC statement of

28th August, it was stated only that those authorities would submit their differences to the arbitration procedure, but the means by which this would be done was left unclear. Since the new statement said only that the ECCY Chairman would "...transmit..." those issues to the Commission which had been "...*submitted* for arbitration...[emphasis added]" and report the decisions back to the Conference, it may be argued that no real change has been made. The "...differences..." would still be submitted by the "...relevant authorities..."and the Chairman would act as a simple intermediary in "...transmitting..." them to the Commission. On this reading, the original "...relevant authorities..." remain the only legitimate source of questions for the Commission.[45]

In practice, however, the Chairman's role was far more active than the above would suggest.[46] Indeed, if the Chairman had been intended to act as a passive recipient of the submitted questions, this would have represented an unnecessary step in the arbitration procedure. It will be shown that the Chairman went beyond the passive role of transmitting questions submitted to him by the Yugoslav republics and formulated his own questions for the Commission. When the relevant authorities submitted questions to the Chairman for transmitting to the Commission, Lord Carrington edited and amended those questions and even refused to refer them at all in some instances. In this sense, he acted as a substantive filter between the issues posed by the relevant authorities and those deemed worthy of the Commission's consideration.[47]

It is difficult to ignore that substantive procedural changes have occurred and that the Yugoslav parties have been placed in a less favourable position by these changes. The framing of questions to be arbitrated is generally decided by negotiations between the disputing parties *inter se*,[48] and the interventionist role undertaken by the ECCY Chairman removed this traditional area of competence. The Yugoslav parties access to the Commission is made indirect and they ceased to be the only legitimate source of questions for the Commission and lost control of the issues which would be decided by the Commission. They also became reliant on the Chairman to accept the referred questions in the form that they were originally phrased, or to accept them as legitimate questions at all. In light of the lack of knowledge about the Chairman's mandate, the Yugoslav parties may have had legitimate concerns about these changes and, indeed, they later played a part in the withdraw of co-operation by certain parties.[49] Nevertheless, because of the difficulties which could have arisen if referral of questions required agreement between the intransigent Yugoslav parties, it is submitted that such an approach is understandable. It may be argued that the continuing participation of the Yugoslav parties in the ECCY process represented acquiescence with these changes but it is possible to participate in a conference without automatically consenting to the role of an organ such as the Commission and it is certainly stretching the notion of consent to argue that the Commission enjoyed the consent of all republics for the role it eventually undertook.[50]

5.3.3 *What Kind of Peaceful Resolution Procedure was Envisaged?*

In the EPC statements of 28th August and 3rd September, there are numerous references to the process of "...arbitration..." and whereas original references are to an arbitration "...procedure..." the statement of 3rd September refers to an "...Arbitration Commission..." and provides greater detail of the intended peaceful-settlement mechanism. The same statement refers to issues to be "...submitted for arbitration..." the Commission's "...deliberations..." and to the "...Arbitrators..." who would conduct those deliberations. Ostensibly, there appears no doubt that the peaceful dispute resolution mechanism involved is arbitration. Subsequent developments showed the rhetoric of the Commission's role to differ from its reality, however.

5.3.4 *What Procedure was the Commission to Use?*

The statement of 3rd September identifies that the Commission's basic rules of procedure were to be supplemented by the arbitrators themselves, "...after taking into account existing organisations in that field". Presumably, the "...field..." in question would be arbitration.

It is not unusual for peaceful dispute resolution organs to follow procedural approaches of other comparable organs in the same field.[51] The comparative approach is circumscribed here, however. New rules of procedure are to be developed after having derived inspiration from "...existing organisations..." in the field. As an *ad hoc* dispute resolution mechanism within the ECCY, the Commission's procedural adoptions may have been intended to be limited to other *ad hoc* organs rather than delving into complex issues surrounding the creation of permanent institutions, whose procedural demands are often far different from *ad hoc* organs.

Indeed, resort is often made to the latter to avoid the procedural rigidities of the former. The Statement, however, refers to "...existing organisations..." which would appear to remove many *ad hoc* organs from its scope, either because they no longer *exist* or because they are incapable of being described as *organisations*. Furthermore, one of the primary advantages of *ad hoc* organs is that they enable the disputing parties to retain greater control over procedural organisation than if they had utilised a pre-established organ.[52] In requiring the arbitrators to supplement existing procedures after consideration of other existing organisations, rather than after consultation and dialogue with the disputing parties themselves, the EPC statement transferred an issue traditionally under the control of the parties to the Commission. The ECCY's role and its Commission thereby moved away from a mere 'good-offices' mission into a more pro-active mechanism, removing traditional areas of control from the disputing parties.[53]

If, as submitted, the Commission was intended to assist in the re-negotiation of Yugoslavia's constitution there exist few, if any, comparable institutions or organisations from which to derive procedural inspiration. The constitutional issues underlying Yugoslavia's crisis have traditionally been jealously guarded as issues of domestic jurisdiction and international involvement viewed as a breach of State sovereignty. Indeed, the Commission's most interesting feature is that it is an anomalous organ epitomising international involvement in intra-State constitutional disputes.[54]

5.4 The Appointment of the Arbitrators

5.4.1 *The Method of Appointment*

The statement of the 28th August makes no reference to the manner in which the EC would appoint its members. Given the complexity of the various EC decision-making processes, this may have affected whether such a decision must be adopted unanimously, by a simple majority or by a qualified majority.[55] Given that the creation of the ECCY and the Commission was not done by any formal Community legislative procedure, however, and represented more of a gentleman's agreement than a formal EC decision,[56] it is likely that selection would have been undertaken in the same manner, on the basis of unanimity within the European Council. ECJ judges are selected by unanimity in order to underline their independence and absence of national allegiances.[57] Assuming this to be the case, the EC Member States, acting under the informal EPC arrangements preceding the CFSP pillar, would have acted by consensus outside the normal institutional framework.[58] The Commission's funding came through the EC's Presidency and not its legislative institutions and, it is submitted, this would also have been the case with the procedural organisation of the Commission and the ECCY. Pellet suggests that the selection was made after the chosen three members were nominated by the EC Council of Ministers, as specified in the statement of the 28th August.[59] It is unclear that the statement dictates such a procedure, however, and Pellet cites no Council proposal nor other source to evidence this. This is to be contrasted with the provisions relating to the Commission's composition under the ICFY, which specified that the EC-chosen delegates were to be selected by the Council of Ministers.[60] Pellet's reference to the Council may mean that the Member States were meeting in the European Council as Member States and not as the Council *per se*, which would appear a likelier explanation.

The statement provides no indication of the manner in which the short-list, if any, of potential arbitrators was drawn up. It is clear that the appointments did not follow the same pattern as the selection of the EC-Troika in June 1991. A Troika is composed of representatives of the current EC Presidency, the past President and the future President, in order to ensure consistency in policy as the Presidency changes hands. In June 1991, the Presidency was held by Luxembourg and the Troika was composed of additional representatives from Italy and Holland, as past and future Presidents. By August, the Presidency had passed to Holland, which would have removed the Italian representative from the Troika and replaced him with the Portuguese representative as the new future President. Neither Holland, Portugal or Luxembourg were represented on the Commission, however. Having taken place within informal EPC arrangements, the nature of the selection process remains unknown. It is likely that the date on which this decision was taken was the 7th September 1991, on which the ECCY was convened.

It has been argued that the selection process in the statement of 28th August was contrary to international practice, since the members were not chosen by the disputing parties, namely Yugoslavia and its constituent republics.[61] Other arbitration tribunals indeed allow the disputing parties greater powers in the selection of arbitrators. The Iran-USA Claims

Tribunal,[62] created in 1981 to resolve compensation issues arising from the hostages crisis, comprises nine arbitrators, three of whom are appointed by the disputing States from their own judicial system and a further three from third countries.[63] Similarly, the Permanent Court of Arbitration allows each party to nominate a maximum of four arbitrators from a pre-established panel of names, and allows all members of the court to be chosen by the parties without any outside interference. In the absence of consensus on the choice of a member to act as umpire, an appointing authority may become involved,[64] but the authority will not normally be asked to nominate any more than one member and never appoints more members than the disputing parties themselves. This is clearly not the case in respect of the Commission, where the EC was designated to appoint the majority of the arbitrators and, in fact, appointed all of them.

Surrounding factual circumstances may justify the Commission's departure form established practice. First, given the lack of co-operation between the Yugoslav parties, it may have proved most difficult to sustain the Commission's credibility if disputes arose regarding the independence of the Yugoslav-appointed arbitrators. This proved to be the case even when the Commission was appointed solely by the EC Member States but it may have been far more problematical if a majority of the Commission was appointed by the Yugoslav parties. The EC's aim may have been to indicate the impartiality of the institution by ensuring that a majority of appointees would avoid accusations of national bias. Second, the fact that the disputing parties in this instance were not different States but elements of one sovereign State may reduce the potency of the argument that any national bias could arise. This applies *a fortiori* if the initial aim of the Commission was, as suggested, to re-draft Yugoslavia's constitution and not to decide issues between independent countries. Nevertheless, the mistrust and nationalistic suspicions which had developed between the Yugoslav republics by this time, combined with the fact that the Yugoslav constitutional court was viewed with suspicion after a series of purportedly pro-Serbian judgments,[65] made it unlikely that accusations of national bias could be completely avoided.

There is a natural, and understandable, reluctance for parties to submit their differences to tribunals consisting solely of foreign judges.[66] Nevertheless, criticisms of the Commission's composition are weakened by the fact that the Yugoslav parties failed to agree on a single arbitrator. Even if the procedure had allowed all arbitrators to be selected by the disputing parties, such selection would not have been possible and it is likely that a default selection power would have fallen on the EC in any case. In order to prevent the work of the Commission being threatened from the outset, therefore, it is submitted that the EC pursued a sensible compromise which failed only as a result of the Yugoslav parties intransigence.

The issue of partiality within the Commission is one which potentially faces any judicial tribunal and is a common reason for challenging the presence of an international arbitrator.[67] Schermers notes that there are a number of ways in which tribunals attempt to pre-empt such accusations, such as appointing judges for long periods of time or creating procedures which minimise the possibility that one State may dominate the selection process.[68] In this instance, however, neither of these options appeared practical. On the one hand, accusations of bias were not directed against any of the EC-appointing States in particular but against the EC's political motives as a whole. Serbia believed that the EC favoured Yugoslavia's division and that the Commission's jurisprudence reflected these political objectives. In such circumstances, the only way of avoiding such accusations would be to remove altogether the EC's role in appointing the arbitrators, which may have prevented the Commission being created. On the other hand, it would be impractical to have appointed the arbitrators for a lengthy period of time since, first, lengthy terms of office do not necessarily prevent national bias and, more pertinently, the Commission was not a permanent judicial organ but an *ad hoc* one, for which such a system of appointment would be unsuitable.

Since, as shown below, the Commission operated on the basis of consensus and did not publish any dissenting opinions or even acknowledge whether such dissents existed, it is difficult to identify any particular arbitrator as having exhibited partiality or bias. Nevertheless, the challenges of bias were not directed at any particular arbitrator, but against the Commission as a whole. It is interesting to note statistics cited by Schermers on the behaviour of national judges when voting in cases involving their appointing State.[69] In a study conducted by Il Ro Suh on the voting behaviour of judges in the Permanent Court of International Justice (PCIJ) and International Court of Justice (ICJ) up to 1969 it was found that they voted in favour of their appointing State's position on 167 occasions and against on only 36 occasions. The national "...orientation..." was even more evident in *ad hoc* appointees, where votes in favour were 108 as opposed to a mere 11 against. Whilst not necessarily indicating any bias on the part of any of these judges, it is interesting to posit the possibility that a 'European' approach may have been brought to the Commission by virtue of the potential candidates that were on offer and that such an approach may have been at odds with what the position of the Yugoslav federal authorities. When the 'European' approach changed from maintaining the SFRY as a sovereign and unified State to accepting the independence of its constituent republics, it is interesting to assess whether a similar change occurred in the jurisprudence of the Commission.

5.4.2 *The Identity of the Arbitrators*

The EC Member States selected their arbitrators from three of the more powerful States within the Community and, although judicial selection assumes that the candidate will act impartially and not seek to reflect the approaches of those selecting him, this may heighten accusations that the Commission was subject to dominant Community policy.[70] The EC-appointed arbitrators were Robert Badinter, President of the French Conseil Constitutionnel, Roman Hertzog, President of the German Karlsruhe constitutional court and Aldo Corasaniti, President of the Italian constitutional court.

Before the Commission was fully composed, the three EC-appointees were required to select the remaining two appointees, because of Yugoslavia's inability to agree on this issue. Madame Irene Petry of the Belgium Cour d'Arbitrage and Mr. Francisco Tomas y Valiente of the Spanish constitutional tribunal were appointed. Although the decision is specified as that of the arbitrators themselves, with no obvious EC involvement, no information is available on other candidates considered for the posts, if any, nor of any unofficial guidance EC-States may have provided.

The fully composed Commission first met in Paris on 11th September 1991, four days after the convening of the ECCY and eight days after the procedural additions in the EPC statement of 3rd September.[71] It was agreed that Monsieur Badinter would act as President. In addition to the benefit of having a French President who was fully conversant in one of the EC's official languages, it is likely that Badinter represented a popular choice given his interest in international arbitration and his pioneering attempts to create a Court of Arbitration and Conciliation within the CSCE mechanism.[72]

5.4.3 *Legal Assistance Provided to the Commission*

The composition of the Commission fails to indicate whether they would be assisted by legal advisors or an equivalent of an Advocate-General. Alain Pellet became the legal advisor of the Commission at some time during the ECCY process, but it has not been possible to ascertain the precise manner and date of his appointment.[73] Paul Szasz later advised the Commission during its time under the ICFY. Both are respected international legal academics.

Although the Commission utilised Rapporteurs for certain purposes, neither these nor legal advisors were explicitly authorised in the written procedure and it appears that such supplementary procedures were developed by the Commission as the need arose. There appears to have been no separate secretariat for the Commission and it must be assumed that the Commission utilised the ECCY's secretariat. This would strengthen arguments against the Commission's independence. It is a truism that "...[t]he independence of a judicial body could be jeopardised if its secretarial work were done by a body responsible to persons other than the judges themselves..."[74] and, at the very least, this creates the appearance of dependence on that other body. Having said this, the point should not be overstated and, it is submitted, this is more problematical when referring to permanent judicial institutions rather than *ad hoc* organs.[75] The Benelux Court of International Justice has a registrar who is also an official of the organisation to which the tribunal belongs, because of the court's relatively small work-load, as do a number of other organisations.[76] The same reasoning may be argued to apply to the Commission.

5.5 The First Meeting of the Fully-Composed Commission

This first meeting decided a number of issues which, although of marginal legal significance, were of vital practical importance to the Commission's day to day functioning.

5.5.1 *Location*

It was decided that all principal meetings would be held in Paris, where the first meeting took place. This decision may have been linked to Monsieur

Badinter's election as President.

5.5.2 *Funding*

In addition to providing premises for the Commission, the EC was required to finance both the ECCY and the Commission. At this first meeting, the Commission decided that the statement of expenses incurred, travel, translation, telephone bills, photocopy bills and all other costs associated with its work, would be transmitted for reimbursement to the appropriate Community body, in this case the Presidency.[77]

5.5.3 *Rules of Procedure*

During this meeting of 11th September, the Commission adopted a set of procedural rules which were not made public.[78] One puzzling aspect of this is the rapidity of such procedural development. Although alacrity is a necessary requirement in many *ad hoc* organs which have to develop their rules of procedure in time to play a significant role in resolving the dispute, the immediacy of this response is noteworthy. Having only been appointed for a matter of days, and having gathered collectively for the first time on the 11th September, to have produced any meaningful procedural changes on that same day would have required some considerable effort and like-mindedness amongst the arbitrators. Even assuming this was possible, it is unlikely to have fulfilled the arbitrator's obligation to have taken account of procedural rules of "...existing organisations in that field". It is submitted, therefore, that there are two possible explanations. Either these new rules were very basic and intended to be supplemented as necessary or the Commission adopted a pre-established procedural organisation, such as the ILC's *Model Rules on Arbitral Procedure*,[79] the 1976 *UNCITRAL Rules*[80] or the *1992 Optional Arbitration Rules of the Permanent Court of Arbitration*.[81] If the new rules were not taken from pre-established organisations, it is unclear whether they were agreed by the arbitrators alone or whether the EC States or ECCY-Secretariat proposed a draft procedural mandate which was adopted by them.

Most *ad hoc* judicial organs are structured around pre-existing procedures rather than being required to create their own procedure.[82] Nevertheless, there would have been little point in the arbitrators hiding the identity of any pre-established procedure adopted and, in light of the incremental way the Commission's procedure appears to have developed, it seems likelier that the new rules were basic and covered issues such as location and funding, mentioned above, rather than the substantive procedural questions discussed below. Pellet also reaches the conclusion that the new rules were designed to allow the Commission to rule on problems as they presented themselves rather than attempting to pre-empt every possible procedural obstacle from the outset.[83]

5.5.4 *Applicable Law*

The rules of procedure provide no indication of the law to be applied by the Commission in resolving differences referred to it. One interpretation is that it fell for the arbitrators to decide this question, as is the case with many judicial organs, both domestic and international.[84] As the Commission's jurisprudence emphasises, the Commission decided that, by the time it received the first referred questions, the parties differences had become international law issues and this was the applicable law. Whether this would have been the case at an earlier stage, when the issues related to constitutional disagreements, remains unclear. Craven suggests that the original intention may have been for Yugoslav law to be the *lex arbitri*,[85] although this begs the question why no Yugoslav judges were permitted to sit on the Commission.

5.6 Yugoslavia's Deteriorating Political Situation

Throughout the initial stages of the SFRY crisis, EC-policy remained committed to Yugoslavia's preservation as a united State and the prevention of territorial disruption at a time when the USSR's future was unstable. The call for a revised Yugoslav constitution evidenced the way in which the EC perceived Yugoslavia's Statehood would be best protected.[86] The ECCY must be seen as the primary political vehicle for negotiating the revision of Yugoslavia's constitution and the Commission as the primary legal organ for ruling on constitutional legal matters during this process. Nevertheless, as the crisis worsened and a united Yugoslavia became an increasingly unfeasible outcome, the EC was forced to accept a new situation which substantially changed the nature of the questions faced by the ECCY and its Commission.

Although the EC's decision to accept "...new relationships and structures..."[87] does not, of itself, indicate an abandonment of the policy to preserve a united Yugoslavia, it must be understood contextually in light of the demands of the disputing parties at this time. Croatia and Slovenia had escalated their constitutional demands towards independence while Bosnia and Macedonia had argued for the confederalisation of Yugoslavia to counter the centralisation underway by Serbia and Montenegro. To omit any preference for a united Yugoslavia and refer instead to the EC's willingness to accept "...any outcome that is the result of negotiations conducted in good faith..." must be seen as an acceptance that Yugoslavia's division was no longer unthinkable. This drastically altered the roles of the EC, the ECCY and the Commission.

5.6.1 *How was the Commission's Role Affected by these Developments?*

These events altered the nature of the dispute between the parties from one where an internal settlement within existing borders was possible to one where new States seemed likely to emerge. This inevitably raises questions of international law, such as those relating to recognition and succession issues, which the Commission was clearly not designed to consider.

The changing nature of the questions facing the ECCY is typified in the EC's response to the takeover of the Federal Presidency by Serbia and Montenegro. EPC Statements not only condemned this but categorised it as "...illegal action..." which was in contravention of "...the constitution of Yugoslavia and the [CSCE's] *Charter of Paris*..."[88] Clearly, the dispute was increasingly involving questions beyond a purely internal nature and were becoming 'inter-mestic' issues.[89]

Whilst EPC statements increasingly acknowledged the international law dimensions of the Yugoslav conflict, with references to self-determination and offers of recognition,[90] they nevertheless emphasised continuing roles for the ECCY and Badinter Commission. One statement, of 6th October 1991, stated that "...[the] right to self-determination of all the peoples of Yugoslavia cannot be exercised in isolation from the interests and rights of ethnic minorities within the individual republics..." and that such interests could "...only be assured through peaceful negotiations for which the [ECCY], including its Arbitration Commission, has been convened".[91] Clearly, the Commission's role was perpetuated by creative reinterpretation of its unclear original mandate.

It will be noted that the contemplated independence of certain Yugoslav sub-State areas is still limited to republics. It is likely, therefore, that the groups allowed to participate in the envisaged negotiations would be limited to republican representatives, again condemning Kosovo and Vojvodina to have their fates decided within the ECCY but without their direct participation. The extent to which those areas held a legitimate interest in Yugoslavia's future was never openly discussed and must be a feature of the ECCY which remains open to doubt, especially since these areas were later to suffer the effects of sanctions imposed against Serbia.

The wisdom, or otherwise, of having retained the services of the ECCY, and the Commission in particular, can in one sense only be assessed in the light of the Commission's jurisprudence. One may wonder, however, why the Commission was not re-established and the composition altered to reflect the fundamental changes which had occurred and the new substantive legal questions involved. At this point, it must have been clear that questions involving issues such as the status of internal boundaries and minority rights would have assumed far greater importance than when an internal settlement seemed possible. Although the EC provided no information on this decision, it is likely that it was discussed at the ECCY meeting of the 4th October, which preceded the aforementioned EPC statements. One possible explanation for retaining the Commission is that the EC saw no need for changing its approach because the *source* of the crisis remained constitutional grievances and the outcome of any resolution must address those grievances, even if they were now phrased as questions of international law. Alternatively, the EC may have perceived no change in the *nature* of the dispute and deemed that the fundamental issues remained the same as when they undertook the mandate to resolve the conflict. In this sense, the blurring of distinctions between internal disputes and international disputes would be evidenced by the maintenance of the same Commission. A more cynical possibility is that the EC wished to avoid any embarrassment caused by dissolving the Commission so soon after it had been offered as the chief legal organ for resolving the dispute. With Yugoslavia representing a dry-run of the EC's forthcoming CFSP pillar, it would have been politically humiliating to be forced into a U-turn so soon into its handling of the crisis. Support for the ECCY process and the Commission was not only forthcoming from EC States, however. The joint statement of 18th October 1991 clearly states the "…full support…" of both the USA and USSR for the Commission even at this stage of the conflict.[92] Furthermore, even when the ICFY replaced the ECCY, the Commission was retained with only modest alterations to its composition.[93] If mistakes were made in allowing the Commission to continue its role, these cannot be portrayed as purely European ones.

Whilst the true reasons behind the retention of the Commission remain unknown, it allows one to consider the manner in which a panel of constitutional lawyers interpreted significant international legal questions. The Commission's jurisprudence represents "... a unique and important examination of the legal issues that attach to the dismemberment of a State..."[94] from a non-international perspective. In the sense that the Commission was experienced in domestic law yet considering international legal issues, it too may be described as 'inter-mestic'.

5.7 The First Questions Referred to the Commission

At the fifth plenary session of the ECCY, on 5th November 1991, Lord Carrington presented his evaluation of the Yugoslav conflict and concluded that fundamental elements of his peace plan were not being observed by all parties. Accordingly, the EC agreed to impose economic sanctions against the SFRY as well as suspending Yugoslavia's participation in a forthcoming G-24 Meeting. Such sanctions were later removed against all republics other than Serbia and Montenegro, and thereby included Kosovo and Vojvodina as units within Serbia.[95] On 20th November, Lord Carrington referred a letter to the Commission containing a number of questions.

5.7.1 *The Referred Questions*

When the ECCY convened on 7th September 1991 Lord Carrington invited the Yugoslav Federal Presidency and republican Foreign Ministers to present him with a list of "...differences..." they wished the Commission to consider.[96] Although it was not made public which republics responded to this,[97] it became clear that at least Serbia asked Lord Carrington to "...transfer..." some issues of concern to the Commission.

From 19th October, a day after the Carrington Plan had been unveiled, Serbia had been calling for the Arbitration Commission to consider the Yugoslav conflict. Expressing surprise that "...no mechanism has been set in motion to put an end to the misunderstandings and blockade inherent in the [ECCY]..." Milosevic expressly endorsed the Commission as the appropriate mechanism for this task. He noted the existence of "...a number of disputes...over issues representing vital principles in *international law* and constituting the entire basis of the world order today...[emphasis added]"[98] and called on the Commission to rule on the following issues.

" 1. Who should be the entity of the right to self-determination - the people or the federal unit?
2. Legality of secession in international law and the conditions under which such secession can be realised.
3. The status of internal or administrative frontiers and of external or State frontiers from the aspect of universal international law, the *Helsinki Final Act* and the *Charter of Paris*...".

At this point, Serbia was insistent that these issues be resolved by the "...eminent group..." of arbitrators and expressed the hope that their deliberations would ensure "...a solution based not only on law but on justice...". He noted with disappointment that "...the Commission was circumvented entirely..." in preference of Carrington's diplomatic plan, which Serbia rejected. He believed the ECCY to be implementing new EC policy favouring Yugoslavia's dissolution and stated that "...[n]one of the participants at the Conference have the authorisation to accede to these arrangements, nor does the Conference as a forum have these rights". In a later Federal Presidency statement,[99] the ECCY was criticised for having exceeded the original 'good offices' role to which the various Yugoslav republics had consented. As EC sanctions became focused solely on Serbia-Montenegro, the FRY grew increasingly convinced of the EC's "...one-sidedness and partiality...".[100] Serbia and Montenegro wished to continue the SFRY's international legal personality and, accordingly, chose to categorise the prospect of independence of certain other republics as secession attempts rather than dissolution of Yugoslavia *per se*. Secessions would reduce Yugoslavia's territories but would leave its international personality intact, whereas dissolution would entail "...the complete disappearance of the predecessor State...".[101] With Serbia having replaced Iraq as the major international pariah State, it was unlikely to be granted EC recognition nor be allowed to join important international institutions such as the UN. Dissolution would, therefore, be politically expensive for Serbia and Montenegro. Equally, it would entail financial consequences, since dissolution would only leave Serbia and Montenegro rights over Yugoslavia's property and assets similar to the other republics, as equal successor States.[102] Whereas the notion of dissolution contradicted Serbia-Montenegro's political stance, the other republics preferred this to references of secession. Croatia, Bosnia and Macedonia each had sizeable minority populations within their territories and, in the event of independence, would seek to prevent loss of these territories. Dissolution would allow these republics to achieve independence without having based this on any 'right' of secession for ethnic groups.

Lord Carrington's letter suggested that recent developments presented the ECCY with a "...major legal question..." and asked the Commission for "...any opinion or recommendation it might deem useful..."[103] on the same. The questions actually referred to in this letter were phrased slightly differently than those submitted by Serbia and it appears that Lord Carrington solicited the opinions of the other ECCY participants before summarising these positions in his letter to the Commission. Thus he stated that "Serbia considers that those Republics which have declared or would declare themselves independent or sovereign have *seceded* or would *secede* from the SFRY which would continue to exist. Other Republics on the contrary indicate that there is no question of secession, but the question is one of the *disintegration* or *breaking-up* of the SFRY as the result of the concurring will of a number of Republics". These latter Republics furthermore considered that "...the six Republics are to be considered equal successors to the SFRY, without any of them or group of them being able to claim to be the continuation thereof". The letter went on to identify two questions based on issues raised by Serbia, which asked first "Does the Serbian population in Croatia and Bosnia-Herzegovina, as one of the constituent peoples of Yugoslavia, have the right to self-determination?" and second "Can the internal boundaries between Croatia and Serbia and between Bosnia-Herzegovina and Serbia be regarded as frontiers in terms of public international law?".

5.7.2 *What was the Nature of these Questions?*

The legal nature of questions referred to arbitral proceedings is confirmed in Lord Carrington's letter, as is the transformed nature of the questions raised by the Yugoslav crisis. These questions are identified by Serbia and Lord Carrington as international law issues and it is difficult to argue against such classification. Thus, having composed the Commission with 'internists' rather than 'internationalists', and with no expectation that they would become involved with international law, the EC's Commission found itself exclusively located in this domain.[104] Furthermore, the questions posed form the essence of factual and legal disagreements between the Yugoslav parties, which traditionally has important implications in respect of the requirement of consent to submit them to judicial scrutiny. More will be said on this below.

5.7.3 *How were the Questions Transferred?*

Serbia's submitted questions were transferred to the Commission via Lord Carrington, in accordance with the procedure of 3rd September. The ECCY Chairman's expanded role, at the expense of the disputing parties, was clearly evidenced in the referral of these questions. First, instead of asking the Commission to consider the legality of secession as a question of international law, the Commission was asked to indicate whether there was in fact any secession occurring in Yugoslavia, a fact disputed by the majority of republics. This must be a legitimate use of the powers granted to the ECCY Chairman, since to require consideration of secession in general would not only involve a major controversial question of international law but would also pre-judge the issue whether this reflected actual events in Yugoslavia. The Commission's intended role must surely have been limited to be to ascertaining and considering the relevant facts and not to have allowed one or more republics to pose questions aimed at securing tacit acceptance of their, opposed, view of events. Second, instead of asking the identity of the 'self' enjoying the right of self-determination, the letter specifically asked whether the Croatian and Bosnian-Serbs enjoyed this right. Again, this narrows the question and avoids abstract consideration of controversial international norms. Third, the final question was limited in a similar way by asking the Commission to consider only whether the boundaries between the specified republics could be considered as international boundaries. Again, it is submitted that it was reasonable for Lord Carrington to have limited the questions to issues involved in the Yugoslav conflict rather than asking the Commission to consider general international law, which was not part of its mandate.

The FRY's legal advisor objected to the loss of control over the phrasing of the questions and correctly noted that "...[t]he parties submitting contentious issues...could not do it in a direct way; they had to do it through the Chairman of the [ECCY]...who decided independently when to submit them for deliberation and who changed their formulation".[105] This loss of control began Serbia's loss of faith in the Commission process.

5.7.4 *Did the Commission's Practice Supplement Previous Procedure?*

Since the Commission's procedural conduct is best evidenced through its practice rather than its brief written procedures - the reality rather than the rhetoric - these questions presents the first opportunity to identify the Commission's procedures in operation.

Although written procedures identified a two-month time-limit within which the commission produce its deliberations, it is unclear whether this period started immediately upon receipt of the questions or only after the Commission was appraised of the respective positions of the Yugoslav parties. One would assume the latter to be the case, however. This may have proved important if the Commission required a lengthy period to deliberate a complex issue, or in the event that one party was intransigent in responding to the request for information. Although the former problem did not occur during the Commission's working-life, the latter became relevant at a later stage.[106] In *Opinion 1*, the Commission notes that it became appraised of these positions through "...the memoranda and documents communicated respectively by the Republics of Bosnia-Hercegovina, Croatia, Macedonia, Montenegro, Slovenia, Serbia, and by the collegiate Presidency of the SFRY". Each of the parties was kept aware of the positions of the others because the Commission copied and faxed these documents to all parties.[107] It must be assumed that, in accordance with the procedure for submitting questions, such information was provided only to those "...relevant authorities..." discussed above. Again, there is no indication that the Commission was appraised of the positions of either of the two previously autonomous regions which had been subsumed within Serbia.

It is unclear whether these documents were transmitted to the Commission via the ECCY Chairman or whether they were solicited from the various parties directly. In the former case, it would be unusual that the Commission did not refer to having received these documents on the 20th November, together with Lord Carrington's letter. In the latter case, the Commission would have opened up the possibility of direct access to the Yugoslav parties for the purposes of submitting their viewpoints on the various issues referred to the Commission despite their inability to pose such questions other than through the ECCY Chairman. Whereas Lord Carrington modified Serbia's original phrasing of the questions in light of the positions of the other republics, it is not clear whether the Commission also engaged in discussions with the republics to cast further light on the positions as summarised in Carrington's letter. The unpublished nature of the Commission's procedure creates certain difficulties in this and other areas.[108]

The Commission organised the proceedings on a written, rather than an oral, basis. This may simply be because the Commission's members were all from continental countries wherein the written procedure is common or because of certain advantages of written proceedings. Generally, such proceedings compel brevity, succinctness and relevancy from the submitting parties which cannot always be guaranteed in oral proceedings and provide an incontrovertible record of the position of the various parties, which can be copied to all other parties. Both the ICJ and the ECJ divide cases into two phases, involving an initial written procedure and a subsequent oral phase, although the former are often treated as the most important.[109]

Whereas most international arbitral tribunals deal with differences between two parties, usually though not inevitably States,[110] the Badinter Commission was clearly dealing with a different situation, in which multiple parties were allowed access to the tribunal. In such circumstances, it is unrealistic to speak of a plaintiff or defendant, as would normally be the case, and it must be assumed that all parties to the arbitration would have been intended to be bound by the Commission's awards. In the event that the Commission is characterised as an advisory organ, there would similarly be no notion of plaintiff or defendant and the advice provided by the organ would be for the benefit of the tribunal's 'parent' organ,[111] in this case the ECCY. In the latter situation there are more convincing arguments for the interposition of an independent member of the 'parent' organ, such as Lord Carrington, to ensure that, whilst issues referred to the Commission reflected the disputing parties differences, they were referred to assist the ECCY in designing a response to these differences rather than as a legal resolution of the contentious issues *per se*. This will be shown to be the manner in which the role of the Commission eventually developed.

5.7.5 *What was the Nature of the Commission's Responses?*

The Commission answered the posed questions in three separate responses. The first of these was returned to Lord Carrington on 29th November and the latter two were returned on 11th January 1992.

The EPC statement of 28th August indicated that the Commission was to give its "...decision..." within two months. Nothing in the statement of the 3rd September indicated that the nature of the Commission's deliberations had changed and, indeed, this again referred to an "...arbitration..." procedure which would presumably produce binding decisions. Nevertheless, a dilution of the Commission's pronouncements is noticeable from the ECCY's inaugural Meeting of 7th September when Lord Carrington asked the Yugoslav parties to submit issues for the Commission's consideration. He noted that the Commission's "...suggestions..." would be reported to the ECCY within two months and asked the Commission merely for "...any opinion or recommendation it might deem useful..." in his letter of the 20th November. Such phraseology indicates a move away from a binding arbitral award towards the Commission's eventual role as an advisory organ. The chief problem with this development is that it does not appear to have been envisaged in any of the procedures published at this time and, as such, would appear outside the mandate the participants had consented to. It is perhaps surprising, therefore, that the Commission chose not to address its competence to provide such advice during its initial opinions and left this issue until its competence was challenged by Serbia.[112]

The likeliest reason for the Commission's changing role is that its intended role was no longer possible. Redrafting Yugoslavia's constitution was a laudable aim but delayed international intervention meant that the conflict had escalated beyond a stage where this would remedy Yugoslavia's crisis. In such circumstances, and given the absence of recognised international legal experience of the arbitrators, it may have been prudent to reconstitute the Commission. In the event, it appears that the option chosen was to reduce the Commission's input into the resolution of the conflict to a purely consultative and advisory capacity.

The nature of the questions posed raised questions about the requirement of consent from the disputing parties. On the one hand, if these were contentious disputes, the procedure would appear to infringe traditional international practice because the posed questions were not agreed between the parties *inter se* and the deliberations of the arbitral organ would fall short of binding awards. On the other hand, if the Commission saw itself in a role comparable with the advisory jurisdiction of the ICJ, for example, it would contradict international practice to issue an advisory opinion where it relates to the substance of an existing contentious dispute between parties that have not consented to such advice.[113] With the only method of establishing such consent being the Yugoslav parties continued participation in the ECCY, this appears a considerable dilution of the notion of consent.

In terms of their appearance, the opinions are remarkably terse given the complexity of the subject matter dealt with therein. Again, this may reflect the adoption of a continental approach and, as Pellet notes, the Commission's opinions are more reminiscent of rulings from the French Conseil d'Etat than any international tribunal. This has caused concern to some writers. Frowein writes that "...[i]f one reads these very short opinions, which apparently are being considered as binding judgments on points of law, one is surprised about the boldness with which very difficult issues of public international law are being decided in a clear-cut manner without much argument".[114] The conversational style of the judgments and lack of definitional clarity is also notable. The Commission's jurisprudence includes references to imprecise terms such as Yugoslavia's "...federal-type..." government and the need to consider its "...sway..." over the population and territory. Finally, the opinions often fail to cite international legal authority for positions adopted therein. Whilst reference is made to the *Vienna Conventions on State Succession*, it is not made clear whether the "...accepted definition..." of succession cited by the Commission is taken directly from these Conventions or other instruments. Equally, no authority was given for the criteria of Statehood, derived from certain "...commonly defined..." requirements referred to by the Commission, despite an accepted definition existing in the *Montevideo Convention on the Rights and Duties of States 1933*. Use of accepted legal authorities grew under the ICFY process, however.[115]

The possibility of dissenting decisions amongst the five-member panel of arbitrators is not discussed in any written procedure, but Pellet states that the meeting of the 11th September agreed that all decisions would be by simple majority without the possibility of abstention.[116] None of the Commission's opinions include any separate decisions, however, neither as dissenting nor concurring judgments, although it is unclear whether this was a procedural requirement or merely an informal arrangement. Perhaps the arbitrators were unanimous in their decisions and never needed to include separate judgments. Alternatively, the Commission may have adopted a procedural model which reflected its members continental approaches to legal proceedings. In the event that the Commission's President played as decisive a role in influencing procedural developments under the ECCY as under the ICFY,[117] the French legal background of Monsieur Badinter would support brief judgments which do not allow dissenting judgments nor identify whether any dissenting votes occurred.[118] Equally, the ECJ is prohibited from including dissenting judgments[119] and, in deference to the EC as the Commission's organisational 'parent' the ECJ's approach may have been adopted. It is most likely, however, that a consensual approach developed because of the damaging effects which dissenting opinions may have on the authority of a tribunal's pronouncements.[120] Given that the Commission would later lose the support of certain Yugoslav parties and would receive only half-hearted adoption of its advice by the ECCY, this was a prudent decision.

5.7.6 *When were the Opinions Delivered?*

The Commission delivered *Opinion 1* on 29th November 1991, merely 9 days after receiving Lord Carrington's letter. However, *Opinions 2* and *3*, dealing with two of the three questions contained therein were not returned until 11th January 1992. All opinions were clearly within the relevant time-limit, even given the possibility that further information may have been solicited from the republics after receipt of Carrington's letter. This begs the question, however, of why the Commission opted to stagger the return of its deliberations in such a manner. Pellet rightly concludes that the decision to answer Lord Carrington's own first question before those posed by Serbia cannot be attributed to deference to the ECCY Chairman's position. Whereas Pellet concludes that the primary reason was the need to determine whether constitutional or international law was applicable, it is submitted that political, rather than legal, logic was the chief factor behind this decision. The Commission's response to the first question, whether events in Yugoslavia indicated a dismemberment of the SFRY or secession of some of its territories, would heavily influence negotiations which followed this response. If the Commission endorsed Serbia's contentions that it was a question of secession, this may have bolstered Serbia's intransigence and convinced it that the international community was prepared to accept the continuation of 'Yugoslavia' in the form of Milosevic's 'Greater Serbia'. Conversely, if the Commission had decided that Yugoslavia's dissolution was a given reality, this may have sparked conflict in areas which had hitherto avoided it, such as Bosnia-Hercegovina and Macedonia. Lord Carrington had already suggested that accepting the independence of individual republics in the absence of an overall arrangement governing issues of succession and future relations would light the fuse on a wider Balkan conflict. The Commission's method of resolving this dilemma was politically prudent, if legally controversial and is discussed further below and in chapter 7.

5.7.7 *Opinion 1*

Opinion 1, having noted the disagreement about whether events in Yugoslavia raised questions of secession or dismemberment, stated that the Commission's response would be based on "...the principles of public international law which serve to define the conditions on which an entity constitutes a State..." This was a factual question, with recognition by other States having only "...purely declaratory..." effect. The Commission found that a State is "...commonly defined as a community which consists of a territory and a population subject to an organised political authority [and] that such a State is characterised by sovereignty". The internal political organisation of a State and its constitutional order were "...mere facts..." although it was necessary to take these into account to "...determine the government's sway over the population and the territory". Where questions arose over the existence or disappearance of a "...federal-type state, which embraces communities that possess a degree of autonomy and, moreover, participate in the exercise of political power within the framework of institutions common to the Federation..." the continued existence of such a State implied that those federal organs "...represent the components of the Federation and wield effective power".

Assessing Yugoslavia's factual situation in light of these principles, the Commission found that, although Yugoslavia had until this point retained its legal personality, notably within international institutions, a number of constituent republics had "...expressed their desire for independence". Reference was made to the referenda in Slovenia and Croatia, which indicated popular support for independence, and Macedonia's referendum "...in favour of an independent Macedonia within an association of

Yugoslav States". Bosnia had adopted a Parliamentary resolution declaring the republic sovereign, although the Commission noted that this had been contested by Bosnian-Serb Parliamentary representatives.

The Commission's crucial factual finding was that "...the composition and workings of the essential organs of the Federation, be they the Federal Presidency, the Federal Council, the Council of the Republics and the Provinces, the Federal Executive Council, the constitutional court or the Federal Army, no longer meet the criteria of *participation* and *representativeness inherent in a federal State* [emphasis added]". This sparked conflict which had caused thousands of deaths and shown the Federal and Republican authorities to be "...powerless to enforce respect for succeeding cease-fire agreements concluded under the auspices of the EC or the UN". This led the Commission to conclude that Yugoslavia was "...in the *process of dissolution*...[emphasis added]" and that, should issues of State succession arise, it would be incumbent on the republics to settle all related problems on the basis of respect for international law, particularly human rights and the rights of peoples and minorities which it described as "...peremptory norms of general international law...". The Commission defined State succession as "...the replacement of one State by another in the responsibility for the international relations of territory..." and noted that this occurred "...whenever there is a change in territory of the State". Again, the Commission noted that this was a question of international law and that the *Vienna Conventions* of *1978* and *1983*, dealing with the succession process, had drawn inspiration from customary international legal principles.

Despite these findings, the Commission indicated that Yugoslavia's dissolution was not yet an incontrovertible fact,[121] and that it remained possible to maintain Yugoslavia's territorial unity if the constituent republics worked together to "...form a new association endowed with the democratic institutions of their choice".

Opinion 1 steers an uneasy course between the contrasting positions of the Yugoslav parties. On the one hand, it does not endorse Serbia's assessment of the situation, which may have resulted in repression of those republics which had not declared their independence. On the other hand, it refutes suggestions that Yugoslavia is no longer a viable unified State and allows for the possibility of negotiations between the parties to re-draft Yugoslavia's constitution and create new democratic institutions which satisfy the demands of all parties. Essentially, the factual situation failed to indicate with any legal certainty whether Yugoslavia was a lost cause and

Opinion 1 placed this decision in the hands of the republics themselves. Nevertheless, the seriousness of the situation was evident in the Commission's findings that a *process* of dissolution had begun which required co-operation of all Yugoslav parties to prevent it becoming *de facto* dismemberment.

In light of these findings, it is perhaps understandable that the Commission delayed examining questions of internal boundaries and self-determination, both of which would depend on whether the dissolution process continued until Yugoslavia no longer existed or whether negotiations salvaged the SFRY. The rights of Serbs in Croatia and Bosnia could not be answered until it was clear whether they remained Yugoslav citizens or citizens of independent successor States and to answer this preemptively could have damaged political negotiations. The rapidity of the Commission's response supports this, since it would be imperative that negotiations continued in the knowledge that any delay could prevent the opportunity to maintain Yugoslavia's territorial integrity. A notable omission from *Opinion 1*, however, is any indication whether the Commission saw itself as an appropriate forum for assisting the suggested constitutional negotiations. Given that this would have ensured a role with which the Commission was more experienced, and similar to the function for which it was originally created, this is surprising.

The dates of *Opinions 2* and *3* are more understandable in light of what has been said above. Delivered on 11th January 1992, following adoption of the *Guidelines on Recognition* and *Declaration on Yugoslavia* and applications for recognition had been received by most Yugoslav republics,[122] it was clear by then that the suggested negotiations were not occurring and that Yugoslavia enjoyed insufficient support for its continuation. The Commission was therefore able to address the remaining issues in Lord Carrington's letter knowing that Serbs living within newly-independent successor States would no longer be Yugoslav citizens and that formerly-internal borders would now be recognised international borders of independent States. This is reinforced by the fact that *Opinions 2-3* were given on the same day as *Opinions 4-7*, on the issue of recognition.

5.7.8 *How were the Opinions Delivered?*

In accordance with the procedure of 3rd September, the Commission's deliberations were "...put back to the Conference through the Chairman".

Lord Carrington received the response to his first question on the 29th November, but it is clear from *Opinion 3* that *Opinion 1* was not published until 7th December, 8 days after it had been transmitted to Carrington.[123] This indicates another aspect of the discretion assumed by the ECCY Chairman and, given the urgent need for negotiations following *Opinion 1*, any decision to withhold it from the Yugoslav parties, even for a short period of time, must be open to question. It is likely, therefore, that Carrington informed the republics of the Commission's findings before publishing them.

5.8 Political Developments Following *Opinion 1*

Despite having called for the Commission's involvement, *Opinion 1* was clearly unpopular with the FRY. The FRY's Foreign Ministry legal advisor considered that it "...reflected the prevailing political thought in the EC that SFRY...should be disintegrated into six new sovereign States, each of which can associate with each other in creating a new State".[124] In a detailed critique of *Opinion 1*, he argues that the Commission applied principles outside the scope of international law, by taking account of constitutional structures within Yugoslavia albeit stating they were "...mere facts..." for international legal purposes. He states that "...[i]nternational theory and practice knows of no case in which the disruption of the functioning of a federal government due to insurrection in some federal units entails the disappearance of the State as a subject of international law...".[125] He suggests that the "...source, beginning and original nucleus of Yugoslavia in the international sense was the Kingdom of Serbia..." and that, as the contemporary form of the foundation of Yugoslavia, Serbia and Montenegro could not be viewed as doing anything other than continuing Yugoslavia's personality, albeit in a diminished form, rather than establishing a new State. The Commission's findings of a process of dissolution could not, therefore, be correct.

It is clear that *Opinion 1* conformed with developments occurring in EC policy towards Yugoslavia. With Serbia unwilling to accept the Carrington plan and intransigent in all discussions which would have secured an overall settlement, the EC gradually accepted the position that Yugoslavia's dissolution was an unavoidable, but regrettable, conclusion. With events in the USSR having indicated the likelihood of its dissolution, the former desire to prevent events in Yugoslavia's causing the Soviet

Union's fragmentation disappeared. Accordingly, the *Guidelines* and *Declaration on Yugoslavia* were adopted.[126] Nevertheless, *Opinion 1* and ongoing attempts to reach an agreement within Yugoslavia's borders showed that this remained a policy to which the EC was, at least nominally, still committed.

With the likelihood of dissolution accepted by the EC, Slovenia and Croatia applied for recognition together with Bosnia and Macedonia which had hitherto been willing to accept a confederalised Yugoslavia.[127]

5.9 *Opinions 2 and 3*

The Commission's responses to the remaining issues in Lord Carrington's letter were delivered on the same day as its advice on the recognition of those republics having applied for recognition. This indicated that the process of dissolution had been met with developments that created a situation of *de facto* dissolution, which was shortly to be acknowledged as *de jure* dissolution.

5.9.1 *Opinion 2*

Opinion 2, dealing with the question of self-determination, was said by the Commission to have been "...put by Serbia..." although it is clear that some modification of the original Serbian question had occurred.[128]

The materials used by the Commission in addressing this question were cited as "...the *aide-memoires*, observations and other materials submitted by the republics of Bosnia-Hercegovina, Croatia, Macedonia, Montenegro, Slovenia and Serbia, by the Presidency of the SFRY and by the 'Assembly of the Serbian People of Bosnia-Hercegovina'". Identical materials were referred to in *Opinion 3*. It is clear that the Commission viewed fact-finding as an inherent part of its mandate and that it was willing to consider sources such as the Bosnian-Serb Assembly's observations to ensure this was fulfilled. No mention is made of information solicited from, or provided by, Kosovo or Vojvodina and, although this is probably because the question posed limited itself to the status of Serbs in Bosnia and Croatia, it indicates how the formerly autonomous regions were effectively given less access than the Republika Srpska which enjoyed no formal status under Yugoslavia's constitution and was the creation of nationalist military conflict.

Chapter 7 discusses *Opinion 2* in greater detail but for the sake of chronology its main points are mentioned here. The Commission did not provide a definition of the 'right' of self-determination nor 'self' to whom that right applies. Instead, it noted that international law failed to spell out all the potential implications of self-determination except that it "...must not involve changes to existing frontiers at the time of independence (*uti possidetis juris*), except where the States concerned agree otherwise...". The Commission used the language of minority rights to explain the rights of Serbs in Bosnia and Croatia and asserted that, within States encompassing one or more ethnic, religious or linguistic communities, those groups had the right to "...recognition of their identity under international law". This built on *Opinion 1*, wherein the Commission described the rights of minorities as *jus cogens.*[129] Serbs in Croatia and Bosnia "...must...be afforded every right accorded to minorities under international conventions as well as national and international guarantees consistent with the principles of international law and the provisions of *Chapter II* of the [Carrington] Draft Convention...which has been accepted by these Republics". Linking the concept of minority rights with self-determination, the Commission noted that the International Conventions of 1966[130] identify self-determination as a concept which safeguards human rights. This led to "...one possible consequence..." that those Serbs could be recognised as having the right to choose their nationality, presumably Serbian, whilst remaining a citizen of the republic in which they are currently residing - in effect a right to dual nationality.

5.9.2 *Opinion 3*

Opinion 3 was clearly decided after *Opinion 1*, since it refers to the applications for recognition by *inter alia* Croatia and Bosnia, which had not occurred when *Opinion 1* was delivered. It reiterated the Commission's stance that, given Yugoslavia's "...fluid and changing situation..." the question of the status of internal boundaries must be "...founded on the principles and rules of public international law". Definitional uncertainties in these statements cause confusion about whether the Commission considered international law applicable *per se* in intra-State conflicts or whether the "...fluid and changing situation..." must involve independence movements and civil conflict before the dispute resolution procedure would be

"...founded..." on international legal principles.

The Commission stated that, "...once the process [of disintegration] in the SFRY leads to the creation of one or more independent States, the issue of frontiers, and particularly those of...[Bosnia and Croatia] must be resolved in accordance with the following principles:

" *First* - All external frontiers must be respected in line with the Principles stated in the *UN Charter*...[and other international instruments].
Second - The boundaries between Croatia and Serbia, between Bosnia and Serbia, and possibly between other adjacent independent States, may not be altered except by agreement freely arrived at.
Third - Except where otherwise agreed, the former boundaries become protected by international law. [...]
Fourth - According to well established principles of international law, the alteration of existing frontiers or boundaries by force is not capable of producing any legal effect".

The Commission cited the *Burkina Faso/Mali (Frontier Dispute) Case*, in which the ICJ noted that the *uti possidetis juris* principle was a general principle of international law which is "...logically connected with the phenomenon of obtaining independence, wherever it occurs. Its obvious purpose if to prevent the independence and stability of new States being endangered by fratricidal struggles".[131] Yugoslav federal authorities had argued that *Article 5* of Yugoslavia's 1974 constitution rendered illegal any attempt to disrupt Yugoslavia's territorial unity. *Article 5* states, *inter alia*, that "The territory of the SFRY is a single unified whole...The territory of a Republic may not be altered without the consent of that Republic...The frontiers of the SFRY may not be altered without the consent of all Republics and Autonomous Provinces...Boundaries between the Republics may only be altered on the basis of mutual agreement...". Whilst the federal authorities emphasised the importance of the consent of all republics before Yugoslavia's external borders could be altered, the Commission's emphasis was on those passages stating that the borders of republics or autonomous regions could not be altered without their consent. Attempts to change those borders forcibly would be legally invalid.

The Commission concluded with a "...well established principle of international law..." that existing borders could not be altered by force, without limiting this statement to inter-State borders. The *Friendly Relations*

Declaration,[132] *Helsinki Final Act* and the *Carrington Draft Convention* were cited as authority for this. The Commission's policy here is quite evident - assuming certain Yugoslav republics were recognised as sovereign States, the next problem would be ensuring that 'internationalising' the situation did not proliferate territorial fragmentation. *Opinion 3* extends *uti possidetis juris* to formerly administrative boundaries while *Opinion 2* seeks to redress potential grievances of Serbs in the successor States by suggesting the creation of a dual-nationality status. In conjunction with the minority rights accepted as part of the conditions for recognition, particularly those creating areas of 'special status' under Chapter II of the Carrington convention, these opinions collectively sought to minimise the destabilising effects of Yugoslavia's dissolution.

These opinions not only correspond with prevailing EC political opinion on Yugoslavia but also appear to borrow from Community ideology in separating the notion of nationality from territoriality, which is a feature of the *Treaty on European Union* (TEU).[133] Furthermore, the illegitimacy of forcible territorial changes is consistent with the *Declaration on Yugoslavia*, in which the EC States emphasised that they were "...determined not to recognise a change to frontiers brought about by force...". These opinions are discussed further in chapter 7.

5.10 The Commission's Changing Mandate

Whilst reflecting the changing nature of the questions posed by the events in Yugoslavia, the *Declaration on Yugoslavia* indicated a continuing role for the Commission. It required the republics seeking recognition to adopt certain constitutional provisions and the Commission to assess whether these had been met. Given the constitutional orientation of the arbitrators, they clearly possessed greater expertise in this role than in answering questions related to international law concepts such as self-determination and *uti possidetis*. Whilst some requirements were essentially political in nature, such as continuing support for the ECCY and the UN peace efforts, many were of a constitutional law nature, such as the adoption of measures to implement the provisions of the Carrington plan. The obligation to refrain from hostile propaganda against neighbouring Community States and the renunciation of territorial claims were expressly required to be adopted in "...*constitutional* and political guarantees...". Effectively, this new role gave the Commission a new mandate.

5.10.1 *How were the Applications for Recognition to be Received?*

The *Declaration* required applications for recognition to be forwarded to the European Council and all applications expressly referred to having done this.[134] It did not, however, dictate the identity of the party capable of forwarding such a request, which was left for the republics to decide. Whereas, in Croatia's case, the application was written by President Tudjman, this task was performed by the Foreign Ministers of Bosnia, Macedonia and Slovenia. The Council was responsible for forwarding these to Lord Carrington, who submitted them to the Commission. This procedure differs from that of the 3rd September in adding the European Council as a 'filter' between the Yugoslav parties and the Commission. This is explainable by virtue of the fact that recognition of new States neighbouring the EC is a process demanding the highest level of political authority and one which was certainly outside the original mandate of the ECCY, its Chairman and the Commission. The issues under consideration were no longer "...differences..." *inter se* between the "...relevant authorities..." but concerned the relationship between individual participants in the ECCY and the EC Member States.

5.10.2 *How were the Commission's Responses to be Delivered?*

An indication of the marginalisation of the ECCY process is evidenced by the fact that the Commission's advice was to be addressed to the Council's President rather than Lord Carrington. As Pellet notes, the Commission at this stage was acting more as an auxiliary to the EC itself rather than the ECCY process *per se.*[135]

5.10.3 *What was the Commission's Role?*

The *Declaration* states that the Commission would provide "...advice..." on the question of recognising the independence of each applicant republic before the implementation of such recognition on 15th January 1992. The Commission's changing mandate is clearly evidenced by the explicit reference to its advisory nature and references to "...decisions..." were notably absent.

As indicated above, the Commission's advice related to the fulfillment of conditions in the *Guidelines* and *Declaration on Yugoslavia*. To this end, the Commission provided, in *Opinions 4-7*, an analysis of a number of instruments which were given in support of the applications of Bosnia-Hercegovina, Croatia, Macedonia and Slovenia. Neither Serbia nor Montenegro applied for recognition as new States. Having argued that recognition of other republics could not affect the ongoing legal personality of Yugoslavia, Serbia and Montenegro felt no need to apply for recognition and announced their intention to continue Yugoslavia's identity as the renamed Federal Republic of Yugoslavia (FRY). Again, the Commission's practice provides more information than any written procedure.

5.10.4 *Procedural Developments*

Opinions 4-7 all refer to a new set of rules of procedure on 22nd December 1991. Again, these were not published and this writer has been unable to obtain them from the ECCY Secretariat. Having been adopted so soon after the *Guidelines* and *Declaration on Yugoslavia*, however, these rules probably related to the manner in which the Commission's new function would be conducted. It is also likely that the Commission agreed on the questionnaire which was sent to all applicant republics.

5.10.5 *Materials Considered by the Commission*

One noteworthy aspect of the Commission's analysis is the width of materials used in assessing whether the applicants had fulfilled the criteria in the EC declarations of 16th December. In considering Bosnia's application, the Commission referred to a questionnaire it had sent to all applicant republics on 24th December, the *1974 Constitution of the Socialist Republic of Bosnia-Hercegovina* (SRBH) and amendments thereto of 1990, the 1974 SFRY constitution and the "...draft constitution currently being prepared...".[136] This last instrument must be taken to mean the Bosnian constitution under preparation, since no evidence exists to suggest that a revised Yugoslav constitution was under preparation and the absence of such was one of the primary factors behind the decision to contemplate recognising the republics.[137] Furthermore, the Carrington plan had now been shelved after Serbia's rejection and the shift in EC policy towards recognition. The Commission also took note of the Memorandum and

Platform of the SRBH Assembly, of 14th October 1991, a letter to Lord Carrington from the President of the SRBH Presidency of 27th December concerning the establishment of an "...Assembly of the Serbian People in Bosnia-Hercegovina...", a letter of the 22nd December from the President of this new Assembly and political decisions published in the *Official Journal* relating to the SRBH government's acceptance of the conditions in the *Guidelines*. On 8th January, the Commission requested further information from the SRBH on its commitment to the conditions for recognition. The Commission finally referred to having taken note of a Rapporteur.

In the applications of other republics, other matters were taken into account. In addition to letters and written informal explanations of the constitutional structures of the other applicant republics, the Commission paid attention to referenda held in those republics prior to their applications for recognition. Again, the Commission availed itself of contradictory opinions on the issues presented in these materials by sending copies of such instruments to the other parties, presumably including Serbia and Montenegro as ECCY participants despite the fact that neither had applied for recognition.[138]

A number of interesting points arise from this practice. First, it is clear that the Commission's task went beyond a simple constitutional analysis of the legal commitments accepted by the republics and that it also extended into assessing political commitments made by them. The use of the statements made by the Bosnian Prime-Minister in the *Official Journal* evidence this as do similar statements made by the representatives of the other applicant republics.[139] The Commission, as a legal rather than a political organ, merely acknowledged the existence of such statements, however, and their sincerity and validity presumably fell to be assessed by the European Council. Given the politically sensitive nature of the recognition decisions, Pellet suggested that the Commission was "...foolish..." to accept its new mandate at all.[140] Nevertheless, the importance of constitutional analysis is evident from the fact that the constitutions of each applicant republic were referred to in each of the four opinions. In respect of Bosnia, the Commission simply noted that "...the current SRBH constitution guarantees equal rights for the nations of Bosnia-Hercegovina - Muslims, Serbs and Croats - and the members of other nations and ethnic groups living on its territory...[and]...guarantees respect for human rights...". In Macedonia's case, however, the analysis was more specific and referred on a number of occasions to specific constitutional provisions. *Article 4*, for example, codified the renunciation of territorial claims against neighbouring States and specified that succession issues required agreement between all Yugoslav republics. *Article 78* described the creation of a Council for Inter-Ethnic Relations which was to consider issues relating to inter-ethnic relations and provide advice to the Macedonian Assembly. In Croatia's case, the Commission's eventual decision to advise against recognition was based directly on the fact that "...the constitutional Act of 4th December does not fully incorporate all the provisions of the [Carrington] draft Convention of 4th November 1991, notably those contained in *Chapter II, Article 2(c)*, under the heading 'Special Status'...". Second, the Commission's analysis clearly did not limit itself to the constitutions of the applicant republics and equally determinative, it appears, were the responses to the Commission's questionnaire. The text of this questionnaire was not published but, from the text of *Opinion 6*, it is clear to see that the questionnaire issued by the Commission followed the EC *Guidelines* almost to the letter.[141] The *Guidelines* required the republics to state their willingness to "...respect...the provisions of the *Charter of the United Nations* and the commitments subscribed to in the *Final Act of Helsinki*, and in the *Charter of Paris*, especially with regard to the rule of law, democracy and human rights". The Commission's questionnaire asked "...what measures Macedonia had already taken, or intended to take, to give effect to the *UN Charter*, the *Helsinki Final Act* and the *Charter of Paris?*". Whilst the Commission's question, and indeed Macedonia's response, did not give special emphasis to the rule of law, democracy and human rights, it is clear it is substantially the same as the *Guidelines* requirements. Other questions on the measures taken, or to be taken, to protect the rights of ethnic and national groups and minorities, to respect the inviolability of all frontiers, to abide by all relevant commitments on disarmament and nuclear non-proliferation and to settle regional disputes and questions of State succession by agreement, were equally reflective of the *Guidelines*. The questionnaire also required the applicants to accept the specific conditions in the *Declaration on Yugoslavia*, including acceptance of the Carrington Convention, specifically *Chapter II* thereof, and the duty to refrain from hostile propaganda against neighbouring EC States. Although the questionnaire makes no reference to the *Declaration*'s requirements that the republics continue support for the peace efforts of the EC, ECCY and UN, such political commitments fell to be assessed by the Council rather than the Commission.

The use of a questionnaire accords with the Commission's previous written procedures. It is uncertain whether the Commission forwarded the questionnaires to the republics via the ECCY Chairman, as were its previous opinions, or whether they were sent directly to the applicants.[142] The latter interpretation would clearly reduce the Chairman's role, which may nevertheless be justified because the issues in question were now between the Yugoslav parties and the EC itself rather than the parties *inter se*. It is clear that the Commission engaged in direct contact with the applicants to the extent that it requested additional information on many of the points addressed in the questionnaire. In Croatia's case, for example, the Commission asked for confirmation of its acceptance of *Chapter II* of the Carrington Convention. Croatia's response came in a letter from President Tudjman which was addressed to Monsieur Badinter directly. This letter stated that it was in response to "...your letter..." which indicates that some communication between the Commission and the parties was done without the interposition of Lord Carrington.

A third notable feature of the materials considered by the Commission is the reliance placed on the referenda of those republics seeking recognition. In the case of Croatia, Macedonia and Slovenia, the Commission referred to the plebiscites which had been conducted to ascertain the will of the population for independence and, in the case of Slovenia, the Commission referred expressly to the large majority which had voted for independence.[143] In Bosnia's case, however, the Commission was concerned that no referendum had occurred and that the Bosnian Assembly's vote for independence had been taken without the participation of the Bosnian-Serbs. Since *Article LXVII* of the SRBH Constitution stated that Bosnia's citizens were entitled to have their opinions reflected through a representative Assembly or by referendum, the Commission was unable to accept that the will of those citizens had been properly established.[144]

A final feature of the materials considered by the Commission is the reference to a Rapporteur. The Commission gives no details about who this person was or what role they played, other than to say that they were "...heard..." Given that references indicate the use of only one Rapporteur it is likely that an inquisitorial, rather than an adversarial, procedure was used, which would again accord with most continental legal systems, including the Commission Chairman's domestic system.[145] It is unknown whether there was one Rapporteur acting on behalf of all republics or whether each republic had their own Rapporteur. In the former case, the Rapporteur's role would be closely aligned with the fact-finding function of the Commission during its advice on recognition and he may have assessed factual situations in the republics having visited them and spoken directly to their governmental authorities.[146] What is clear, however, is that use of a Rapporteur represents a deviation from the Commission's previous insistence on a written procedure, although since the Commission refers neither to the Rapporteur's precise role nor his findings, it is impossible to know the extent of this deviation. The Commission's distinct fact-finding role during *Opinions 4-7* is evidenced in the fact that the Rapporteur system was only used during these opinions.

5.10.6 *Time-Limits*

The *Declaration* clearly states that implementation of the EC's recognition of applicants would occur on 15th January 1992 and that all applications must be made by 23rd December. Given that the period in which the Commission's advice would be sought is a mere 23 days, this is clearly short of the two-months provided for in the Commission's original mandate. Even assuming applications were received by the European Council on the same day the *Guidelines* were published, this gave the Commission only a further week to receive the applications from Lord Carrington, solicit the necessary information and advise the Council in time for them to have formulated a policy on recognition for the 15th January. It is submitted, therefore, that the Commission's influence in the recognition decisions was intended to be nominal and that the EC had already decided on the action it intended to take in respect of the various applicants. Germany had already undermined the *Guidelines* attempts to coordinate recognition by announcing, on 23rd December 1991, that it had decided to recognise Croatia and Slovenia but would wait until the 15th January 1992 to implement this decision.[147] This obviously represented a serious undermining of the Commission's advice on these questions

As mentioned earlier, Pellet argued that the initial two-month time-limit was restrictive but, since the *Declaration* effectively halved the time available for the Commission to consider applications for recognition from four republics, this applies *a fortiori* to *Opinions 4-7*. Nevertheless, the Commission provided its advice well within the allotted time and, having received the applications on the 19th and 20th of December, published *Opinions 4-7* by 11th January, a total of just 23 days.

5.10.7 *The Nature of the Commission's Findings*

The *Declaration* states that the Commission was to provide only "...advice..." on the issue of recognition and Germany's actions clearly created pressure for this advice to concord with growing EC pressure to recognise certain republics. *Opinions 4-7*, however, offer the best evidence that the Commission remained independent of such pressure. The relationship of these opinions with the Commission's other jurisprudence on Yugoslavia's "...dissolution process..." is discussed further in chapter 7.

5.10.8 *Opinion 4 - Bosnia-Hercegovina*

Having considered the materials mentioned above,[148] the Commission considered Bosnia's application for recognition to be insufficient to the extent that it had not expressed the true will of the entirety of the republic's population. Accordingly the Commission suggested that Bosnia remedy this situation "...possibly by means of a referendum of all the citizens of the SRBH without distinction, carried out under international supervision". When the Bosnian authorities organised a referendum under CSCE supervision on 1st May 1992, it was boycotted by Bosnian-Serbs but almost all Bosnian-Muslims and Bosnian-Croats voted in favour of independence, which ensured an overall majority of 63% of Bosnia's entire population. Bosnia was recognised by the EC on 6th April 1992, sparking off disastrous conflict in that republic.[149]

5.10.9 *Opinion 5 - Croatia*

The Commission found that certain provisions of the Carrington Convention, "...notably those contained in *Chapter II*, *Article 2(c)*, under the heading 'Special Status...'[150] had not been fully incorporated in the Croatian constitution and consequently concluded that Croatia had not fulfilled the criteria for recognition. Although, in a later "Comment" given by the Commission on 4th July, Croatia's amended Constitution was said to satisfy "...the requirements of *general international law* regarding the protection of minorities...[emphasis added]", the Commission still felt the Carrington Convention's provisions on autonomy had not been fully incorporated. Nevertheless, this comment stated that the Commission's view in *Opinion 5* was that "...Croatia satisfied the conditions for recognition by the Member

States of the EC set out in the joint statement on Yugoslavia and the *Guidelines*...". It is clear from *Opinion 5*, however, that this was not the case and that the Commission engaged in some historical revisionism on this point. The reasons for this may be related to the way in which its advice was treated by the Council, which is discussed below.

5.10.10 *Opinion 6 - Macedonia*

The Commission found simply that Macedonia "...satisfies the tests in the *Guidelines*...and the *Declaration on Yugoslavia*...". Realising that Greece objected to the use of the name 'Macedonia' the Commission explicitly referred to legal and political guarantees in which Macedonia renounced all territorial claims and agreed to refrain from hostile propaganda against any neighbouring State. Whilst falling short of explicitly recommending the recognition of Macedonia, which remained a political decision for the EC, the Commission's advice could not have been more favourable.

5.10.11 *Opinion 7 - Slovenia*

The Commission referred to Slovenia's referendum which produced an overwhelming vote in favour of independence[151] and the Slovenian constitution before concluding that the republic satisfied the criteria for recognition. Again, it refrained from directly recommending recognition.

5.10.12 *Responses to the Commission's Findings*

On 15th January, the European Council announced its decision to recognise Slovenia in accordance with *Opinion 7*. It also appeared to follow the Commission's advice in announcing that Bosnia's application left "...important matters to be addressed..."[152] and that the Council unanimously supported the Commission's suggestions of a referendum. Nevertheless, on the questions of Croatia and Macedonia, the Council clearly failed to follow the Commission's recommendations by rejecting Macedonia's application whilst accepting Croatia's.

The reasons for these decisions are understandable only in light of the contextual political setting surrounding them. With EPC soon to be replaced by the new CFSP pillar, EC Member States were keen to avoid divisions that might threaten the ratification of the *TEU* and were susceptible to pressures imposed by individual Members who threatened to withdraw support for the treaty. In respect of the Croatian application, such pressure was applied by Germany who argued that 'internationalising' the situation would allow the full force of international law to be applied to a conflict which had hitherto been deemed internal. Equally, Greece's objections to the use of certain emblems on the Macedonian flag, together with fears over the use of the name 'Macedonia', accounted for the inclusion of certain requirements in the *Declaration* and were responsible for the rejection of Macedonia's application.[153] Whilst these political pressures created unity, it was "...the unity of a chain gang. When one member pushed hard on the chain...the other 11 had to move".[154]

Although the Commission's role had been reduced to a consultative remit by this time, it is arguable that EC Member States should have taken more account of the Commission's findings in this area. Whilst non-binding, advisory opinions can create a moral imperative to follow their reasoning. Schreur argues that "...there is at least a duty to consider them in good faith".[155] Since the expertise of the Commissioners was clearly in the field of constitutional law and since *Opinions 4-7* involved an analysis of constitutional documents, it is submitted that the compelling nature of the Commission's findings should have been more obvious than any of its other opinions. Instead, political considerations dominated the recognition process and the Commission's credibility was damaged by such action. It would have been far better to have left the recognition decision solely to EC Member States than to create a legal façade which discredited the Commission's role in the ECCY. Perhaps the EC simply assumed that the Commission would be aware of prevailing political opinion on recognising the respective republics and formulate its advice accordingly. If so, the Commission at least retained some credibility in terms of its independence.

The Commission evidenced its independence from the political pressures which affected EC policy during this period by deviating from what was openly expected of it. Despite the potential for national, or rather supra-national "...orientation..." in *ad hoc* tribunals,[156] it appears that no such phenomenon occurred in *Opinions 4-7* at the very least. To the extent that the EC's decisions conflicted with the Commission's advice, except where the political objectives of the former coincided with the recommendations of the latter, it is clear that the Commission's opinions were neither determinative of EC policy nor prejudiced thereby.

5.11 Events Following *Opinions 2-7*

Responses to the Commission's second batch of opinions were varied. Naturally, Slovenia agreed entirely with the Commission's endorsement of its political and constitutional framework. Croatia, whilst doubting the Commission's objections to its constitutional guarantees on minority rights, was obviously delighted, though not totally surprised, to receive EC recognition despite such reservations. Bosnia, whilst dissatisfied with its rejected application, nevertheless accepted the Commission's reasoning and organised a referendum on the issue of independence. Macedonia perhaps had the greatest cause for concern, having received the Commission's legal endorsement of its application yet having been rejected for overtly political reasons emanating from one EC Member State. These concerns were, to some extent, alleviated when the republic was subsequently recognised as the Former Yugoslav Republic of Macedonia (FYROM). Although neither Serbia nor Montenegro had applied for recognition as new States, *Opinions 2-7* perturbed the FRY because they denied the legality of forcibly implementing territorial changes to create a 'Greater Serbia' out of Bosnia and Croatia and limited the right of self-determination for Serbs in those republics to protection of their ethnic identity rather than legitimising secession once independence was recognised. This was worsened by *Opinions 8* and *10*, which concluded that the FRY could not claim Yugoslavia's legal personality and would have to apply for recognition as a successor State.[157]

Even before *Opinions 2-7* were published on 11th January 1992, the Yugoslav Federal Presidency had published its own views on the questions posed in Lord Carrington's letter of 20th November. It was argued that the right to self-determination, including the right to seek independence or secession, could not be exercised by sub-State regions of existing States unless those regions were populated by only one 'people', a nation. To hold otherwise would define the 'right' as "...self-determination of *citizens*, instead of *peoples*... [emphasis added]".[158] The Presidency concluded that Yugoslavia's constituent nations enjoyed the right of self-determination, up to and including secession, which was guaranteed by Yugoslavia's Constitutions of 1946, 1963 and 1974, but that this could not be implemented unilaterally and required "...constitutional and legal..." regulation. This meant that none of Yugoslavia's republics could achieve independence without the consent of all republics and, having attempted to do so, Serbs within those secessionist republics could seek to leave them to remain within the FRY. A later position, published on 30th December 1991,[159] addressed the issue dealt with in *Opinion 3* and argued that, in seeking EC recognition, Croatia and Bosnia had breached Yugoslavia's 1974 Constitution.[160] The possibility for territorial fragmentation was evident when the Presidency threatened that "...if the Republic of Croatia should become an independent State, without a prior adjustment of the administrative border between this republic and Montenegro to make Prevlaka an integral part of Montenegro, the sovereignty of Yugoslavia, and of Montenegro, over a part of its territory, the Boka Kotorska Bay, would be threatened".

This latter position reveals further elements of the Commission's practice since it refers to questions posed to the republican leaders by Monsieur Badinter, asking whether they considered republican boundaries to constitute international legal borders. The Presidency's position was that, from medieval times, these internal borders had been "...very vaguely defined..." and were currently based on formulations resulting from war-time conditions, under which "...it was impossible to apply with any consistency ethnic, economic, political or other principles relevant to the charting of internal borders".[161] When the Presidency's position was not reflected in *Opinion 3* and when the EC recognised Croatia and Slovenia despite warnings that this would constitute "...gross interference in the internal affairs of a sovereign State...[a] violation of international law [...] and a dangerous precedent in international relations...", Serbia and Montenegro issued a jurisdictional challenge against the Commission. Such challenges are common from those who perceive that their interests are not being protected by the organ in question and indicate a loss of faith in the relevant dispute resolution process.[162] To the extent that arbitration is traditionally dependent on the consent of the disputing parties, this may have hindered the Commission's consideration of these issues.[163] To the extent that the Commission enjoyed a dual mandate, however, the consultative remit of which did not necessitate consent of the Yugoslav parties, this withdrawal of cooperation was legally, if not politically, irrelevant.

5.12 Comments on Croatia's Constitutional Amendments and Lord Carrington's Second Letter

Following *Opinion 5*, Croatia amended its constitution to redress the Commission's reservations about its fulfillment of the Carrington Convention and these constitutional amendments of 8th May 1992 were forwarded to the Commission by Lord Carrington on 3rd June. Why the ECCY Chairman felt the need to ask the Commission for advice relating to the criteria for recognition when Croatia had already been recognised is confusing. The Commission's response refers to a letter sent to President Tudjman by the President of the European Council on 22nd February, some time after recognition was granted, which expressed reservations over inadequacies in the Croatian constitution law highlighted by the Commission. This indicates that, despite rejecting the Commission's advice against recognition for essentially political reasons, the EC implicitly acknowledged the Commission's constitutional law expertise by pressuring Croatia to remedy those constitutional lacunae identified by the Commission in *ex post facto* constitutional amendments.

The Commission offered a 'Comment' in response to these amendments, which is a category of response not envisaged in any written procedure. The anomalous status of these deliberations is perhaps best explained by the fact that they were ultimately irrelevant, recognition having already been granted, and because Carrington's letter of 3rd June contained neither "...differences..." of the Yugoslav parties awaiting the Commission's "...decision..."nor applications for recognition awaiting the Commission's "...advice...".

Despite the Comment's anomalous status, the Commission considered materials broadly similar to those used in *Opinions 4-7* and referred to the text of the amended constitution, in English and French, the Croatian authorities comments thereupon and an English translation of the Croatian electoral law of 9th April 1992.[164] This confirms that the working languages of the Commission must have been both French and English as was also the case under the ICFY.[165]

The Commission concluded that the requirements of the *Carrington Convention* were still "...not entirely reflected in the constitutional Law adopted by the Croatian Parliament on 8th May 1992". This again illustrates the degree to which the Commission was determined to maintain its independence by refusing to sanction any inadequacies in the Croatian constitution even after recognition had already been granted by the EC. The Commission nevertheless concluded that, whilst falling short of the Carrington requirements, Croatia's constitution satisfied the "...requirements of general international law regarding the protection of minorities...". Again, the Commission's definitional inadequacies fail to explain the differences between the *Carrington Convention* conditions and the purported international legal requirements regarding minorities.

The Badinter Commission's continuing role in the peaceful resolution of disputes amongst the Yugoslav parties, even after EC recognition of a majority of the former-Yugoslav republics, was evidenced by a letter sent to the Commission by Lord Carrington on 18th May 1992. Carrington's second letter sought the Commission's advice on questions formulated on the initiative of Portuguese Foreign Minister De Deus Pinheiro in light of Serbia and Montenegro's attempts to continue Yugoslavia's international legal personality.[166] The letter's three questions are reprinted below.

> "1. In terms of international law, is the FRY a new State calling for recognition by the Member States of the EC in accordance with the joint statement on Yugoslavia and the *Guidelines*...?
> 2. In *Opinion 1* of 29th November 1991, the Arbitration Commission was of the opinion that 'the SFRY (was) in the process of dissolution'. Can this dissolution now be regarded as complete?
> 3. If this is the case, on what basis and by what means should the problems of the succession of States arising between the different States emerging from the SFRY be settled?"

Before the Commission considered these important international legal issues, however, it received a jurisdictional challenge from the FRY.

5.13 The First Jurisdictional Challenge

Having adopted legal and factual positions which were consistently at odds with the Badinter Commission's findings it was unsurprising that the FRY challenged its jurisdiction to rule on the questions in Lord Carrington's second letter, which involved consideration of the FRY's legal status. It was clear that the Commission process had increasingly transferred control of areas traditionally reserved for the disputing parties into the hands of the EC and ECCY Chairman. Given that the most obvious advantage of arbitration is the control it gives disputing parties over the resolution process, the Commission was clearly failing to fulfill these advantages.

A letter from the Presidents of Montenegro and Serbia was sent directly to Monsieur Badinter on 8th June informing the Commission that the FRY considered the new questions outside the Commission's competence. The letter contained three grounds for challenge which are reproduced below.

> "1. These questions did not fall within the mandate given to the EC under the terms of the Brioni agreement;
> 2. Outstanding matters between the FRY and the other Yugoslav Republics should be resolved by means of an overall agreement between them;
> 3. Those which could not be resolved by agreement should be submitted to the ICJ".[167]

In line with previous practice, the Commission informed the other republics of these objections and Croatia, Macedonia and Slovenia each sent observations to the Commission on 18th and 19th June contesting the FRY's challenge, which were in turn copied to the FRY. Although it has not been possible to obtain the texts of these observations, Pellet convincingly argues that the other republics based their challenges to the FRY's position on the fact that the FRY was not a recognised successor State to the SFRY and that Serbia and Montenegro had accepted the Commission's jurisdiction from the outset of the ECCY.[168] The FRY then argued that the Commission possessed no power to decide on its own jurisdiction and competence, raising questions about the applicability of the German legal principle of *kompetenz-kompetenz* or the French principle of *competence de la competence*, by which a judicial organ is implicitly allowed to rule on its own competence.[169]

The Commission issued an "Interlocutory Decision" on 4th July which began by stating that it was for the Commission to ascertain its competence to rule on its own jurisdiction before examining the other substantive aspects of the FRY's challenge. The Commission's conclusions on its own "...legal nature..." nevertheless also strayed into substantive areas of the FRY's challenge. Thus, the Commission noted that it was "...established not by the Brioni Agreement...but by the joint statement on Yugoslavia adopted at an extraordinary meeting of Ministers in the context of European Political Co-Operation on 27th August 1991". This EPC *Declaration* described an "…'arbitration procedure', which was not defined but which was to lead to 'decisions'…" and it was accepted by all Yugoslav republics at the convening of the ECCY on 7th September 1991. The Commission noted that, despite the summary nature of its early procedural instruments, "…it is clear from the terminology used and even the composition of the Commission that the intention was to create a body capable of resolving on the basis of law the differences which were to be submitted to it by the parties…". This was "…precisely…the definition of arbitration…" and the ICJ's jurisprudence in the *Arbitral Award of 31st July 1989 Case*[170] was cited as authority for this. The Commission also cited the *Nottebohm (Preliminary Objections) Case*,[171] wherein the ICJ stated that "…since the *Alabama Case*, it has been generally recognised that…in the absence of any agreements to the contrary, the international tribunal has the right to decide as to its own jurisdiction and has the power to interpret for this purpose the instruments which govern that jurisdiction. […] This principle, which is accepted by general international law in the matter of arbitration, assumes particular force when the international tribunal is no longer an arbitral tribunal constituted by virtue of special agreement between the parties for the purpose of adjudicating on a particular dispute, but is an instrument which has been pre-established by an international instrument defining its jurisdiction and regulating its operation". Implicitly, the Commission appears to identify itself as falling within the latter category, although one may argue that the international instrument(s) governing the Commission's competence provide scant information about its jurisdiction and operation. Clearly considering these cases sufficient authority for its position, albeit without saying that it considered itself bound by them, the Commission concluded that it possessed the implied power to rule on its own competence. This is clearly in accordance with traditional international law.[172] Pellet suggests that the citation of ICJ jurisprudence may also have been intended to prepare the ground for a later argument in which the Commission makes certain parallels between itself and the ICJ by asserting that the ability to make *consultative* and *advisory* opinions did not detract from the Commission's characterisation as an arbitral tribunal capable of making *decisions* on *contentious* legal questions.[173]

Since the FRY's challenge was not directed individually at any of Lord Carrington's questions and must, therefore, be taken as applying to all three questions, the Commission dealt with its jurisdictional competence in one individual decision rather than in relation to each posed question. The Commission noted that its initial mandate of 27th August was "...supplemented and clarified..." by later texts and by "...the practice followed by the [ECCY] and by the responsible authorities in the various Yugoslav Republics". As evidence of such supplementary texts, the Commission reiterated the procedural developments contained in the EPC statement of the 3rd September which had been accepted by all Yugoslav Republics.[174] The Commission also noted that it was Serbia that had taken the initiative to refer questions to Lord Carrington for the Commission's attention and that, of the three questions referred, two of these were dealt with by the Commission. The Commission noted that all republics had informed it of their opinions on the issues under consideration with "...none...[making] the least mention of any incompetence on the Commission's part". This was interpreted as indicating that all participating republics accepted "...an identical interpretation of its mandate, and thereby recognising its competence in *consultative* issues as well". This latter statement presumably refers to Lord Carrington's dilution of the Commission's role by asking for an "...opinion or recommendation..." rather than a "...decision...".

Returning to the question of its constitutive remit, the Commission observed that it had been created within the ECCY framework, whose task was to "...establish peace for all in Yugoslavia and to achieve lasting solutions which respect all legitimate concerns and legitimate aspirations".[175] The Commission's role was to "...enlighten the Conference on the legal aspects of problems which it encounters in carrying out this mission..." and that it would require "...conclusive reasons..."[176] to prevent it replying to questions posed by the ECCY Chairman. The Commission saw no such reasons for refusing to consider those questions dealt with in *Opinions 1-3*, nor those in Lord Carrington's second letter, which remained "...fully within the role entrusted to it by the EC and its Member States on the one hand and the six Republics on the other".

Reinforcing its legal nature, the Commission noted that it could "...give a judgment only in law..." and that "...far from constituting an obstacle to the Arbitration Commission's exercising its competence...[the legal nature of the posed questions] is, on the contrary, a justification...[of such competence]". The Commission concluded that it had "...decided..." it was competent to assess its own jurisdiction and that it possessed the competence to rule on the issues in Carrington's letter. The fact that the

Commission ruled in favour of its ability to assess its own competence is not surprising. Given a similar challenge, it would be unusual for a judicial organ to consider itself unable to rule on this issue even if it subsequently ruled itself incompetent to address the relevant substantive issues. Indeed, this has been suggested to be a general rule of international institutional law.[177] Nevertheless, one must note that it is usual for jurisdiction to be interpreted alongside the initial arbitration *compromis*, which did not exist in this case. The importance of the notion of consent[178] of the parties appears, therefore, to have been ignored by having extended the Commission's functions to providing advisory opinions.[179] The ICJ refuses to issue Advisory Opinions they would circumvent the requirement of consent if the case were tried on its merits,[180] yet this appears precisely the situation in respect of the new questions posed in Carrington's letter.

The FRY's jurisdictional challenge is curious in a number of ways. First, reference to the Brioni Agreement, which pre-dated the Commission's creation by over a month, is unlikely to have convinced the Commission that its jurisdictional mandate was governed by the Accord rather than subsequent EPC statements and declarations. Second, the assertion that questions of succession could only be resolved by the Yugoslav republics *inter se* and through negotiation ignores the fact that the Commission's advice would not displace the need for negotiations but provide guidelines within which those negotiations would take place. Legal advice and political negotiations are not mutually exclusive options but complementary. Indeed, in *Opinion 9*, the Commission required negotiations to continue between the Yugoslav parties *as part of its advice*. Third, reference to the ICJ is curious because neither Serbia nor Montenegro, nor indeed the SFRY, had subscribed to the *ICJ Statute's Optional Clause* nor acknowledged the ICJ's competence in other ways. The possibility of an *ad hoc* referral could not, of course, be excluded, but reference to the ICJ probably represented nothing other than a sign of the FRY's frustration regarding the Commission's previous opinions and its desire to move the decision-making process away from that organ. In this sense, it is ironic that precisely the same motivations lay behind the Serbia's earlier demands to shift the decision-making process away from political negotiations within the ECCY and towards the "...eminent group..." of jurists within the Commission.[181] The origin of the complaint, however, indicates that the FRY would have preferred an institution such as the ICJ where they could control the nature and wording of issues referred for settlement. Fourth, a notable omission from the jurisdictional challenge is reference to the international law concept of *rebus sic stantibus*. This principle legitimises a State's decision to vary its international legal obligations as the result of a radical transformation in circumstances surrounding those obligations. Whilst it is usually discussed in relation to the termination of treaties,[182] it is not conceptually difficult to imagine its application in respect of accepting the jurisdiction of an organ such as the Badinter Commission. On this basis, it may have been possible to argue that a "...radical transformation..."[183] of factual and legal circumstances had occurred following the recognition of certain former-Yugoslav republics. Having joined the ECCY process at a time when the preservation of Yugoslavia was stated EC policy and, if earlier suggestions are correct, having accepted the Commission's jurisdiction when its intended function was to assist in a constitutional resettlement, the recognition of Yugoslavia's dissolution radically alters the essence of the ECCY process and the Commission's role therein. The policy of maintaining a united Yugoslavia may be argued to have represented "...an essential basis of the consent of the parties..."[184] and changing EC policy may have justified the withdrawal of cooperation and the jurisdictional challenge against the Commission, whose continued activities may arguably be *ultra vires*. Such arguments were not made, however.

Procedurally, a number of other interesting points arise. First, having termed its response a "...decision..." and used the language of decision-making in its deliberations, this clearly contrasts with previous consultative recommendations and represents a new category of response from the Commission.[185] This must be thought appropriate, since the jurisdictional competence of an arbitral tribunal must be established beyond doubt and 'advice' or 'opinions' on this issue would not have sufficed for these purposes.[186] Second, the materials considered reflect the binding nature of this decision. Whereas earlier opinions generally failed to cite established international case-law on issues considered therein, this decision contained two direct quotations from ICJ cases. This indicates that, even in the absence of any binding doctrine of precedent, the Commission felt obliged to establish its competence in accordance with established international institutional rules, on which greater consensus may be possible than on the other substantive issues of international law considered by the Commission. Third, it was clear that the Commission was willing and able to continue proceedings even in the absence of participation by a number of key parties to the disputes, namely Serbia and Montenegro. Despite having failed to respond to the issues posed in Lord Carrington's letter and having instead forwarded the challenge outlined above, the Commission felt able to proceed with its consideration of those issues.[187] Fourth, the Commission confirms that its ability to issue advisory opinions does not detract from or remove its legal identity as an international arbitral tribunal capable of issuing binding awards in the appropriate circumstances. Fifth, the Commission's Interlocutory Decision was delivered within the established two-month time-limit and, since it was delivered at the same time as the Commission's opinions on the issues in the second letter, on 4th July 1992, must have been decided some time before this date.

5.14 *Opinions 8-10*

The final Opinions delivered by the Commission during its role within the ECCY were those delivered on 4th July 1992, on the same day as the Interlocutory Decision.

5.14.1 *Opinion 8*

Opinion 8 addressed the question whether Yugoslavia's dissolution process had come to an end.[188] The Commission dealt with Lord Carrington's second question first because "...the answers to the first and third questions depend on the answer given to the second".

The Commission began by reiterating its findings of *Opinion 1* that the "...intrinsic requirements of a federal State regarding participation and representativeness..." were not satisfied in Yugoslavia and that, although the pronouncement of a State's dissolution has "...major repercussions in international law...[and] calls for the greatest caution..." a number of factual developments indicated that the dissolution process was complete. Chief among these was the fact that a number of the Yugoslav republics had constituted themselves as sovereign and independent States recognised by the EC, other Yugoslav republics and other States. This had "...seriously compromised..." Yugoslavia's international personality and meant that federal authority could no longer be exercised. Whilst the Commission emphasised that recognition had "...only declarative value...", it noted that this bore testament to the fact that the entities so recognised possessed certain international rights and obligations and that the Yugoslav federal authorities "...no longer held sway on the territory of the newly constituted States...". The Commission also noted the creation of the FRY, which it called a "...new State..." and noted the existence of a number of international legal instruments referring to "...the *former* SFRY... [emphasis added]..." as well as a UN Security Council resolution stating that the FRY's attempts to automatically continue the SFRY's legal personality had "...not been generally accepted".[189] This was compounded by the fact that Bosnia, Slovenia and Croatia had all become UN Member States on 22nd May 1992.

Notably, the Commission refrained from providing advice on whether the FRY fulfilled the criteria laid out in the *Guidelines* and *Declaration*. This is prudent given that, first, it had not been asked to rule on this issue and, second, its advice in respect of other republics had already been ignored by the EC.

5.14.2 *Opinion 9*

Opinion 9, dealing with the question of State succession, followed on from *Opinion 8* by saying that all new States arising from the dissolution process were equal successors to the SFRY and that no individual republic, nor group thereof, could claim to continue Yugoslavia's legal personality. The Commission noted that all republics had accepted that the *Vienna Conventions* of 1978 and 1983 should be the "...foundation..." for State succession negotiations and that such negotiations must lead to "...an equitable outcome...". Nevertheless, any such solution must ensure that it is in accordance with the requirements of general international law and particularly the fundamental rights of peoples and minorities. Again, the Commission referred to the European Council's decision of 27th June 1992, at which it was stated that the EC would not recognise the FRY as Yugoslavia's legal successor "...until the moment that decision has been taken by the qualified international institutions...". Although this fails to state the identity of the relevant international institutions, given the nature of the question considered in *Opinion 10*, the Commission itself may arguably have been intended to fall within this definition. It is more likely, however, that the institutions referred to would be the UN General Assembly and Security Council. The Commission therefore concluded that Yugoslavia's successor States must settle all aspects of succession *inter se* by way of an equitable agreement based on the principles of the *Vienna Conventions* which takes account of the "...principle of equality of rights and duties between States in respect of international law". The Commission noted that, since no specific question on succession had been submitted, it could not offer an opinion on "...the very real problems associated with the succession to the former Yugoslavia". Nevertheless, it offered some broad principles which may assist the subsequent negotiations on this issue in the ECCY process.

First, "...property of the SFRY located in third countries must be divided equitably between the successor States..." as must Yugoslavia's assets and liabilities. Any issues which could not be settled by agreement must be resolved peacefully "...in line with the principles laid down in the *UN Charter*..." which effectively required all parties to seek such resolution "...by means of inquiry, mediation, conciliation, arbitration or judicial settlement". Whilst not stating that it considered itself suitable for any arbitration which may be chosen by the parties, it is submitted that, in light of the Commission's familiarity with the Yugoslav crisis, it could represent a possible dispute resolution mechanism for States accepting its jurisdiction in this area. Nevertheless, as emphasised in the Interlocutory Decision, the choice of peaceful-settlement procedures remains one for the disputing parties to decide.

5.14.3 *Opinion 10*

Opinion 10 dealt with the FRY's claim to be Yugoslavia's sole legal successor and asked whether the FRY was in fact a new State which would have to satisfy the conditions in the *Guidelines* and *Declaration on Yugoslavia* to achieve EC recognition. One obvious difficulty in the prospect of the FRY having to fulfill these conditions was that the *Declaration* specified that applications for recognition must have been received by the European Council by 23rd December 1991 and implemented by 15th January 1992. Having recognised Bosnia in April 1992 and the FYROM in May 1992 it is clear that these dates remained flexible in terms of implementation, although whether the same would apply to the application date was uncertain, since only Serbia and Montenegro had failed to respond by the relevant date.

The Commission began by noting the FRY constitution adopted on 27th April 1992 and reiterating its findings that none of the republics could claim to be Yugoslavia's sole legal successor. The Commission stated that the FRY was "...a new State...[which] does not *ipso facto* enjoy the recognition enjoyed by the SFRY... [and that] recognition by the Member States of the EC would be subject to its compliance with the conditions laid down by general international law for such an act and the joint statement and *Guidelines* of 16th December 1991". The Commission again emphasised the declaratory nature of recognition but also noted that recognition, as "...a discretionary act...", could be subject to whatever conditions other States chose to impose, subject only to the requirements of international law and particularly that any conditions could not ignore the prohibitions on the use of force in inter-State relations nor the guarantees of the rights of ethnic, religious or linguistic minorities. It went on to state that the FRY met the international legal criteria of Statehood, described in *Opinion 1*, without commentating on the fulfillment of the criteria in the *Guidelines* and *Declaration*. This evidences the divergence between the minimal factual criteria for Statehood described in *Opinion 1* and the more burdensome conditions for recognition within the *Guidelines* and *Declaration*. The Commission qualified its opinion somewhat by stating that such qualifications were met only "...within the frontiers constituted by the administrative boundaries of Montenegro and Serbia in the SFRY...", which was plainly intended to reiterate the Commission's insistence that no further territorial disruption should occur and that the Serbian concern over Serbs in other republics could not be addressed by their incorporation into the FRY. Again, however, it condemns Kosovo and Vojvodina to remain as part of Serbia and allows the FRY to avoid the constitutional scrutiny that the other republics had undergone. The perpetuation of a repressive political system, in which ethnic Albanians and Hungarians in Kosovo and Vojvodina were routinely discriminated against, eventually led to the outbreak of a civil conflict in Kosovo and highlighted the problems caused by the absence of political pressure to encourage reform in the FRY.[190] Whether the international legal requirements for recognition of guaranteeing minority and group rights were met in the FRY, therefore, remains doubtful.

5.14.4 *Procedural Issues Arising from Opinions 8-10*

Procedurally, these opinions offer little by way of innovation. It is clear that the Commission referred to papers from each of the republics continuing participation in the 'arbitration' process as well as materials other than those submitted by the Yugoslav parties, such as the EC and UN declarations challenging the FRY's claim to be Yugoslavia's sole legal successor. These latter materials show that the Commission considered itself competent to use declarations of international organisations in a manner which may evidence a position in international law. An example of this is the explicit reference to the *UN Charter* and the obligation contained therein for States to settle their disputes by pacific means.[191] The Commission reiterated that it was operating in the sphere of international law by referring to the requirements of general international law throughout *Opinions 8-10* and *Opinion 10* specifically required the Commission to deliberate "...in terms of international law...". The opinions evidence the Commission's desire to maintain a thread of consistency through its jurisprudence, by cross-referring its earlier jurisprudence. In *Opinion 8* the Commission reiterated the requirements inherent in a federal State and how these were not met in the former Yugoslavia, which were originally detailed in *Opinion 1*. *Opinion 9* also reiterated the findings of *Opinion 1* that issues of State succession must be settled on the basis of principles embodied in the *Vienna Conventions* and must reflect the Commission's long-standing requirement of respect for "...the fundamental rights of the individual and of peoples and minorities". In all other respects, the procedural conduct of *Opinions 8-10* accords entirely with earlier opinions, excluding the slight differences during *Opinions 4-7*.[192]

5.15 Political Developments Following *Opinions 8-10*

On 1st April 1992, the EC and USA issued a joint statement declaring that they wished to coordinate policy on the issue of the FRY. The EC and its Member States explicitly referred to *Opinion 10* to justify their decision not to recognise the FRY as the legal successor to Yugoslavia and to require the FRY to apply for recognition in a manner comparable to the other republics.[193]

In respect of the Commission's recommendation in *Opinion 9* that "...the SFRY's membership of international organisations must be terminated according to their statutes..." the international response was far from a clear endorsement of this advice. The CSCE, on 8th July 1992, suspended Yugoslavia's participation from all CSCE meetings, despite having no such constitutional provision for suspending membership and the FRY's participation in the General Assembly was suspended under *UNSC*

Resolution 777.[194] In neither case was Yugoslavia formally expelled, which confirms the extent to which the Commission's recommendations were overruled if political considerations dictated an alternative result.

5.16 Conclusions

It was submitted at the outset of this chapter that the most important feature in assessing the practice and procedure of an organ is the function it is intended to perform. The merits and demerits of a body such as the Badinter Commission must be considered contextually and in light of its envisaged role. It has been argued that the Commission was originally conceived as a body to assist in the restructuring of Yugoslavia's constitution at a time when maintaining the SFRY was EC policy. This fact is reflected in the Commission's composition and the fact that the differences between the Yugoslav parties at this time were constitutional in nature. This being the case it is, in one sense, impossible to evaluate the success or failure of the Commission against its intended function, since political developments outpaced the EC's response to Yugoslavia's constitutional crisis and altered the nature of the questions posed thereby. It is impossible to speculate whether the constitutional expertise of the Commission's members would have allowed them to devise a settlement which could have preserved Yugoslavia and secured the agreement of all Yugoslav republics. In its purest sense, therefore, the Commission failed to fulfill its objectives through no fault of its own. It was ultimately utilised for a task for which it was not created and one with which its members were not experienced. Nevertheless, the decision to retain the Commission, despite the modification of its mandate this entailed, allows a new kind of analysis. The consideration of controversial international legal doctrines, such as self-determination, *uti possidetis*, recognition and State succession, by a panel of lawyers with little experience of the traditional international legal approach to such questions allows one to consider these doctrines from a new perspective. At a time when intra-State problems are becoming the predominant source of international unrest and when many writers are arguing for a new international approach which delves further into the domain of State sovereignty than ever before, the Badinter Commission may be argued to be a microcosm of a much wider debate. Presented with problems which have vexed international legal academics and tribunals for decades, it is unrealistic to expect the Commission to have resolved these issues to the satisfaction of all. The Commission's analysis often differed from that which may have been offered by a Commission composed of international lawyers. One may take this as meaning that the Commission erred in its advice to the ECCY or, alternatively, that such advice offers a fresh and challenging outlook on international legal norms in a world where the dividing lines between internal and international issues are increasingly blurred. Chapter 7 discusses the Commission's early jurisprudence further and argues for the latter interpretation.

Although it is common ground that advisory opinions such as those from the Badinter Commission are non-binding, even when originating from such eminent judicial authorities as the ICJ,[195] such opinions are not necessarily devoid of legal effects and may be used as a way of encouraging development of international law instead of merely describing it.[196] It has, indeed, been said that advisory opinions are often 'nothing else than an unenforceable judgment'.[197] To avoid rhetorical innovations in international law exceeding the realities of international practice, however, one must evaluate how the Commission's opinions were actually treated by the international actors involved. The manner in which the Commission was viewed by the various parties involved in the crisis differed as factual circumstances in Yugoslavia changed over time. Initially, the SFRY federal authorities sought to maximise the Commission's role as a way of shifting attention away from political negotiations within the ECCY. Nevertheless, those same parties later sought to prevent the Commission ruling on issues which followed the Commission's opinions on the dissolution process. The EC Member States initially appeared to pay great attention to the Commission's analysis of the crisis and negotiations following *Opinion 1* were clearly influenced by the Commission's analysis. Nevertheless, the status of the Commission's responses was downgraded when it was realised that the issues involved had become those traditionally dealt with by international law. Whether it was prudent to maintain the Commission in an advisory role, rather than disbanding the Commission and reconstituting it with international legal experts remains open to doubt, especially since the EC blatantly ignored the Commission's findings when recognising Croatia and refusing to recognise Macedonia. Ironically, these opinions involved the Commission in a fact-finding exercise of constitutional law, for which it would be difficult to imagine a more competent panel of experts. It is difficult to believe that the EC could not have foreseen some international legal problems arising, since constitutional negotiations had already broken down between the parties and referenda in favour of independence had been held in Croatia and Slovenia two months before the creation of the ECCY and five months before any questions were referred to the Commission. States outside the EC, such as America and the USSR, also offered support for the Commission, although it is submitted that this may have had more to do with supporting the EC's growing involvement with foreign policy and security issues than the Commission *per se*. Finally, the Commission appeared to receive only partial support from other international institutions, such as the CSCE and UN, who failed to terminate Yugoslavia's membership in accordance with the Commission's recommendations. The FRY considered that the Commission's opinions "...served as a basis for making concrete decisions on relevant issues concerning the Yugoslav crisis".[198] Pomerance also speaks of "...the authoritativeness, *bordering on binding force*, attributed to the Commission's decisions by the EC, its Members and other international organisations [emphasis added]".[199] It is submitted however that the Commission experienced support for its advice only insofar as it conformed with the political agendas of those to whom it was addressed.

In terms of its procedural organisation, a number of difficulties presented themselves. First, the EPC declarations creating the ECCY and the Commission provided barely any information on the way in which the Commission would operate. Where they did provide an explicit description of the Commission's role, such as where the Commission was stated to provide "...decisions..." on the issues presented to it, subsequent practice often deviated from what was specified. Second, although the Commission was required to adopt its own supplementary rules of procedure, having taken account of "...existing organisations in the field...", it is unclear whether this was actually done. Although it is reported that the Commission adopted rules of procedure on 11th September 1991 and 22nd December 1991, none of these were published and no indication is given whether procedures from other organisations have been used and, if so, which procedures were adopted from which organisations. Furthermore, it has proved impossible to obtain such information from the ECCY Secretariat, despite numerous attempts. Many questions remain, therefore, in respect of the role of legal advisors to the Commission, the Rapporteur system used in *Opinions 4-7*, the manner in which judgments were adopted, the ability of Kosovo and Vojvodina to participate in the ECCY and Commission process and other unresolved issues.

The Commission's practice clearly deviated in many respects from what would be expected of an international arbitral tribunal. As traditionally understood, arbitration offers the disputing parties the opportunity to tailor the resolution process to their own demands, albeit resulting in a decision which binds those parties. International arbitration was described in the *1899 Hague Convention for the Pacific Settlement of Disputes* as "...the settlement of differences between States by judges of their own choice and on the basis of respect for law".[200] This reinforces the fact that traditional international arbitration involved legal disputes between States who retained control over the composition of the Commission and whose consent was required to proceed with the arbitration process.[201] Such consent is generally given in the form of a *compromis*. On the first point, nothing approaching the specificity of an arbitral *compromis* was ever agreed between the disputing parties and Serbia's jurisdictional challenges correctly note that control of the Commission remained firmly in the hands of the ECCY rather than the Yugoslav parties. Whilst this initially resulted from a failure of those parties to agree on any appointments to the Commission, it does not explain subsequent diminution of the Yugoslav parties control over the 'arbitration' process. Control over the issues to be considered by the Commission was shifted from the Yugoslav parties and replaced by a procedure which gave greater powers to the ECCY Chairman. Equally, the recipient of the Commission's advice eventually became the ECCY itself or the European Council, rather than the Yugoslav parties. It is also clear that, since the Commission's initial opinions were given at a time before any of the Yugoslav republics were recognised as independent States, this was not a traditional case of inter-State arbitration but more akin to an intra-State process, at least during the early stages of the dissolution process. In the absence of an award directly binding on the disputing parties *per se*, it is difficult to describe the Commission's function as arbitration. The Commission maintained in its Interlocutory Decision that it was an arbitral tribunal which also possessed advisory powers which, as it happened, was the only function it was ever asked to perform. This dual mandate was confirmed when the Commission was reconstituted under the ICFY, discussed in chapter 6. Nevertheless, on no occasion did the Commission come close to performing an arbitral role.[202] It issued no binding awards and the only pronouncement falling into the category of a 'decision' was the Interlocutory Decision of 4th July, which was a procedural rather than a substantive matter. Taken collectively, these features of the Commission mean that it clearly fell short of representing a "...procedure for the settlement of disputes between States by a binding award on the basis of law and as the result of an undertaking voluntarily accepted".[203] It is perhaps more accurate to describe the Commission as a panel of experts who provided advice to a diplomatic conference, albeit experts in a field other than that with which the conference found itself involved.

The rhetoric which surrounded the creation of the Commission exceeded the reality of the Commission's actual functions. Political decisions ensured the retention of the Commission at a time when it should perhaps have been replaced by another organ and resulted in the EC ignoring the Commission's advice on constitutional issues - the only issues it was competent to rule on authoritatively. It is unfortunate that the Commission was not established in its original form at a much earlier time, when debate in Yugoslavia centred around the redrafting of Yugoslavia's constitution and before independence became the sole aim of certain Yugoslav republics. Only then would it be possible to evaluate the Badinter Commission against the mandate it was originally intended to perform.

The idea of international assistance in resolving internal constitutional crises is an interesting one which failed not because of any inherent flaw but because of the timing of the initiative. The jurisprudence of the Commission offers some valuable insights into the way international law may be used by 'constitutionalists' rather than 'internationalists' and the creation of the Commission represented a unique stage in EC foreign affairs and the way in which security threats were handled in the immediate post-Cold War years. It is hoped that ways will be sought to improve the type of international intervention which was attempted in Yugoslavia rather than resorting to the familiar response that internal matters are inappropriate for international intervention. Clearly, 'internationalising' the situation by recognising Croatia and Slovenia did little to prevent the spread of conflict and tensions in the former Yugoslavia and, as a potential avenue for resolving disputes within States, the Badinter Commission offers us some interesting food for thought.

Notes

1 Pellet, A., 'Note sur la Commission d'Arbitrage de la Conférence Européene pour la Paix en Yougoslavie', (1991), 37 *AFDDI*, 329; Craven, M.C.R., 'The European Community Arbitration Commission on Yugoslavia', (1995), 66 *BYIL*, 333, at 409.

2 Schermers, H.G. and Blokker, N.M., (eds.) *International Institutional Law*, (1995), Nijhoff, 18.

3 See for example Bailey, S., *The General Assembly of the United Nations: A Study of Procedure and Practice*, (1960) Clarendon; Rosenne, S., *The World Court: What it is and How it Works - Fifth Edition*, (1994), Nijhoff; McGoldrick, D., *The Practice and Procedure of the Human Rights Committee Under the ICCPR*, (1991), Clarendon; Pogany, I., 'The Role of the President of the UN Security Council', (1982) 31 *ICLQ*, 231; Berthoud, P., 'The United Nations Development Programme, Framework and Procedures', (1970) 4 *JWTL*, 155.

4 See for example Lasok, K.P.E., *The European Court of Justice: Practice and Procedure*, (1984), Nijhoff; Remington, R.A., *The Warsaw Pact - Case Studies in Communist Conflict Resolution*, (1971), Clarendon; Lambrinidis, J.S., *The Structure, Function and Law of a Free-Trade Area*, (1965), Stevens; Dunnett, D.R.R., 'The European Bank for Reconstruction and Development: A Legal Survey', (1991), *CMLRev*, 571; Sveinsson, T.H., 'Activities of the Nordic Council 1990-92', (1993), 36 *GYIL*, 495.

5 See chapter 1, sections 1.2.2. and 1.2.3.

6 See, for example, Chowdhuri, R.N., *International Mandates and Trusteeship System: A Comparative Study*, (1955), Stevens; Campbell, A.I.L., 'The Attitudes and Practices of the Specialised Agencies and the UN Organs and the Interpreting of Their Basic Constitutions', (1986), 2 *JRev*, 177; Shihata, I.F.I., *The European Bank for Reconstruction and Development: A Comparative Analysis of the Constituent Agreement*, (1990), Routledge; Rasmussen, H., *On Law and Policy in the European Court of Justice: A Comparative Study in Judicial Policy-making*, (1986), Nijhoff.

7 Rama-Montaldo, M., 'International Legal Personality and Implied Powers of International Organisations', (1970), *BYIL*, 111, at 145.

8 Schermers, supra n.2, 1192-3. Rama-Montaldo, ibid, 144, refers to this as "...[t]he principle of functional limitation". See also White, N.D., *The Law of International Organisations*, (1996), MUP, 2-7, on functionalism in legal analysis.

9 Chapter 4, section 4.3.6. for the ECCY's part in the peace-efforts in Yugoslavia and the list of participants.

10 EC Bulletin 7/8 (1991), 115-6.

11 Although this "...arbitration procedure..." has been referred to as the Carrington Commission, this writer refers to it as the Badinter Commission, in recognition of the fact that Lord Carrington merely utilised the Commission and did not preside over it. See Weller, M., 'The International Response to the Dissolution of the Socialist Federal Republic of Yugoslavia', (1992), 86 *AJIL* 569, at 596. Cf.

reference to the Arbitration *Committee* in Ragazzi, M., 'Conference on Yugoslavia Arbitration Commission: Introductory Note', (1992), 31 *ILM*, 1488, at 1489. For discussion of whether the procedure was really "...arbitration..." at all, see below, section 5.16 and chapter 6, section 6.11.

12 See chapter 4, section 4.3.5.

13 Shaw, M.N., *International Law*, (1997), CUP, 717. On the importance of negotiations as a means of avoiding or resolving conflicts, see Merrills, J.G., *International Dispute Settlement: Second Edition*, (1991), Grotius, 1-26.

14 See below, section 5.13.

15 The *Statute of the International Court of Justice, Article 34(1)* states that "Only States may be parties in cases before the court".

16 *EC Treaty, Article 164.*

17 *Report of CSCE Experts on Peaceful Settlement of Disputes, Section XII*, reprinted in (1991) 30 *ILM*, 382-95.

18 Ragazzi, supra n.11.

19 Pellet, supra n.1, 331.

20 Craven, supra n.1, 337. For the text of these rules, see *GA Resn. 1262(XI) 1958.* For an example of an inter-State *compromis* between UK-France in 1975, see Merrills, supra n.13, 263.

21 The *Treaty of Ghent* Arbitration, in 1814 specified that, in the event of disagreement over the appointment of arbitrators, a disinterested third party would hold the power of appointment. Note, however, that, in the Yugoslav case-study, the possibility of all arbitrators being appointed by the parties themselves is not envisaged. The *Jay Treaty of Amity, Commerce and Navigation 1794* specified that the UK would appoint one of the three-man arbitration commission, the USA the second man and the third would be appointed by agreement between the arbitrators chosen by the disputing parties. In the event that agreement was not possible, they would "...each propose one person and, of the two names proposed, one [would be] drawn by lot in the presence of the two original Commissioners". For details, see Moore, J.B., *International Adjudication - Volume One*, (1929), OUP, 3. For an example of the problems which may be caused in the absence of such a default-mechanism, see *Interpretation of Peace-Treaties Case*, [1950], ICJ Rep, 3, where the ICJ was faced with the problem of whether to allow the UN Secretary-General to appoint a representative to a Commission when certain of the parties to the Treaties had not yet appointed their own representatives.

22 Merrills, supra n.13, 82-3.

23 Section 5.7.5.

24 Although the House of Lords may be argued to have considerable experience in deciding questions with tremendous constitutional significance, it is nevertheless distinct in character from true constitutional courts such as the French Cour de Cassation or the German Bundesverfassungsgericht. For an example of a case where the House of Lords has resolved a question of constitutional importance, see *R v Secretary of State for Transport, ex parte Factortame*, (1989), 2 CMLR, 46.

25 Cf. the phraseology used within the ICFY. See chapter 6, section 6.3.1.

26 See section 5.7.2.

27 See section 5.4.

28 Etinski, 'Has the SFR of Yugoslavia Ceased to Exist as a Subject of International Law?', (1992), 32 *JRMP*, 4.

29 See chapter 2, section 2.6.

30 Although this phraseology differs from the requirements of *Article 36(2)* of the *Statute of the ICJ*, which requires a "...dispute..." to exist, it is submitted that it accords with the International Court's interpretation of this requirement; namely that such a test is met when there is "...a disagreement over a point of law or fact, a conflict of legal views or interests between two persons". See *Mavrommatis Palestine Concessions Case (Jurisdictional Hearing)*, (1924), PCIJ, Series A, at 11.

31 Schermers, supra n.2, 440.

32 Craven, supra n.1, at 338, n.29.

33 Ibid, 340.

34 Ibid, 340, n.45.

35 Chapter 4, section 4.3.6.

36 Id.

37 Note that Lord Carrington's tenure as ECCY Chairman was not formally announced until an EPC statement of 3rd September, but the statement of 28th August referred to his role as the EC's special-envoy to Yugoslavia, which made him prime candidate for the ECCY Chairmanship. See EC Bulletin 9 (1991), 48 and 63. For discussion of events surrounding Lord Carrington's ECCY Chairmanship, see Owen, D., *Balkan Odyssey,* (1995), Victor-Gollancz, 23-5.

38 Arbitration was defined by the *Hague Convention 1907, Article 37*, as "...the settlement of disputes between States by judges of their own choice and on the basis of respect for law". The International Law Commission also defined arbitration as "...a procedure for settling disputes between States by a binding award on the basis of law and as a result of an undertaking voluntarily accepted". See *Yearbook of the ILC, Volume II*, (1953), 202.

39 Alternatively, reference may be made to an "...award [which is] final and binding upon the parties..." *Hague Convention 1907, Articles 81* and *84*.

40 Merrills, supra n.13, 86. *Article 23* of the Permanent Court of Arbitration's *Optional Rules for Arbitrating between Two States*, reprinted in (1993), 32 *ILM*, 572, states that such a time-limit should "...not exceed ninety days. However, the arbitral tribunal may set longer time-limits, if it concludes that an extension is justifiable".

41 See Pellet, supra n.1, 331.

42 See above, chapter 4, section 4.3.3.

43 See EC Bulletin 9 (1991), 63. Interestingly, in the light of the lack of public information about the Commission's mandate, the mandate of the ECCY Chairman was also not made public.

44 Ibid.

45 One interesting point of speculation is whether the Chairman could have defined the notion of "...relevant authority..." to include Kosovo and Vojvodina. It has

been noted above that these areas were probably excluded from the definition envisaged in the EPC statement of 28th August, but this may not have prevented a creative and expansive definition being provided by Lord Carrington, especially given the creative interpretation adopted by Lord Carrington to his own role in the arbitration proceedings.

46 See section 5.7.1.

47 Pellet, A., 'L'Activité de la Commission d'Arbitrage de la Conférence Européene pour la Paix en Yougoslavie', (1992), 38 *AFDDI*, 220.

48 Merrills, supra n.13, 87.

49 Etinski, supra n.28, 2.

50 Craven, supra n.1, 348, suggests that, in respect of questions relating to Yugoslavia's existence or disappearance, it is difficult to identify the necessary "...organic relationship..." between the remit of the ECCY and the work of the Badinter Commission and that to have pronounced on these issues was "...highly inappropriate..." in the absence of explicit consent from the Yugoslav parties.

51 Many of the ECJ's procedural rules, for example, derived from the earlier rules of the ICJ. See Plender, R. 'Rules of Procedure in the International Court and the European Court', (1992) 3 *EUZW*, 1.

52 See Fox, H., 'States and the Undertaking to Arbitrate', (1988), 37 *ICLQ*, 1.

53 A 'good-offices' mission exists where a third party seeks to redress the severance of diplomatic relations between the disputing parties and to "...bring the parties together so as to make it possible for them to reach an adequate solution *between themselves*...[emphasis added]". Sohn, L.B., *The Future of Dispute Settlement*, (1986), OUP, 1124.

54 A committee of international legal academics was appointed by the Quebec National Assembly to report on the international legal issues surrounding the possible attainment of independence by Quebec. This panel of experts considered issues such as self-determination and uti possidetis and, in this respect, bears some similarity to the Badinter Commission. The existence of a genuine conflict in the Yugoslav scenario, the status of the arbitrators as constitutional experts rather than international legal academics and the judicial capacity in which the Badinter Commission operated, however, serve to distinguish it from this panel of experts. See generally, Joffe, P., *Sovereign Injustice: Forcible Inclusion of the James-Bay Crees and Cree Territory into a Sovereign Quebec*, (1995), Grand Council of the Crees Publication, discussed further in chapter 7.

55 For details on the various EC decision-making processes, see generally Tillotson, J., *European Community Law: Text, Cases and Materials*, (1994), Cavendish, 95-127; Craig, P. and DeBurca, G. (eds.), *EU Law Text, Cases and Materials: Second Edition*, (1998), OUP, 105-63; Bermann, G.A., Goebel, R.J., Davey, W.J. and Fox, E.M. (eds.), *Cases and Materials on European Community Law*, (1993), West, 922-26.

56 Craven, supra n.1, 341.

57 Schermers, supra n.2, 457.

58 See chapter 4, section 4.3.1. Within the normal EC framework, the Commission usually begins the legislative process with a proposal. This would not be the case

under EPC provisions, where the Member States retain greater sovereignty and operate outside the EC's supra-national institutional structures. Equally, whereas the *TEU* requires the European Parliament to be "...consulted..." on the issues under consideration, the *SEA* required Parliament merely to be "...informed..." of those issues and for the Presidency to ensure that such views are taken into consideration. See Bermann, supra n.55, 926.

59 Pellet, supra n.1, 332.

60 See chapter 6, section 6.3.1.

61 Etinski, supra n.28, at 2. Again, it should be noted that this definition of the parties to the dispute contains no reference to the autonomous areas of Kosovo and Vojvodina, although this writer has argued that they had as much at stake as the republics which were allowed representation at the ECCY.

62 For further reading see Khan, R., *The Iran-United States Claims Tribunal*, (1990), Nijhoff; Avanessian, A.B., *The Iran-US Claims Tribunal in Action*, (1993), G&T; Mapp, W., *The Iran-US Claims Tribunal: The First 10 Years. An Assessment of the Tribunal's Jurisprudence and it's Contribution to International Arbitration*, (1993), MUP; Alrdich, G.H., *The Jurisprudence of the Iran-US Claims Tribunal*, (1996), Clarendon.

63 Schermers, supra n.2, 442.

64 For example, *Article 6(2)* of the PCA's *Optional Rules*, supra n.43, allow the Secretary-General of the PCA to designate a default appointing-authority, in the event that the parties themselves are unable to agree on the appointment of the arbitrators. The Secretary-General of the International Centre for the Settlement of Investment Disputes (ICSID) has an equally important role in the appointment of arbitrators. See Parra, A.R., 'ICSID and New Trends in International Dispute Settlement', (1993) 87 *ASIL*, 2; Morera, R., 'The Appointment of Arbitrators by the International Court of Arbitration', (1996), 2 *ICC/ICA Bull*, 32.

65 See above, section 5.2.1.

66 Plender, supra n.51, 5.

67 Tupman, W.M., 'Challenge and Disqualification of Arbitrators in International Commercial Arbitration', (1989), 38 *ICLQ*, 26. Lack of expertise is another common reason, which may also prove relevant in the Badinter Commission's case.

68 Schermers, supra n.2, 458.

69 Id, 458-9.

70 See below, the accusations of Etinski, supra n.28, 2. Bermann, supra n.55, 925, notes that it is not unusual for a Troika such as this to include representatives from one or more of the larger Member States, although this is not inevitable.

71 Cf. Silber, L., and Little, A., *The Death of Yugoslavia*, (1995), Penguin, 220, where the authors state that the Badinter Commission was not appointed until November 1991.

72 The court was created under the *Stockholm Convention on Conciliation and Arbitration 1992*, reprinted at (1993), 4 *EJIL*, 24. Monsieur Badinter became the President of the new court, which became operational in September 1996. For discussion of this French proposal, see Condorelli, L., 'En Attendent la 'Cour de Conciliation et D'arbitrage de la CSCE: Quelques Remarques sur le Droit

Applicable', in Dominicé, C., Patry, R. and Reymond, C. (eds.), *Études de Droit International en L'Honneur de Pierre Lalive*, (1993), RCADI, 457.

73 In his first article on the work of the Commission, Pellet appears to write as an admiring outsider rather than an integral part of the Commission's organisation. Nevertheless, he has managed to amass a great deal of information which this writer has been unable to obtain, despite numerous attempts at contacting the Secretariat of the ECCY, which may indicate that he already had some involvement with the ECCY and Commission process. See generally, Pellet, supra n.1.

74 Schermers, supra n.2, 460.

75 Schermers explains the need for such a separation on the basis that it could prove embarrassing for a court to have to pronounce on the legality of acts of the institution when the secretariat of the same institution also organises the work of the tribunal. This is clearly not the case with the Badinter Commission, which was in no way required to act as a constitutional tribunal within the ECCY itself.

76 Schermers, ibid, lists the UN, ILO, World Bank, IMF and OAS administrative tribunals, as well as the UN human-rights committees.

77 Pellet, supra n.1, 331-2.

78 Ibid, at 332. See also Craven, supra n.1, 336.

79 *GA Resn. 1262 XIII*. Nevertheless, these have not been used very often and one commentator has argued that "...if the Model rules are the highwatermark of legal scholarship in the field of international arbitration, they also represent a point far removed from what the majority of States are willing to apply in settling their disputes". Pinto, M.C.W., 'Thoughts on the 'Essence' of International Arbitration', in Muller, S., and Mijs, W., *The Flame Rekindled - New Hopes for International Arbitration*, (1993), Leiden, 46.

80 See UNGA Resn. 31/98 (1976); *UN Commission on International Trade Law Model Rules of Arbitration*, (1977), UNDPI; Holtzman, H.M. and Neuhaus, J.E. (eds.), *UNCITRAL Model Law on International Commercial Arbitration*, (1989), Kluwer; Hermann, G., 'The UNCITRAL Model Law: Its Background, Salient Featues and Purposes', (1985), 1 *ArbInt.*

81 See (1993), 32 *ILM*, 572; *Permanent Court of Arbitration: The First Conference of the Members of the Court*, (1994), IBPCA.

82 Schermers, supra n.2, 440.

83 Pellet, supra n.1, 332.

84 The Iran-USA Reparations Commission, for example, is charged with applying "...such choice of law rules and principles of commercial and international law as the Tribunal determines to be applicable". See supra n.62, for details. Judge Ruda, who is President of this Tribunal, later became a member of the reconstituted Badinter Commission. See chapter 6, section 6.3.1.

85 Craven, supra n.1, at 340, n.44. See also Pomerance, M., 'The Badinter Commission: The Use and Misuse of the International Court of Justice's Jurisprudence', (1998), 20 *MichJIL*, at 33.

86 Chapter 4, section 4.3.2.

87 Ibid, section 4.3.6.

88 See EPC statement 5th October 1991, cited in EC Bulletin 10 (1991), 86.

89 Chapter 3, section 3.5.1.

90 Chapter 4, section 4.3.8.

91 See EC-Bulletin 10 (1991), 86.

92 Chapter 4, section 4.3.6.

93 See chapter 6, section 6.3.1.

94 Craven, supra n.1, 409.

95 See chapter 4, sections 4.3.4.-4.3.7.

96 Pellet, supra n.1, 333.

97 Despite this writer having requested this information from the Secretariat of the ECCY, no information has been forthcoming.

98 President Milosevic's address to the ECCY, 18th October 1991, after having rejected the Carrington Plan. Quoted in Trifunovska, S. (ed.), *Yugoslavia Through Documents: From its Creation to its Dissolution*, (1994), Nijhoff, 363-5.

99 Kostic, B., 'FRY Position on the European Communities Conference on Yugoslavia', (1991), 42 *RIA*, 14.

100 Etinski, supra n.28, 3.

101 Parry, C. *et al* (eds.), *Encyclopaedic Dictionary of International Law*, (1986), Oceana, 98.

102 See section 5.14.2. on *Opinion 9* and chapter 6 on *Opinions 11-15*, dealing with succession issues.

103 *Opinion 1*, cited in 31 *ILM* (1992), 1494, and discussed in section 5.7.7. below and chapter 7, section 7.4.

104 Pellet, supra n.1, 333.

105 Etinski, supra n.28, 2.

106 See section 5.13.

107 Pellet, supra n.1, 332.

108 Pellet, supra n.1, at 333, notes that although the written procedure of the 3rd September implies that only the Chairman of the ECCY could submit something to the Commission, the practice was orientated in a totally different manner - "...une direction assez différents...". He fails to embellish on this, however, and it remains uncertain whether the Commission received these documents directly or via Lord Carrington.

109 See Plender, supra n.51, at 19-23.

110 The ICSID tribunal, for example, deals with cases between individuals and companies against States. See *ICSID Basic Documents*, ICSID Publications, 34.

111 Schermers, supra n.2, 464. An analogy may be made with requests from the General Assembly and World Health Assembly for advisory opinions from the ICJ on the legality of the threat or use of nuclear weapons. See *Advisory Opinion on the Legality of the Threat or Use of Nuclear Weapons*, (1996), ICJ Rep.,1.

112 See below, section 5.13.

113 See, for example, the PCIJ's refusal to offer an Advisory Opinion on a dispute between Finland and Russia in the *Eastern Carelia Case*, [1923], PCIJ Series B, 28-9.

114 Frowein, J.A., 'Self-Determination as a Limit to Obligations in International Law', in Tomuschat, C. (ed.), *Modern Law of Self-Determination*, (1993), Nijhoff, 211, at 216.

115 See chapter 6, section 6.7.

116 Pellet, supra n.1, 332.

117 See chapter 6, section 6.4.

118 Dickson, B., *Introduction to French Law*, (1994), Pitmans, 11-12.

119 *Statute of the Court of Justice of the European Communities, Article 32.*

120 Hambro, E., 'The Authority of the Advisory Opinions of the International Court of Justice', (1954) 3 *ICLQ*, 2, at 20; Schermers, supra n.2, 466, notes that separate judgments tend to "…undermine the persuasive force of judgments...and weaken the solidarity…[of a judicial organ]".

121 In doing so, the Commission distanced itself from the position adopted by Croatia in its Assembly decisions of 8th October 1991, wherein the disappearance of the SFRY appears to be taken as a political truism and is referred to as "…the *hitherto* federation of the SFRY…". Cited in Etinski, supra n.28, at 2, n.9.

122 See chapter 4, section 4.3.8.

123 *Opinion 3*, paragraph 1, reprinted in (1992), 31 *ILM*, 1499.

124 Etinski, supra n.28, 2.

125 Ibid, 31.

126 See chapter 4, section 4.3.8.

127 The position of the Bosnian republic, which closely reflected that of Macedonia, is evident from the Platform of the Bosnian Assembly of 14th October 1991, which is referred to in *Opinion 4*, paragraph 2, reprinted in (1992), 31 *ILM*, 1502. The conditions upon which Bosnia was prepared to remain within a united SFRY were that:

"(i) the new Community must include Serbia and Croatia at least; and

(ii) a convention must be signed at the same time recognising the sovereignty of the SRBH within its present borders…".

128 See above, section 5.7.1.

129 The *Vienna Convention on the Law of Treaties, Article 53,* defines such a right as "…a peremptory norm of international law…a norm accepted and recognised by the international community of States as a whole as a norm from which no derogation is permitted and which can be modified only by a subsequent norm of general international law having the same character". See also *Article 64*. See also Jennings, R., and Watts, A., *Oppenheim's International Law: Ninth Edition Volume I*, (1992), Longmans, 4-7; Weisburd, M., 'The Emptiness of the Concept of Jus Cogens as Illustrated by the War in Bosnia-Hercegovina', (1995), 17 *MichJIL*, 1.

130 The *International Convention on Civil and Political Rights* (ICCPR) and the *International Convention on Economic, Social and Cultural Rights* (ICESCR) both include the same opening article which states that "All peoples have the right to self-determination. By virtue of that right, they freely determine their political status and freely pursue their economic, social and cultural development".

131 [1986] ICJ Rep, 554, at 565.

132 See chapter 1, section 1.2.3. for references to *GA Resn. 2625 (XXV)*.

133 Pellet, supra n.1, 340, speaks of "...une dissociation très remarquable entre la nationalité et la territorialité...". EU citizenship, is, however founded on the nationality of a Member State to the EU. See Closa, C., 'The Concept of Citizenship in the Treaty on European Union', (1992) *CMLRev*, 137.

134 See for example *Opinion 4*, paragraph 1, reprinted in (1992), 31 *ILM*, 1501.

135 Pellet, supra n.1, 335.

136 *Opinion 4*, paragraph 2. See Trifunovska, supra n.98, 290 *et seq*, for texts of the various republican constitutions.

137 This interpretation is confirmed in *Opinion 4*, paragraph 4, where reference is made to the new Constitution being framed by the SRBH and the commitment of the SRBH authorities to ensure that this instrument would "...provide full guarantees for individual human rights and freedoms".

138 Pellet, supra n.1, 332.

139 In *Opinion 5* and *7*, the Commission considered statements of the Croatian Parliament and Presidency and the Slovenian Assembly.

140 Pellet, supra n.47, 227. Cf. however, the same writer's agreement with the Commission's *Interlocutory Decision*, discussed in section 5.13., where it stated that it would take "...conclusive reasons..." for it to refuse to participate in the provision of legal advice when asked to do so by the ECCY. Presumably, this difference is explained by the fact that Pellet would have considered such conclusive reasons to have existed as a result of the politically sensitive nature of these recognition applications. Cf. the practice of the ICJ, which has stated that, in principle, it should not refuse a request to give advice, unless "...compelling reasons..." exist. *Interpretation of Peace Treaties Case with Bulgaria, Hungary and Romania [First Phase]*, [1950], ICJ Rep, at 72; *Western Sahara Case*, [1975], ICJ Rep, at 21.

141 Cf. Pellet, supra n.1, 335.

142 All of the opinions state simply that the questionnaires were "...sent to the Republics concerned on 24th December..." without any indication of who exactly forwarded them.

143 *Opinion 7*, paragraph 1, reprinted at (1992) 31 *ILM*, 1513, cites Slovenia's figures of an 88.5% vote in favour of independence and 4% against.

144 *Opinion 4*, paragraph 4.

145 See Dickson, supra n.119, 19-20.

146 Pellet, supra n.1, 332, notes that although the Commission made provision for elected delegates to visit the places concerned in order to ascertain a more objective opinion of the situations under consideration, this was never used. Similarly, he notes that the Commission refused a request for a hearing by one of the parties, without providing details of the nature of the requested hearing or the requesting party. This would tend to indicate that the Rapporteur's duties were other than suggested above.

147 See chapter 4, sections 4.3.7.-4.3.8.

148 See Section 5.9.5.

149 See chapter 2, section 2.6.3.

150 *Article 2(c)* stated that areas in which persons belonging to a national or ethnic group form a majority would enjoy 'special status' which allowed such areas to, "...have and show the national emblems of that group; the right to a second nationality...in addition to the nationality of the republic; an education system which respects the values and needs of that group; a legislative body; an administrative structure, including a regional police force; [and] a judiciary responsible for matters concerning the area which reflects the composition of the population of that area". See Trifunovska, supra n.98, 359.

151 See supra n.143.

152 *EC Presidency Statement on the Recognition of Certain Yugoslav Republics*, reprinted in Trifunovska, supra n.98, 501.

153 See McGoldrick, D., 'Yugoslavia: The Responses of the International Community and of International Law', (1996), 49 *CLP*, 375, at 382-3.

154 Buchan, D., *Europe: The Strange Superpower*, (1993), Dartmouth, 80.

155 Schreur, C.H., 'Recommendations and the Traditional Sources of International Law', (1977), *GYIL*, 103, at 118. See also Hambro, supra n.120.

156 See above, section 5.4.1.

157 See below sections 5.14.1-5.14.3.

158 *Yugoslav Federal-Presidency Position, 18th December 1991*, reprinted in Trifunovska, supra n.98, 475-8.

159 Ibid, 481-5.

160 See above, section 5.9.2.

161 Trifunovska, supra n.98, 482.

162 The withdrawal of American participation in the *Nicaragua v USA Case* evidences this point perfectly. See also Joffe, supra n.54, 239; Schermers, supra n.2, 467.

163 Higgins, R., *Problems and Process*, (1995), Clarendon, 186.

164 Reprinted in (1992) 31 *ILM*, 1506.

165 Chapter 6, section 6.4.

166 Pellet, supra n.47, 220.

167 Reprinted in (1992) 31 *ILM*, 1518.

168 Pellet, supra n.47, 224.

169 Park, W.W., 'Kompetenz-Kompetenz', (1996), 12(2) *ArbInt*, 137. In the *Tadic Case,* the ICTY received a jurisdictional challenge and concluded that it was competent to decide its own competence. For the text of this, see (1996) 35 *ILM*, at 32 *et seq*. See also Rowe, P., 'The International Criminal Tribunal for Yugoslavia: The Decision of the Appeals Chamber on the Interlocutory Appeal on Jurisdiction in the Tadic Case', (1996) 45 *ICLQ*, 691. *Article 19* of the *Statute of the Permanent International Criminal Court* provides that the court shall "...satisfy itself that it has jurisdiction in any case brought before it...".

170 ICJ Rep, [1991], 70.

171 ICJ Rep, [1953], 119.

172 Simpson, J.L. and Fox, H., *International Arbitration: Law and Practice*, (1959), Stevens, 68-75; Fachiri, A., *The Permanent Court of International Justice: Its Constitution, Procedure and Work*, (1925), OUP, 85; Schermers, supra n.2, 149.

The PCIJ, in the *Interpretation of Greco-Turkish Agreement of December 1st 1926 Case*, (1928), PCIJ Rep., Series B, at 20, stated that "...as a general rule, any body possessing jurisdictional powers has the right in the first place itself to determine the extent of its own jurisdiction...". Cf., however, *Hague Convention 1907, Article 73*, which states that an arbitral tribunal may interpret its own competence "...by interpreting the *compromis*". To the extent that no such *compromis* existed, the Commission's case is different to what would normally occur in international practice.

173 Pellet, supra n.47, 223. Cf. Pomerance, supra n.85.

174 See above, section 5.3.1.

175 Section 6.3.

176 "...raisons décisives...". Cf. the ICJ's reference to "...compelling reasons..." for refusing to answer a question referred for an Advisory Opinion, supra n.139.

177 Schermers, supra n.2, 463, notes that it is a general principle of law that judicial organs may decide on their own jurisdiction, and cites *Article 36(6)* of the *Statute of the International Court of Justice*, *Article 2(3)* of the *Statute of the UN Administrative Tribunal* and *Article 2(6)* of the *Statute of the International Labour Organisation Administrative Tribunal*, in support of this assertion.

178 In the *Eastern Carelia Case*, supra n.113, at 27, the PCIJ stated that "...no State can, without its consent, be compelled to submit its disputes with other States either to mediation, or to arbitration, or to any other kind of pacific settlement".

179 In the *Peace Treaties Case*, supra n.140, at 65, the ICJ said that "The situation [regarding consent] is different in regard to advisory proceedings even where the request for an Advisory Opinion relates to a legal question actually pending between States. The Court's reply is only of an advisory character...It follows that no State...can prevent the giving of an Advisory Opinion...".

180 See for example the *Western Sahara Case*, supra n.144, 12.

181 See above, section 5.7.1.

182 See, for example, the *Fisheries (Jurisdiction) Case* [1973], ICJ Rep, 3.

183 Ibid, at 21.

184 *Article 62* of the *Vienna Convention of the Law of Treaties 1969*, which "...in many respects..." codifies customary law on this issue. Ibid, at 18.

185 The Commission, in announcing its interlocutory findings, "...decided..." that it possessed the competence in question. This may be contrasted with *Opinions 1-3* where the Commission expressed its "...opinion..." or "...view...". Whereas, under fact-finding mandate involved in *Opinions 4-7*, the Commission fell short of offering any explicit decision on the question of recognition, which was to be taken ultimately by the EC Council, it nevertheless maintained its preference for expressing an opinion or a view, and in *Opinions 8-10*, discussed below, the same is true.

186 Cf. the Commission's 'Reactions' to the second jurisdictional challenge in chapter 6, section 6.7.

187 Although the Commission took note of papers from Bosnia, Croatia, Slovenia, Macedonia, Montenegro and Serbia, it is likely that the reference to papers referred to by these last two republics are limited to those supporting the

challenge to the Commission's jurisdiction and not as to the substantive issues considered thereafter. Indeed, it would be most unusual for these republics to have challenged the Commission's jurisdiction and then to have referred papers to the Commission in the event that it rejected such a challenge.

188 Reprinted at (1991) 31 *ILM*, 1523.

189 This contrasted with the position of Russia, which continued the USSR's legal personality in the UN Security Council. A number of factors have been cited to differentiate between the cases of the FRY and Russia, including the incomparable proportions of territory, populations, resources and armed forces maintained by each State. The most obvious legal difference, however, would appear to be that those States arising from the dissolution of the USSR consented to Russia's assumption of the USSR Security Council seat, in contrast to the resistance encountered by the FRY's claim to continue Yugoslavia's legal personality. Legal advisers to the US State Department recalled that the American decision to differentiate between the two cases were based on the idea that the alternative was "...politically unpalatable - the US was no more inclined to bless Serbia-Montenegro as the legitimate heir to the SFRY than it was to allow Croatia to abandon existing treaty obligations". See Williamson, E.D. and Osborn, J.E., 'A US Perspective on Treaty Succession and Related Issues in the Wake of the Breakup of the USSR and Yugoslavia', (1993) 33 *VJIL*, 261, at 270. The authors also cited *Opinion 9* in support of this view. See also Blum, Y., 'Russia Takes Over Soviet Union's Seat at the UN', (1992), 3 *EJIL*, 254; Blum, Y., 'UN Membership of the 'New' Yugoslavia: Continuity or Break?', (1992), 86 *AJIL*, 830; Scharf, M., 'Musical Chairs: The Dissolution of States and Membership in the UN', (1995), 28 *Cornell JIL*, 29; Mullerson, R., 'The Continuity and Succession of States by Reference to the Former USSR and Yugoslavia', (1993), 42 *ICLQ*, 473.

190 Within the ICFY, a special group for Kosovo was created within the Working Group on Ethnic and National Communities and Minorities. See chapter 6, section 6.2.

191 *Opinion 9*, paragraph 4, reprinted in (1992), 31 *ILM*, 1525.

192 See above, sections 5.10.8.-5.10.11.

193 Ragazzi, supra n.11, 1490.

194 See chapter 4, sections 4.4.5. and 4.5.15.

195 See Hambro, supra n.120, 5.

196 Higgins, supra n.163, 25-28. See also White, supra n.8, 92-7.

197 Judge Zoricic in his dissenting opinion in the *Peace Treaties Case*, supra n.140, at 101.

198 Letter from FRY's Deputy Prime Minister and Foreign-Affairs Minister to ICFY Chairmen, 2nd July 1993, reprinted in (1993), 32 *ILM*, 1584.

199 Supra n.85, at 48.

200 *Article XV*.

201 Dixon, M. and McCorquodale, R. (eds.), *Cases and Materials on International Law*, (1995), Blackstones, 605, describe arbitration as "...a device for leaving

the settlement of disputes as much in the hands of the parties as possible". See also *Eastern Carelia Case*, supra n.113, 34.

202 Shaw, supra n.13, 743-4.

203 ILC Offical Records of the General Assembly, 8th Session, Supplement No.9, paragraph 16, reprinted in Simpson, supra n.172, 1.

6 The Badinter Commission under the International Conference on the Former Yugoslavia

6.1 Introduction

This chapter examines the Badinter Commission's role under the International Conference on the Former Yugoslavia (ICFY), which superseded the ECCY. The methodology adopted is accordingly similar to that of chapter 5. A brief description of the ICFY will be followed by key events involving the Commission during the lifetime of the conference. The Commission delivered five opinions under the auspices of the ICFY and, although the contents of such opinions cannot be ignored, it must be remembered that this book is limited to consideration of the Commission's role in relation to the *dissolution* of Yugoslavia. Since the dissolution process was acknowledged as having come to an end during the lifetime of the ECCY, opinions under the ICFY relating to succession issues *after* Yugoslavia's dissolution are of marginal relevance to the dissolution process *per* se. *Opinions 11-15* also lack the doctrinal depth and width of *Opinions 1-10* but a brief analysis of these opinions helps to provide a more holistic appreciation of the Commission's role in the peace process as a whole.

Chapter 5 argued that the Commission never performed the function for which it was initially created and that this posed a number of problems in terms of its procedural organisation and its jurisprudence. This chapter suggests that the Commission's intended function was far clearer by the time the ICFY supplanted the ECCY and this allowed a number of procedural ambiguities to be redressed. In many ways, the Commission had already undergone its most testing period because its members, composed solely of constitutional law experts, had provided a series of opinions on difficult international legal issues and outlived the ECCY process itself, despite the FRY's jurisdictional challenge and a half-hearted support of the

Commission's jurisprudence from the conference's founders. By the time the ICFY peace process began, the Commission was clearly aware that it would be considering questions of international law, it had already asserted its dual mandate which allowed it to provide advisory opinions as well as ruling on contentious issues, it had already performed a unique role in offering legal advice contemporaneously to the dissolution of a sovereign State - this task being even more perplexing during the period of legal uncertainty which accompanied the New World Order - and it had remedied its rudimentary written procedural mandate by developing new rules of procedure as problems presented themselves. In this respect, the developing procedural organisation of the Commission under the ICFY owes much to its experiences under the ECCY.

6.2 The London Conference and the ICFY

With the Bosnian conflict spiraling out of control during the later stages of the ECCY, a new initiative was announced by the UK's EC representative. Having assumed the EC Presidency from the Dutch in December 1991, the UK felt that the peace process required intensification and, more specifically, a greater coordination of policy between the EC and UN. Clearly, the EC's attempts to resolve the Yugoslav crisis single-handedly had been unsuccessful and it was felt that the UN's political authority and experience in dispute resolution would benefit the peace process. Accordingly the UK's incumbent Prime Minister, John Major, announced the creation of the London Conference, held from the 26th to 28th August 1992. The London Conference represented "...the first time that the UN's and EC's efforts have been so closely coordinated..."[1] and the ICFY, the most important creation of the London Conference, was said to be "...a complete joint effort by the UN and the EC".[2]

Having felt betrayed by the EC's decision to recognise Slovenia and Croatia in the absence of an overall political settlement,[3] Lord Carrington had retired as ECCY Chairman and the UK recommended Lord David Owen to represent the EC at the ICFY. Despite initial French complaints that Owen's comments on the Yugoslav crisis had shown him to be anti-Serb and incapable of operating effectively as mediator, his candidature was accepted and he was appointed to work alongside Cyrus Vance, the UN Secretary-General's representative, as Co-Chairman of the ICFY's Steering

Committee.[4]

The London Conference was structured on the basis of a set of rules of procedure which discussed *inter alia* the participants, the procedural mandate of the conference's permanent Co-Chairmen,[5] the role of the conference's secretariat, the manner of recording the results of the conference, the procedural organisation of meetings to be held and the possible creation of task forces for discussion of specific issues.[6] It is interesting to compare the extent to which procedures were pre-established and readily identifiable for this conference with the way in which the Badinter Commission's *ad hoc* procedural developments occurred under the ECCY. The conference adopted a statement of principles emphasising the need for all parties to cease hostilities and to negotiate a political settlement on the basis of certain stated principles. Amongst those principles was an obligation relating to "...implementation of constitutional guarantees of the human rights and fundamental freedoms of persons belonging to ethnic and national communities and minorities, the promotion of tolerance and the right to self-determination in accordance with the commitments entered into under the CSCE and in the ECCY".[7] It has been suggested above[8] that the Badinter Commission was originally intended to assist in the redrafting of Yugoslavia's constitution as a way of seeking a resolution of the crisis within existing borders. It is clear that this policy is still being pursued to prevent further fragmentation amongst Yugoslavia's successor States. Another principle by which all negotiations were to be conducted was that all participants were required to "...respect the inviolability of *all frontiers*...[emphasis added]". This is in accordance with earlier EC declarations on Yugoslavia and appears to endorse the Commission's opinion on *uti possidetis*.[9] Equally, the requirement to settle State succession issues by "...consensus or arbitration..." and the duty to share equitably Yugoslavia's assets and responsibilities endorse the Commission's ECCY jurisprudence.[10] A number of other documents were produced during the London Conference, dealing with more specific aspects of the Yugoslav conflict.[11]

The multilateral and inclusive approach adopted in the ICFY process is evident from the creation of the 31-nation Steering Committee including members of the EC and CSCE Troikas which had already been involved in the crisis, representatives of the permanent members of the UN Security Council,[12] a representative from the Organisation of the Islamic Conference (OIC), two representatives from States neighbouring the former

Yugoslavia[13] and Lord Carrington. Such wide-scale participation meant that the ICFY could truly be described as "...an innovative exercise...".[14] In addition to the Steering Committee, six Working Groups were created, each with their own Chairman and membership, to ensure intense discussions on specific policy issues and prevent non-cooperation on one issue stalling negotiations on other issues. Thus, Working Groups were created on Bosnia-Hercegovina,[15] Humanitarian Issues,[16] Ethnic and National Communities and Minorities,[17] Succession Issues,[18] Economic Issues[19] and Confidence and Security-Building and Verification Measures.[20] It was decided at the first meeting of the Steering Committee that each Working Group should be allowed to develop its own rules of procedure and mode of operation and that flexibility of approach would benefit the negotiations process. The ICFY was to be based in Geneva and, as a reflection of the intensified nature of the peace process, it was to sit in continuous session, in contrast to the ECCY which sat on discrete occasions when deemed necessary.

6.3 The Commission's Role within the ICFY

The London Conference's Work Programme made only brief reference to the Badinter Commission, stating that the ICFY would "...seek the continued assistance of the Arbitration Commission". This cursory statement raises far more questions than it answers, as is often the case with materials dealing with the Commission. Although it is clear that the Commission is to be retained in some capacity, in light of the jurisdictional challenge received by the Commission during its time within the ECCY,[21] it is unclear whether the "...assistance..." sought by the ICFY is in the form of advisory opinions similar to those given under the ECCY or as an arbitral tribunal *per se*, for the resolution of disputes between the Yugoslav parties. Whilst the Work Programme refers to the "...*Arbitration* Commission...[emphasis added]" it is likely that this is merely a reference to the name given to that organ under various ECCY documents and not in any way determinative of the functions the Commission performed during that conference. The decision to retain the Commission may be argued to be an endorsement of its earlier jurisprudence. Alternatively, hidden political factors may have influenced this decision, as it was suggested they influenced the EC's decision to retain the Commission even at the point when its envisaged role could not be performed. Having declared the ICFY's intention to "...build on the work already done by the [ECCY]..."[22] it would have been a glaring omission to exclude the Commission from the ICFY and one which could have been interpreted as an implicit criticism of the EC's attempts at dispute resolution.

Having announced the decision to retain the Commission, the Steering Committee Co-Chairmen (SCCC) soon attempted to modify the Commission for its role in the ICFY. On 27th January 1993, the SCCC published a revised set of procedures for the Commission, based on proposals they had made on 27th October 1992.[23] Cyrus Vance had already met with Monsieur Badinter on 18th September and it is likely that discussion began during this meeting on the Commission's role within the ICFY.[24] These new rules dealt with two main areas - the Commission's composition and its competence and legal nature. These will be examined in turn.

6.3.1 *Composition*

The new Terms of Reference noted that the Commission would be composed of:

"(a) Three Members designated by the Council of Ministers of the EC from among incumbent Presidents of Constitutional Courts existing in Member States of the EC or from among members of the highest courts in those States, it being understood that for the present these members are those from France, Germany and Italy;
(b) One member designated by the President of the ICJ from among the former members of the Court or persons possessing the qualifications required by *Article 2* of the Statute of the Court;
(c) One member of the European Court of Human Rights, designated by the President of the Court".

In accordance with general international practice, no two members of the Commission were to hold the same nationality, and each member was to serve on the Commission "...as long as he or she holds the office on the basis of which the designation was made". The Terms of Reference also made provision for the appointment of *ad hoc* members in certain circumstances, discussed further below.

These provisions raise a number of issues but, in light of the secrecy surrounding the motives behind many of the procedural changes during the transition from the ECCY to the ICFY, much of this analysis is speculative.

The first question is why the Commission's composition was altered at all. This answer falls to be deduced from the changes actually made, which essentially replaced two constitutional-court judges with a former judge, or potential judge, of the ICJ and an incumbent judge of the European Court of Human Rights. Clearly, the aim appeared to be to increase the Commission's competence and experience in questions of international law and human rights *per se*, rather than as an adjunct of the constitutional expertise Commission's original members. Given that the nature of questions had changed from constitutional to international ones during the ECCY and that this was confirmed by the recognition of a majority of those former Yugoslav republics and an acknowledgment that, even in the absence of recognition, the FRY was a State which fulfilled traditional international legal criteria for Statehood, this must have influenced the decision to reconstitute the Commission.[25] In conversations with this writer at an international legal conference on Yugoslavia in July 1996,[26] Professors Christopher Greenwood and John Dugard both expressed reservations about the Commission which may epitomise the feeling behind the need to alter its composition. Greenwood considered that the Commission's opinions were not a shining light of international legal jurisprudence and Dugard lamented simply that he wished Badinter had known more international law. Frowein has written that he is "...not convinced that the whole [Badinter Commission] system will add credibility to international dispute settlement in critical cases..." and Pomerance considers that the "...long-range results of the Commission's application of ICJ law could more plausibly harm than facilitate the goal of having self-determination questions adjudicated in judicial and quasi-judicial fora".[27] It appears that some force lay behind the feeling that the Commission's original composition was insufficient for dealing with the issues which fell to be decided by it.

The next question is why any of the original arbitrators were retained if the aim was to increase the Commission's experience in international legal matters. Although the Belgian and Spanish judges were removed from the Commission after January 1993, those from France, Germany and Italy remained.[28] First, one may note that, despite the criticisms mentioned above, other commentators have considered *Opinions 1-10* to have been innovative and interesting rather than illegitimate and uninformed.[29] Second, political factors may have encouraged the EC-UN representatives to refrain from appearing to capitulate to the FRY's demands to see the Commission's work draw to an end. By maintaining some of the original arbitrators, and in particular the President whose name had become synonymous with the Commission, the ICFY gave the impression that the Commission enjoyed a level of continuity and evolution rather than a completely new beginning. Third, this allowed the Commission's new members to be aware of the approaches of the various Yugoslav parties during the ECCY and the ways in which they had participated with the Commission and the peace process as a whole up to this point in time. One must then consider how the new composition balanced the conflicting demands for consistency and greater international legal experience. One approach may have been to maintain the current five-man composition and simply add additional members with greater international law experience. The obvious problem with this, however, is the fact that decision-making processes generally become more difficult as the numbers involved expand. Accordingly, the preferred approach was to retain the five-man composition whilst substituting two constitutional judges for international law judges. This still leaves the original members of the Commission in a majority and, in the event that decision-making was to be taken on a majority basis, this may have been significant.[30] It is likely that the two original members who were replaced were not removed because of any inability to perform the task of arbitrator or advisor within the Commission but rather as a reflection of their initial mode of appointment.

The Belgian and Spanish judges were appointed after the other three arbitrators, and indeed by the other arbitrators, in default of any nominations from the Yugoslav parties. The ICFY may have been influenced to retain the original three members because they were appointed by the EC itself and, since their role in the ICFY was to act as the Commission's EC-appointed representatives, preference should be given to these members. Alternatively, the expiry of national judicial mandates of the Belgian and Spanish representatives has been suggested to be the primary reason.[31] It is interesting that the criteria specified for the EC-appointed members has now changed to the extent that it no longer requires incumbent residents of EC Member States constitutional Courts and now extends to "…members of the highest courts in those [EC] States…" Accordingly, the Commission could now include representatives from States without constitutional courts, such as the UK,[32] although given that the appointments were specified to have been made in favour of the French, German and Italian members, this appears little more than a cosmetic change.

The next question relates to the manner in which the new members were chosen. The rules specified that one of these appointees must be a former member of the ICJ or a person who possesses the qualifications to have been such a member. Such qualifications are contained in *Article 2* of the *Statute of the ICJ*, which requires ICJ members to be "...independent judges, elected regardless of their nationality from among persons of high moral character, who possess the qualifications required in their respective countries for appointment to the highest judicial offices, or are jurisconsults of recognised competence in international law". In practice, consideration of these requirements did not come into play since Jose Maria Ruda, Argentina's former ICJ-President, was appointed. Judge Ruda is also President of the Iran-USA Arbitration Claims Tribunal and the ILO Administrative Tribunal. With the apparent aim being to increase the Commission's international legal expertise, one could not imagine a more suitable candidate. More interesting, perhaps, is the second non-EC representative, who was to be designated by the President of the European Court of Human Rights from amongst the court's incumbent members. The intention here cannot have been to increase the Commission's experience of international law *per se*, since the essence of the ECHR's work is to assess the compatibility of States domestic laws with the *European Convention on Human Rights*. Even in the event of an inter-State case, which are far fewer than cases taken by individuals against their own State, the issue remains essentially constitutional rather than international.[33] Nevertheless, such an appointment would provide the Commission with expertise on human rights and the ways in which civil and political rights may be protected in various States. In this sense, the ECHR member brings a comparative analysis to the Commission's work which may remedy some of the problems caused by the original Commission's lack of knowledge of the Yugoslav constitution or eastern-European approaches to constitutional issues. The European Court's Swedish member, Elizabeth Palm, was chosen as the final member of the newly-composed Commission.

In theory at least the Commission could now call upon a vast array of experience from different areas of law which may influence the issues to be faced during the post-dissolution phase of the peace process. Constitutional issues remained to be addressed in the case of the FRY, which had still not applied for EC recognition, human rights issues fell to be decided within a number of the successor States and international law issues would impact on the process of State succession.

The final noteworthy aspect of the Commission's new composition is the provision made for the appointment of an *ad hoc* member by any of the "...contending parties..." under the Commission's contentious proceedings. Clearly, this was intended to redress the imbalance caused by having removed the Yugoslav parties ability to select two members of the Commission's original composition. It also brings the Commission into line with established international practice regarding arbitration proceedings.[34] What is undefined, however, is whether it is possible for there to be more than two "...contending parties..." so that the Commission may be influenced by the inclusion of numerous State appointed arbitrators. Given that each of the questions considered in *Opinions 1-10* prompted a response from each of the six republics, and the Bosnian-Serb Assembly, it may have been possible for a similar situation to arise under the ICFY's contentious proceedings and for the State-appointed arbitrators to outvote the Commission's permanent members. In reality, however, the Commission's contentious proceedings were never utilised and accordingly no *ad hoc* members were ever appointed.

6.3.2 *Terms of Reference*

Many of the procedural rules adopted during the ICFY conform to the Commission's practice under the ECCY. Nevertheless, the ICFY generally provided clear written conformation of the procedures involved and did not rely on deductive analysis from the Commission's practice alone.

The Terms of Reference highlighted the continuing legitimacy of the Commission's arbitral role in contentious proceedings whilst also acknowledging its advisory role, thereby legitimising the dual mandate proclaimed in the earlier *Interlocutory Decision*.[35] The Commission was declared competent to:

> "(a) Decide, with binding force for the parties concerned, any dispute submitted to it by the parties thereto upon authorisation by the...[SCCC];
> (b) Give its advice as to any legal question submitted to it by the...[SCCC]."

Disputing parties could appoint *ad hoc* members during contentious proceedings and such appointees must either be former ICJ members, or possess the requisite qualities for such membership, or current members of the ECHR. A new source from which disputing parties could appoint *ad hoc* arbitrators was also included. Appointments could be made from incumbent members of the constitutional or highest court of any of the CSCE's Member States, thus allowing the disputing parties to opt for members outside the EC States. This was probably intended to remedy the fears of certain republics that the EC agenda was inherently biased against their position. For proceedings of an advisory nature there existed no such provision for *ad hoc* members because the Commission's opinions would act merely as advice for the ICFY and would not *stricto sensu* bind the former Yugoslav parties. Nevertheless, given that the advice would probably dictate much of the approach of negotiations within the ICFY and that the parties risked sanctions or other penalties for failing to cooperate in these negotiations, it may be argued that the parties were bound indirectly by advisory opinions. In some cases the ICJ has allowed States to nominate *ad hoc* judges even on advisory opinions, where it felt that the State had a sufficiently direct interest in the issue,[36] but the Commission's procedure clearly prevents such a possibility in the absence of an extremely creative interpretation.

6.4 The Commission's Procedural Rules of April 1993

The SCCC's new Terms of Reference for the Commission concluded by stating that the Commission would establish its own rules of procedure. This again followed the practice adopted under the ECCY but, on this occasion, the adopted rules were published in a written constitutional form on 26th April 1993. This indicates that the Commission not only reviewed its ECCY-practice in keeping its procedures secret and developing them as the need arose but also that the Commission took almost three months to adopt its new procedural mandate. The lengthier deliberations preceding the adoption of these procedures, in comparison with the speedy adoption of the Commission's ECCY procedures, may have been caused by greater heterogeneity in the Commission's membership under the ICFY or simply by the Commission's desire to redress some of the procedural uncertainties marking its tenure under the ECCY. These new procedures sought to address questions pre-emptively and addressed various procedural difficulties in discrete sections.

Section 1 required the arbitrators to be "...completely independent and impartial in the performance of their duties". This is a standard provision for judicial institutions and a working presumption in *ad hoc* tribunals,[37] and it must be assumed that such a presumption operated within the Commission under the ECCY. Explicit references to the requirement of impartiality may be as a result of the FRY's jurisdictional challenge, in which it appeared to consider the Commission to be involved in an EC conspiracy to divide Yugoslavia. The section also noted that *ad hoc* members appointed for contentious proceedings would participate in the Commission on "...exactly the same terms..." as the permanent members. Again, this is reflective of general international practice, and to suggest that an *ad hoc* appointee would be given lesser rights than permanent members would undermine the value of having the power to appoint such a person. The section goes on to state that "...[e]ach member of the Commission may appoint an expert to assist him..." although it offers no indication as to what kind of assistance is envisaged. It is unclear whether any such experts were appointed,[38] but the Commission does not refer to any such assistance in its opinions under the ICFY. Finally, the section states that all Commission members, together with the secretariat and any appointed experts, shall maintain "...absolute secrecy in respect of the [Commission's] proceedings...". This makes no distinction between the contentious and advisory jurisdictions of the Commission and would appear to follow previous practice under the ECCY.

Section 2 dealt with the Chair of the Commission, who was to be elected by the permanent members for a period of 3 years. The length of time of such an appointment may be an indication of the Commission's expected working-life and it is the only appointment which is specified in any temporal sense. A new Chair would be elected in the event that the elected Chair left before the end of such a period. The Chair's role was to "...direct the deliberations of the Commission and, between meetings...[to] take any decisions required for the proper conduct of the proceedings". In the event that the Chair was unable to perform these tasks, they would be given to another member of the Commission and, although the section does not specify this, it is likely that this member would be required to be a permanent rather than an *ad hoc* member, in light of the need for procedural consistency. This section appears to afford the Chair some discretion in developing the Commission's procedures. There appears, for example, no requirement that any "...decisions..." taken by the Chair be ratified by the other permanent members of the Commission.

Section 3 dealt with the Commission's secretariat and the official languages to be used in proceedings. The secretariat was to consist of "...a Secretary, assisted by the necessary staff..." who were to be "...under the sole authority of the Commission".. In light of what was said about the possibility that the Commission under the ECCY may have utilised the secretariat of the Conference rather than enjoyed its own secretariat,[39] this is a welcome confirmation of the Commission's administrative independence under the ICFY. In keeping with practice under the ECCY, English and French were declared the Commission's official languages and all proceedings, pleadings, decisions and opinions were to be in either of these languages. Nevertheless, section 3.2. allowed any Commission member to request simultaneous interpretation into their native language, provided such a request were made before the relevant Commission meeting. Judgments would be produced in either English or French and, although translation into both would be made, the original version in whichever language would be the sole authentic text. This is standard practice which prevents the possibility that linguistic differences in the translated version might distort the original meaning of the Commission's findings.

Section 4 dealt with the Commission's meetings and affirmed the previous practice of holding all meetings in Paris. Presumably, having found premises which had housed the Commission under the ECCY, there appeared no reason to move to another venue. The procedure does not specify a set number of meetings. The presumption was that the Commission would meet only as required. It is specified that all meetings shall "...normally be attended by all members". Nevertheless, the provision allows for one "...or at most two..." of the members to miss a meeting without preventing it being held. There appears no distinction between permanent members and *ad hoc* members in this respect. In this sense, the procedure creates a quorum which was not evident from any previous practice. It is in line with ICJ procedures, however, which allows a meeting to take place with only nine of the fifteen judges present.[40] The Commission's procedure differs to the extent that any absent member would receive a report of the meeting within forty-eight hours and would be required to vote on the issues decided. Another rule reflecting ICJ procedures was the requirement that any member unable to act with the "...requisite impartiality..." on any question or contentious proceedings must refrain from participating in such proceedings. Given any doubt on this, the Commission would decide.[41]

Sections 5-8 dealt with the various proceedings before the Commission. Section 5 began with some general rules stating that all proceedings shall be "...as informal as possible..." Given the ill-defined discretion of the Chairman to take "...decisions..." on the Commission's procedure outside full meetings, it is unclear how this requirement would be resolved in practice. The section goes on to state that any procedural problems arising would be settled by "...the Commission and its Chairperson..." but again provides no indication of the respective power of these distinct entities. All such settlements should, however, pay "...due regard for the need to ensure completely equal treatment of the parties and to avoid unnecessary costs and waste of time". Section 5 continued that the Commission may instigate "...whatever preparatory inquiries it deems appropriate..." and that this power may be used either upon a request from one of the parties or of the Commission's own volition. Whilst the section fails to define precisely what preparatory inquiries are envisaged, this is perhaps understandable given the need to ensure interpretive flexibility in procedures which are established before proceedings arise in which they will be used. Section 5 affirmed the requirements of secrecy in Section 1, stating that "...proceeding and pleading documents shall be treated as confidential until the opinion or the decision has been disclosed..." This appears to differ from previous procedure, under which the Commission routinely transmitted the respective views of all parties to the other relevant authorities concerned.[42] Whilst the Commission may decide against such secrecy "...after consulting the parties..." there appears to be a presumption that routine disclosure would not be the norm. The section concluded by stating that each party would be required to bear its own costs. Whilst previous procedure made no reference to the issue of costs, it must be assumed that this is in accordance with procedure under the ECCY. Whilst the EC may be expected to pay for the functioning of the Commission as an integral part of the ECCY, this does not extend to paying for the preparatory costs of each party for proceedings before the Commission. Such an approach would be in accordance with the ICJ procedures.[43] Given the move towards greater use of non-written materials, discussed further below, such costs may be potentially far higher under the ICFY than the exclusively written procedure of the ECCY.

6.4.1 *Contentious Proceedings*

Section 6 dealt in more detail with contentious proceedings. It required a notification of the dispute to be given to the SCCC and for such notification to indicate that the parties agreed to the formulation of the question(s) and recognised the Commission's jurisdiction to rule on such question(s). This was clearly an attempt to avoid jurisdictional challenges similar to that which the Commission encountered under the ECCY. Given that the majority of issues left to be decided were between the FRY, on the one hand, and the other former Yugoslav republics on the other hand, it is unsurprising that such contentious proceedings were never actually initiated. Whereas such absence of practice makes it impossible to state for certain what kind of "...dispute..." was envisaged, it is submitted that, in light of the Commission's composition and other sections which show an adherence to the *ICJ Statute*, these would be limited to *legal* disputes.[44] Section 6 confirmed that each party to the dispute was entitled to nominate an *ad hoc* member and noted that the Commission would invite such parties to "...state their case in writing within a time that...[the Chairperson]...shall appoint". It is clear that the requirements of secrecy in respect of pleadings, mentioned in section 5, do not apply rigidly to contentious proceedings and, as one might expect, each party was entitled to receive a copy of the case of all other parties to the dispute. The secrecy of pleadings cannot extend to preventing parties to a contentious issue from knowing the position of the other parties involved. A reply was to be expected from the parties upon the communication of this opposing position, again within a time limit to be decided by the Chairperson.

A modification to the previously exclusive use of a written procedure[45] is noticeable in the fact that the Commission was to decide, after having received the replies of the parties and engaged in "...consultation..." with them, whether the parties needed to be heard. Although the section does not state this explicitly, it must be thought that, in the event that such a hearing was required, it would be offered to both parties and not simply one of them, since this might breach the need to ensure "...completely equal treatment of the parties..." as required by Section 5. The rules on contentious proceedings concluded with the time-limits within which the Commission must give its "...decision..." These were clearly in excess of those under the ECCY process and were stated as being within four months of the closure of written proceedings, albeit capable of being extended to six months. Again, no indication was given as to whether the decision to extend would be that of the Chairperson or the Commission as a whole, although it is likely that the latter would be the case for such an important decision.

6.4.2 *Advisory Proceedings*

Section 7 dealt with the Commission's advisory mandate and stated that a request for an advisory opinion, emanating from the SCCC, would "...normally be exclusively in writing..." Again, however, the shift away from an exclusively written procedure is identifiable in this section. Provision was made for "...representatives of the parties concerned..." to be heard in exceptional circumstances or even "...other persons..." No indication is given as to who such other persons might be, although it is likely that it refers to expert witnesses to assist the arbitrators. The Commission would appoint one of its members as a rapporteur upon receipt of such a request, although no description of the role of the rapporteur is provided. All parties concerned with the issue under consideration may be asked to make "...observations..." within a time-limit set by the Chairperson and these would be sent to all parties concerned for replying observations to be made, within a time-limit decided by the Chairperson. Although this does not prevent such documentation being categorised as 'confidential', it is unclear to the extent that it limits the potential for such observations to situations in which they are deemed "...necessary..." The section again provides no indication of whether such a determination fell to be made by the Chairperson alone or by the Commission as a whole. Section 7 concluded by stating the time-limits within which any advisory "...opinion..." must be made. Such temporal limits were shorter than in the case of contentious proceedings and were restricted to three months from the date of receiving the request. Again, however, the limits were extendible in exceptional circumstances to four months, though no indication is given of the decision-maker in such circumstances. In the case of advisory opinions, the integral role of the ICFY itself may have allowed the SCCC to have granted such a prolongation, or this power may have been intended for the Commission's Chairperson or the Commission as a whole.

Section 8 concluded the Commission's procedural rules and dealt with the nature of decisions and opinions. Both were to be taken by a majority vote and members of the Commission were not allowed to abstain from voting. The section would appear to have taken account of the, albeit unlikely, possibility that a contentious issue may involve an odd number of parties, each of whom would be entitled to appoint an *ad hoc* member to the Commission which would result in an organ with an even number of arbitrators. Such an event is anticipated in the *ICJ Statute* to the extent that it allows the President of the Court to have the casting vote in the event of an equality of votes,[46] and comparable provision is made in respect of the Chairperson of the Commission. Decisions and opinions were, predictably, to state the grounds on which they were made[47] but no record was to be taken of the number of votes which constitute a majority, nor of the manner in which individual Commission members voted. This is contrary to ICJ procedures but coincides with procedures adopted by the ECJ.[48] Allowance is made for those members who wish to attach a dissenting opinion, although such dissents were required to be "...brief...". Similar provision for members to make a concurring judgment were not adopted, however. In reality, none of the opinions adopted after these rules of procedure saw the arbitrators adopt separate judgments. The rules of procedure concluded by stating that the recipients of the Commission's deliberations would differ according to the nature of the proceedings involved. In contentious proceedings, the parties to those proceedings would be given the results of the deliberations in addition to the SCCC whereas, in the case of advisory proceedings, only the latter would receive the Commission's advice and publication would be at their discretion.

6.4.3 *Initial Conclusions on the New Rules of Procedure*

The approach taken by the Commission under the ICFY clearly deviates in a number of respects from ECCY practice. First, in adopting a fairly comprehensive set of procedural rules before receiving any questions, the Commission decided to tackle tough procedural problems pre-emptively rather than reactively. The publication of such procedures is a welcome development for anyone researching the Commission and redresses some of the problems encountered as a result of the ECCY's secrecy. Second, substantive changes were made to the way in which the Commission was to operate. In addition to changes to composition, there is a perceptible move away from the exclusivity of written procedure under the ECCY. Third, the Commission's procedure in contentious cases and the possibility of *ad hoc* appointees to the Commission is something which was not a feature of earlier practice. Perhaps this is because the Commission never actually acted in a manner comparable to contentious proceedings under the ECCY and, in the event that it had, a similar system may have been created. This is speculative, however. The Commission's procedures under the ICFY in this respect bring it into line with traditional arbitral practice whereby the disputing parties are entitled to appoint a member of the tribunal hearing the dispute and, in the case of arbitration, often appoint the whole panel.

In other respects, the new procedural rules simply codify the Commission's practice under the ECCY. The duality of the Commission's role is emphasised and traditional expectations of judicial impartiality are spelt out. The powers of the Chairman are defined and appear to follow the ECCY model, where the Chairman appeared to have had a decisive influence on many aspects of the Commission's practice. The manner of referring questions to the Commission also appears identical to the ECCY model - advisory opinions would originate in a request from the Conference Chairman, in this case the ICFY Steering Committee Co-Chairmen, and contentious proceedings would originate from the disputing parties, but would require the "...authorisation..." of the Co-Chairmen.

In order to comment further on these procedural developments, it is necessary to view them in operation. This is done in the following sections.

6.5 The First Questions Referred to the Newly-Composed Commission

The above procedural mandate was adopted at a meeting of the Commission in Paris on 26th April 1993. Nevertheless, it must be assumed that discussions and preparatory work had been conducted into these revised rules from the time when the SCCC announced, in the Terms of Reference of 27th January, that the Commission would establish its own procedures. Assuming such preparation to have been continuing throughout this period, it would have been interrupted by the referral of a letter to the Commission from the SCCC on 20th April 1993. This letter contained a series of questions relating to the work of the ICFY and its various Working Groups, particularly the Working Groups on Succession and Economic Issues. The questions posed are reprinted below.

"1. In the light of the inventory in the report by the Chairman of the Working Group on Economic Issues, what assets and liabilities should be divided between the successor States to the former SFRY during the succession process?
2. On what date(s) did succession of States occur for the various States that have emerged from the SFRY?
3. (a) What legal principles apply to the division of State property, archives and debts of the SFRY in connection with the succession of States when one or more of the parties refuses to cooperate?
   (b) In particular, what should happen to property
   - not located on the territory of any of the States concerned, or
   - situated on the territory of the States taking part in the negotiations?
4. Under the legal principles that apply, might any amounts owed by one or more of the parties in the form of war damages affect the distribution of State property, archives and debts in connection with the succession process?
5. (a) In view of the dissolution of the SFRY, is the National Bank of Yugoslavia entitled to take decisions affecting property rights and interests that should be divided between the successor States...?
   (b) Have the central Banks of the States emerging from the dissolution of the SFRY succeeded to the rights and obligations of the National Bank of Yugoslavia deriving from international agreements concluded by the latter, in particular the *1988 Financial Agreement* with foreign commercial banks?
   (c) On what conditions can States, within whose jurisdiction property formerly belonging to the SFRY is situated, oppose the free disposal of that property or take other protective measures?
   (d) On what conditions and under what circumstances would such States be required to take such steps?"

Clearly, these questions all related to the succession process taking place in the aftermath of Yugoslavia's dissolution and the legal difficulties which had marked this dissolution process were not complete, even after recognition of most of the Yugoslav republics as sovereign States. Many of them are of a more practical and less theoretical nature than those considered by the Commission under the ECCY, although it will be seen that the Commission was required to produce some important theoretical principles on State succession during its deliberations.

It is likely that the questions were prompted by developments which had already occurred in discussions of the Working Group on Succession

Issues. Difficulties were bound to arise in relation to the FRY's claim to be Yugoslavia's sole legal successor and in respect of Bosnia-Hercegovina, much of whose territory, assets and property were beyond the control of its governmental authorities because of the war in that republic. Having suggested that these problems arose because of political differences within the Working Group negotiations, it is clear that they are not referred in accordance with the Commission's contentious proceedings, contained in section 6 of its rules of procedure. This section effectively required the disputing parties to agree a *compromis* agreeing the formulation of the questions posed and recognising the Commission's jurisdiction in such issues. One explanation for this is that the SCCC's letter was given to the Commission six days before the Commission's rules of procedure were published and that, accordingly, the letter could not have anticipated these procedural requirements. Nevertheless, even in the Co-Chairmen's note to the ICFY Steering Committee, in which the Commission's new Terms of Reference were contained, they appeared to make a distinction between issues which were referred by the SCCC for advice to assist the ICFY and its Working Groups and disputes "...submitted...by the parties thereto...". These questions contained no indication of any specific disputes nor the parties involved therein. Instead, they sought assistance for the Working Groups on Succession and Economic Issues as constituent parts of the ICFY and, in doing so, must be deemed requests for advisory opinions.[49] As will be seen below, the procedural rules followed by the Commission during its deliberations confirm this suggestion.

Before the Commission was able to consider these issues, however, a second jurisdictional challenge was delivered by the FRY in a statement of the 30th April 1993. Again, since the Commission would not have been able to consider these issues in the event of a successful jurisdictional challenge, logic dictated that it was necessary to consider this challenge before going on to deal with the issues in the SCCC's letter.

6.6 The Jurisdictional Challenge of April 1993

The FRY statement began by reiterating its stance in the first jurisdictional challenge, namely that "...the FRY does not recognise the jurisdiction of the Arbitration Commission, known as the Badinter Commission, in the assets and liabilities division procedure..." The FRY noted that it was "...not agreed that the Commission issue advisory opinions on the principles on the basis of which succession of States would be effected between the SFRY, as the predecessor State on the one hand, and the secessionist former Yugoslav republics, as successor States on the other".

This brief introduction makes clear a number of points. First, the Commission had indeed been asked to issue advisory opinions rather than decisions to contentious issues. Second, the FRY appeared to have paid no attention to the Commission's previous deliberations. The FRY clearly ignores the gist of the Commission's *Interlocutory Decision*,[50] in which it stated that consent of the parties was not a prerequisite for advisory proceedings. A request from the Chairman of the ECCY was sufficient to warrant a response from the Commission, assuming the absence of "...conclusive reasons..." to the contrary. It must be thought highly unlikely that the Commission would view its advisory mandate under the ICFY in a radically different manner. Third, the republics may be argued to have accepted the advisory competence of the Commission by having agreed to the various procedural changes which led in this direction and by continuing participation in the Commission's activities. The same may be said of the acceptance of the new Terms of Reference which clearly envisage a continuation of the Commission's advisory mandate. One may argue that it was possible for the FRY to accept the ICFY process without accepting the Commission's jurisdiction *per se*.[51] Nevertheless, the Terms of Reference made it clear that the Commission would continue playing an important role in providing legal advice upon which basis the ICFY negotiations process would proceed and it is unlikely that a State could accept negotiations without acknowledging the legitimacy of the Commission's role in this respect. Finally, the FRY ignored the Commission's findings in *Opinions 1*, *8* and *10*, in which it stated that events in Yugoslavia led to a "...process of dissolution..." leaving all republics equal successors to the SFRY and not, as alleged by the FRY, episodes of secession which would allow Yugoslavia's legal personality to survive.

The FRY considered it unacceptable that principles of succession "...be discussed before any body, prior to substantial discussion of these principles within the Succession Group of the [ICFY]...". Again, this is open to criticism, in that it seems to imply that the principles of succession should not come into operation at the outset of the negotiations but only after the parties had arrived at some agreement *inter se*. Whilst the principle of State sovereignty may give successor States as much latitude as necessary to arrive at agreements between themselves, such agreements must nevertheless be compatible with general international legal requirements on the principles of succession, on which the Commission was being asked to deliberate. In this sense, it seems logical that those principles should be clearly established before negotiations in the Working Groups began and that the agreements reached in those Working Groups should seek to remain compatible with those pre-established principles. From the tenor of the SCCC's letter, it appeared that certain real problems had already made themselves apparent in the positions of the parties and, if negotiations were not to be stalled, the Commission's advice on such problems would be extremely important.

The FRY argued that "...in the sense of international law, the Arbitration Commission was not established or composed for arbitration purposes..." and that "...its work within the [ECCY] so far has been seriously in breach of both the law of procedure and the implementation of material law". This is again open to a number of criticisms. First, the statement offers nothing above bland assertions of procedural and substantive legal irregularities which fail to evidence these with specific examples. More puzzling is the fact that the statement appears to misunderstand the nature of the Commission's role under the ECCY and in the present proceedings. By alleging that the Commission was not created for arbitration purposes, the FRY seems to ignore the fact that the Commission's original arbitration mandate was extended to include advisory functions conceptually different from arbitration. To the extent that any procedural irregularities may have been perceived, therefore, this may be because the FRY authorities were comparing the advisory procedure of the Commission with traditional arbitral proceedings. In relation to the present proceedings, the FRY failed to appreciate that the Commission was not being used for "...arbitration purposes..." but for advisory purposes and that the successor States are, at best, secondary parties to such proceedings. They are instigated by, and intended for the use of, the SCCC and, despite the ability of the Yugoslav parties to submit memoranda and observations to appraise the Commission of their respective positions, this does not translate an advisory opinion into traditional arbitration proceedings. This confusion is perpetuated in the FRY's assertion that "...all disputes that may arise vis-à-vis the division of assets and liabilities should be referred by agreement either to the Permanent Court of Arbitration in the Hague or to an *ad hoc* arbitration court". The existence of a dispute between the Yugoslav parties demanded "...proceedings before a court of law in the sense of general international law and not as proceedings before the Arbitration Commission presided by Mr. Badinter". One notes that references to the ICJ, included in the first jurisdictional challenge, have been dropped, no doubt reflecting the FRY's acknowledgment fact that neither it nor the SFRY had never been party to the ICJ's Optional Clause.[52] Reference to the Permanent Court of Arbitration (PCA) was at least more understandable given that Yugoslavia had been a party thereto[53] although, since the FRY's claim to continue Yugoslavia's legal personality had not been accepted, such referral may have been more complicated than may at first appear. Alternatively, the FRY was willing to see issues be referred to "...an *ad hoc* arbitration court..." which again indicates the FRY's confusion as to the nature of the Badinter Commission.

The FRY's objections to the Commission appear to be based on the irregularities described above but, as has been argued, these were not irregularities of an arbitration tribunal but an entirely different procedure altogether, as a result of the Commission's dual mandate. To indicate acceptance of an alternative *ad hoc* arbitration court, which would presumably operate procedures more in line with traditional arbitral proceedings is to ignore the fact that the Commission could have done this in the event that its contentious proceedings mandate was utilised by a referral from the parties themselves. It is far likelier, therefore, that the real reasons for the FRY's objections to the Commission's continuing role lay not in procedural irregularities but in a loss of confidence in the Commission's willingness to accept the FRY's factual and legal positions regarding events in Yugoslavia. This loss of confidence was apparently not redressed by the admission of the former ICJ President and current ECHR judge to the Commission.

The FRY concluded its objection by stating that it "...considers the opinions of the Commission doctrinary in the sense of *Article 38(d)* of the *Statute of the ICJ*, which do not constitute a legal ground for any valid decision...[and that]...the FRY shall consider null and void and non-binding any opinion of the Commission adopted in the procedure to which it has not agreed".[54]

This statement was forwarded to the SCCC together with a letter from the deputy-head of the FRY's ICFY delegation, dated 5th May. It was transmitted to the Commission on 11th May and the Commission's response was contained in a statement entitled "Reactions of the members of the Arbitration Commission...to the statement made by the FRY Government on its competence".

6.7 The Commission's Reactions to the Second Jurisdictional Challenge

The Commission's deliberations regarding the FRY's letter were returned to the SCCC on 26th May 1993.[55] The Commission noted that, "...although the FRY did not send this statement to the Arbitration Commission itself...", unlike the first jurisdictional challenge which was addressed to Mr. Badinter directly, it represented "...an appropriate opportunity to set out the scope and limits of its competence". The FRY's letter could not be viewed as anything other than a direct objection to the continuing mandate of an integral part of the ICFY, and one which must be dealt with before deliberations on the SCCC's questions could begin.[56]

The first point of interest in this statement is its legal status and the description given to it by the Commission. In contrast with the *Interlocutory Decision* of 4th July 1992, reference to "...[r]eactions of the members..." of the Commission appears to give it a less authoritative collective status and a more personal character. It will be recalled that the Commission's procedural rules of 26th April make no reference to the decision-making process in the event of a jurisdictional challenge, which was a curious omission given earlier experiences. Nevertheless, it may be assumed that the issue fell to be decided by the Chairperson's discretion to "...settle any procedural problems which may arise, with due regard for the need to ensure completely equal treatment of the parties and to avoid unnecessary costs and waste of time".[57]

The 'reactions' of the Commission's members bear a remarkable similarity to the style of the earlier *Interlocutory Decision*. A number of international legal materials are considered, including ICJ case-law and the ICJ's Statute, and the 'reactions' are in fact delivered in the form of a single reasoned argument, with no indication that any dissent occurred.[58] Naturally, had dissenting opinions arisen, it may have fallen for the Chairmen to have decided whether, in accordance with procedures for advisory and contentious proceedings, dissenting opinion would be allowed. In effect, the informal title of the Commission's response does not prevent it being viewed as an authoritative statement of its competence similar to the *Interlocutory Decision*. Nevertheless, the Commission appeared to make a distinction between the formality of this earlier decision and the "...clarification..." provided in this statement.

The response began by noting that, in accordance with the new Terms of Reference, these issues had clearly been referred by the Co-Chairmen under paragraph 3(b) thereof, whereby the Commission would "...give its advice to any legal question submitted to it by the Co-Chairmen...". The Commission reiterated that its advisory mandate stemmed not from the consent of the parties, "...but from the mere fact of referral...". Since such an opinion would fall to be interpreted and acted upon, or not, by the SCCC it had "...only an advisory character...[and]...no binding force". The ICJ Advisory Opinion in the *Interpretation of Peace Treaties Case*[59] was cited as authority and, perhaps more clearly than the *Interlocutory Decision* emphasised that this was a different question to the status of the Commission as an arbitral tribunal. Thus, the Commission noted that such advice was given "...in order to furnish...[the Co-Chairmen]...with information they needed to take decisions..." and that the decision to request such advice was entirely at the Co-Chairmen's discretion, who could not be prevented from doing so by any of the ICFY participants. The Commission agreed with the FRY's description of the opinions as doctrinary, in that they fulfilled the criteria of *Article 38(d)* of the *ICJ Statute*, and clearly saw nothing improper about conceding their opinions such a status.

Having noted that advisory opinions did not bind the parties themselves, but served as "...points of reference..." upon which negotiations may be conducted, the Commission explained that it was open to the parties to refer any matter which could not be resolved by negotiations to the Commission under paragraph 3(a) of the Terms of Reference. The discretion inherent in referring an issue to contentious proceedings meant, however, that such referral could alternatively be to "...any other adjudicatory or arbitral body of their choice". The importance of consent in truly contentious proceedings is thereby acknowledged.

In terms of the FRY's objections vis-à-vis the alleged procedural and substantive irregularities, the Commission rejected these by stating that it was only because the FRY refused to continue participation after its first jurisdictional challenge that *Opinions 8-10* were made without the Commission being aware of the FRY's position on those issues. The Commission had "...always acted in a completely impartial manner, strictly following the adversary method which guarantees equality between the parties concerned". Whereas references to impartiality are unsurprising, reference to the adoption of an adversary procedure is more perplexing. This procedure is commonly understood to rely heavily on the use of oral evidence and oral examination of witnesses by legal representatives of the parties involved, and is most familiar to common-law systems such as the UK.[60] It contrasts directly with the inquisitorial procedure of the continental civil legal systems, whereby the inquiry is led by the arbitrators rather than the parties own representatives.[61] All evidence would tend to indicate that the mainly written procedure of the Commission was of an inquisitorial, as opposed to an adversarial, nature and instances such as the questionnaire sent to the republics by the Commission and requests for additional information would tend to affirm this.[62] Reference to the adversary procedure is also confusing because the Commission's role had hitherto been limited to advisory proceedings to furnish advice to the ECCY-Chairman. To the extent that no contentious proceedings had arisen and existing procedure better reflected an inquisitorial system, it is submitted that the Commission's categorisation is confusing and probably inaccurate.

The Commission's final comments indicate the informal nature of its response. It was stated that the "...clarification..." contained in the 'reactions' "...in no way prejudices either the competence of the Commission in this matter if it is challenged on grounds which they deem justified, nor the replies it may be led to give on the substance of the questions posed by the Co-Chairmen...". This confirms the anomalous nature of these findings and can only be explained by the fact that the Commission did not treat the FRY's statements as a *stricto sensu* jurisdictional challenge, in comparison with the earlier challenge of 8th June. Nevertheless, it has been suggested that the Commission's pronouncements may be of use not only in relation to its own jurisdiction but also to international arbitration tribunals in general.[63]

6.8 Political Developments Following the Commission's Reactions

Having again had its position regarding the Commission's jurisdiction rejected, the FRY decided to cease cooperation with the Commission. In a letter to the SCCC of 2nd July 1993, the FRY's Deputy Prime-Minister and Foreign Minister, Vladislav Jovanovic, identified a "...serious problem...concerning the Working Group on Succession Issues, owing to the renewed activities of the so-called Badinter Commission".[64] He indicated the FRY's decision to withdraw from this Working Group "...pending discontinuation of the work of the so-called Badinter Commission for the reasons we have indicated on several occasions". This letter reiterated the FRY's jurisdictional objections and repeated a number of the allegations which were criticised above in relation to the FRY statement of 30th April. Again, the letter rejected the Commission's mandate for the "...settlement of disputes through arbitration..." without taking account of the fact that the mandate under discussion was the Commission's advisory, rather than contentious, procedure. It asserted that "...it is a fact that the Commission has not been established in accordance with international law..." and that "...in its *Opinions Nos. 1-10*, the Commission has essentially violated the legal norms of international law, in respect of both procedure as well as the implementation of material law".

The FRY also considered that "...in practice, the opinions of the Commission, as an advisory body of the ICFY, on the basis of which the Yugoslav participants were to adopt relevant decisions by consensus taking also into account the Commission's opinion, were taken as judgments and served as a basis for making concrete decisions on relevant issues concerning the Yugoslav crisis". This is interesting, since it indicates that the FRY believed the Commission to possess considerable influence in terms of EC and UN policy. The extent to which this is true is debatable and has been discussed elsewhere.[65] To the extent that the Commission's opinions "...served as a basis for making concrete decisions on relevant issues..." it is submitted that this is perfectly compatible with its advisory mandate since, although the opinions may have been a basis for such decisions, they were ultimately taken by the responsible political authorities in the various conferences and international institutions.

Having expressed confidence that the SCCC would understand the FRY's position, and presumably expecting them to recommend the requested "...discontinuation..." of the Commission, the FRY must have been most upset to find that the Commission continued its deliberations on the substantive issues in the SCCC's letter and gave a series of opinions in July 1993.

6.9 *Opinions 11-13*

On 16th July 1993, the Commission delivered three opinions dealing with a number of issues raised in the SCCC's letter. In keeping with established practice, the Commission found it legitimate to re-order these questions to make its deliberations more logical and understandable.

6.9.1 *Opinion 11*

Opinion 11 dealt with the dates of succession of the various States arising out of Yugoslavia's dissolution process. The obvious implication of dealing with this first is that the answers to this question may impact on the responses to other questions involving the division of assets and responsibilities. These issues of succession of property must be viewed as different to the question of succession of legal personality, particularly within international organisations, which the Commission dealt with briefly in *Opinion 9*.[66]

The Commission noted that "...[n]one of the State parties to the proceedings has contested the Commission's right to answer questions referred to it". This may be interpreted as meaning that the second jurisdictional challenge was not, *per se*, an official one or, more convincingly that, given the FRY's absence from these proceedings, all *participating* parties had accepted the Commission's jurisdiction. The Commission observed that "...[t]he FRY has submitted no memorandum or observations on the questions referred...", which left it to consider only those documents supplied by Bosnia-Hercegovina, Croatia, FYROM and Slovenia. Despite having received no information from the FRY, the Commission is at pains to highlight the continuing equality which must be preserved between all parties, including the FRY, by stating that all information received had been passed on to all the successor States.

The analysis continued by adopting the definition of succession provided in the *1978 Vienna Convention on Succession of States in Respect of Treaties*[67] and the *1983 Vienna Convention on Succession of States in Respect of Property, Debts and Archives*,[68] which had been referred to in previous opinions.[69] Neither of these treaties has received the requisite number of ratifications to allow them to enter into force and reliance on them is, in this sense, noteworthy. One explanation is that the Commission felt them sufficiently reflective of existing customary law to allow inspiration to be drawn from them. This is unlikely, however, since the conventions are widely recognised as having adopted an approach "...pertaining more to the *development* of existing customary international law than to its *codification.*

[emphasis added]".[70] A more relevant fact was that the relevant former Yugoslav authorities had agreed during the ECCY that the conventions would form the basis for negotiations on succession issues.

The conventions provided that the date of succession was "...the date upon which the successor State replaced the predecessor State in the responsibility for the international relations of the territory to which the succession relates".[71] From these uncontroversial foundations, the Commission noted that particular problems were caused by the Yugoslav case, since the SFRY had disappeared as a legal entity and none of the successor States was entitled to consider itself sole legal successor to Yugoslavia's international personality. Furthermore, unlike the dissolutions of the USSR and Czechoslovakia, Yugoslavia's dissolution process had occurred in the absence of an agreement between the parties on succession issues. Nevertheless, the Commission confirmed, in line with its previous opinions, that the dissolution process had started on 29th November, when it issued *Opinion 1*, and concluded on 4th July, when it issued *Opinion 8*. These circumstances must be taken into account in applying the principles laid down in the two *Vienna Conventions*,[72] but did not establish the dates for State succession in respect of individual republics. This issue could only be determined by the date on which the respective republics "...became States..." which was "...a question of fact...to be assessed in each case in the light of the circumstances in which each of the States concerned was created". Here, the Commission appears to endorse its earlier findings that recognition is merely declaratory and that the dates on which the republics achieved Statehood are not necessarily those on which EC recognition was forthcoming. Nevertheless, whilst recognition may not be legally constitutive the Commission said nothing about the quasi-constitutive effect of the decision to establish diplomatic relations. This is discussed in chapter 7.[73]

The Commission adopted a subjective approach and placed great emphasis on the relevant republic's desire to sever relationships with the SFRY.[74] Thus, the date for succession in respect of Slovenia and Croatia was deemed to be the 8th October 1991 when the suspension of their declarations of independence, agreed in the Brioni Accord, expired.[75] Only then did they "...definitively break all links with the organs of the SFRY...and become sovereign States in international law". Macedonia had asserted its "...right..." to independence on 25th January 1991, but the Commission noted that it was not until after the results of the referendum held on 8th September 1991 that it actually declared this right to have been implemented. The effects of this declaration were incorporated into the Macedonian constitution of 17th November 1991, which again established the absence of any "...institutional link..." with the SFRY and represented the date of Macedonian succession. In terms of Bosnia, the relevant date was the 6th March, when the results of the referendum of 29th February were officially promulgated. Since that date, the Commission noted that, despite the conflict in that republic "...the constitutional authorities...have acted like those of a sovereign State in order to maintain its territorial integrity and their full and exclusive powers...". In relation to the FRY, the Commission was faced with the problem that the FRY still considered itself to be the continuation of Yugoslavia rather than a successor State and had, accordingly, not applied for recognition as a new State in line with *Opinion 10*. This caused the Commission "...particular problems..." since the FRY's claim was "...not a position that can be upheld". The Commission cited concurring opinions of "...all the international agencies which have had to state their views on this issue..." without identifying these institutions explicitly. The Commission nevertheless took account of the fact that the FRY's constitution was adopted on 27th April 1992 and that this date also signalled the time at which the relevant international institutions began to refer to "...the former SFRY...", which affirmed that the dissolution process was completed and that this was the relevant date of succession for the FRY.

Having decided the different dates for succession, the Commission correctly noted that it was aware of the practical problems which may arise as a result of these different dates and because of "...the long-drawn-out process whereby the SFRY was dissolved". One implication of the existence of different dates of succession was that different dates would apply for the transfer of State property, rights and liabilities, but the Commission noted that the rules on State succession were "...supplementary..." and did not preclude the parties themselves resolving the practical difficulties by agreements which would ensure "...an equitable outcome...".[76] In the absence of such agreements, however, the expressed dates were those on which the successor States were entitled to claim their respective rights to Yugoslavia's property, assets, archives, debts and other rights and duties. Having been asked only to provide the guiding principles on succession, the Commission made no attempt to consider the practical implications this would have on each successor State. Presumably, this would be a task for the Working Group on Succession Issues.

Opinion 11 raises a number of important points. First, the different dates of succession are problematical in the sense that they could complicate the division process being negotiated within the Working Groups. This is a difficult factual situation which has little previous practice to draw from. Second, the dates on which the republics became States are clearly different from the dates on which recognition was granted, and thus reinforces the point that the recognition implementation dates were not necessarily the dates on which succession occurred. One problem with this is that the Commission's dates are difficult to reconcile with its earlier declarations that the republics gained their independence as a result of a "...dissolution process..."[77] and not by secession. The reasoning inherent in such a suggestion is that the former republics did not secede from Yugoslavia but that Yugoslavia's dissolution led to the independence of the new States. The Commission's dates of succession, however, make it clear that the SFRY dissolution process had not been completed at the time that such independence was obtained and that Yugoslavia must, therefore, have remained a sovereign State with ongoing legal personality when the republics achieved Statehood. The independence of Slovenia and Croatia, effective from 8th October 1991, occurred some nine months before the 4th July, on which the dissolution process was said to have been completed. The case of the FRY illustrates this position most clearly. The Commission stated on the one hand that the dissolution process was not complete until *Opinion 10*, on 4th July 1992, yet it acknowledged the independence of the FRY as a State, albeit an unrecognised one, on the 27th April. By noting that certain international institutions began to refer to the former Yugoslavia at this point, it was compelled to find that the date of FRY independence was the date upon which "...the process of dissolution of the SFRY had been completed". This date was, however, some time before *Opinion 10*, which the Commission had said marked the end of the dissolution process. If the independence of the former republics did not occur by way of secession but as a result of Yugoslavia's dissolution it is difficult to see how Yugoslavia can have retained international personality until the end of the dissolution process whilst the republics gained their independence before the completion of that process. Third, although the Commission reiterates its findings in *Opinion 9* that the result of any negotiations must achieve an "...equitable outcome...", references in *Opinion 9* to the need to ensure such an outcome complied with "...the fundamental rights of the individual and of peoples and minorities..." are omitted. Clearly, the newly-constituted Commission felt less willing to make pointed reference to such rights, which had characterised its early jurisprudence under the ECCY, and was unwilling to repeat its assertion that such rights were "...now peremptory norms of international law".[78]

6.9.2 *Opinion 12*

Opinion 12 dealt with the legal principles applicable to the division of assets, rights and obligations in the event that one or more of the Yugoslav parties refused to cooperate and whether, and on what conditions, third States controlling property which formerly belonged to Yugoslavia could block the free disposal of such property or take protective measures in relation thereto.

The Commission again began with a statement relating to the second jurisdictional challenge and noted that the FRY had submitted no information for the Commission to consider. All other former republics had submitted memoranda and observations. It then referred to *Opinion 9*, which was echoed in *Opinion 11*, stating that, although there are "...few well-established principles in international law applicable to State succession...[t]he fundamental rule is that States must achieve an equitable result by negotiation and agreement". In the event that one or more States refused to fulfill this fundamental requirement of cooperation and negotiation, it would be "...liable internationally with all the legal consequences this entails, notably the possibility for States sustaining loss to take non-forcible counter-measures, in accordance with international law".[79] Whilst there currently appears no general international legal duty for States to negotiate on every dealing with other States,[80] there are a number of exceptions to this. First, such an obligation exists in *Article 33* of the *UN Charter*, where the dealings involve "...*any dispute*, the continuance of which is likely to endanger international peace and security [emphasis added]". Second, the subject matter of the dealings in question may create an international legal obligation to negotiate. Thus, in the *North Sea Continental Shelf Case*, the ICJ noted that States involved in maritime delimitation were "...under a duty to conduct themselves so that the negotiations are meaningful, which will not be the case when either of them insists on his own position without contemplating any modification of it..."[81] The Commission's deliberations provide no indication whether it perceived the succession issues in question to represent a source of conflict which could endanger international peace and security or whether succession issues *per se* create a duty to negotiate.[82]

In the event of non-cooperation by one or more successor States, all other successor States must endeavour to continue cooperation *inter se* to achieve an agreement which reaches "...a comprehensive equitable result, reserving the rights of the State or States refusing to cooperate". Such an agreement would have the status of "...*res inter alios acta*..."[83] between those States which had achieved the agreement as well as the non-cooperating State(s) and all other third States. *Article 34* of the *Vienna Convention on the Law of Treaties*, however, enshrines the principle that "...a treaty does not create either obligations or rights for a third State without its consent...". Accordingly, third States in whose territory such property may be situated could not be *required* to take action in pursuance of such agreements but they may not be precluded from *choosing* to give effect to this agreement, provided it was one which had been freely reached by agreement and achieved a comprehensive equitable result. In the absence of any such agreement, third States may adopt "...interim measures of protection as are needed to safeguard the interests of the successor States..." and they may be *required* to adopt such measures if "...an international agency with powers in the matter..." took decisions which were binding on them. The Commission does not identify the existence of any such international agency although it must be thought that, given the institutional framework behind the ICFY process, the UN or EC would be the institutions in mind.[84] Pellet rightly concludes that this would create a system of collective counter-measures which, in the absence of a right deemed *erga omnes*,[85] would extend international law beyond its current boundaries.[86] Since the rights involved in instances of State succession necessarily involve the rights of only those States involved in the succession process, it is unlikely that they could be categorised in this manner.

Opinion 12 effectively adopts a position which prevents the continuing intransigence of certain parties from blocking the necessary negotiation process within the ICFY, and in this sense is a functional judgment, similar to many of those delivered previously by the Commission. It provides a warning to the FRY authorities that, even in their absence, an agreement on succession issues could be adopted by the other former Yugoslav republics. It nevertheless seeks to maintain impartiality towards the parties, even those refusing to cooperate, by maintaining that the interests of such non-cooperating States must be respected and protected in any succession agreement.

6.9.3 *Opinion 13*

Opinion 13 dealt with the possibility that certain successor States may seek to influence the succession process by taking account of any damages owed by other parties, in respect of war damages in particular, in deciding the division of assets to the State(s) owing such damages. This is a difficult issue since it is obviously a legitimate consideration for those States whose territories and economies have been destroyed by conflicts arising out of the dissolution process yet it is also one which, in the absence of participation by all parties, could unduly affect the non-cooperating State(s). This is especially so in light of the fact that the non-cooperating FRY delegation would be the party against which most such war damages were claimed.

Having reiterated the FRY's absence from the proceedings, the Commission affirmed that succession problems were determined largely on a "...case by case..." basis "...depending on the circumstances proper to each form of succession..." with few well-established international rules to assist in the process. Nevertheless, the *Vienna Conventions* of 1978 and 1983 were referred to again as offering "...some guidance..." on these issues and, in the case of succession arising out of a dissolution process, *Articles 18*, *31* and *41* were relevant.[87] The Commission refined its earlier pronouncements that the agreement on division of assets and liabilities be equitable, by stating that "...these articles do not require that each category of assets or liabilities be divided in equitable proportions but only that *the overall outcome* be an equitable division [emphasis added]".

On the issue of war damages, the Commission noted that these rules, relating to State *responsibility*, were conceptually and practically distinct from the question of State *succession*, on which the equitable outcome must be achieved. To the extent that they formed different questions, therefore, "...[t]he equitable division of assets and liabilities...must...be effected without the question of war damages being allowed to interfere in the matter of State succession". The amounts which may be owed in war damages should, therefore, have "...no direct impact on the division of State property". This was subject to the possibility that the States concerned may conclude agreements to the contrary, or that such a decision may be imposed on them by "...an international body". Again, no definition of such an international body is given, though it must be thought that this refers either to the UN, EC or possibly even the ICFY. It was, furthermore, made clear that the ruling was in no way prejudicial to the respective responsibilities of the various parties in terms of war damages and "..[t]he possibility cannot be excluded in particular of setting-off assets and liabilities to be transferred under the rules of State succession on the one hand against war damages on the other". This latter sentence is somewhat confusing, in the sense that it appears to contradict much of what has gone before. On the one hand, the question of war damages should have no direct impact on the division of assets, yet the same question may allow the possibility of setting-off transferable assets against war damages. It is perhaps best understood as indicating the conceptual difference between the initial agreement on the division of assets, which should remain free from questions of war damages, and the practical implementation of that division, which may legitimately take account of the respective parties' responsibility and any war damages owed. This appears to achieve a workable compromise on the sensitive nature of the issues being decided.

6.9.4 *Reflections on Opinions 11-13*

Collectively, *Opinions 11-13* lay the fundamental ground-rules for the ongoing negotiation process within the Working Groups. State succession issues are difficult from an international legal perspective because the paucity of consistent State practice in this politically-charged area means there are few established customary legal rules[88] and the *Vienna Conventions* are neither in force nor capable of binding any successor State.[89] The latter of these problems was avoided when the former Yugoslav parties accepted the conventions as the basis for negotiations, but the Commission was still faced with the problem that the conventions were heavily influenced by the necessities of decolonisation[90] which did not necessarily correspond to the demands of the Yugoslav scenario. Nevertheless, the Commission attempted to build on the principles contained in the *Vienna Conventions* whilst ensuring that its rulings were, on the whole, consistent with its earlier jurisprudence. Accordingly, *Opinions 11-13* rely heavily on reasoning in *Opinion 9*, which noted the importance of an equitable distribution of assets and liabilities, and *Opinion 10*, which dealt to some extent with succession of legal personality in international institutions and concluded that no successor State(s) could claim to continue Yugoslavia's legal personality.

The Commission was not forced to deal with the question of succession to treaties since, to a large extent, this had been dealt with by the terms of the *Guidelines on Recognition*. These required the republics to have "...accepted the appropriate international obligations..." including respect for the *UN Charter* and *Charter of Paris*, guarantees for the rights of ethnic and national groups and minorities, the inviolability of all frontiers and commitment to nuclear non-proliferation.[91] Nevertheless, the Commission's opinions appear to endorse the policy that successor States arising from the dissolution of a sovereign predecessor State should not benefit from the 'clean slate' theory of State succession but that succession should operate under a presumption of continuity of legal obligations.[92] This is not to say that those obligations may not require modification and some level of re-negotiation, to account for the inevitable disruption of affairs following the dissolution of a State,[93] but simply that some level of obligation is likely to continue.

The opinions confirm that non-participation by any State(s) in the negotiations process may not affect the conclusion of any agreement on succession issues, provided the non-participating States have their rights and interest protected within it. They specify an implicit duty to negotiate issues of succession, albeit failing to indicate the source of such an obligation, and provide an indication of the appropriate remedy in the event of a breach of this obligation. They confirm that any State suffering loss as a result of such non-cooperation would be entitled to pursue non-forcible counter-measures to remedy that loss and that property located in third States may be protected for all successor States, either by a decision of the State in which it is located or a decision imposing such protective measures taken by the relevant international agency or institution. Nevertheless, they provide no indication of such authorised institutions and cite no evidence in support of the ability of a third party State, in the absence of a financial interest in the property situated on its territory or the existence of an *erga omnes* right, to take counter-measures in respect of such property. Finally, they clarify that, although the question of State responsibility should not affect the nature of the equitable conclusion reached, it may nevertheless affect the practical distribution of assets after the conclusion of agreements on succession and war damages.

The remaining questions in the letter of 29th April dealt with the identity of the assets and liabilities to be divided between the successor States and the role of Yugoslavia's National Bank following the SFRY's dissolution. These questions arguably relate less to the *principles* of succession than to the *practicalities* of the succession process. In view of the conceptual difference between the questions, it was perhaps prudent of the Commission to have dealt with the principles first, allowing the negotiation process to proceed in the light of the Commission's advice, and to have left the practical issues until a later date.[94] This explains the fact that the remaining questions were delivered almost a month after *Opinions 11-13*. Nothing of any significance happened to the Commission during this interim period.

6.9.5 *Procedural Issues Arising from Opinions 11-13*

The Commission's procedure, whilst containing no radical departures from earlier practice, is noteworthy because of the procedural changes which occurred under the ICFY process. It is clear that the questions posed were of an advisory, as opposed to a contentious, nature and that, accordingly, the Commission's mandate under the ICFY remained essentially the same as under the ECCY in such proceedings. The issues were referred through the SCCC after having ascertained the basis for existing or potential issues of disagreement between the parties which may have obstructed the work of the ICFY's Working Groups.

The absence of the FRY's participation in the Commission's proceedings first occurred under the ECCY after the first unsuccessful jurisdictional challenge and continued under the ICFY after a second challenge. Whereas *Opinions 8-10* do not make it clear that the FRY failed to submit observations on the issues considered therein, *Opinions 11-13* contain a standard paragraph noting the continued support for the Commission from all other States and that it was forced to consider the issues in the absence of observations from the FRY. The Commission's new rules of procedure stipulate that advisory proceedings shall invite the observations of the parties only "...if necessary..."[95] although the Commission appears to have continued its practice of soliciting the views of the parties, including the FRY, as a matter of course.

The sources used by the Commission as authority for some of its pronouncements were similar to those used under the ECCY procedure, such as ICJ case-law and the *Vienna Conventions*. On a number of occasions, the Commission also referred to its earlier opinions and built on them . The importance of questions of fact involved in the process of succession, stated in *Opinion 1*, is confirmed, as is the need to achieve an equitable solution to the division of assets and liabilities, contained in *Opinion 9*. This must be taken as a reaffirmation of the Commission's early jurisprudence which, in light of the new membership, indicates that the original Commission, albeit composed of constitutional legal experts, correctly assessed many difficult international law areas. *Opinion 11*, however, appears to conflict somewhat with *Opinion 1*, by confusing the issue whether the successor States achieved their independence by virtue of the dissolution process, which apparently was not complete until 4th July 1992, or by something closer to secession, with Yugoslavia remaining a sovereign State at the times of their independence.

The opinions remain terse and succinct, in spite of the addition of members from the ICJ and ECHR, where judgments are usually lengthier and more thoroughly reasoned. The language used is discursive and similar to that in earlier opinions and it was common for the Commission to express a "...view..." on issues rather than offering more definitive conclusions. The fact that these questions were referred under the Commission's advisory mandate may have limited the Commission's ability to offer more concrete findings, however.

The Commission's new procedural rules of 26th April 1993 specified a number of interesting features of advisory proceedings. It is clear that the parties had no right to appoint any *ad hoc* representatives to the Commission. In this sense, the former Yugoslav republics were potentially more disadvantaged than under the ECCY process where they enjoyed the right to have nominated two permanent representatives to the Commission. Failure to agree on these appointments render the ECCY's advantages theoretical, however. Although the proceedings were to be normally "...exclusively in writing...", provision was made for the appointment of one of the Commission members as a rapporteur.[96] It is unclear whether this was done and, if so, who the designated member was and what their functions were. It was also specified that the parties observations were to be submitted within a time-limit to be set by the Commission's Chairperson, although no such limits are known. Similarly, the potential for appointing an expert for each of the Commission members is envisaged in Article 1.3 of the new rules, but it is unclear whether any such appointments were made or whether the Commission undertook any "...preparatory inquiries..."[97] before producing its opinions. No reference is made to such actions in the Commission's opinions.

The opinions were delivered on 16th July, having been received by a letter of 20th April. The new time-limits specified that all advisory opinions be delivered within three months of having been received, although this was extendible to four months, on conditions which were not made clear. Clearly, the opinions fell within the time-limit, although only by a few days. It is submitted that, given the jurisdictional challenge which occurred in the period between the Commission having received the letter and delivered its opinions, this was not an unreasonable delay. *Opinions 14-15*, were reserved until 13th August, however, and clearly required the Commission to have extended its deliberations to four months. The reasons for such a postponement and on whose authority this decision was taken remain unknown.

No indication is given that the opinions were based on anything other than unanimity amongst the Commission's members, although the new rules of procedure make provision for dissenting opinions.[98] Since no record was to be made of the way in which the members voted,[99] and the proceedings were kept secret, one is left unaware of any disagreements which may have arisen vis-à-vis the wording used or emphasis given in the opinions. One explanation is that such issues are unknown by virtue of the overriding requirement contained in Article 1.4. of the procedure of the 20th April, that "...absolute secrecy..." shall be maintained in respect of all Commission proceedings.

6.10 *Opinions 14-15*

The remaining questions dealt with certain practical issues surrounding the succession process and asked about the identity of the assets and liabilities to be shared amongst the successor States and the status of the central SFRY National Bank and central banks of the successor States.

6.10.1 *Opinion 14*

Opinion 14 dealt with the identity of the assets and liabilities to be shared amongst the successor States, and again included the standard paragraph on FRY non-participation. It noted the existence of a *Draft Single Inventory of the Assets and Liabilities of the SFRY As At 31st December 1990*, which had been compiled by the ICFY Working Group on Economic Issues on 26th February 1993, as one of the fundamental documents for the Working Group on Succession Issues. This document was compiled with the assistance of those States participating in the former Working Group and was divided into two areas - agreed items and non-agreed items, the latter obviously representing the more contentious succession issues.

Assuming there to be no further need for discussion on those items within the 'agreed' list of the Draft Inventory, the Commission made no comment upon these. In considering the non-agreed issues, the Commission stated tersely that it did "...not have sufficient information on which to base a decision as to each asset and liability..." and that, even if it did possess such information, "...it considers that these are not legal issues which it could profitably seek to resolve as part of its consultative remit and that it should confine itself to determining the legal principles to be applied". The Commission nevertheless noted the existence of a "...well-established rule of State succession law..." that immovable property situated on the territory of any of the successor States should pass exclusively to that State regardless of the origin or initial financing of such property or any loans or contributions made in respect of it.[100] This principle of *locus in quo* would be subject to possible compensation to be made by the successor States if such property was divided "...very unequally..." between them. This principle obviates the need to assess, and the relevance of, the actual ownership of such property and the method by which it was initially or subsequently financed, which can be extremely complicated factual issues.

In terms of movable property, debts and archives another "...commonly agreed principle..." enshrined in the *1983 Vienna Convention* required such property to be divided equally between successor States, assuming that it belonged to Yugoslavia on the date of succession of each of those States. Again, the question of initial financing, loans or contributions made in respect of such property was irrelevant.[101]

The question of ascertaining ownership presented further problems, however. Whilst the Commission stated that this should be determined by domestic law, and particularly Yugoslavia's 1974 constitution, the concept of "...social ownership..." in Tito's Yugoslavia meant that the constitution would not always categorically resolve such issues. First, the constitution expressly transferred certain items of property to the republics themselves and these could not be regarded as Yugoslavia's property for the purposes of succession "...whatever their origin or initial financing". Second, many "...associated labour organisations..." with their own legal personality existed within the republics, and the Commission noted that "...if, and to the extent that, other organisations operated 'social ownership' either at federal level or in two or more republics, their property, debts and archives should be divided between the successor States in question *if they exercised public prerogatives on behalf of the SFRY or of individual republics*.[emphasis added]". If such organisations did not exercise public prerogatives on behalf of the republics concerned or on behalf of the SFRY, they should be considered private-sector enterprises and excluded from the rules of State succession. This appears to be in accordance with PCIJ case-law in the *German Settlers Case,* where it was stated that "…[p]rivate rights acquired under existing [national] law do not cease on a change of sovereignty".[102]

Realising that these questions raised more complicated factual issues than many of the previously referred questions, the Commission concluded that its advice was without prejudice to the possibility that compensation may be required after the application of these principles to ensure the overall agreement remained equitable, as required by *Opinions 9* and *13*. Affirming its earlier position that such practical problems may form the basis of contentious proceedings, the Commission felt it inappropriate to address them whilst operating under its "…consultative function…" In the event that a dispute arose over a specific item of property, or of ownership thereof, it would be for the relevant States to "…resort to arbitration or some other mode of peaceful settlement of their disputes…" Whilst falling short of suggesting that it considered itself capable of acting in a contentious capacity in this area, it is submitted that the Commission must have felt competent to do so.

This opinion contains a number of interesting features, most notably the Commission's decision to refrain from providing anything other than "…general principles…" on State succession and its refusal to offer advice on issues which may represent contentious proceedings between the parties. In doing so the Commission showed considerable restraint which was consistent with the "…consultative remit…" under which these questions had been referred. This was the first time the Commission refrained from answering any question which had been put to it by the Conference Chair. Presumably and, it is submitted, correctly, the Commission saw in this instance "…conclusive reasons…" for doing so.[103] Having lost the confidence and participation of the FRY, the Commission could ill-afford to lose the confidence of the other parties by agreeing to consider a potentially contentious issue under its consultative mandate, which did not allow any of the interested parties to formulate the question referred, nor to appoint an *ad hoc* member to the Commission or to have the opportunity of an oral hearing before the Commission.[104]

6.10.2 *Opinion 15*

Opinion 15 dealt with the respective rights of the National Bank of Yugoslavia (NBY) and the central banks of the successor States and could not avoid consideration of specific factual problems.

The opinion began by considering whether the NBY was entitled to take decisions affecting the property, rights and assets of the former Yugoslavia after its dissolution. The Commission affirmed the findings of *Opinion 1*, without explicitly referring thereto, that municipal laws are "...merely facts in international law..." which must nevertheless be taken into account in assessing the structure and responsibilities of the NBY. The Commission cited the ICJ case of *Certain German Interests in Upper Silesia*[105] in support of this position. Accordingly, the Commission referred to the *1989 Statute of the NBY* and the *1974 SFRY Constitution* to conclude that the NBY "...participated in the exercise of the prerogatives of sovereignty...[of the SFRY]". Since the NBY was a composite of the central, republican and provincial banks, and enjoyed "...close institutional relations with Parliament..." it was clear that it "...partook of the State power of the SFRY...". Evidence of this was cited in the fact that the NBY acted on behalf of Yugoslavia in carrying out currency, credit and foreign exchange policies. Accordingly, the NBY, as an intrinsic part of the SFRY, must have been subject to the same dissolution process which befell Yugoslavia's other federal institutions. Therefore, "...[n]one of the organs of the NBY...can take legitimate decisions in respect of property, rights and interests that should be divided between the successor States of the SFRY...[and]...no decision in such matters taken by the Governor of the NBY on his own authority would have any legal validity once the former collective organisation has ceased to exist". This would be otherwise, however, if collaboration between the central banks of the successor States and the NBY had continued since Yugoslavia's dissolution "...outside the preexisting institutional framework...". In such circumstances, the NBY may legitimately be viewed as "...a coordinating agency acting on their behalf for the purposes of *jurisdictio inter volentes* to effect - rather than obstruct - the division of the property, rights and assets of the former SFRY". The very fact of referral by the SCCC indicated that such collaboration was non-existent, however, and the lack of FRY cooperation at other levels was duplicated in respect of the NBY. The Commission accordingly noted that the above situation was "…not the case…" and that the NBY had no continuing authority to take decisions affecting the property of the former SFRY.

Moving on to consider whether the central banks of the successor States had succeeded to the NBY's rights, the Commission noted that such rights must be divided equitably. Accordingly, the rights and obligations deriving from international agreements entered into by the NBY during Yugoslavia's existence fell to be divided amongst the successor States. This did not mean that such rights would automatically devolve to the central banks of those successor States, however, since it was "…for each of the successor States to determine by virtue of its sovereign constitutional powers, how these rights are to be exercised and these obligations discharged". Thus, any successor State could choose to retain its share of the NBY's rights and obligations as a governmental power, or instruct any other authority to act on its behalf, rather than exercising such powers through its central bank. However, the applicability of the rules of State succession would depend on whether those international agreements were entered into by the NBY acting as a Yugoslav federal organ or whether they were ordinary commitments entered into with the NBY acting "…as a bank with its own legal personality". In the latter case, the relevant rights and duties would be excluded from the State succession process. Essentially this was a question of fact which must be decided on a case-by-case basis. Whereas such questions of fact were avoided in *Opinion 14*, however, this question had specifically asked the Commission to rule on the status of a 1988 financial agreement between the NBY and foreign commercial banks, in relation to the manufacturers Hanover Ltd.

The Commission noted that this agreement was entered into with the NBY acting for the international creditors of Hanover Ltd. and that it had "…acted together with other Yugoslav banking institutions presenting themselves expressly as legal persons accepting on their own behalf the obligations deriving from the agreement".[106] Similarly, all parties to the agreement had made the discharge of their obligations subject to the law of a third State and to the jurisdiction of the ordinary Yugoslav courts or other foreign courts in the event of disputes arising regarding the agreement or its obligations. Accordingly, the Commission noted that it was "…for the parties to refer it to one of the courts that have jurisdiction under the agreement itself…" in the event that any dispute arose and made no further observations. This reinforces the Commission's earlier refusal to delve into potentially contentious matters without express referral by the relevant parties under the contentious proceedings of the Commission. In this case, however, the Commission appeared to indicate that it did not consider itself competent to act as an adjudicatory body, since the appropriate judicial mechanisms for such a task had already been specified. Far from representing any abdication of responsibility, such restraint should be recognised as the appropriate response to any question which may have cast further confusion on the Commission's role within the ICFY.

6.10.3 *Reflections on Opinions 14-15*

The Commission's findings in respect of the division of immovable and moveable property are difficult to criticise.[107] They provide certain supplementary rules to govern the succession process, whilst emphasising that these are capable of being deviated from by agreement between the parties, subject to the overriding requirement to reach an equitable overall settlement, which may require compensation if assets are disproportionately located throughout the successor States. Essentially, they provide further legal advice on which basis negotiations between the parties continuing cooperation with the Working Group on Succession Issues could continue to work towards an agreement, without ever attempting to resolve actual disputes which may occur during those negotiations.

6.10.4 *Procedural Issues Arising from Opinions 14-15*

Opinions 14-15 provide further evidence of the Commission's continuing willingness to flout political pressure to ensure its independence was retained. The issues dealt with therein involved specific factual questions which were conceptually different from SCCC's other questions and which could easily have formed the basis for contentious proceedings. Whereas such factual issues may be argued to fall within the definition of "*…any* legal question…"[108] for the purposes of legitimising the SCCC's request for an advisory opinion, it is submitted that the Commission would have blurred the distinctions between the various aspects of its dual mandate if it had provided the type of advice sought in their letter. Merely because none of the parties had issued contentious proceedings was no excuse to circumvent the requirements of consent by addressing them in advisory opinions.

Accordingly, the Commission was right to limit its role to supplying general legal principles applicable to the succession process and, in the case of the *NBY-Hanover Ltd. Agreement* to have indicated that the Commission was not the appropriate forum for any contentious proceedings. It is regrettable that the SCCC forced the Commission to appear to shy away from these issues by erroneously submitting them under its advisory remit.

In all other respects, the procedure employed was no different from that discussed in respect of *Opinions 11-13*.[109] Most importantly, these opinions represented the end of the Commission's active participation within the ICFY and the completion of the Commission's jurisprudence. After this point, although the Commission was not formally discontinued,[110] no further questions were referred under either of its dual remits, despite many requests from private individuals and NGO's asking it to make a declaration on different legal issues relating to the Yugoslav conflict.[111]

6.11 Conclusions

It has been suggested that, at the time the Yugoslav crisis clearly became one which would involve international legal issues such as self-determination, recognition of States and *uti possidetis*, political motives lay behind the EC's decision to retain the Commission in its original form. Having performed its role in respect of providing legal advice on issues relating to the dissolution of Yugoslavia, the change from the ECCY to the ICFY offered the ideal opportunity to conclude the Commission's work and constitute a new organ to deal with the post-dissolution aspects of the conflict. This was not done, however, for reasons that remain purely speculative. Nevertheless, having decided to retain the Commission, the ICFY allowed further examination of its practice and procedure in a new form and in a new role.

From a procedural perspective, the Commission did not undergo a radical transformation during its transfer to the ICFY. Despite a reconstitution of its members, a majority of the newly-composed Commission's members remained those from the ECCY. Many of the procedures adopted in the new Terms of Reference and rules of procedure did little more than codify unpublished practices during the ECCY. In some areas, however, procedural changes occurred during the transition to the ICFY. There is a perceptible move away from the exclusivity of the written procedure and the need for the consent of the relevant parties for any contentious proceedings is made far clearer. There is clearly an attempt to deal with potential procedural problems prospectively rather than reactively, the latter of these having characterised the Commission's ECCY approach. Many of these procedures remained unused because no disputes were referred under the Commission's contentious proceedings mandate. Despite the greater clarity provided by the written procedural rules, a number of areas of uncertainty remained. Having characterised the FRY's second jurisdictional challenge as something less than a formal challenge, the Commission's 'Reactions' are of uncertain legal character, and are not contemplated in any procedural instruments. The role of rapporteurs and experts and the possibility of embarking on preliminary inquiries before proceedings are all features of the new procedural mandate, but nothing in the Commission's practice provides any indication of how they were to work. The identity of certain parties entitled to take decisions such as prolonging the length of deliberations was also unclear. Finally, the Commission's oblique reference to it having always adopted an adversarial style of proceedings is curious.

From a jurisprudential perspective, it is submitted that the Commission provided competent legal advice in difficult circumstances. State succession is a vexatious area of international law and one in which there exists little incontrovertible practice or custom. Furthermore, such practice often relates to the problems of earlier periods in international relations, such as the decolonisation process, where the demands of the succession process were not the same as those in the Yugoslav case study. The dissolution of a sovereign State into numerous new States, each of which achieved independence at a different time and most of which have a certain antipathy towards certain other successor States, is a difficult factual scenario. This was further complicated by the FRY's claim to be continuing Yugoslavia's legal personality and its decision to withdraw cooperation with the Commission and other elements of the ICFY when this claim was not endorsed. Nevertheless, the Commission's jurisprudence steered an acceptable route through these legal and political difficulties and succeeded in providing guiding principles on succession which were of direct influence on the negotiations which followed them.

Substantively, having now completed its roles under the respective conferences, it is possible to say with confidence that the epithet of 'arbitration' was entirely inappropriate for the functions performed by the

Badinter Commission. Despite having proclaimed a dual mandate in its ECCY *Interlocutory Decision* and in its ICFY Terms of Reference, the Commission never approached what could be described as arbitration proceedings in the traditional sense of that term. Having lost the confidence of Serbia and Montenegro under the ECCY, it was unlikely that the contentious procedures unveiled in the new Terms of Reference would ever be used, since contentious proceedings would invariably involve these parties. Wisely, the Commission refrained from dealing with issues which could have formed the basis of contentious proceedings, had the relevant parties consented thereto, when asked to provide advisory opinions on certain factual problems involved in the succession process. Accordingly, the Commission issued nothing other than advisory opinions during its working life under both conferences, notwithstanding the '*Comments*', '*Interlocutory Decision*' and '*Reactions*' discussed herein and in chapter 5. This is not to deny the importance of the Commission's opinions. At a practical level, they influenced, to varying degrees, the political approaches of the conferences under which they operated and, under the ICFY, assisted the Working Group on Succession Issues in establishing principles on which to base the negotiations process. At a more abstract level, the Commission's jurisprudence offers a unique insight into the legal problems surrounding the dissolution of a State and the practical problems of succession in the aftermath of such dissolution. The inventiveness of the Commission, especially in its earlier jurisprudence, offers academics the opportunity to review traditional international law approaches to these issues and to assess the approaches adopted by those more experienced in constitutional affairs. In light of the blurring of boundaries between inter-State problems and intra-State problems, this is a task whose importance cannot be underestimated.

Having said that the Commission's earlier jurisprudence emanated from those with little or no international legal experience and that they have been subject to some criticism, it is interesting to note that the Commission's ICFY jurisprudence does little to contradict its earlier opinions. It is true that *Opinion 11*, considering the various dates of succession and suggesting that Yugoslavia retained international personality until a time after which all republics had become independent States, is difficult to reconcile with *Opinion 1*, which denied the existence of any secessions in Yugoslavia and declared any independent States to have arisen as a result of a dissolution process. It is also true that the Commission refrained during its later jurisprudence from repeating earlier declarations that the rights of individuals, peoples and minorities were peremptory norms of international law. Certain aspects of the Commission's jurisprudence remain frustratingly imprecise, as a result of their conversational style, such as the vague references to an "...international agency having powers...[to require third States to take counter measures to protect Yugoslav property on their territory]". Nevertheless, on a number of other occasions, the Commission specifically refers to its earlier jurisprudence in an approving and quasi-precedential manner. *Opinions 9* and *10* are repeatedly relied upon to reinforce the need to arrive at an equitable succession agreement and to deny the legitimacy of the FRY's claim to continue Yugoslavia's international legal personality. For those who criticise the Commission's jurisprudence as lacking any knowledge of international law, it is a salutary reminder that one of the new members of the Commission was formerly the President of the ICJ and currently an active member of the Iran-USA Claims Tribunal. Equally, Monsieur Badinter's reputation following his role as the Chairman of the Commission appears to have suffered no irreparable harm, and he has since been appointed as President of the OSCE's new Court on Conciliation and Arbitration.

In summary, this writer considers the Commission's jurisprudence to have offered a new insight into many areas of international law. Chapter 7 will now attempt a rationalisation of the Commission's jurisprudence in respect of the dissolution of Yugoslavia and offer some observations on how its opinions may offer a new approach to the problems facing contemporary international society.

Notes

1. Private letter from John Major to Lord David Owen, reprinted in Owen, D., *Balkan Odyssey*, (1995), Victor Gollancz, 18.
2. Boutros-Ghali, B., *Report of the United Nations Secretary-General on the ICFY*, (1992), UN Doc. S/24795, 1, partially reprinted in (1992), 31 *ILM*, 1549-1577.
3. Owen, supra n.1, 29.
4. For an interesting example of how the demands of one EC Member State may impact on the policy of the organisation as a whole, see Owen, ibid, 24, where he describes how these initial French concerns dissolved when it became clear that the French government needed British help in seeking to address domestic public opposition to the ratification of the TEU.

5 The incumbent UN Secretary-General, Boutros Boutros-Ghali, and President of the EC Council, John Major, were Co-Chairmen of the London conference and ICFY.

6 For the full text of the rules of procedure, see *International Conference on the Former Yugoslavia: Documents Adopted at the London Conference*, (1992), 31 *ILM*, 1531-3. See also Ramcharan, B.G. (ed.), *The International Conference on the Former Yugoslavia Official Papers*, (1997), Kluwer.

7 Ibid, 1533-4.

8 Chapter 5, section 5.2.2.

9 See Chapter 5, section 5.9.2. and Chapter 7, section 7.4.

10 See Chapter 5, sections 5.14.2 and sections 6.9.1.-6.10.3. below.

11 A *Statement on Bosnia*, a series of *Specific Decisions by the London Conference*, reports detailing *Conclusions on the Implementation of Existing Sanctions*, a *Programme of Action on Humanitarian Issues*, a discussion of *Confidence, Security-Building and Verification Measures* and a specific paper produced by the Co-Chairmen of the London Conference on *Serbia and Montenegro* were agreed. For the text of these agreements, see (1992), 31 *ILM*, 1537.

12 China, France, UK, USA, USSR (now Russia).

13 These two seats were sub-divided into EC-states and non-EC states. Italy and Greece occupied the EC-states seat, on a six-monthly rotation system. Non-EC states agreed to hold the position for a period of three months before it rotated, on an alphabetical basis, from Romania to Albania, Austria, Bulgaria and Hungary.

14 *Report of the UN Secretary-General on the ICFY*, supra n.2, 1.

15 This Group's task was to "...promote a cessation of hostilities and a constitutional settlement in Bosnia..." A Mixed Military Working Group was created to orchestrate communications between the warring Bosnian factions, several military crises were negotiated to varying degrees of success and a series of constitutional proposals were produced for a new Bosnian constitution.

16 To "...promote humanitarian relief in all its aspects, including refugees". This Group was chaired by the UN High Commissioner for Refugees, Sadako Ogata, and dealt with the estimated 3 million dependent upon external assistance for their survival. Negotiations for securing the provision of humanitarian aid, preventing harassment of minority populations and the return of all refugees and internally-displaced persons were all part of the Group's agenda.

17 To "...recommend initiatives for resolving ethnic questions in the former Yugoslavia..."A number of sub-groups were created for each republic and special groups on Kosovo and Vojvodina were also created. Serbia and Montenegro did not participate in this Working Group. Close links were made between the efforts of this Group and those of the CSCE. See Rossanet, B., 'Protecting the Rights of Ethnic and National Communities and Minorities: The Experience of the ICFY', (1994), 2 *IJGR*, 79.

18 To "...resolve succession issues arising from the emergence of new states on the territory of the former Yugoslavia". In addition to questions of succession

involving property, this Group also looked at the question of citizenship for people finding themselves in a newly-independent State.

19 To "...address economic issues arising from the emergence of new states..." Close links existed between this Group and the Working Group on Succession Issues. The Economic Issues Group prepared an inventory of State assets and liabilities which formed the basis of negotiations on succession issues. See below, section 6.10.1. The Group also considered measures necessary to rebuild the shattered economies of the various republics.

20 To "...develop confidence-building measures covering military movements, arms control and arms transfers and limitations, and measures for their monitoring and verification". This Group discussed specific military incidents which were preventing negotiations from continuing and more general agreements allowing international supervision of military positions by UNPROFOR and the ECMM.

21 See Chapter 5, section 5.13.

22 UN Secretary-General's Report, supra n.2, 1.

23 See (1993), 32 *ILM*, 1572-8, for details.

24 UN Secretary-General's Report, supra n.2, 4.

25 Pellet, A., 'L'Activité de la Commission D'arbitrage de la Conférence Européene pour la Paix en Yougoslavie', (1992), 38 *AFDDI*, 220, at 235, notes that "...si l'époque à laquelle ella avait été créé justifiait cette orientation 'constitutionnaliste', il n'en allait plus ainsi à partir du moment où la dissolution de la RSFY étant acquise".

26 *Justice in Cataclysm*, Brussels, 20th July 1996.

27 Frowein, J.A. 'Self-Determination As A Limit to Obligations Under International Law', in Tomuschat, C. (ed.), *Modern Law of Self-Determination*, (1993), Nijhoff, 211, at 216. These comments are made in respect of the Commission's ruling on *uti possidetis* and the same author later concedes, at 217, that "...a lot can be said for the approach made by the Badinter Committee...". See also Pomerance, M., 'The Badinter Commission: The Use and Misuse of the International Court of Justice's Jurisprudence', (1998), 20 *MichJIL*, at 32.

28 The original Italian representative, Aldo Corasaniti, was replaced by Francisco Paolo Casavola when the former retired.

29 See for example Kingsbury, B., 'Claims by Non-State Groups in International Law', (1992), 25 *Cornell JIL*, 481, at 505-6; Pellet, A., 'Note sur la Commission D'arbitrage de la Conférence Européene pour la Paix en Yougoslavie', (1991), 37 *AFDDI*, 329; Pellet, A., 'The Opinions of the Badinter Arbitration Committee: A Second Breath for the Self-Determination of Peoples', (1992), 3 *EJIL*, 178. Craven, M.C.R., 'The European Community Arbitration Commission on Yugoslavia', (1995), 66 *BYIL*, 333, at 413, considers that, even if one accepts certain limitations on the jurisprudence of the Commission, it nevertheless provides "...an indication as to the direction in which the various aspects of international law are developing...".

30 See Chapter 5, section 5.7.5. on decision-making under the ECCY. Although the rules of procedure adopted by the Commission within the ICFY allowed for

majority decision-making and dissenting judgments, this does not appear to have been the case in the Commission's practice.

31 Pellet, supra n.25, 235.

32 See Chapter 5 section 5.2.2.

33 Cf. Merrills, J.G., *The Development of International Law by the European Court of Human Rights: Second Edition*, (1993), MUP.

34 Pellet, supra n.25, 236,

35 See Chapter 5, section 5.13.

36 See Pomerance, M., The Admission of Judges Ad Hoc in Advisory Proceedings: Some Reflections in the Light of the Namibia Case, (1973), 69 *AJIL*, 446.

37 Schermers, H.G. and Blokker, N.M., (eds.), *International Institutional Law*, (1995), Nijhoff, 458, note that "...judicial organs should be as independent as possible". *Article 2* of the *ICJ Statute*, requiring judges to be "...independent..." has already been mentioned.

38 The writer was unable to obtain information on this point from the Secretariat of the ICFY, despite repeated requests.

39 Chapter 5, section 5.4.3.

40 *ICJ Statute, Article 25(3).*

41 *ICJ Statute, Article 24* requires any member considering himself unable to participate in a particular case to notify the President but, in the event of disagreement on this issue, it is for the court to decide.

42 Of course, documents may still be categorised as 'confidential', even if they are circulated to the parties concerned.

43 *ICJ Statute, Article* 33 states that the court's costs shall be borne by the UN, whereas *Article 64* states that each party shall bear its own costs unless otherwise decided by the court. The Commission's approach appears to leave it no discretion in this latter aspect.

44 *ICJ Statute, Article 36(2)* accordingly limits all disputes to those of a legal nature. In the *Mavrommatis Case*, [1924], PCIJ Series A, No.2, at 11, the PCIJ defined a legal dispute as "...a disagreement over a point of law or fact, a conflict of legal views or of interests between two persons". This was recently confirmed in the *East Timor Case*, [1995], ICJ Rep, 32. The ICJ has consistently held that this is a matter for "...objective determination...". See, for example, *Interpretation of Peace-Treaties Case*, [1950], ICJ Rep, 65.

45 Although *Opinions 4-7* refer to the use of a rapporteur, there is no indication that this person was intimately linked to any of the parties involved in the issues under consideration, unlike the position apparently adopted here.

46 *ICJ Statute, Article 55(2).*

47 *ICJ Statute, Article 56* makes similar provision.

48 The *Statute of the ECJ, Article 32*, prohibits dissenting opinions. The *1991 Rules of Procedure of the ECJ, Chapter 5(6)* state simply that "...[d]ifferences of view on the substance, wording or order of questions, or on the interpretation of the voting shall be settled by decision of the Court...". Schermers, supra n.37, 466 notes one case in which the ECJ was forced to debate an issue for six months before it could arrive at a decision with which all members were satisfied, which

is a direct result of the inability of such members to express a dissenting opinion. For details, see *ICI v Commission (Dyestuffs) Case*, [1972], ECR, 619.

49 In its response to the challenge of the FRY, the Commission explicitly referred to paragraph 3(b) of these Terms of Reference, which would tend to support the position offered above.

50 Chapter 5, section 5.13.

51 See Pomerance, supra n.27, at 48-50.

52 Sahovic, M., 'The Former Yugoslav Federation and International Law', in McDonald, R. (ed.), *Essays in Honour of Wang Tieya*, (1994), Nijhoff, 619.

53 Ibid, 627.

54 *Article 38(1)* of the *ICJ Statute* is widely acknowledged as the classic definition of the sources of international law. *Article 38(1)(d)* includes amongst these sources "...judicial decisions and the teachings of the most highly qualified publicists of the various nations, as subsidiary means for the determination of rules of law".

55 *Opinion 11*, reprinted (1992), 31 *ILM*, 1587.

56 Cf., however, the Commission's 'Reactions' in section 6.7. below, in which it stated that it did not rule out the possibility that a direct challenge may be made by the FRY on grounds which the Commission deemed justified. This would tend to indicate that the Commission treated the second challenge as an informal one, in light of the fact that it was not communicated directly to the Commission's Chair, and would justify the informality of the response provided.

57 Section 5, discussed in section 5.2. below.

58 *Opinion 11* confirms this suggestion by stating that "...the Commission unanimously adopted a document reacting to the assertions made by the FRY...".

59 [1950] ICJ Reports, 71.

60 Lee, E., *Dictionary of Arbitration Law and Practice*, (1986), Mansfield, 24.

61 Ibid, 90.

62 See Chapter 5, section 5.10.5.

63 Pellet, supra n.25, 234.

64 Reprinted at 32 *ILM*, (1993), 1584-5.

65 See Chapter 5, section 5.16.

66 Chapter 5, section 5.14.2.

67 Reprinted at (1978), 72 *AJIL*.

68 Reprinted at (1983), 22 *ILM*.

69 See Chapter 5, section 5.7.7.

70 Mullerson, R., 'The Continuity and Succession of States, by Reference to the Former USSR and Yugoslavia', (1993), 42 *ICLQ*, 473. Equally, Vagts, D.F., 'State Succession: The Codifiers View', (1993), 33 *VJIL*, at 295, notes that "...[r]eferences to the *Vienna Convention on Treaty Succession* as codifying custom are rare".

71 This definition is taken from *Article 2*, common to both conventions, whose precise wording states that succession is "...the replacement of one State by another in the responsibility for the international relations of territory". Jennings R. and Watts, A., *Oppenheim's International Law*, (1992), Longmans, 208, use

similar phraseology, stating State succession to occur "...when one or more international persons takes the place of another international person, in consequence of a change in the latter's condition".

72 The Commission cites *Articles 18, 31 and 41* of the *1983 Vienna Convention* as authority for this position.

73 Chapter 7, section 7.5.

74 Pellet, A., 'L'Activité de la Commission D'arbitrage de la Conférence Internationale pour L'Ancienne Yougoslavie', (1993), 39 *AFDDI*, 294.

75 Chapter 4, section 4.3.3.

76 State practice from the dissolution of the former USSR tends to support the requirement of an overall equitable outcome. Thus, the *1991 Treaty on Succession to the Soviet Union's State Debts and Assets*, cited in Mullerson, supra n.69, 479, required the successor States to agree on "...an appropriate, fair and ascertained share of the property [of the former USSR]..." Jennings, supra n.70, 220-21, cites State practice for the assertion that such an agreement must achieve "...proportionality..." between the successor States. Cf. Kreca, M., Succession and the Continuity of Yugoslavia, (1992), 39 *JRMP*, 178.

77 Chapter 5, section 5.7.7.

78 See Chapter 5, section 5.9.1.

79 The reference to taking counter-measures "...in accordance with international law..." must be taken as referring to the requirements of having first attempted to seek a peaceful settlement, having ascertained that the counter-measures are necessary and, finally, ensuring the proportionality of such measures. See the *Naulilaa Case*, (1928), 2 UNRIAA, at 1011.

80 See Rogoff, M.A., 'The Obligation to Negotiate in International Law: Rules and Realities', (1994), 16 *Mich JIL*, 141.

81 [1969] ICJ Rep., 46-7.

82 Rogoff, op cit, 160, suggests that an obligation to negotiate may exist "...where the extent of the rights of States are limited by the rights of other States". This would appear to include issues of succession, where the interests of all successor States are inextricably linked. If this were the case, one may consider the implications of practice in the dissolution of the USSR, where a number of former Soviet republics refuse to take place in certain aspects of the succession negotiations. See Mullerson, supra n.69, 480, for discussion of the non-participation of certain former Soviet republics in negotiations on non-military ships. See also White, G., 'The Principle of Good Faith', in Lowe, V. and Warbrick, C. (eds.), *The UN and the Principles of International Law*, (1994), Routledge, 230.

83 The full maxim *res inter alios acta alteri nocere debet* means that a transaction between others does not produce legal effects for those who are not parties thereto. Osborn, P.G., *Concise Law Dictionary*, (1947), S&M, 89.

84 Pellet, supra n.73, 297, suggests that this could only really occur if the UN Security Council adopted a Resolution under *Chapter VII* of the Charter.

85 In the *Barcelona Traction Case*, [1970], ICJ Rep, at 32, the ICJ distinguished between rights between rights which exist only between specific identifiable

States and those in which "...*all States* have a legal interest in their protection...". The latter are deemed rights *erga omnes*. See also *Vienna Convention on the Law of Treaties 1969, Articles 53* and *64* and the ILC's *Draft Articles on State Responsibility, Article 19*, (1980), 2 Ybk.ILC, 30.

86 Pellet, supra n.73, 298. Effectively, it would widen the *locus standi* of those allowed to enforce the property rights.

87 Craven, supra n.29, 398, notes the "...more circumspect view..." of the conventions taken by the Commission during these later opinions, in comparison with its reference to the same instruments having "...drawn inspiration from the general principles of international law..." in *Opinion 1*.

88 Jennings, supra n.70, 210, states that "...[n]o general rule can be laid down concerning all the cases in which a succession occurs, and each needs to be examined separately". O'Connell, D.P., 'Reflections on the State Succession Convention', (1979), 24 *ZAORV*, 725, at 726, goes so far as to say that "...State succession is a subject altogether unsuited to the process of codification". One generally accepted customary rule is enshrined in *Article 11* of the *1978 Vienna Convention* and establishes that succession cannot, as such, affect a boundary created by a treaty.

89 Mullerson, supra n.69, 474.

90 Ibid, 473.

91 See Chapter 4, section 4.3.8. The *Guidelines* would tend to support the assertion that "...where a State divides into constituent parts, the [State] practice supports the continuity of existing treaty rights and obligations". Williamson, E.D. and Osborn, J.E., 'A US Perspective on Treaty Succession and Related Issues in the Wake of the Dissolution of the USSR and Yugoslavia', (1993), 33 *VJIL*, 261, at 263. Naturally, not having applied for EC-recognition, the FRY had not accepted these obligations. Nevertheless, the FRY had, along with the other former Yugoslav republics, accepted the *Vienna Conventions* as the basis for conducting negotiations on succession and, accordingly, it is likely that *Article 34* of the *1978 Vienna Convention* would apply. This states that any treaty, applicable to the whole predecessor State, which was in force at the date of succession continues to bind each new successor State. This is subject to modification, by agreement between all successor States, and subject to the proviso that this principle may be incompatible with the object and purpose of some treaties and would not therefore apply. The *1968 Nuclear Non-Proliferation Treaty*, applying only to 'nuclear' States, is thus clearly inapplicable to all non-nuclear States arising from the dissolution of the USSR. In the event that the FRY considered itself the continuation of the SFRY, therefore, it would be bound to accept all pre-existing obligations of the SFRY and, in the event that it were considered a successor State, as indicated in *Opinion 10*, it would still be bound by those treaties which applied to the whole of the territory of the former Yugoslavia, by virtue of its acceptance of the conventions as the basis for negotiations. One possible counter-argument is that *Article 6* of the 1978 convention and *Article 3* of the 1983 convention both stipulate that the conventions apply only to those instances of succession which have occurred "...in conformity with international

law and, in particular, with the principles of law embodied in the *Charter of the United Nations*...". The FRY would presumably maintain its argument that the illegal 'secessions' of the various newly-independent States claiming succession rights were illegal from an international law perspective and that, accordingly, the operative terms of the conventions were inapplicable.

92 On the 'clean-slate' theory and the alternative 'universal succession' theory, see O'Connell, D.P., *State Succession in Municipal and International Law: Volumes I-II*, (1967), CUP, 6-8. Schachter, O., 'State Succession: The Once and Future Law', (1993), 33 *VJIL*, 253, at 258 notes that "...as a matter of policy, the case for presuming continuity makes sense today when the State system is increasingly fluid".

93 Mullerson, R., 'New Developments in the Former USSR and Yugoslavia', (1993), 33 *VJIL*, 299, at 317.

94 Nevertheless, the Commission's later opinions did also include further principles of succession and largely attempted to become embroiled in specific factual questions.

95 See above section 6.4.

96 See section 6.4.

97 Ibid.

98 Ibid.

99 Ibid.

100 Jennings, supra n.70, 232, cites a wealth of State practice in support of this view.

101 This is in contrast to the position in respect of 'newly-independent' States under the 1983 convention. The term newly-independent State under the *Vienna Conventions* on succession, however, refers to something other than had occurred in the case of Yugoslavia's dissolution and is limited to "...a successor State the territory of which immediately before the date of succession was *a dependent territory for the international relations of which the predecessor State was responsible* [emphasis added]". See *Articles 7-18*. The influence of the decolonisation period during which the conventions were drafted is self-evident. See Vagts, supra n.69, 275. For discussion of succession issues in times before the decolonisation era, see generally Feilchenfeld, E.H., *Public Debts and State Succession*, (1931), Macmillan.

102 [1928] PCIJ Rep, Series B, at 36. *Article 6* of the 1983 convention also excludes the rights, obligations and property of natural and juridical persons from its provisions on succession.

103 See above, section 6.6.

104 See section 6.4.

105 [1926] PCIJ Reports, Series A, 12.

106 Specific sections of the relevant agreement were cited in evidence of this position. These are relatively unimportant if one seeks merely to highlight the principles advised by the Commission.

107 Cf. Craven, supra n.29, 401, where he states that the Commission stated the rule of *locus in quo* too broadly and that the Commission suggested that "...any moveable property found on a successor State's territory would automatically

pass to that State". It is submitted, however, that the Commission's comments, in stating that "...public property passes to the successor State on whose territory it is situated..." were given in the context of a paragraph discussing only *immoveable* property and that they must be understood accordingly. No similar reference is made in the passage discussing moveable property.

108 See section 6.4.

109 See section 6.9.

110 For evidence of this, see references to the Commission in Reports of the ICFY Co-Chairmen. Amongst these are Report numbers S/1994/1074, 19th September 1994, S/1994/1124, 3rd October 1994, S/1994/1454, 29th December 1994 and S/1995/175, 2nd March 1995. See generally Owen, D., *Balkan Odyssey: CD ROM,* (1995), Victor Gollancz, accompanying the book of the same name.

111 Pellet, supra n.25, 30.

7 The Dissolution of Yugoslavia and Self-Determination

"It will raise hopes which can never be realised. It will, I fear, cost thousands of lives. In the end, it is bound to be discredited, to be called the dream of an idealist who failed to realise the danger until too late to check those who attempt to put the principle into force. What a calamity the phrase was ever uttered!".
R. Lansing (American Secretary of State) commenting upon the post-war self-determination policy of President Woodrow Wilson.

7.1 Introduction

Self-determination is an important international legal concept about which much has been written yet little agreed upon.[1] When evaluating the wealth of material in this area, one cannot help but be struck by the division of opinion as to the meaning, applicability and, ultimately, the usefulness of this concept. Cassesse notes self-determination's "...Janus-like nature..." and comments that "...its ideological origins render it a multi-faceted but also an extremely ambiguous concept".[2] It is submitted that this lack of clarity causes confusion in academic debate and practical implementation of self-determination.[3] One identifiable feature, however, is that the 'law' of self-determination has developed alongside political events to which it has been applied. This is true of the concept of nationality, the precursor to self-determination, Wilsonian self-determination following World War I and the post-World War II decolonisation process. Self-determination in the contemporary era not only faces the problem of intellectual differences regarding its purposes, but also the practical difficulties faced by international norms at a time when the international system itself is in a state of flux. Uncertainties in the legal system in which a norm operates inevitably create uncertainties in those norms themselves.[4] The challenge is to adapt legal concepts to ensure they maintain relevance in the era in which they must operate, whilst retaining their normative foundations.[5] Since all international legal concepts are inter-related,[6] developments in one norm will have an impact on development of other norms. Self-determination has already impacted on other international norms[7] and its continuing evolution may prove to have a great impact on the international system as a whole.

The Yugoslav case study offers an opportunity for re-evaluating self-determination in a contemporary contextual setting where claims for self-determination have different origins and different demands than earlier manifestations of the same 'right'. Problematic questions surrounding the concept remain fundamentally the same. What does self-determination entail and to whom does it apply? How is it to be exercised and what is the role of the international community in the process? How, if at all, has the principle adapted to new political conditions and what is its standing in the current international legal system? The Commission's responses to such questions differ from the traditional approach and any challenge to established ways of thinking is bound to provoke scepticism. It is submitted, however, that the Commission's jurisprudence offers an interesting appraisal of a controversial international norm from the perspective of those outside the discipline, which challenges many traditional preconceptions about self-determination.

The chapter describes the historical development of self-determination before highlighting how the Commission's theoretical framework builds on self-determination's evolutionary development.[8] A brief reiteration of the problem of self-determination in Yugoslavia precedes an analysis of the opinions relevant to the dissolution process.

7.2 A Brief History of Self-Determination

Just as one cannot understand contemporary conflicts without an appreciation of certain historical facts,[9] one cannot understand disagreements over the 'correct' application of a specific norm without an appreciation of its history. This section seeks to highlight the various manifestations of the 'right' to self-determination and show that there are discrete manifestations of the 'right' which dealt with the prevailing contextual problems of international society during different eras. Nevertheless, certain underlying foundations may be identified, relating to the notion of legitimate governance, which are developed in the Commission's juisprudence.

7.2.1 *Pre-World War I*

Self-determination first arose as a political postulate rather than a legal right. In a domestic sense, it is credited as having developed from the philosophies of Hobbes, Locke and Rosseau.[10] Its evolution into an international philosophy is evidenced in references to the concept in the American Declaration of Independence of 1776 and in the post-revolution French Constitution of 1791.[11] Its roots are traceable to the principle of nationality and the quest to be free from despotic government, whether an overseas ruler or an authoritarian monarch.[12] The principle became synonymous with the creation of European nation States.

7.2.2 *Post-World War I*

Lenin was "...the first forceful proponent of the concept at the international level...".[13] He used it to justify the Soviet socialist revolution and to prevent the influence of capitalism disrupting the socialist experiment. The rhetoric of self-determination was often betrayed by the reality of communist dictatorship, however, and self-determination was subjugated, re-defined or ignored if it conflicted with the USSR's desire to exert political control over its neighbouring States or the struggle against the bourgeoisie.[14] The banner of self-determination presided over the Soviet annexation of the Baltic States in 1940. Nevertheless, believing self-determination to be entirely compatible with communist ideology, Lenin is credited as having played a major role in including the principle in the *UN Charter*.[15]

Ironically, America's President Wilson also strongly supported the concept of self-determination, but had entirely different ideas about what it meant.[16] Wilsonian self-determination relied on consent of the governed as the source of political legitimacy. Wilson also believed minority rights to be linked with this concept and included many minority protection schemes in the post-war territorial realignment. Equally, however, Wilson's rhetoric was displaced by the protection of colonial interests in post-war territorial settlements. Thus, "...self-determination was deemed irrelevant where the people's will was certain to run counter to the victor's geopolitical, economic and strategic interests".[17] Self-determination was deemed inapplicable in respect of the victors. Concern about the "...destabilising effects of international recognition of the doctrine of self-determination..."[18] led to its exclusion from the *Covenant of the League of Nations*.

7.2.3 Self-Determination and the UN

The *UN Charter* was the first universal Treaty to refer to self-determination and marked a critical juncture in its development as a legal right.[19] Although it was referred to only as a 'principle' and not as a 'right', *Article 1(2)* included as one of the UN's Purposes the developing of international relations based on respect for "...the principle of equal rights and self-determination of peoples...". *Article 2(4)* requires Members to refrain from acting in any manner inconsistent with these Purposes and *Article 55* identifies areas for the UN to promote in its task in ensuring the respect for self-determination.[20] *Article 56*, a "...significant provision...",[21] obliges States to take "...joint and separate action to achieve the purposes set forward in *Article 55*". Continuing disagreement about the precise meaning of the concept meant, however, that State practice was required to clarify what this obligation would entail.[22]

Decolonisation represented the first real State practice on self-determination. Colonialism, at the time of signing the Charter, was not yet perceived as illegal and Churchill had entered World War II on the pretext of guaranteeing the freedom to choose ones own government whilst excluding this right to British colonies.[23] *Chapters XI* and *XII* of the Charter, however, dealt with Non-Self-Governing Territories and territories held under the International Trusteeship System, both of which were intended to undergo "...progressive development towards *self-government*...".[24] Although reference to self-determination is avoided, these Chapters were clearly linked to the concept.[25] The *Declaration on the Granting of Independence to Colonial Countries and Peoples* stated that "...*all peoples* have the *right* to self-determination; by virtue of that *right* they *freely determine their political status* and *freely pursue their economic, social and cultural development* [emphasis added]".[26] This was followed by a clause on territorial integrity, a standard inclusion in resolutions on self-determination, stating that "Any attempt at the partial or total disruption of national unity and territorial integrity of a country is incompatible with the purposes and principles of the Charter...".[27] A *Declaration on Principles Relating to Non-Self-Governing Territories* specified the kinds of political status which were available to Non-Self-Governing territories; these were "...(a) Emergence as a sovereign independent State; (b) Free association with an independent State; or (c) Integration with an independent State".[28] State practice saw almost every former colony opt for independence and the number of independent States grew concomitantly from the immediate post-war years onwards.[29] While stressing the applicability of a "...right..." of self-determination to "...all peoples...", the reality again fell short of the rhetoric and it was generally only cases of "...salt-water colonialism..."[30] which attracted support for self-determination claims.[31] Repression of populations by domestic governments such as the USSR and many newly-independent States in Africa attracted little support for the applicability of self-determination. Although the ICJ, in the *Namibia Case*[32] and the *Western Sahara Case*[33] confirmed self-determination as a right rather than a political principle, it must be remembered that these advisory opinions were, respectively, considering issues relating to Non-Self Governing territories and decolonisation. These were specific contextual manifestations of the 'right' to self-determination and not the sum total of the doctrine. Equally, in the *Nicaragua Case*, where the ICJ said that it "...could not contemplate a new rule opening up a right of international intervention by one State against another on the ground that the latter has opted for some particular ideology or political system..."[34] one must remember that this was said in the context of the use of force in one State by another during the ideologically divided Cold War period. Recent contentious proceedings in the *East Timor Case* also involved a Non-Self-Governing Territory and failed to proceed to the merits of the case because of the absence of Indonesia's consent to jurisdiction.[35] The ICJ, however, conceded that the categorisation of self-determination as an *erga omnes* right was "...irreproachable...".[36]

The next major development occurred in 1966, with the adoption of the *International Covenant on Civil and Political Rights* (*ICCPR*) and the *International Covenant on Economic, Social and Cultural Rights* (*ICESCR*). Common *Article 1* confirmed that "*All peoples* have the *right* to self-determination [emphasis added]". It added that "All peoples may, for their own ends, freely dispose of their natural wealth and resources...".[37] The inclusion of self-determination, in light of the concept's ambiguity, rendered *Article 1* the "...most controversial provision..."[38] in the Covenants. Discussions in the Commission of Human Rights and the Third Committee, indicate that it was impossible to reach a common understanding on the scope, contents or meaning of the concept.[39] Nevertheless, *Article 1* was taken as confirming the right of self-determination outside the colonial context and identifying it as a free-standing human right. The *ICCPR* included a number of other clauses which may explain self-determination's meaning in that Covenant. *Articles 2-3* cover non-discrimination on various grounds, *Articles 18-19* cover freedom of thought, conscience, religion and expression, *Articles 18-19* cover the right to peaceful assembly and association and *Article 26* guarantees equality before the law. Of special significance are *Articles 25* and *27*. *Article 25* guarantees "...the right...(a) To take part in the conduct of public affairs, directly or through freely chosen representatives; (b) To vote and to be elected at genuine periodic elections which shall be by universal and equal suffrage and shall be held by secret ballot, guaranteeing the free expression of the will of the electors; (c) To have access, on general terms of equality, to public service...". *Article 27* requires that "In those States in which ethnic, religious or linguistic minorities exist, persons belonging to such minorities shall not be denied the right in community with the other members of their group, to enjoy their own culture, to profess and practise their own religion, or to use their own language". Cassesse concludes simply that the Covenants supplemented the *UN Charter's* references to self-determination and that, following them, "...there is no self-determination without *democratic decision-making* [emphasis added]".[40] Nevertheless, he concludes that the 'self' to whom this 'determination' applies can only mean the entire population in independent States or States yet to achieve independence and populations living under foreign occupation. He specifically excludes the applicability of the right to minorities, who are given only the protection offered in *Article 27*.[41] Distinctions drawn between self-determination and minority rights have generally continued.

The *Friendly Relations Declaration 1970*[42] also demonstrated that self-determination existed outside of the colonial context. It noted the duty of States to "...refrain from any forcible action which deprives peoples...of their right to self-determination and freedom and independence". Peoples against whom such force was used were entitled to "...seek and receive support in accordance with the purposes and principles of the Charter...". Furthermore States had the duty to "...promote, through joint and separate action, the realisation of the principle of equal rights and self-determination of peoples...". Some new elements were introduced in this declaration. First, the options available to the 'peoples' seeking self-determination were widened from those under the colonial declarations to include "...any...political status freely determined by a people...". Second, the territorial integrity clause was altered. Nothing in the declaration should be construed as authorising or encouraging activities which would undermine the territorial integrity of States "...conducting themselves in compliance with the principle of equal rights and self-determination...and thus *possessed of a government representing the whole people belonging to the territory without distinction as to race, creed or colour* [emphasis added]". This declaration has been called "...the most authoritative interpretation of the right to self-determination under the *UN Charter* and customary international law".[43] State practice shows how the new anti-racist features of self-determination was used to condemn apartheid in South Africa as a violation of the principle of equal rights and self-determination.[44] Similar resolutions were made in respect of South Rhodesia, albeit a few years before this declaration was adopted.[45] The declaration was heavily influenced by these situations and it has been suggested that it only applies to such racist regimes, rather than to repressive regimes *per se*.[46] Nevertheless, it represented a significant development in the concept of 'internal' self-determination, by requiring a government which was, at least in the racial sense, *representative* of its entire population.[47] This marked the beginning of a growing focus on the internal features of States and their governments which, to some degree, blurs the distinction between earlier manifestations of self-determination and protection of domestic populations through human rights and minority rights.

Further developments in this direction were made when the General Assembly adopted the *Declaration on the Rights of Persons Belonging to National or Ethnic, Religious and Linguistic Minorities* in 1992. This entitles minorities to enjoy their own culture, practice their own religion, use their own language and specifies "...the *right to participate effectively* in decisions on the national and, where appropriate, regional level concerning the minority to which they belong or the regions in which they live...[emphasis added]".[48] Its Preamble also refers to the realisation of the rights of minorities as "...within a democratic framework based on the rule of law...". This will be seen to be closely linked with the Commission's framework.

The 1993 *Vienna Declaration and Programme of Action*[49] was adopted by consensus following a World Conference on Human Rights, at which all UN Member States and many NGO's participated. Section 1 noted that "...the denial of the right of self-determination...[was] a violation of human rights..." and expanded on the definition of representative government in the 1970 Declaration by describing those States acting in compliance with self-determination as having "...a government representing the whole people belonging to the territory *without distinction of any kind* [emphasis added]". Clear links between self-determination and democracy were also made in Section 8, which described democracy, development and respect for human rights as "...interdependent and mutually reinforcing..." and defined democracy as "...the *freely expressed will of the people to determine their own political, economic, social and cultural systems* and their *full participation* in all aspects of their lives [emphasis added]". This built upon earlier pro-democracy resolutions such as that entitled *Enhancing the Effectiveness of the Principle of Periodic and Genuine Elections*.[50]

The applicability of self-determination to indigenous peoples represented a new manifestation of self-determination. *ILO Convention 169 on Indigenous Tribal Peoples in Independent Countries*, entering into force in 1991, referred to indigenous populations as 'peoples' but stated that that term should not be construed as implying the applicability of international legal rights of 'peoples' under general international law, namely self-determination.[51] A *Draft Universal Declaration on the Rights of Indigenous Peoples*, was adopted by the UN Sub-Commission on Prevention of Discrimination and Protection of Minorities in 1994.[52] It includes the right to self-determination and aims to allow indigenous peoples to maintain their traditional socio-economic, cultural and legal systems whilst retaining the right to participate fully in the life of the State.[53] Whether the provisions of the Draft Declaration will survive in the adoption of a declaration by the full Commission remains to be seen.

Whilst self-determination has clearly evolved during the UN's lifetime, continued fears about its inherently destructive consequences have hindered its development in respect of peoples living within sovereign States. Since earlier manifestations of the right resulted in independence for areas which were colonised or under alien occupation, States fear that granting the right to sub-State groups will endorse secessionism. State practice has generally denied the legitimacy of secession because of the principle of State sovereignty and territorial integrity. The Nigerian civil war, based on the uprising of Ibo communities in Biafra, was "...largely ignored by the UN..."[54] and the UN waited until after the *de facto* resolution of Bangladesh's secession before becoming involved. It will be argued, however, that a fresh approach is required to meet the contemporary demands of self-determination within existing States and that it is possible to develop an approach which guarantees self-determination whilst preserving territorial integrity.

7.2.4 *Other Instruments Dealing with Self-Determination*

The CSCE *Helsinki Final Act* of 1975 includes as one of its Principles the equal rights of peoples and their right to self-determination, in conformity with the *UN Charter*. The *HFA* provisions appear to go further than the instruments considered above, however, in stating that such rights mean that "…all peoples always have the right, in full freedom, to determine, when and as they wish, their internal and external political status, without external interference…".[55] The emphasis on internal self-determination as a continuing right goes beyond those earlier instruments and is not in any way limited to colonial situations, foreign invasions or racist regimes. Having been designed for the European States party to the *HFA*, it is intended to apply to existing sovereign States in a region where territorial disruption is unlikely. The reference to "…full freedom…" has been suggested to refer to the complementarity of other basic human rights with self-determination, mainly political rights such as freedom of expression and rights to participate in the election of governments and other public affairs.[56] Although the *HFA* is non-binding, political accountability may arise from non-compliance with this principle and State practice in conformity with the *HFA* may be used as evidence of a growing customary norm.[57] The *1990 Charter of Paris for a New Europe* is more circumspect in its provision on self-determination, stating only that the CSCE Members support the right "…in conformity with the Charter of the United Nations and with the relevant norms of international law, including those relating to the territorial integrity of States".[58] Nevertheless, emphasis on democracy and the importance of minority rights protection was indicated by the creation of an Office for Democratic Institutions And Human Rights (ODIHR) and a High Commissioner On National Minorities (HCNM) to provide "…early warning' and, as appropriate, 'early action'…in regard to tensions involving national minority issues…".[59] The Helsinki Summit noted that all CSCE countries took democracy as "…the basis for their political, social and economic life…"[60] and the Copenhagen Meeting on the Human Dimension, required CSCE governments to be "…representative in character…[and] accountable to the elected legislature or the electorate".[61]

Other non-European regional instruments have included the right of 'all peoples' to self-determination, including the *African Charter on Human and Peoples Rights 1981*.[62] Some organisations have also emphasised the right to representative government. In 1991, for example, the Organisation of American States (OAS) adopted a resolution requiring the political representation of its Members to be based on "...effective exercise of representative democracy".[63] Cassesse also makes reference to the 1976 *Algiers Declaration on the Rights of Peoples*,[64] although given the fact that this involved only NGO's and not States, it is unlikely that it may be taken as evidence of developing customary law.[65]

7.2.5 *Conclusions*

It has been suggested that there are "...good arguments..." for considering 'self-determination' as part of customary law and the existence of a 'law' of self-determination has been said to be "...beyond debate". State practice and ICJ jurisprudence confirm its legal character, at least in certain manifestations. It is widely, though not universally, accepted that self-determination has achieved the status of *jus cogens*.[66] The International Law Commission has agreed with this and included the denial of self-determination as an example of an international crime.[67] Self-determination has impacted on other international norms and, for example, "...no legal title to territory can be acquired in breach of self-determination".[68] *Article 2(4)* of the Charter, prohibiting the use or threat of force in international relations, does not apply when force is used to realise self-determination.[69] The ICJ has recently stated that suggestions of self-determination's status as an *erga omnes* right were "...irreproachable...".[70]

Such statements are ironic, given that self-determination's evolution from a political postulate to a legal right has done little to clarify exactly what is meant by the concept. Its inclusion in the *UN Charter* and other international instruments marked a critical turning point from the perspective of the concept's legal status but, due to continuing divisions about its meaning, these instruments contain only broad definitions, representing the low common denominators on which opposing interpretations of the doctrine could agree.

Self-determination has been used to pursue various political ideologies during different time-periods in international relations. The demands of decolonisation, prohibition of alien occupation and illegality of apartheid have all been dealt with under the rhetoric of self-determination. Although disparate, it is submitted that they all relate in some way to the notion of *legitimate governance*. Alien occupation clearly breaches State sovereignty and territorial integrity but colonialism and apartheid, although acceptable at one stage of international relations, became illegal during the UN's lifetime. Clearly, self-determination is flexible enough to adapt to new international problems and may cause a once-accepted practice to become a new manifestation of illegitimate governance. Despite many self-determination situations having been dealt with on a case-by-case basis with little consistency in State practice,[71] it is generally accepted that colonialism, foreign occupation and apartheid are no longer acceptable means of governing a State.

Academic debates about self-determination reflect political disagreements on what is meant by the concept. Whereas it is widely accepted that self-determination rights in respect of decolonisation, freedom from external invasion, and illegality of apartheid and racist regimes have crystallised through State practice, the question of self-determination within sovereign States remains controversial. States are reluctant to acknowledge the right of self-determination within their territories because they associate the doctrine with territorial fragmentation. International law is not a "...suicide-club".[72] These fears, and the lines drawn between self-determination and minority rights, arise because the bulk of State practice has been related to decolonisation and alien occupation, where independence is the only viable remedy.[73] Even in these situations, territorial fragmentation arose not because of the implementation of self-determination but because of a *denial* of self-determination.[74] Each of them represented a form of illegitimate governance which was, or became, illegal during the UN's lifetime.

Decolonisation remains relevant to international relations - Namibia was admitted to the UN in 1990 and issues such as East Timor and Gibraltar remain outstanding - but its relevance should not be overstated. Equally, threats of alien occupation cannot be considered moribund,[75] but these no longer represent the prime source of self-determination claims, nor the major threats to contemporary international peace and security. These threats are now most common from self-determination claims arising from sub-State groups in a world composed of ethnically-heterogeneous independent States.[76] A growing focus of internal self-determination, intensified by the tendency to focus on internal affairs in the aftermath of the Cold War,[77] means that such claims are likely to continue to grow. Demands for secession have been made by Biafrans, Katangans, West New Guineans, Southern Sudanese, Eritreans, South Moluccans, Pathans, Nagas, Corsicans, Basques, Sikhs, Kurds, Tamils and Quebecois.[78] Claims for greater political rights short of secession are even more widespread.[79] Responsibility for developing a coherent legal response rests on the international community and its organisations. The outdated demands and consequences of decolonisation should not prevent the search for a new manifestation of self-determination which will "...to steer a course between encouraging the break-up of viable nations...and...rejecting all further claims by oppressed minorities".[80] The problem of self-determination in independent States must be 'promoted' to the top of the international agenda.

Higgins notes that "There is a general assumption that self-determination is to do with independence".[81] To this, one might add that there is a further assumption which considers self-determination related to independence *and nothing else*. It is submitted that this attitude must be altered if any constructive developments in the concept are to be made.[82] As White suggests, it is time that the UN and the international community turned its attentions to the plight of encapsulated minorities within States.[83] Although most episodes of self-determination have resulted in the creation of new States, self-determination is not limited to independence and does not automatically authorise secessionism. Outside the decolonisation context and the occupation of a State by foreign forces, self-determination *must* mean something other than simply the right to independence and secession.[84] If not, the *Friendly Relations Declaration* and the *Vienna Declaration* would make little sense, since they deny the legitimacy of secession in cases where the State is conducting itself in accordance with self-determination. To hold that self-determination *must* include the right of secession is to give these 'saving paragraphs' no meaning. The question, therefore, is finding what self-determination *does* mean in reference to minorities and sub-State groups within independent States.

It is increasingly common to refer to self-determination not as a 'right' but as a 'bundle of rights' whose aims and outcomes may differ from other aspects of self-determination.[85] It has been suggested that decolonisation, alien occupation and apartheid are merely specific manifestations of a wider right, whose foundations lie in the concept of legitimate governance. To prevent progress on developing a solution to the problems of group rights within States by reference to the disruptive effects of these earlier manifestations is to confuse the aspect of self-determination in question. The demands of groups within sovereign States are different - most seek only non-discrimination and equal participation in their State's political structures[86] - and the results of implementing self-determination would also be different. This is not to deny the possibility that sub-State groups may seek independence. However, this is generally done as a last resort, after attempts at modifying the internal State structures have failed. What is needed is an approach which addresses the threats to international peace and security arising from internal repression of populations whilst avoiding unnecessary territorial disruption which also threatens peace and security.

An approach with increasing support is based on the linkage of self-determination and human rights, including minority rights. Those sub-State groups who enjoy participation in a representative government and live free from repression are least likely to give their support to nationalist claims for independence. Self-determination has been described as a prerequisite for the enjoyment of human rights, but human rights are also a prerequisite for the fulfilment of self-determination.[87] This is implicitly recognised in some of the international instruments discussed above, particularly those dealing with the need to ensure a *non-discriminatory* and *representative* political system which guarantees *participation* for all members of society, essentially on the basis of democracy. There is an increasing emphasis on 'internal' aspects of self-determination which, nevertheless, remain loyal to its underlying foundations of ensuring legitimate governance. Focus on the legitimacy of internal governmental structures has been evident since the anti-apartheid elements of self-determination were developed but it may be that current international relations allow this legitimisation process to develop beyond the extreme example of apartheid.

Writers disagree as to the appropriate manner to implement such an approach under the banner of self-determination. Some argue for a 'federal' right of self-determination, it being specified that the granting of autonomy rights cannot be seen as the first step towards independence and secession.[88] Others advocate autonomy without the emphasis on the federal aspects.[89] Others argue for a democracy-based approach which gives "...the whole people of every State...the right freely to choose its rulers, through a democratic and pluralistic process and in particular by means of free and genuine elections".[90] The essence of this writer's hypothesis is that it is less important which approach one prefers - and this cannot realistically be discussed outside the contextual requirements of an individual case-scenario - than the realisation of the need for a distinct approach to these questions. Numerous contextual ways of implementing such an intra-State approach are possible,[91] but it is changing the emphasis towards focusing self-determination claims within a State that is crucial. One exception to this, however, is this writer's disagreement with those who advocate greater leniency towards secession as a means of addressing these issues. It has been suggested, for example, that "Wherever ethnic minorities are suppressed they have a right, under international law, to secession".[92] To argue this case is not only to approach the question from the wrong angle - it implicitly accepts the impossibility of resolving such issues within existing State structures - but also hinders developments in State practice by reinforcing States' pre-conceptions about the inherently destructive nature of self-determination. One proponent of the need for a theory of secession nevertheless notes that "...the exercise of self-determination may take many forms, with secession...being only the most extreme. [...] Experimentation with new forms of 'semi-autonomy' or 'limited-autonomy' is what is needed".[93] It is necessary to disassociate the aims of contemporary self-determination from its destructive past. This is only possible with greater definitional clarity as to what is meant by the concept.

Even amongst writers who acknowledge the existence of the multiple aspects of self-determination and support the idea that minority rights and 'internal' self-determination mark the way forward, it is commonplace to hear references to its devastating effects without distinguishing between these different aspects. Cassesse thus notes that "Indiscriminately granting *the right*...to all ethnic groups and minorities would bring about a major disruption of international relations, a serious threat to peace and the fragmentation of States into a myriad of entities that would often be unable to survive [emphasis added]".[94] This remains true only if "...*the right*..." necessarily entails the right to independence. Such a position forces the writer to acknowledge that secession and self-determination claims from sub-State groups within independent States are simply "...a fact of life, outside the realms of law...".[95] Whatever uncertainties remain about the best way to approach these issues, it is submitted that these are in no way as dangerous as the suggestion that the primary threats to international peace and security operate outside the legal system intended to guarantee that security.

State practice and the Badinter Commission's jurisprudence concerning the dissolution of Yugoslavia exhibit an interesting approach to these issues. Whilst characteristically lacking in definition, the opinions constitute a theoretical framework addressing some of the more important aspects of how self-determination may operate in the New World Order. The growing emphasis on *representative* and *participative* government is evidenced and *minority rights* and *non-discrimination* are shown to be capable of operating as part of the self-determination concept, rather than as a weak alternative thereto. A new manifestation of *legitimate governance* may be emerging.

7.3 Self-Determination and the Dissolution of Yugoslavia

The major factual causes of Yugoslavia's dissolution have been addressed elsewhere.[96] This section seeks to assert the legal relevancy of the 'right' to self-determination to those events, by which it is meant an international legal right and not a right arising under national legislation.[97] A number of prominent authors have cast doubt on this by contending that events in Yugoslavia had nothing to do with self-determination and cannot, therefore, teach us anything about the doctrine.[98] It is contended that this is not the case. The likeliest cause of such disagreement is differing definitions of the concept of self-determination. A major problem with analysis of self-determination is that "...many writers judge the legality on the basis of a personal definition. The task...[however] is not to discover if international practice is consistent with one's definition, but if the international practice which States are willing to characterise as a principle having legal effect exists, even if that characterisation is at odds with the definition that the writer prefers".[99]

In light of the need for transparency in legal analysis,[100] this writer has already indicated that a definition encompassing a right to *legitimate governance*, with specific links between self-determination, human rights and minority rights, is preferred. Many reject this suggestion and thereby exclude the dissolution of Yugoslavia from the sphere of self-determination. There arises a circular definitional argument - Yugoslavia may offer lessons about self-determination because self-determination is applicable in such situations, or Yugoslavia's dissolution occurred outside international law *because* self-determination cannot apply. To maintain that international law has nothing to say about such matters is not only to render it impotent in the face of new threats to peace and security but is to abdicate the responsibility of the international law academic to assist in the development of international norms.[101] A number of writers agree that Yugoslavia's problems were directly related to self-determination[102] and others consider that the concept "...certainly influenced..." those events.[103] Even under traditional definitions of self-determination, the events in the SFRY would fall to be considered as an issue of self-determination, although it may be decided that the 'right' was inapplicable in this case. The existence of territorially-defined ethnic groups seeking independence from a sovereign State would surely locate the problem, if not the solution, within the sphere of self-determination.

The preamble of the *1974 Federal Constitution of Yugoslavia* states that Yugoslavia was formed according to the free will of the constituent nations "...proceeding from the right of every nation to self-determination, including the right to secession...".[104] Events involving the revocation of such consent must raise issues of self-determination. This was obviously the opinion of the republics seeking to influence Yugoslavia's constitutional arrangements by basing their demands on the historic right of self-determination. As early as December 1990, when the Croatian leaders indicated their willingness to accept greater political and economic autonomy, as opposed to independence, Croatia's new constitution declared its position to be "Proceeding from...the inalienability and indivisibility, non-transferability and non-consumability of the right of the Croatian nation to self-determination...".[105] Similarly, Slovenia's Declaration of Independence of 25th June 1991 stated that it's actions were taken "On the basis of the right of the Slovene nation to self-determination..."[106] Slovenia declared it would recognise the right of all other Yugoslav republics, nations and nationalities to self-determination, whilst seeking to continue harmonious relations based on an association of democratic States with no changes to Yugoslavia's internal or external borders. Macedonia later produced a *Declaration for the Sovereignty of the Socialist Republic of Macedonia*, in which it confirmed that its actions were based on "...the right of the Macedonian people for self-determination, including the right of secession".[107] The Yugoslav federal authorities also acknowledged the existence of a self-determination question.[108] In assessing the impact of the Slovenian and Croatian declarations of independence, the SFRY authorities consistently identified self-determination as the source of the conflict, albeit disagreeing as to the manner of implementation and implications of the right. They argued that the right had already been exercised by the Yugoslav peoples when they decided to create the SFRY and could now only be considered as belonging equally to all Yugoslav peoples and capable of being exercised only through an agreed constitutional process. The relevancy of self-determination is evident in the Yugoslav Presidency's submission to the Badinter Commission, in response to the Serbian question regarding ethnic Serbs in Croatia and Bosnia-Hercegovina, where it argued that Serbs in those Republics, as a constituent nation of Yugoslavia, possessed the right to self-determination.

The relevance of self-determination was also acknowledged by the EC. Early EPC declarations, and the Brioni Accord, emphasised that the decision of the peoples of Yugoslavia as to the future of the country was to be exercised in accordance with international principles, including self-determination.[109] The *Guidelines on Recognition* and *Declaration on Yugoslavia* also made explicit reference to self-determination, albeit at a stage when independence was being sought.[110]

The positions of academics, the Yugoslav parties and international institutions not only indicate that this was a question of self-determination, but also show that the automatic association of self-determination with a quest for independence is incorrect. References to self-determination were made by the Yugoslav republican leaders when seeking a looser constitutional structure within Yugoslavia's existing borders.[111] Equally, the EC's references to self-determination were made at a time when it sought to retain Yugoslavia as a unified State. However one defines self-determination, in terms of its consequences and applicability, there appears no doubt that the events in Yugoslavia required discussion of the concept. Other sub-State groups will continue to use the language of self-determination and instead of denying that these are problems of self-determination, because they differ from previous manifestations of that 'right', it is more productive to seek a definition which addresses the demands of contemporary self-determination problems. Whether Mr. Lansing likes it or not, the terminology of 'self-determination' is here to stay, albeit in a new sense.

Yugoslavia illustrates how many contemporary self-determination scenarios involve claims for a re-negotiation of political or territorial structures *within the parent State* and not independence or secession. The rise of nationalism following Tito's death, assisted by the political vacuum created at the end of the Cold War, intentionally-crafted historical divides between the Southern Slavs and contemporary political disagreements over economic and political power, still led only to calls for greater autonomy within Yugoslavia. The federal authorities intransigence, and the fact that politicians who had constructed their political support on the basis of nationalism risked political suicide if they appeared to compromise their electorate's interests, soon escalated those demands towards independence, however. Wars of independence followed, with the bloodshed and destruction which inevitably accompany them. The absence of any international response before the situation had deteriorated to this extent is acceptable, indeed encouraged, if one accepts such situations to occur outside the international law of self-determination. Unfortunately, it delays intervention until claims of independence occur, by which time levels of mistrust between the parties may prevent the solution being resolved within existing borders. In the name of State-sovereignty, international law takes a neutral position until such time as that sovereignty may no longer be salvageable. Territorial integrity is not protected by this approach but threatened by it.

Yugoslavia highlights the dangers of leaving the resolution of self-determination claims solely in the hands of the relevant parties. The first Kosovo crisis developed because Serbia feared demands of independence from its Albanian-populated autonomous region. In response, Serbia pursued a policy of repression in Kosovo and revoked Kosovo's and Vojvodina's constitutional autonomy. This confirmed fears of further centralisation in other Yugoslav republics who, in return, sought greater autonomy. Negotiations among the parties failed to achieve agreement because their political agendas were juxtaposed and the situation deteriorated until independence became the preferred option. Whilst an agreement freely reached between disputing parties is likelier to be adhered to than one proposed by external actors, it is equally true that, without external pressure to reach such an agreement, domestic channels of dispute-resolution appear ineffective. The same may be said of the Bosnian crisis, where the warring factions were unwilling to debate constructively and agree a comprehensive peace-deal until international pressure coerced them into doing so. The international community may assist by pressuring the parties to reach an agreement and acting as a scapegoat upon whom compromise may be blamed. It appears the most effective way of redressing the alternative, a foreseeable domestic stalemate.

Naturally, State sovereignty cannot be ignored and the ability of the international community to intervene in a State's sovereign affairs is both legally and politically limited, for good reason.[112] Sovereignty is not an immutable concept, however, and growing international involvement in affairs once unreservedly within the domestic domain has been a consistent feature of the post-UN international environment. If, as will be suggested, sovereignty now requires some semblance of legitimacy as well as the factual requirements of Statehood, intervention in such issues may be more legitimate then ever before. Indeed, if self-determination is an *erga omnes* right as the ICJ has noted, the international community enjoys an interest in the outcome of situations of this kind, especially in light of the peace and security threats they now pose. Furthermore, it is ironic to claim that non-intervention respects State sovereignty if it allows political problems to intensify to such a level that the relevant State loses part of its territory or disappears altogether, as in Yugoslavia's case.

The tardiness of international intervention in Yugoslavia, forcing the EC into a crisis-management rather than a crisis-aversion role, has been discussed elsewhere.[113] Equally, a lack of clarity when referring to self-determination in EPC resolutions perpetuated confusions about the consequences of this 'right' in the Yugoslav context.[114] Had those resolutions specified that contemporary self-determination claims must be resolved within existing borders, on the basis of a participative, representative and democratic government which guarantees equal rights and minority protection, all Yugoslav parties would have been aware of the need for compromise. The Badinter Commission would have been able to assist in redrafting the Yugoslav constitution to address the conflicting political aspirations as far as possible. The massive amounts of money spent in tackling the wars in Slovenia, Croatia, Bosnia and Kosovo, and averting conflict in Macedonia, may have been spent instead on addressing Yugoslavia's economic problems. The atrocities and displacement of thousands of Yugoslavs may have been averted. Instead, the resolutions were interpreted, on the one hand, as legitimising a claim to independence for the republics and, on the other hand, as encouraging the federal authorities intransigence on the question of constitutional change.

The EC's approach contained a number of interesting aspects, however. First, the Brioni Accord clearly addressed the chief obstacles to the resumption of negotiations, namely Slovenia and Croatia's declarations of independence and the conflict in Slovenia. The Accord, also emphasised that any negotiated settlement must be based on the principles of the *Helsinki Final Act* and *Charter of Paris*, "... in particular respect for human rights, *including* the right of peoples to self-determination, in conformity with the Charter of the United Nations and with relevant norms of international law, including those relating to territorial integrity of States...[emphasis added]".

This confirms self-determination as a human-right whilst emphasising that its implementation must respect territorial integrity. Second, EC resolutions spoke of the "...illegal..." use of force by the JNA and the UK had already referred to the attempted "...territorial conquests..." of certain republics by federal forces. The emphasis is clearly on protecting the SFRY's internal boundaries as well as its external boundaries. This was confirmed by an EC-USA-USSR joint statement rejecting the use of force to change boundaries "...whether internal or external...". Finally, acceptance of 'external' self-determination for certain republics resulted only after it became clear that the federal authorities were unwilling to contemplate any internal constitutional settlement. It also followed the characterisation of Yugoslavia's federal organs, by the constitutional law experts of the Badinter Commission, as unrepresentative and non-participative and the use of force by federal authorities against its own population. Recognition required a host of obligations to be accepted, including the establishment of a political system which redressed the problems of Yugoslavia's structures and explicit guarantees on protection of human rights and minority rights. In this sense, independence was accepted only as a last resort, only after the legitimate governance aspect of self-determination had been denied to the republics and only after those republics undertook to ensure such legitimate governance in their independent States. All of these features will be shown to be reflected in the Commission's opinions on the dissolution process, discussed next.

7.4 The Badinter Commission Opinions Dealing with the Dissolution of Yugoslavia

All of the Commission's jurisprudence under the ECCY dealt in some way with the dissolution of Yugoslavia, as opposed to the succession issues considered under the ICFY, and collectively they create a theoretical framework on issues surrounding sub-State self-determination claims. Whilst the questions posed to the Commission, and indeed its responses, do not always refer to 'self-determination' *per se*, it will be shown that questions relating to international legal personality and recognition of States are inter-related and have close links with self-determination. Since judicial consideration of self-determination is limited, and generally relates to decolonisation, these opinions offer an exciting opportunity to assess how self-determination claims in the contemporary legal environment may be addressed.

Opinion 1, considering whether the events in Yugoslavia represented instances of secession or dissolution, began by describing the traditional criteria for Statehood. The Commission referred to "...a community which consists of a territory and a population subject to an organised political authority...[and] characterised by sovereignty". This largely conforms with the traditional requirements of the *1933 Montevideo Convention on the Rights and Duties of States*,[115] requiring States to possess "...(a) a permanent population; (b) a defined territory; (c) government; and (d) capacity to enter into relations with other States". The latter of these is perhaps more correctly described as a *consequence* of Statehood, as opposed to a *pre-requisite* for Statehood,[116] and it has been suggested that a more appropriate requirement would be independence and freedom from external control by another State.[117] It is in relation to the notion of government that the Commission's findings are most interesting.

The Commission noted that the internal political organisation of a State and its constitutional arrangements are "...mere facts...". This is again in accordance with traditional international law. In the *Western Sahara Case*, the ICJ noted that "No rule of international law...requires the structure of a State to follow any particular pattern, as is evident from the diversity of the forms of States found in the world today".[118] States constitutional structures have traditionally been deemed outside the legitimate scope of international law, as a result of "...the agnosticism of the Westphalian system..."[119] and the sovereign-equality doctrine. Nevertheless, the Commission appeared to deviate from this absolute position by declaring that such facts were relevant to "...determine the government's sway over the population and the territory". It is perhaps unsurprising, in light of the Commission's composition, that its members should choose to focus upon Yugoslavia's internal structures and constitutional organisation. It is not clear what is meant by "...the government's sway..." though two distinct possibilities arise. It may refer to the traditional *effective* government criterion which has traditionally been international law's focus.[120] It is submitted, however, that the Commission's next paragraphs require something over-and-above a merely *effective* government. The Commission stated that in a "...federal-type State which embraces communities that possess a degree of autonomy and, moreover participate in the exercise of political power within the framework of institutions common to the

Federation..." the existence of that State is contingent on it continuing to "...*represent* the components of the Federation *and* wield effective power [emphasis added]". Having found that Yugoslavia "...no longer met the criteria of participation and representativeness *inherent* in a federal State...[emphasis added]", the Commission alluded to the federal authorities powerlessness to ensure respect for cease-fires before declaring that a "...process of dissolution..." had begun.[121]

Suggestions of a new manifestation of self-determination, requiring *representative* and *participative* government would appear confirmed by this. The agnosticism of the traditional approach is discredited, if not abandoned. Reference to "...effective power..." is followed by a description of the nature of such power, requiring Yugoslavia to "...*represent* the components of the Federation...". The notion of a right to representation is enhanced by reference to the various "...communities..." comprising the State, lending a more humanistic interpretation to the "...components..." requiring representation. Yugoslavia's Statehood appeared conditional on the maintenance of a political system which secured representation for its constituent communities. Failure to do so resulted in the onset of a dissolution process which eventually destroyed Yugoslavia's international legal personality. The only way to avoid this was for the constituent regions to redraft the constitution and "...form a new association endowed with the democratic institutions of their choice". Statehood was thus viewed as more than the fulfilment of certain factual requirements and was treated as a *process* of maintaining representative and participative constitutional structures. Reference to the "...emerging emphasis on internal self-determination as a *pre-condition* for Statehood..."[122] is increasingly common. It is not intellectually problematic to consider the logical conclusion of such a development as requiring the ongoing implementation of self-determination to *maintain* Statehood.[123] Just as entities seeking recognition as States have sometimes been required to fulfil certain human rights criteria, as was the case with the Yugoslav successor-States, existing States, such as Yugoslavia, may find themselves compelled to demonstrate a commitment to representative and participative governance to maintain their legal personality. Whilst this is undeniably value-laden, it must be noted that the concept of Statehood has always been value laden and even the factual requirements of the *Montevideo Convention* have been used to deny the Statehood of indigenous nations in Africa, such as Madagascar, because their type of government did not represent the western model of effective control.[124] The Commission's version is no less value-laden but much more transparent in its objectives.

Having provided a fresh view on Statehood, *Opinion 2* considered whether Serbs in Croatia and Bosnia enjoyed the right to self-determination. This was a "...loaded question..."[125] and, if self-determination was equated with independence, a potentially explosive issue. To acknowledge the 'right' of self-determination for the Serb communities, without clarification of what this meant, could have encouraged a secessionist conflict. To deny the 'right', without clarification, may have encouraged repression and a denial of the political and human rights of those Serbs. Neither prospect is attractive - it perpetuates the problems encountered in Yugoslavia, either in respect of political repression or territorial fragmentation.

Instead of making such assumptions about the 'all-or-nothing' approach to self-determination,[126] however, the Commission noted that "...international law as it currently stands does not spell out all the implications of the right to self-determination". This may mean that international law offers no real explanation of what self-determination means, and therefore does not "...spell out..." its implications, or that the potential manifestations of self-determination have not yet been exhausted and that other ways, short of independence, exist to implement this 'right'. In this sense, international law does not limit, or "...spell out...", those methods of implementation, but merely the normative foundations of the 'right'. Appearing to adopt the latter of these positions, the Commission noted that, by virtue of its inclusion in the ICCPR and ICESCR it could be said that "*...the principle of the right to self-determination serves to safeguard human rights*.[127] By virtue of that right, every individual may choose to belong to whatever ethnic, religious or language community he or she wishes". This meant that "Where there are one or more groups within a State constituting one or more ethnic, religious or language communities, they have the *right to recognition of their identity* under international law [emphasis added]".

The question specifically required discussion of self-determination, yet the Commission makes only oblique reference thereto. One may argue that this opinion relates to minority rights rather than self-determination. This is acceptable, however, only if one views the concepts as mutually-independent and maintains that self-determination must always allow the possibility of independence. This is clearly what was sought by Serbia, but the Commission did not adopt such an approach.

Opinion 1 indicated the way in which self-determination could be implemented to save Yugoslavia's territorial integrity. *Opinion 2*, decided after the *Guidelines* had been published and when recognition of certain republics was likely, indicated how the newly-recognised States could implement self-determination to save their territorial integrity. Essentially, they would be required to implement a series of obligations which ensured they redressed the political problems within Yugoslavia's political structures. The Commission correctly noted that the loss of Statehood has "...major repercussions in international law...[and]calls for the greatest caution..." This situation only arose, however, because of Yugoslavia's failure to implement self-determination in the form of a participative and democratic government. Secession of Serb-populated areas in successor States would not be allowed because self-determination would be guaranteed therein by the obligations accepted under *Guidelines* and the Carrington Convention.[128]

Emphasis on territorial integrity and non-fragmentation was given in the statement that "...whatever the circumstances, the right of self-determination must not involve changes to existing frontiers at the time of independence (*uti possidetis juris*) except where the States concerned agree otherwise". Whereas denial of self-determination in Yugoslavia allowed *uti possidetis* to be 'trumped', its guaranteed implementation in the successor States would allow territorial integrity to be protected by *uti possidetis*.

The implementation of self-determination was done through individual and group rights, including minority rights, which had been identified as *jus cogens* in *Opinion 1*. Deeming these rights binding on the successor States, the Commission stated that the Serb communities in question "...must therefore be afforded every right accorded to minorities under international conventions as well as national and international guarantees consistent with the principles of international law and the Provisions of *Chapter II* of the [Carrington] draft Convention of 4th November 1991...".

In light of the fact that self-determination is a bundle of rights, the implications of which must be assessed contextually in specific cases, the right to recognition of identity was merely "...one possible consequence..." of self-determination. The Commission was not required to consider *all* the implications of self-determination, merely the ones which appeared to be relevant in this scenario. The implementation of self-determination here effectively created a right of dual-nationality, allowing Serbs in other republics to maintain their Serbian nationality alongside that of the parent-State.

Opinion 3, dealing with the nature of the internal boundaries between Serbia, Croatia and Bosnia, confirmed the well-established rule that the external boundaries of a State must be respected. The Commission also felt that borders between the specified republics "...and possibly between other adjacent independent States..." could only be altered by agreement freely arrived at between the relevant States. Otherwise, the boundaries would become "...protected by international law..." by virtue of international law's respect for the territorial *status quo* and, specifically, the principle of *uti possidetis juris*. This clearly aimed at preventing further territorial fragmentation if successor States were recognised.

The Commission's role in respect of the recognition procedure required it to assess the constitutional and legal obligations accepted by those republics seeking recognition and to see whether they fulfilled the criteria in the *Guidelines*. The Commission's advice has been mentioned elsewhere.[129] For present purposes, the interesting feature is how the decision to condition recognition on the fulfilment of criteria which are suggested to be related to *legitimate governance* may affect the nature of recognition.

Although the Commission considered recognition to possess "...only declarative value..." it nevertheless "...bears witness to these [recognising] States' conviction that the political entity so recognised is a reality and *confers on it certain rights and obligations under international law* [emphasis added]".[130] Similarly, the decision to recognise, albeit discretionary, was subject to "...compliance with the imperatives of general international law, and particularly those prohibiting the use of force in dealings with other States or *guaranteeing the rights of ethnic, religious or linguistic minorities* [emphasis added]".[131] This links with the description of those rights as *jus cogens*. It appeared that recognition could not be legitimate in the absence of respect for these rights and that, whilst declaratory, recognition conferred certain legal obligations and rights and allowed them to be exercised in the international arena. This is at variance with the pure declaratory theory of recognition, which holds that recognition is in no way constitutive of such international rights and obligations and that they arise *per se* merely from fulfilling the factual requirements of Statehood. Since the successor States were required to fulfil the legitimate governance criteria of self-determination, however, the role of the international community is enhanced to the extent that it is required to assess whether these criteria have been met. This is different from the mere factual possession of territory and population, since qualitative assessment must be made of the entities governmental structures and human rights guarantees.

The Commission's recommendation not to recognise Bosnia was explicitly based on non-participation of Bosnian-Serb delegates in the Bosnian Assembly and the absence of a referendum consulting all Bosnian communities on the question of independence. Accordingly, "...the will of the peoples of Bosnia..." was not fully established. Representation and participation are again explicit requirements.[132] This corresponds to the ICJ's advice in the *Western Sahara Case*, where self-determination was said to require "...a free and genuine expression of the will of the peoples concerned".[133] Advice concerning Croatia's application focused on deficiencies in the Croatian constitution which did not fulfill the Carrington Convention, especially in respect of the creation of autonomous areas for ethnically-homogenous regions. Again, self-determination had not been correctly implemented. In contrast, the Commission's favourable advice regarding Macedonia and Slovenia noted correct implementation of the Carrington Convention and the existence of referenda which supported the decision to seek independence. The Commission also noted, in *Opinion 8*, that recognition of the FRY as a successor State of the SFRY would be subject to its compliance with the *Guidelines*.

7.5 Evaluation of the Commission's Framework

Academic commentary on the Commission's opinions has been varied, as is to be expected. Some have described them as "...an interesting blend of traditional and innovative law..."[134] whilst others have said that they were "...not a shining light of international legal jurisprudence..."[135] and lamented that they "...wished Badinter had known more international law...".[136] It has been suggested that the opinions are "...propositions that would not be generally accepted by international lawyers..."[137] although it is submitted that this again depends on the definitions of international law held by those lawyers and many have cited the Commission's findings approvingly.[138]

In respect of self-determination as a pre-requisite for Statehood, academic approval has already been cited.[139] For the specific links between self-determination and minority rights, similar support exists.[140] The suggestion that a new manifestation of self-determination is now emerging is also evidenced by increasing support for the right to democratic, representative, participative and legitimate governance.[141] Questions remain, however, about the timing of the Commission's decision to announce the onset of the "...process of dissolution...". Hannum considered this finding premature and believes that it aggravated the political situation at a difficult time.[142] With the extermination of Statehood arguably representing the ultimate in international legal sanctions, it must be presumed that this would occur in extremely few cases. Even given Yugoslavia's lack of democratic representation and participation,[143] Serbia's unconstitutional behaviour in blocking the rotation of the federal Presidency and the intransigent position taken by the federal authorities in constitutional negotiations, one must ask whether this is sufficient to justify the Commission's findings, especially since the conduct of other republican leaders was not entirely blameless. Most probably, the key factual criterion was the use of force against Yugoslav populations which had already been condemned by the EC as illegal. The UK's Foreign-Secretary had already qualified EC support for Yugoslavia's territorial integrity by saying that it was no longer legal to "...keep a State together by shooting its citizens..."[144] and it appears that the Commission felt likewise.[145] Given that the Commission's framework specifically endorsed Yugoslavia's continuing Statehood in the event of a constitutional agreement securing democratic institutions, one may have hoped for a longer period of time for EC pressure to encourage such a settlement but it appears that German pressure for recognising Croatia and Slovenia prevailed.[146] This is a fault of the EC's practice, however, and not the Commission's framework. Nevertheless, the Commission's advice is curious in that it appears to limit the requirement of representative and participative democracy to "...federal-type..." States. This may suggest that non-federal States were exempt from the suggested new manifestation of self-determination which would be an illogical and unacceptable distinction.[147] It is dangerous to base a fundamental right such as self-determination on pre-existing levels of autonomy because these may change, as shown by revocation of Kosovo and Vojvodina's autonomy, and to limit the right to cases where such autonomy exists would discourage States from devolving political power, which can often resolve sub-State demands.[148] It is likelier that these references were relevant only in the context of discussion about Yugoslavia and that the Commission was not limiting self-determination territorially.

The Commission's recommendations regarding self-determination of

Serbs in Bosnia and Croatia are suggested to represent a contextual example of how self-determination may be exercised by sub-State groups within existing boundaries. The right of dual-nationality has been described as "...an innovative concept [which] could constitute a further element capable of contributing to the solution of the question of ethnic groups and minorities".[149] Self-identification has been said to be "...directly linked to the right of self-determination..."[150] and the right to determine nationality has been deemed "...an essential aspect of self-determination...".[151] Recognition of such identity is crucial in providing the *locus standi* necessary for protection of group-rights, many of which rely on the distinct ethnic character of the group in question from the majority population.[152] Even those who criticise the Commission's advice on this issue admit that it is a "...novel development...".[153] It suggests a distinction between 'citizenship' and 'nationality' similar to the EU notion of citizenship.[154] It must be emphasised, however, that the Commission did not 'create' a new international legal right to dual-nationality but merely stated that this was "...one possible consequence..." of self-determination which could be agreed amongst the parties. Whilst self-determination may dictate the need for representative and participative governmental structures and adequate minority-right protection, it is a question for the parties how to implement this. Given that those Serb populations felt their identity to be under threat in successor States where they represented minorities, the Commission's suggestion appears appropriate. This remedies the 'international-law-as-rules' approach with a pragmatic contextual solution which respects the underlying normative requirements of self-determination.[155] Some commentators have shown concern over the Commission's description of individual, human and minority rights as "...peremptory..." norms. Cassesse considers this statement "...too sweeping..."[156] whilst nevertheless stating that the Commission's opinions indicate a move towards the status of *jus cogens*.

The Commission's application of *uti possidetis* to internal borders has been criticised by some writers.[157] Others consider that it represented the only viable way to prevent further fragmentation upon the independence of the successor States.[158] Given the bloodshed which often accompanies attempts to alter established boundaries, it is submitted that the Commission's advice on this issue was prudent. Provision was made for territorial adjustments to be made by agreement between the parties which presumably applied both to international boundaries between the successor

States and internal boundaries within new States.[159]

The issue of recognition has caused most academic concern. It is submitted, however, that the problems of recognition relate more to the EC's actions than to the Commission's opinions. The *Guidelines* clearly linked recognition with democratic governance and, in one sense, linked the new manifestation of self-determination with the acquisition of Statehood.[160] The Commission repeatedly made references to the declaratory effect of recognition and the Commission's later opinions clarify that recognition cannot have been constitutive. *Opinion 11*, considering the various succession dates of the successor States, noted that Slovenia and Croatia became States on 8th October 1991, which preceded even Germany's recognition of 23rd December 1992 and was some 3 months before EC recognition was granted. Croatia's constitutional provisions were still considered to be short of the demands of the Carrington Convention in the Commission's Comment of 4th July 1992, yet it had been recognised by the EC since January. The FRY, despite not having received, or indeed requested, recognition was clearly considered to have fulfilled the factual requirements of Statehood, as is confirmed by its appearance before the ICJ in the *Bosnia Genocide Case*.[161] A pure constitutive theory is insupportable. Nevertheless, the Commission's comment that recognition "...bears witness..." to the attainment of Statehood and that such recognition "...confers certain rights and obligations under international law..." is irreproachable.[162] The *Guidelines* addressed the question of establishing diplomatic relations rather than Statehood *per se*[163] but it is submitted that recognition is crucial in the contemporary international legal order to *exercise* the rights of a State.[164] Unrecognised States are completely excluded from the international community and may even enjoy less recognised legal personality than certain national liberation movements.[165] Instances of non-recognition have been fatal to the relevant State's ability to act on the international stage.[166] Whilst a birth-certificate, passport, driving-licence, national-insurance number, credit-cards and electoral-registration do not 'constitute' a person, they are vital to his ability to function in the modern world. The same may be said for recognition of States. A purely declaratory theory is also insupportable therefore. The effect of recognition is perhaps best described as 'quasi-constitutive'. This is supported by the Commission's reference to Yugoslavia's continued membership of the UN as evidence that it had retained its international legal personality.[167]

Criticism of the EC's recognition policy is centred on the fact that the *Guidelines*, whilst "...profoundly innovative...",[168] largely ignored the traditional *Montevideo* requirements of Statehood. Although recognition was said to be "...subject to the normal standards of international practice and the political realities in each case..." the *Guidelines* clearly did not include traditional factual requirements.[169] In particular, the requirement of effective control was obviously lacking from Bosnia, whose government didn't control a third of its territory, and possibly Croatia.[170] The Commission, however, was not mandated to consider the factual requirements of Statehood and was limited to assessing fulfilment of the *Guidelines*. The Commission limited itself to these functions and on no occasion actually recommended the recognition of any former Yugoslav republic. Instead, it recognised that these were political decisions to be taken by the appropriate political organs of the EC in accordance with the political wishes of the EC's Member States. Any suggestions of premature recognition[171] are criticisms of the implementation of the conditional-recognition policy and are not capable of being blamed on the Badinter Commission.[172] To argue otherwise would be to ignore the fact that the Commission's advice was blatantly ignored in respect of Croatia and Macedonia.

The Commission's framework not only challenges international law to re-conceptualise traditional theories of Statehood, self-determination and recognition but also changes the role of the international community in contemporary self-determination conflicts. The first role of the international community should be to take note of the existence of such disputes at an early stage. The 'early-warning' capabilities of the international community have grown tremendously in recent decades[173] and institutions such as the OSCE's ODIHR or the HCNM[174] and the UN's Centre for Human Rights are merely examples of bodies which could produce country-specific and thematic reports on self-determination issues. The importance of NGO's should also be emphasised. It is true that "...one would be well-inspired to initiate structures designed to *prevent* conflicts from degenerating rather than call in the lawyers, like firemen, to dampen a raging fire".[175]

Having become aware of a self-determination claim, the next role should be to advise the parties involved that a negotiated political settlement is the only legitimate method of resolving them. This should be accompanied with a clear statement emphasising the need to resolve such issues within existing borders and on the basis of the legitimate governance aspect of self-determination. This favours neither a pro-independence movement nor encourages State-authorities to believe they are entitled to forcibly suppress legitimate claims for representative and participative government. Emphasis should be placed on the need for the parties to reach an agreement *inter se* on the basis of meaningful negotiations, although the 'good-offices' of the international community should be offered to ensure the respective opinions of the disputing parties are understood. Even in the absence of such international involvement, it should be specified that any settlement must respect the new demands of legitimate governance.

If an agreement is reached between the parties, it remains incumbent upon them to exercise their respective obligations in good faith - *pacta sunt servanda* is as important in respect of such settlements as in international treaties.[176] Similarly, although involving an initial outlay, it would be sensible for the international forum involved in brokering the deal to maintain a role in supervising fulfilment of these obligations. Nothing heightens distrust between parties and reduces the likelihood of progress than a series of broken promises. Furthermore, promises made by the international community to facilitate the agreement must be honoured if the process is to maintain any credibility.

The international community may also have a role in supervising the agreement and ensuring that it is fulfilled in substance, not merely form. This means that State authorities must not be allowed to retract or delay implementation of constitutional changes but also that sub-State groups do not attempt to seek autonomy as a step towards secession. Widespread international involvement under the Dayton Agreement is disappointing only because it exists after violent conflict occurred and not preventatively.[177] More positive involvement could see the international community play a role in organising and supervising elections or referenda and assisting in constitutional restructuring.[178]

In the event that the parties cannot reach an agreement *inter se*, the international community may require a more interventionist role. One possibility is the creation of an impartial organ which could advise on self-determination in specific cases. Blix notes that "...if...dangerous fragmentation of States is to be avoided and...the rule is to have practical significance, there needs to be a third party to assess concrete cases and apply the rule".[179] The *Aaland Islands Case* perhaps represented the first time such a referral was made to an International Committee of Jurists and Rapporteurs.[180] The *Western Sahara*, *Namibia* and *East Timor* cases, referred to the ICJ, have already been mentioned and further Advisory opinions may be an option. The Badinter Commission also represents an *ad hoc* way of allowing such a referral. A number of proposals for the creation of international monitoring mechanisms have been made,[181] including allowing access to the Human Rights Committee to sub-State groups,[182] a new role for the UN Decolonisation Committee,[183] the formation of "...a scientific body composed of independent experts from different disciplines and countries...[184] and roles for the General Assembly, Security Council or regional organisations.[185] The creation of a UN *Rapid Reaction Diplomacy Team*, accompanied by a Fact-Finding Mission to establish an impartial assessment of the situation may be another possibility, or the establishment of a Self-Determination Council composed of representatives from the chief international organisations.[186] Whilst important questions remain to be addressed about the precise role and mandate of such mechanisms, and how to ensure that they are free from political abuse and partiality, this debate is more constructive than the continued absence of an institutional framework for self-determination claims which compels reliance on self-help and categorises such claims as existing outside international law.

Questions remain over what factors may affect the type of self-determination which may legitimately be sought by sub-State groups. The Commission's characteristic ambiguity offers no underlying theory, although it may be said that it was not the Commission's role to construct grand theories but simply to address the Yugoslav scenario. However, given the emphasis placed on representative and participative democracy, and the importance of minority-protection, their absence should be used to indicate potential breaches of legitimate governance. The appropriate remedy is related to the degree that self-determination is breached. Again, this will be a question of political compromise between parties with vested interests in either maximising or minimising the level of political change. Other relevant factors may relate to the bargaining positions and actions of the various parties. Has the State refused to contemplate *any* constitutional restructuring to meet these demands? Has the sub-State group refused to abandon plans for secession in spite of a constitutional package proposed by the State? Has the State used force against its own populations to quell demands for political representation? Has the sub-State group ignored constitutional negotiations in favour of terrorist tactics? Whilst these questions require answers to extremely difficult factual situations,[187] self-determination claims involving political disputes are negotiated in a political process within existing boundaries. Concrete results would arise slowly through case-law and State practice.

The 'internal' aspects of self-determination are increasingly supported by State practice. In South Africa, the constitution adopted after the dissolution of apartheid committed itself to democracy, non-discrimination and the right to "...a conception of self-determination by any community sharing a common cultural and language heritage...".[188] This latter provision was accompanied by the creation of a constitutional court to mediate disputes between central government and provinces and was intended to address demands for autonomy in KwaZulu. The Israel-PLO Agreement of 1993 provides that Palestinians in the West Bank and Gaza Strip may "...govern themselves according to democratic principles..."[189] and provides for the creation of Israeli-Palestinian Liaison and Economic-Cooperation Committees. Although no specific reference is made to self-determination in this case, it was clearly made "...in the perspective of self-determination..."[190] and represents a contextual settlement. In Italy, rising racial tensions prompted the creation of a consultative body - known as the *parliamento* or miniature parliament - upon which elected representatives of minority racial communities sit and propose bylaws, demand answers from the municipal administration and request direct access to municipal representatives to gain information on issues particularly affecting them.[191] The Human Rights Committee's practice under *ICCPR Article 1* also shows that virtually no State refuses to provide information on its structures for ensuring political participation and representation are guaranteed to its various communities.[192] A panel of international legal experts created by the Quebec National Assembly to provide advice on the international law issues surrounding Quebec's possible secession from Canada also touched upon the status of Cree Indians within Quebec in such an event. They concluded that the aboriginal Crees possessed the right to self-determination but that this didn't entitle them to independence.[193] Crees claimed only certain linguistic and cultural rights within Quebec and, in 1977, the Quebec riot-police were involved in quelling civilian demonstrations, which increased demands for greater autonomy. Subsequent negotiations, however, resulted in the *Charter of the French Language*, which recognised Inuit, Cree and Naskapi language rights and defused these tensions.[194] In Sri Lanka, the first truce in the 5-year civil war was achieved only when agreement was reached to begin negotiations and the government had conceded to discuss the possibility of extensive autonomy, falling short of Statehood.[195] The breakdown in negotiations which followed this and the return to military tactics highlight the difficulties of the political path and emphasise the need to ensure negotiations *before* the issue has become a military, rather than a political one. Recent events in Northern Ireland provide not only an example of the power-sharing solutions which are increasingly being used to meet self-determination claims but also the difficulties in ending a cycle of violence once it has begun.[196] Many more examples exist[197] and numerous UN resolutions condemning anti-democratic practices in various countries provide further evidence of State practice.[198] Focus on legitimate governance may also be seen within regional organisations.[199]

Contextual solutions will invariable differ but the fact remains that States possessing democratic political systems and constitutional structures which provide for minority representation and participation in State affairs are less likely to wage war on each other and less likely to encounter secessionist self-determination claims. This is completely opposite to the thinking of many States who fear that increased autonomy would cause greater risks of territorial fragmentation.[200] "Governments that remain repressive out of fear of unleashing self-determination movements must be persuaded that such efforts are ultimately self-defeating".[201] Denial of equal-rights to Ossetians and Ajerbaijanis, and the revocation of South Ossetia's autonomy, within newly-recognised Georgia led to civil war.[202] Yugoslavia's descent into war followed a similar path.

Assuming a negotiated settlement is not achieved, what role exists for the international community? Again, one must assess the factual situation. It has been said that "…in democratic countries, different ethnic groups have more opportunities to gain independence but less incentive to do so".[203] Under the framework proposed here, one may also add they have less *right* to do so. Thus in a case such as Quebec, where political representativeness is acknowledged and no oppression exists, self-determination is fulfilled by the democratic nature of the political system.[204] Where the requirements of legitimate governance appear to be breached, however, self-determination may require international enforcement. Perhaps, as in the case of succession negotiations,[205] a duty to negotiate in good faith may be identified whose breach would legitimise international measures against the recalcitrant party. Against State authorities, these could involve economic or political sanctions. In regimes such as Iraq, self-determination may require the international enforcement of safe-havens.[206] It has been suggested that widespread repression of minorities may justify secession.[207] Taking this one step further, as in the Yugoslav case, political domination of State structures by one sector of the population combined with revocation of autonomy of other Yugoslav territories, intransigence in constitutional negotiations and the use of force against domestic populations, the only viable remedy may be to sanction the dissolution of the State.[208] This is one step beyond accepting secession, since the State itself disappears, rather than simply losing a portion of its territory. Reference has been made to "...internal colonialism..."[209] in such circumstances. Intransigent sub-State groups insisting on secession could be informed of the unlikelihood of recognition, which will affect its ability to act on the international stage. The system of measures outlined above will be referred to as the *dissolution doctrine*, because of its potential to legitimise the disappearance of Statehood.

At present, where a group claims the right to self-determination there exists no coherent framework in which such claims are assessed and the group "...still has no means of legal redress other than resort to armed violence...".[210] The collectivised enforcement of self-determination provided by the *dissolution doctrine* remedies this problem. It is contextual in the sense that many implications short of dissolution may be pursued and there is naturally a strong bias against widespread acceptance of dissolution. Less serious breaches of self-determination will result in less interventionist methods of enforcement. Questions arise about the extent of violation which would be required to contemplate legitimising secession. State practice would be crucial in deciding such issues but one initial possibility may be to use the Human-Rights Commission's model of *Resolution 1503*,[211] requiring "...a consistent pattern of gross and reliably attested violations...[of self-determination]". An alternative might be if a States exhibits "...clear, gross and uncorrected violations..." of self-determination.[212] Again, this would need a legitimate organ to answer such questions.

The Commission's framework includes a number of important definitional problems which may hinder development in the legitimate governance manifestation of self-determination. How does one define a representative and participative government and what is democracy?[213] Which international organisations would be responsible for creating mechanisms to assess self-determination claims? Is the international community the proper assessor of such claims? Could self-determination claims be dealt with at a regional level if this resulted in divergent views of its requirements? The magnitude of these problems cannot be underestimated but they should not prevent the process of re-conceptualising self-determination. The Commission's framework allows one to see the direction in which the norm is travelling but leaves many difficult questions to be resolved. Nevertheless, none of these difficulties are as harmful as the current international law approach to sub-State self-determination claims which delays intervention until those claims have developed a military dimension.

Despite certain shortcomings, the Commission's framework has much to recommend it. The questions posed in the introduction to this chapter are all capable of being answered within the framework. Self-determination is a norm whose underlying foundation aims to ensure legitimate governance. Its traditional concerns with decolonisation, alien-occupation and apartheid have been supplanted by growing sub-State claims for 'internal' self-determination. It applies outside the colonial context to "...all peoples...". It has been said that a 'people' cannot decide its political future until someone decides who is a 'people'.[214] Several studies have attempted to define what is a minority or a people[215] but there remains no clear answer to this question, which is crucial under the traditional approach to defining the rights of the group in question. A case-by-case approach appears to be the favoured option,[216] although this creates difficulties in identifying generally applicable criteria. Many writers define a 'people' as "...the *whole people* of an established State..."[217] in the sense of a State's total population. If a 'people' were the whole population of a State, however, self-determination would be moribund in the post-colonial world.[218] Continued reference to self-determination, in instruments such as the *1993 Vienna Declaration* and academic literature, and proliferating sub-State claims for self-determination indicate this is not so. On policy grounds, this position is flawed since it weakens the international protection of 'peoples' rights.[219] From a common-sense perspective, "It should be possible to call a people, in the ethnic sense, a people, in the legal sense, without having to fear that such recognition entails devastating consequences".[220] Failure to differentiate between different manifestations of the self-determination 'right' has traditionally prevented this, however.

International law has generally adopted a "...pedigree-orientated approach...".[221] The Commission's opinions at last allow a 'people' to be identified in an ethnic sense. The divergence between sociological and legal definitions of 'peoples' are narrowed because the Commission chooses not automatically equate self-determination with a right to independence - making classification as a 'people' crucial - but accepts sociological definitions of a 'people' and concentrates on what is meant by the 'right' of self-determination to these groups. Since self-determination does not necessarily, and will not usually, entail independence of these groups, the Commission is able to avoid the traditional conflict-orientated approach to self-determination epitomised by Pomerance when he states that "…the grant of self-determination to one self entails the denial of it to another…".[222] Mullerson is thus incorrect to ask "…why is the population of Bosnia-Hercegovina more of a people than are the ethnic-Serbs who live in Bosnia-Hercegovina?" Equally, Pomerance asks "If the secession of the republics from the SFRY was permissible because the Federation was disintegrating, on what *legal* grounds could further secession from those republics be legitimately be opposed. Why was one unit's self-determination more sacrosanct than that of another?"[223] It is hoped that the foregoing analysis has shown the way in which such questions may be answered.

The Commission's framework utilises self-determination as a cohesive, rather than a divisive, force a principle of inclusion rather than exclusion. It focuses self-determination claims within existing borders and requires negotiation between the disputing parties. It also encompasses an enforcement-mechanism, which has been called the *dissolution doctrine*, implemented by the international community against any State or sub-State group breaching the requirements of legitimate governance. What remains is to discuss the standing of this new self-determination right in current international law. In order to be anything more than an intellectual construct of this writer's imagination, the Commission's framework must be evidenced by State practice.

State practice in this sense relates primarily to the dissolutions of Yugoslavia, Czechoslovakia and the USSR, since previous practice relates to other self-determination manifestations. Yugoslavia offers the best instance of State practice because of the highly coordinated and institutionalised approach of the international community in this case and the Commission's jurisprudence which accompanied this practice. ICJ case-law confirming the concept's *erga omnes* status and academic suggestions of its *jus cogens* status do not refer to the notion of legitimate governance discussed here.

International legal developments occur generally through treaty or customary law and State practice is relevant to both. The *Vienna Convention on the Law of Treaties, Article 31*, notes that subsequent practice may be used to interpret a treaty-right and case-law indicates how practice may form customary law. Both of these are relevant to the

Commission's framework, since self-determination is contained in numerous international instruments and features like the *dissolution doctrine* could only be considered under customary law. The ICJ considered customary law in the *Nicaragua Case* where it stated that "...the conduct of States should, in general, be consistent with such rules, and...instances of State conduct inconsistent with such rules should generally be treated as breaches of that rule...".[224] Additionally, such practice must be "...accompanied by the *opinio juris sive necessitatis*. Either the States taking such action or other States in a position to react to it, must have behaved so that their conduct is "...evidence of a belief that this practice is rendered obligatory by the existence of a rule of law requiring it".[225]

Some of the Commission's positions are clearly reinforced by State practice. The wealth of State practice on 'internal' self-determination has been mentioned earlier. Similarly, the *dissolution doctrine* may be argued to enjoy some support in contemporary practice. The EC suspended $1billion of economic aid to the USSR after it used force against the Baltic States to repress their claims to revival of Statehood and suspended economic deals and arms-trade with Yugoslavia in July 1992.[226] The recent adoption of a "...ladder of measures..." by the Commonwealth countries, to be used against States denying human rights to their citizens also corresponds to the tenets of the *dissolution doctrine*.[227] The reverse would see those same States willing to fund pro-democratic trends in other States, which also enjoys some support in State practice. The EU has begun to hold biannual Pan-European Summits to defuse ethnic tensions in areas where they were seen to be building up.[228] CSCE mechanisms also endorse this early-warning approach.[229]

Many important aspects of the framework are not evidenced by consistent State practice, however. It was suggested that the maintenance and acquisition of Statehood may now require fulfilment of the criteria of legitimate governance, as exemplified in the *Guidelines*. The dissolutions of the USSR and Yugoslavia resulted in the creation of 20 new States, recognition of which was conditional upon satisfying the *Guidelines*. This could have provided a wealth of State practice to support the Commission's framework, but recognition of Croatia against the Commission's advice and non-recognition of Macedonia clearly deviate from the framework's requirements. The Statehood of the FRY has not been questioned, despite its failure to seek recognition or fulfil the *Guidelines*' requirements. Problems of non-majority populations in the successor States have attracted less international response than those of the SFRY. Outside the Yugoslav scenario, support for a universal obligation of legitimate governance is patchy. Many States retain governments which would fail the criteria of representation and participation, yet non-intervention remains the norm.[230] Furthermore, when Czechoslovakia dissolved, no referendum was held and opinion-polls indicated that the majority of people favoured unity.[231] This practice is clearly not "...both extensive and virtually uniform..."[232] as would be required to substantiate a peoples right to legitimate governance. Equally, the Commission's findings that the SFRY had disappeared and that the FRY was a successor State, rather than a continuance of Yugoslavia, is only partially evidenced by international practice. Although the UN Security Council agreed that the SFRY had ceased to exist, the General Assembly endorsed these findings without actually expelling Yugoslavia from the UN itself, as advised in *Opinion 9*, and the CSCE had similarly 'suspended' Yugoslavia's participation in certain CSCE organs rather than terminated its membership.[233]

In addition to equivocal State practice, there appears no evidence that the necessary *opinio juris* was present. As discussed elsewhere,[234] the EC followed the Commission's framework only insofar as it corresponded with existing Community policy. Recognition was clearly subject to political pressure, the *Guidelines* were "...clearly not designed as binding legal rules..."[235] and the imposition of economic and political sanctions, including recognition of Yugoslavia's dissolution were clearly considered political options rather than legal obligations. Nevertheless, State practice endorses the Commission's vital findings that Yugoslavia's dissolution came as a result of its internal constitutional failings. Recognition was conditional upon new States possessing the representative and participative government which was lacking in Yugoslavia and protecting individual, group and minority rights. A specific question on the applicability of the right of self-determination to Serbs within those new States was addressed with suggestions of rights short of independence. It is difficult to argue that the events in the SFRY show nothing about the attitude of the international community towards sub-State self-determination questions, even if they currently consider the Commission's approach *de lege ferenda* rather than *lex lata*.[236]

If the EC's approach in Yugoslavia had shown sufficiently consistent State practice and *opinio juris*, it may have been suggested that any customary norm of legitimate governance was regional and limited to the

EC/OSCE region. Equally, customary law is always subject to the 'persistent-objectors rule'[237] whereby States could refuse to be bound by the custom. Neither of these would present a significant problem, however. Many international legal concepts have originated in Europe and subsequently become accepted as universal custom - State-sovereignty being perhaps the most famous example. Equally, the 'persistent-objectors rule' would undoubtedly allow a State to declare its opposition to the notion of representative and participative government which protects human rights and minority rights but it is highly unlikely that those States who feared such a norm would advertise their non-democratic political system by persistently objecting to it in the international arena.

7.6 Conclusions

The essence of this chapter is that self-determination problems are not primarily due to irreconcilable ethnic hatreds but are *political disputes* requiring *political solutions*. Self-determination is a concept which remains relevant to international relations, albeit in a new sense. Its history shows that it has been used for implementing a number of related, but distinct, political agendas. Many of these, such as decolonisation, apartheid and illegality of foreign-occupation, retain only marginal relevance in contemporary global affairs. Other aspects, such as the rights of indigenous tribal peoples, remain to be developed.[238] The abundance of claims for self-determination, however, currently originate from sub-State groups dissatisfied with existing State structures and seeking constitutional change. These represent the major contemporary threat to international peace and security and can no longer be viewed as having only on domestic effects. An international response is necessary if these threats are to be met and territorial fragmentation prevented. Yugoslavia, therefore, represents an emerging international phenomenon and cannot simply be ignored as *sui generis*.

The Commission's opinions, whilst radical from one perspective, borrow heavily from self-determination's historical legal evolution. Earlier manifestations of self-determination have been shown to relate to the notion of *legitimate governance* and the Commission's framework marks a further expansion of this concept. Insistence on the right to independence as a corollary of self-determination leaves international law no constructive role to play. In a multi-cultural world where at least 5,000 identified ethnic languages and cultures exist, associating a 'peoples' right with independence is dangerous and impractical.[239] The former USSR had over 140 'ethnic' groups within its borders and Nigeria currently has over 200, all of whom clearly cannot conceive to have a 'right' to independence.[240] Avoiding the difficult questions about precisely what 'right' they do possess and describing sub-State self-determination claims as having occurred outside international law's realms is a dangerous option. Leaving such claims to be resolved solely between the disputing parties doomed many to fail and, in the event that independence is achieved by a sub-State group, problems often remain as regards non-majority populations in these new States.[241] A more constructive approach is to develop an international response addressing these claims within existing State boundaries.

The Commission's deliberations offer an innovative contextual response to the contemporary demands of self-determination claims whilst also incorporating elements of previous self-determination practice. Links with the political principle of nationality are revisited and combined with Wilsonian notions about consent of the governed as the ultimate source of legitimacy. Equal rights, including protection of minority rights, are protected by self-determination and representative and participative government is crucial. Self-determination is specifically identified as a human rights principle, enjoying clear links with political-rights contained in the *1966 Conventions*. Territorial integrity is supported for those States with representative and participative governments, but territorial disruption cannot be excluded if this is not the case.

The Commission's framework, although containing some critical lacunae, adds greater definitional clarity to the self-determination debate which may help States to view the concept with less suspicion and may facilitate more constructive academic debate. Discussions about whether the 'right' was *jus cogens* would be required to identify which aspect of self-determination they referred to. Whereas decolonisation and freedom from foreign occupation may secure widespread support for being *jus cogens*, the right to legitimate governance is clearly not in the same category. Ultimately, despite the intellectual attractions of the Commission's framework, inconsistent State practice and an absence of *opinio juris* are fatal to its claims to represent existing international law. In this sense, the Commission's opinions may be viewed as illegitimate from a positivist perspective. Once more, the rhetoric exceeds the reality. The rhetoric is, however, a much more attractive position. Another, more optimistic, interpretation is that they are ahead of their time and challenge academics to refrain from perpetuating territorial, sociological and conceptual limitations on self-determination and States to show the political will necessary to create a binding norm of legitimate governance.[242] The application of rules by judicial organs such as the Commission increases their determinacy which in turn increases their legitimacy.[243] It is hoped that the increasing emphasis on legitimate governance continues and that State practice eventually reaches the levels of the Commission's rhetoric. As Pomerance notes, "A new dawn…is not heralded simply by wishing that it had already arrived…"[244] but unless considerable effort is dedicated to modifying existing State practice, the new dawn may not arrive at all.

Notes

1 For an indication of the amount written on this issue, see Knight, D.B. and Davies, M. (eds.), *Self-Determination: An Interdisciplinary Annotated Bibliography*, (1987), Garland. In the years since this book was compiled, much more has been written and a mere fraction of these writings will be referred to throughout this chapter.

2 Cassese, A. *Self-Determination of Peoples: A Legal Re-Appraisal*, (1995), CUP, 5.

3 Cf. Schachter, O. and Joyner, C.C. (eds.), *United Nations Legal Order: Volume One*, (1995), CUP, 372, where the authors state that "...definition of the beneficiaries of that right, its scope and content, and the methods through which it is to be exercised can be established with some clarity".

4 See chapter 3, section 3.4.

5 See chapter 1, section 1.2.2.

6 Ibid, section 1.2.3.

7 See Cassese, supra n.2., 165-204, for examples.

8 This chapter largely limits itself to political self-determination and does not cover economic self-determination. On economic self-determination, see Ofuatey-Kodjoe, 'Self-Determination', in Schachter, supra n.3, 349, at 363-7; *Declaration on Permanent Sovereignty over Natural Resources, GA Resn. 1803* (1962). Paust, J., 'Self-Determination: A Definitional Focus', in Alexander, Y. and Friedlander, R.R. (eds.), *Self-Determination: National, Regional and Global Dimensions*, (1980), 13, describes political self-determination as "…the collective right of people to pursue their own political demands, to share power equally and, as the correlative right of the individual, to participate freely and fully in the political process". See also Cassese, A., 'Political Self-

Determination: Old Concepts and New Developments', in Aan den Rijn, A. (ed.), *UN Law and Fundamental Rights*, (1979), Sijthoff, 137.

9 See chapter 2, section 2.1.

10 Anderson, M., *Frontiers*, (1996), Polity, 37-8; Musgrave, T.D., *Self-Determination and National Minorities*, (1997), OUP.

11 Simma, B., *The Charter of the United Nations: A Commentary*, (1994),OUP, 58.

12 Mullerson, R., *International Law, Rights and Politics*, (1994), Routledge, 58; Shaw, M.N., *International Law*, (1997), CUP, 177.

13 Cassese, supra n.2., 15.' '

14 Simma, supra n.11, 59.

15 Cassese, supra n.2., 19.

16 Whelan, A., 'Wilsonian Self-Determination and the Versailles Settlement', (1994), 43 *ICLQ*, 99; Franck, T.M. 'The Emerging Right to Democratic Governance', (1992), 86 *AJIL*. 46, at 53-4.

17 Cassese, supra n.2., at 23. Pomerance, M., *Self-Determination in Law and Practice*, (1982), Nijhoff, at 1, calls Wilsonian self-determination "...an imprecise amalgam of several strands of thought...". For details of the Wilsonian treaties, see Hannum, H., *Autonomy, Sovereignty and Self-Determination: The Accommodation of Conflicting Rights*, (1990), PenUP, 52-5.

18 Eastwood, L.S., 'Secession: State Practice and International Law After the Dissolution of Yugoslavia', (1993), 3 *Duke JCIL*, 299, at 313.

19 Gayim, E., *The Principle of Self-Determination: A Study of its Historical and Contemporary Legal Evolution*, (1990), NIHR, chapters 1-2.

20 *Article 55* includes the promotion of "...higher standards of living, full employment, and conditions of economic and social progress and development; solutions of international economic, social, health, and related problems; and international cultural and educational cooperation; and universal respect for, and observance of, human rights and fundamental freedoms for all without distinction as to race, sex, language, or religion".

21 Shaw, supra n.12, at 205. Cf. Cassese, *International Law in a Divided World*, (1986), Clarendon, 151-2. This obligation was also included in the *Vienna Declaration*.

22 Gayim, supra n.19, 91.

23 Pomerance, supra n.17, 48.

24 *Article 76*. See Hall, D., *Mandates, Dependencies and Trusteeships*, (1948), OUP.

25 The 1966 International Covenants, common *Article 1*, specified that all States or organs responsible for Non-Self-Governing and Trust territories must "...promote the realisation of the right of self-determination..." •

26 GA Resn. 1514(XV), (1960), *Article 2*.

27 Ibid, *Article 6*.

28 GA Resn. 1541(XV), (1960), *Principle VI*.

29 See White, R.C.A., 'Self-Determination: Time for a Reassessment?', (1981), 28 *Neth ILR*, 168.

30 Pomerance, supra n.17, 15.

31 Cassese, supra n.2., 79-81, describes the cases of Goa and West Irian to show that UN practice in respect of colonial situations also demonstrates situations where self-determination has been blatantly ignored.

32 [1971] ICJ Rep., 31.

33 [1975] ICJ Rep., 12.

34 *Military and Paramilitary Activities In and Against Nicaragua*, [1986], ICJ Rep 14, at paragraph 263. Crawford, J., 'Democracy and International Law', (1994), 65 *BYIL* , 113, at 121-2, notes that "Since 1986 the world has itself undergone vast changes. In particular there has been a significant change in the democratic balance. In the last decade, the proportion of States with democratic systems...has increased sharply. With this change has come a new stress on democracy as a value, even a dominant value, in national and international affairs. The same is true of the law regulating those affairs".

35 [1995] ICJ Rep, 90. For details, see Chinkin, C., *The East Timor Case*, (1996), 45 *ICLQ*, 712.

36 Ibid, paragraph 29.

37 See Cassese, supra n.2., 56-7, for an explanation of the events behind the introduction of 'economic' self-determination.

38 McGoldrick, D., *The Human Rights Committee: Its Role in the Development of the ICCPR*, (1991), Clarendon, 14. See id, 247-67 for practice of the HRC in respect of the right of self-determination. See also Nowak, M., *UN Covenant on Civil and Political Rights: Commentary*, (1993), Engel, 5-25.

39 *Report of the Third Committee*, UN Doc. A/3077, cited in Michalska, A., 'Rights of Peoples to Self-Determination in International Law', in Twining, W. (ed.), *Issues of Self-Determination*, (1991), AbUP, 71, at 86.

40 Cassese, supra n.2., 55. Nowak, op cit, 23 describes the ICCPR as creating a right of 'internal' self-determination "...based on a democratic element, which is to be exercised together with the Covenant's other political rights and freedoms". Emphasis is placed on the concepts of autonomy and participation in the decision-making process.

41 See also Thornberry, P., 'Self-Determination, Minorities, Human Rights: A Review of International Instruments', (1989), 38 *ICLQ*, 867.

42 *GA Resn. 2625(XXV)*, reprinted at (1970), 9 *ILM*, 1292. See chapter 1, n.26 for references on this declaration.

43 Ofuatey-Kodjoe, supra n.8, 360.

44 See SC Resns. 418 (1977) and 556 (1984).

45 See, for example, SC Resns. 216 and 217 (1965), 221 (1966), GA Resn. 2379 (1968).

46 Cassese, supra n.2, 113-5.

47 For definitions of 'internal' and 'external' self-determination, see Pomerance, supra n.17, 37-42. Thornberry, P., 'The Principle of Self-Determination', in Lowe, V., and Warbrick, C. (eds.), *The United Nations and the Principles of International Law*, (1994), Routledge, at 175, states that "...the external dimension defines the status of the people in relation to another people State or empire, whereas the democratic or internal dimension should concern the

relationship between a people and its own State or government". See also McCorquodale, R., 'Self-Determination: A Human Rights Approach', (1994), 43 *ICLQ*, 857, at 864.

48 UNGA Resn. 47/135 (1992), *Article 2(3)*. See generally Phillips, A. and Rosas, A. (eds.), *The UN Minority-Rights Declaration*, (1993), Turku.

49 Reprinted in (1993), 32 *ILM*, 1661.

50 GA Resns. 45/150 (1990) and 46/137 (1991), discussed in Salmon, J., 'Internal Aspects of the Right to Self-Determination: Towards a Democratic Legitimacy Principle?', in Tomuschat, C. (ed.), *Modern Law of Self-Determination*, (1993), Nijhoff, 252.

51 *Article 1(3)*, reprinted in (1989), 28 *ILM*, 1382. Cf. reference to 'populations' in *ILO Convention 107* 1957.

52 Reprinted in (1994), 32 *ILM*, 911.

53 Id, *Article 4*.

54 Tomuschat, C., 'Self-Determination in a Post-Colonial World', in Tomuschat, supra n.50, 5.

55 *HFA, Principle VIII*.

56 Cassese, supra n.2., 287.

57 Ibid, 291-2.

58 Reprinted in (1991), 30 *ILM*, 190.

59 *Helsinki Document: The Challenges of Change*, (1992), CSCE Publications, *Chapter II(3)*. See McGoldrick, D., 'The Development of the Conference on Security and Co-Operation in Europe (CSCE) After the Helsinki 1992 Conference', (1993), 42 *ICLQ*, 411.

60 *Helsinki Declaration*, ibid, 5.

61 Reprinted in (1990), 29 *ILM*, 1305. See Salmon, supra n.50, 271, for discussion.

62 *Article 20*.

63 *OAS Res. 1080*, cited in Salmon, supra n.50, 272.

64 Cassese, supra n.2., 296-301.

65 Crawford, J., 'Review of Self-Determination of Peoples: A Legal Reappraisal', (1996), 90 *AJIL*, 331, at 332, notes that the declaration "...can only realistically be assessed within the framework of NGO activity in this field".

66 See Espiell, H.G.G., *Study for the UN Sub-Commission on Protection of Discrimination and Protection of Minorities of the Commission of Human Rights*, (1977), UN Doc. E/CN.4/Sub.2/390, 17. See also Buchheit, L.C., *Secession: The Legitimacy of Self-Determination*, (1978), YUP, 55; Espiell, H.G.G., 'Self-Determination and Jus Cogens', in Cassese, A. (ed.), *UN Law, Fundamental Rights*, (1979), Clarendon, 167. Cf. Pomerance, supra n.17, 70, where he states that because "...self-determination is not really *jus*...it is difficult to see how it can be presumed to be *jus cogens*...".

67 *Draft Code on State Responsibility, Article 19(3)(b)*, reprinted in (1980), YbkILC, 32.

68 Cassese, supra n.2., 188-9, cites East Timor as authority.

69 Pomerance, supra n.17, 50.

70 *East Timor Case*, supra n.36, paragraph 29.

71 Pomerance, supra n.17, 26.

72 Thornberry, P., 'The Democratic or Internal Aspect of Self-Determination With Some Remarks on Federalism', in Tomuschat, supra n.50, 101, at 118.

73 Jennings R. and Watts, A., *Oppenheim's International Law*, (1992), Longmans, 712.

74 Kimminich, O., 'A Federal Right of Self-Determination?', in Tomuschat, supra n.50, 83, at 100, correctly refutes the fact that self-determination is inherently destructive and notes that conflicts has been caused by a *denial* of self-determination rather than its correct implementation.

75 See for example Iraq's invasion of Kuwait in 1990 and references thereon in chapter 1, section 1.2.2.

76 Guelke, A., 'International Legitimacy, Self-Determination and Northern Ireland', (1985), 2 *Rev Int Stud*, at 41, notes that only Swaziland, Lesotho, Botswana and Somalia have ethnically homogenous populations.

77 Chapter 3, section 3.5.1.

78 See generally Buchheit, supra n.68; Pomerance, supra n.17, 15.

79 For a review of such claims, see Halperin M.H. and Scheffer, D.J., *Self-Determination in the New World Order*, (1992), Carnegie, 123-60.

80 Franck, supra n.16, 90.

81 Higgins, R., *Problems and Process*, (1994), Clarendon, 111.

82 Higgins, ibid, 122, argues that "...self-determination can be exercised through many ways, including an open and pluralistic political process". Halperin, supra n.81, 46-7, notes that "...the full exercise of self-determination need not result in the outcome predicted by those who would discredit the principle - independent statehood for every ethnic group. Rather, the full exercise of self-determination can lead to a number of outcomes, ranging from minority rights...to cultural or political autonomy, to independent Statehood".

83 See White, supra n.29, 168.

84 Cf. Tomuschat, supra n.54, at 11, where he says "It is the attraction, but also the tragedy of self-determination that...it *necessarily* includes a right to independent statehood".

85 White, supra n.29, 168. Cf. Kimminich, supra n.75, at 90.

86 Hannum, H., 'The Limits of Sovereignty and Majority Rule: Minorities, Indigenous Peoples and the Right to Autonomy', in Lutz, E.L., Hannum, H. and Burke, K.J. (eds.), *New Directions in Human Rights*, (1989), PenUP, 3; Hannum, H., 'Rethinking Self-Determination', (1993), 34 *VirgJIL*, 1, at 63-6.; (1994), 53 ICJur, 67, where it is described how the Greek delegate to the *Draft Declaration on Indigenous Peoples* wrote an explanatory note saying that "...most indigenous groups did not seek secession from existing states, nor did they aspire to separate statehood. What was rather envisaged was the recognition of a special right to a degree of territorial or functional autonomy...within the framework of co-operation with the State".

87 Thornberry, P., 'The Democratic or Internal Aspect of Self-Determination', in Tomuschat, supra n.50, 101, at 111-3.

88 Tomuschat, supra n.54, 14.

89 Hannum, supra n.17; Murswieck, D., 'The Issue of a Right of Succession Reconsidered', in Tomuschat, supra n.50, 21; Hall, R.L. (ed.), *Ethnic Autonomy: Comparative Dynamics,* (1979), Pergamon; Steiner, H.J., 'Ideals and Counter-Ideals in the Struggle Over Autonomy Regimes for Minorities', (1991), 66 *NDLRev.*, 1539.

90 Cassese, supra n.2., 311; Salmon, supra n.50.

91 See below, section 7.5.

92 Frowein, J.A., 'Self-Determination as a Limit to Obligations in International Law' in Tomuschat, supra n.50, 211, at 213. A more nuanced description was given by a rapporteur of the UN Sub-Commission on Prevention of Discrimination and Protection of Minorities who suggested that while self-determination cannot be taken as granting an "...unlimited right of secession..." the right of secession "...unquestionably exists...in a special, but very important case: that of peoples, territories and entities subjugated in violation of international law". Cristescu, A., *The Right to Self-Determination: Historical and Current Development on the Basis of UN Instruments* (1981), UN Doc.E/CN.4/Sub.2/404/Rev.1, paragraph 173. 'Remedial secession' in such circumstances has been suggested to possess the characteristics of a right of self-defence. Murswieck, supra n.92, 26. See also Buchanan, A., *Secession: The Morality of Political Divorce from Fort Sumter to Lithuania and Quebec,* (1991), Westview; Eastwood, supra n.18; Brilmayer, L., 'Secession and Self-Determination', (1991), 16 *YJIL*, 177; Osterland, H.A., 'National Self-Determination and Secession: The Slovak Model', (1993), 25 *CWRJIL*, 655.

93 Buchanan, ibid, 21.

94 Cassese, supra n.2., 328

95 Ibid, 340.

96 See chapter 2.

97 For discussion on the right to self-determination under Yugoslav domestic law See Iglar, R.F., 'The Constitutional Crisis in Yugoslavia and the International Law of Self-Determination', (1992), 15 *Boston JICL*, 213, at 218-21; Cassese, supra n.2., 264-9; Bagwell, B., 'Yugoslav Constitutional Questions: Self-Determination and Secession of Member Republics', (1991), *GAJICL*, 489.

98 Cassese, supra n.2, at 273, states that "The birth of new States in the former Soviet Union and Yugoslavia has occurred outside the realm of both municipal and international law...". Likewise, Higgins, supra n.83, 125, concludes that there is a lacuna in international law in respect of secession from independent states.

99 Ofuatey-Kodjoe, supra n.8, 350, n.1.

100 See chapter 1, section 1.2.6.

101 Ibid, section 1.2.3.

102 McCorquodale, supra n.47, at 861 and 873-7; Stromseth, J.E., 'Self-Determination, Secession and Humanitarian Intervention by the UN', (1992), 86 *ASIL*, 370; Bieber, R., 'EC Recognition of Eastern European States: A New Perspective for International Law?', (1992), 86 *ASIL*, 374.

103 Mullerson, supra n.12, 87.

104 Reprinted in Trifunofska, S., *Yugoslavia Through Documents from its Creation to its Dissolution*, (1994), Nijhoff, 224.

105 Ibid, 252, 299.

106 Ibid, 286.

107 Information paper supplied by the Macedonian Foreign Embassy in London. *Republic of Macedonia: Independence Through Peaceful Self-Determination*, (1992).

108 See *Position of the SFRY Presidency*, a letter from the SFRY Vice-President, Branko Kostic, of 18th December, reprinted in (1992), 43 RIA, 21.

109 See chapter 4, sections 4.3.2. and 4.3.3.

110 Ibid, section 4.3.8.

111 Murswieck, supra n.92, 32-3.

112 See Warbrick, C., 'The Principle of Sovereign Equality', in Lowe and Warbrick, supra n.47, 204.

113 See chapter 4, section 4.5. For criticism of this term, see McGoldrick, D., 'Yugoslavia: The Responses of the International Community and of International Law', (1996), 49 *CLP*, 375, at 378.

114 Ibid.

115 165 LNTS 19, *Article 1*. See also Jennings, supra n.75, 120-23; Crawford, J., *The Creation of Statehood in International Law*, (1979), OUP, 93-182.

116 Rama-Montaldo, M., 'International Legal Personality and Implied Powers of International Organisations', (1970), 41 *BYIL*, 111, at 133. Cf. Cassese, supra n.2., 169.

117 Fawcett, J., *The British Commonwealth in International Law*, (1963), Stevens, 92.

118 Supra n.33, 43-4.

119 See Koskenniemi, M., 'National Self-Determination Today: Problems of Legal Theory and Practice', (1994), 43 *ICLQ*, 241, at 252.

120 Shaw, supra n.12, 140; Crawford, supra n.117.

121 Cf. Kreca, M., 'Succession and the Continuity of Yugoslavia', (1992), 39 *JRMP*, 178; Iglar, supra n.99; Eastwood, supra n.18, at 315.

122 Koskenniemi, op cit, at 245 n.22; McCorquodale, supra n.47, at 865, n.46; Crawford, supra n.117, 105-6.

123 Shaw, supra n.12, 145-6, considers that "...systematic and institutionalised discrimination might invalidate a claim to Statehood". It is not intellectually difficult to consider that breaches of other manifestations of self-determination may do likewise.

124 Vagts, D.F., 'State Succession: The Codifiers View', (1993), 33 *VJIL*, 275, at 277.

125 Koskenniemi, supra n.121, 266.

126 See Crawford, supra n.34, 129; Murswieck, supra n.91, 39.

127 Cf. McGoldrick, D., 'Sustainable Development and Human-Rights: An Integrated Concept', (1996), 45 *ICLQ*, 796, at 802-3, who states that "...self-determination is essentially a territorial principle to which a human rights mantle has been added".

128 Chapter 4, sections 4.3.7.-4.3.8.

129 Chapter 5, sections 5.10.8-11 and 5.10.12.

130 *Opinion 8*, paragraph 2. See also *Opinion 1*, paragraph 1.

131 *Opinion 10*, paragraph 4.

132 One should note that it appears only the *potential* for participation which is required. When Bosnian-Serbs boycotted the later referendum, this could not prevent its legitimacy, since these communities had at least been given the opportunity to participate.

133 Supra n.33, paragraph 55.

134 Kingsbury, B., 'Claims by Non-State Groups in International Law', (1992), *Cornell JIL*, 481, at 505.

135 Conversation with Professor Christopher Greenwood at *Justice in Cataclysm* conference, Brussels, 20th July 1996.

136 Conversation with Professor John Dugard, ibid.

137 Kingsbury, op cit.

138 Koskenniemi, supra n.121, 266-7; Rich, R., 'Recognition of States: The Collapse of Yugoslavia and the USSR', (1993), 4 *EJIL*, 36, at 50; Pellet, A., 'The Opinions of the Badinter Arbitration Committee: A Second Breath for the Self-Determination of Peoples', (1992), 3 *EJIL*, 178; Cassese, supra n.2., 332.

139 See supra n.124-5.

140 Thornberry, supra n.40, 867, states that "Self-determination and the rights of minorities are two sides of the same coin". See also Fox, G.H., 'Self-Determination in the Post-Cold War Era: A New Internal Focus?', (1995), 16 *Mich.JIL*, 733, at 724-5; Cassese, supra n.2., 350.

141 The seminal work remains Franck, supra n.16. See also Crawford, J., *Democracy in International Law,* (1994), CUP; Shaw, supra n.12, 218; Mullerson, supra n.12, 58-91; Fox, G.H., 'The Right to Political Participation in International Law', (1992), 86 *ASIL*, 249; Grossman, C., 'The Right to Political Participation in International Law', (1992), 86 *ASIL*, 257; Paust, J., 'Democracy and Legitimacy: Is There an Emerging Duty to Ensure a Democratic Government in General and Regional Customary International Law?', (1991), 85 *ASIL*, 98; Van Boven, T., 'Is There an Emerging Right to Good Governance?', (1995), 13(3) *NethQHR*, 304; Shelton, D., 'Representative Democracy and Human-Rights in the Western Hemisphere', (1991), 12 *HRLJ*, 353; Boutros-Ghali, B., 'Democracy: A Newly Recognised Imperative', (1995), 1 Global Governance, 3; Franck, T.M., 'Democracy as a Human Right', in Henkin, L and Hargrove, L (eds.), *Human Rights: An Agenda for the Next Century,* (1994), ASIL, 73.

142 Hannum, H., 'Yugoslavia and Europe: Old Wine in New Bottles?', (1993), 3 *TLCP*, 57, at 64.

143 Cf. Iglar, supra n.99, 237.

144 Silber, L. and Little, A., *The Death of Yugoslavia*, (1995), Penguin, 177.

145 See Weller, M., 'The International Response to the Dissolution of the SFRY', (1992), 86 *AJIL*, 569, at 572 *et seq* for discussion.

146 See chapter 4, section 4.3.8.

147 Rich, supra n.140, 63.

148 Mullerson, supra n.12, 78-9.

149 Cassese, supra n.2., 358.

150 Joffe, P., *Sovereign Injustice: Forcible Inclusion of the James-Bay Crees and Cree Territory Into a Sovereign Quebec*, (1995), Grand Council of the Crees Publication, 33.

151 Chan, J.M.M., 'The Right to Nationality as a Human Right', (1991), 12 *HRLJ*, 1, at 12.

152 Ibid, at 1. See also Inter-American Court on Human Rights decision in *Re Amendments to the Naturalisation Provisions of the Costa Rica Constitution*, (1984), 5 HRLJ, 167, paragraph 32, where it was stated that "Not only is nationality the basic requirement for the exercise of political rights, it also has an important bearing on the individual's legal capacity".

153 Frowein, supra n.94, 217. Cf. Bieber, supra n.104, 377, who considers it "...doubtful whether EC policy has contributed to determining the implications of the right to self-determination beyond what is already established in international practice".

154 Pellet, supra n.140, 180.

155 See chapter 1, section 1.2.2.

156 Cassese, supra n.2., 133.

157 See Joffe, supra n.152, 190-99 for a review of academic criticism of the Commission's opinions on *uti possidetis*. Kingsbury, supra n.137, 507, believes the Commission's advice to be inconsistent with State practice. Frowein, supra n.94, 216-7, acknowledges that this may represent "...a feasible solution..." but questions whether international law currently reflects this situation.

158 Shaw, M.N., 'The Heritage of States: The Principle of Uti Possidetis Juris Today', (1996), 67 *BYIL*, 77, at 99, considers it "...beyond question..." that it is a rule of general international law and cites the Commission's jurisprudence approvingly. See also Higgins, supra n.82, 122-4; Mullerson, supra n.12, 148; Schachter, O., 'State Succession: The Once and Future Law', (1993), 33 *VJIL*, 253, at 256; Cassese, supra n.2., 190-3; McCorquodale, supra n.47, 878-80.

159 The re-drawing of Bosnia's 'ethnic' boundaries under the Dayton Agreement may be explained as a voluntary departure from *uti possidetis*. On consensual modification of *uti possidetis* rules, see Shaw, op cit, 141-50.

160 Shaw, supra n.12, 145-6 notes that "...conditions required for recognition may...especially when expressed in general and not specific terms...in practice be interpreted as additional to the criteria for Statehood". Warbrick, C., 'Recognition of States', (1993), 41 *ICLQ*, 473 and 42 *ICLQ* 432, at 475, notes that Community policy in Yugoslavia made "...inter-relations between statehood and recognition and statehood and self-determination...hard to untangle".

161 *Case Concerning Application of the Convention on the Prevention and Punishment of the Crime of Genocide (Bosnia v FRY)*, [1993], ICJ Rep, 3. *Article 34(1)* of the ICJ's Statute confirms that "Only States may be parties in cases before the Court".

162 Joffe, supra n.152, 232, cites the Quebec National Assembly Committee's similar conclusions, which considered effective control the essence of Statehood whilst deeming recognition "...a test of this effectivity". See infra, n.193.

163 The *Guidelines* stated that fulfilment of the conditions "...opens the way to recognition by the Community...*and* to the establishment of diplomatic relations [emphasis added]". It seems clear that the two concepts were fused in this case.

164 Jennings, supra n.74, 128-9, note that, "...in practice, recognition is necessary to enable every new State to enter into official intercourse with other States. [...] It marks the beginning of the effective enjoyment of the international rights and duties of the recognised community".

165 Dugard, J., *Recognition and the United Nations*, (1987), Grotius, 123.

166 Ibid, 81-163, for examples. See also Jennings, supra n.74, 185-90.

167 *Opinion 1*, paragraph 2. Binder, G., 'The Case for Self-Determination', (1993), 29 *Stan.JIL*, 223, at 265, notes that membership of international organisations may provide political, as well as economic, credit. Franck, T.M., *The Power of Legitimacy Among Nations,* (1990), OUP, 228, also notes the value of membership in "...pedigreed institutions".

168 Cassese, supra n.2., 266.

169 Murswieck, supra n.91, 30-31; Gray, C., 'Self-Determination and the Breakup of the Soviet Union', (1992), *YbkEL*, 465, at 477; Koskenniemi, supra n.121, 268.

170 Shaw, supra n.12, 309; Koskenniemi, id; Warbrick, supra n.162, 441.

171 See Mullerson, supra n.12, at 130; Rich, supra n.140, at 58. Cf. Detter, I., *International Legal Order,* (1994), Dartmouth, 40, who argues that recognition of Bosnia and Croatia was not premature because the organs of a State need only show they are *potentially* capable of exercising effective government, not that they are currently fully-functioning.

172 Cf. Pomerance, M., 'The Badinter Commission: The Use and Misuse of the International Court of Justice's Jurisprudence', (1998), 20 *MichJIL*, at 49; Szasz, P., 'Peacekeeping in Operation: A Conflict Study of Bosnia', (1995), 28 *CornellJIL*, 685. Koskenniemi, supra n.104, at 267, argues that the reason for the recognition policy's failure was "...not that it made the recognition of self-determination units...conditional upon their being constituted on a democratic, peaceful and negotiated basis [but] that the policy was used to attain that very situation which it set out as a precondition for its application". Turk, D., 'Recognition of States: A Comment', (1993), 4 *EJIL*, 66, at 69, commends the Commission's "...accurate and consistent..." advice on recognition.

173 See generally Ramcharan, B.G., *The International Law and Practice of Early-Warning and Preventive Diplomacy,* (1991), Nijhoff;. Nowak, M., 'Country-Orientated Human Rights Protection by the UN Commission on Human Rights and its Sub-Commission', (1991), 36 *Neth YIL*, 39.

174 See section 7.2.4.

175 Pellet, supra n.140, 181. See also Hannum, H., 'Minorities, Indigenous Peoples and Self-Determination', in Henkin and Hargrove, supra n.143, 1, at 11-13.

176 See *Vienna Convention on the Law of Treaties 1969, Article 26.*

177 See chapter 4, section 4.5.7.

178 For a review of UN practice in such affairs, see Beigbeder, Y., *International Monitoring of Plebiscites, Referenda and National Elections: Self-Determination and Transition to Democracy*, (1994), Nijhoff. For the OSCE's role, see 'ODIHR Semi-Annual Report', (1998), Spring, OSCE, 5-22. For suggestions that the Badinter Commission should have been asked to propose a constitutional solution to the Bosnian conflict, see Turk, supra n.174, 70.

179 Blix, H., *Sovereignty, Aggression and Neutrality*, (1970), A&W, 13-14.

180 (1920), LNOJ, Supp.4.

181 Cassese, supra n.2., 357.

182 Ofuatey-Kodjoe, supra n.8, 387; McCorquodale, supra n.47, 885, proposes additional protocols to the ICCPR, ECHR and *American Convention on Human Rights*, allowing access to sub-State groups in self-determination claims. For further details on sub-State access to the HRC, see McGoldrick, supra n.38, 247-268.

183 Tomuschat, supra n.53, 17-18; Schachter and Joyner, supra n.3, 387.

184 Gayim, supra n.19, 95.

185 Kimminich, supra n.75, 96; Tomuschat, supra n.53, 17-18.

186 See suggestions made at the Saskatoon International Conference on Self-Determination for the creation of a *Sub-Commission on Self Determination* with its own Rapporteur, reprinted in (1994), January CommLB, 340. See also Osterland, supra n.94, 674-5.

187 For an attempt, see Kirgis, F.L., 'The Degrees of Self-Determination in the United Nations Era', (1994), 88 *AJIL* 304, at 309. The author depicts, in the form of a graph, a simplified version of the factors which would be taken into account in deciding the 'remedy' permissible to achieve self-determination in various circumstances. See also Halperin, supra n.80, 74-80 and 85-93; White, supra n.29, 168-192. Iglar, supra n.99, 229, even suggests that the exercise of self-determination must avoid causing "...undue economic and political impact on the parent State".

188 Quoted by Bindman, G., 'The New South Africa: A Revolution in the Making', (1994), *NLJ*, May 13th, 648.

189 *Article III* of the agreement, cited in Cassese, A., 'The Israel-PLO Agreement and Self-Determination', (1993), 4 *EJIL*, 564-71, 568. See also Benvenisti, E., 'The Israeli-Palestinian Declaration of Principles: A Framework for Future Settlement', (1993), 4 *EJIL*, 542.

190 Cassese, Id.

191 Solomon, B., *Migrants Get Hint of Power in Turin's Mini-Parliament*, (1995), August 5th, *Guardian*.

192 Higgins, supra n.82, 116-7.

193 Joffe, supra n.152, 48. The panel of experts was composed of Thomas Franck, Rosalyn Higgins, Alain Pellet, Malcolm Shaw and Christian Tomuschat, all of whose works have been cited in this chapter. See 229-47 for details of the report.

194 Id, 153-5.

195 Putman, D., *Cease-Fire Holds in Sri Lanka's 11-Year War*, (1995), January 9th, *Guardian*.

196 Walker, M., *Massacre of the Innocent: Britain and Ireland Vow to Crush Splinter IRA*, (1998), August 17th , *Times*.

197 Hannum, supra n.17, 99-102.

198 See Beigbeder, supra n.180, 99-125; Fox, supra n.142, at 753, n.98.

199 See section 7.2.4.

200 Higgins, supra n.82, 116; Hannum, supra n.17, 71.

201 Halperin, supra n.80, 8-9.

202 Brook, S., *Claws of the Crab: Georgia and Armenia in Crisis*, (1992), Picador.

203 Ibid, 70.

204 Joffe, supra n.152, 86-106, cites the findings of the Quebec National Assembly panel of experts, and many other writers, that self-determination was already being exercised by the Quebecois by virtue of Canada's representative and participative political system. The experts noted that self-determination exists "…in many forms…" and may operate at "…various levels…". Id, 319. See also the recent *Canadian Supreme Court Decision Regarding the Legality of Secession of the Canadian Province of Quebec*, (1988), available from http://www.droit.umontral.ca/doc/csc-scc/en/index.html, in which the court found that, at paragraph 126, that a 'right' of 'external' self-determination arises only in "...extreme cases and, even then, under carefully-defined circumstances". The court also noted, at paragraph 130, that there was "...no necessary incompatability between the maintenance of the territorial integrity of existing States...and the right of a 'people' to achieve a full-measure of self-determination". The court conducted a thorough examination of Quebec's constitutional position within Canada and concluded that, since it was fully represented in federal structures and was not denied access to government, self-determination was being fulfilled within existing borders. This appears to be the same type of analysis as the Badinter Commission conducted, albeit resulting in a different answer.

205 See chapter 6, section 6.9.2.

206 Cassese, supra n.2., 361.

207 Supra n.94.

208 Cf. Iglar, supra n.99, 237-9, who argues that Yugoslavia possessed a representative government, whilst acknowledging that the non-Serbian republics were "…unequally treated…" Joffe, supra n.152, 112 argues that "…self-determination and democracy were gravely denied when the Serbian Communist government blocked the regular rotation of the Presidency and prevented the Croatian representative from becoming the first non-Communist President of Yugoslavia".

209 Hannum, supra n.17, 9; Mullerson, supra n.12, 64-7.

210 Cassese, supra n.2., 169.

211 See McGoldrick, D., 'The Principle of Non-Intervention: Human Rights', in Lowe, supra n.47, 85, at 98, *et seq* for details.

212 *Prague Document on Further Development of CSCE Institutions and Structures: Safeguarding Human-Rights, Democracy and the Rule of Law*, (1992), 31 *ILM*, 976, at 987.

213 See Beetham, D. (ed.), *Defining and Measuring Democracy*, (1994), SAGE, for various ways of conducting a 'democratic audit'. See also Kazancigil, A. (ed.), *Rethinking Democracy*, (1991), Blackwells; Denitch, B., *Legitimation of Regimes: International Frameworks for Analysis*, (1979), SAGE; Beetham, D., *The Legitimation of Power*, (1991), Macmillan.

214 Jennings, I., *The Approach to Self-Government*, (1956), CUP, 56.

215 The most famous is perhaps the report prepared for the Human Rights Commission. See generally Capotorti, F., *Study on the Rights of Persons Belonging to Ethnic, Religious and Linguistic Minorities*, (1979), UN Publications, Doc.E.78.XIV.1. For alternative definitions, see Joffe, supra n.152, 1-35; Lim, C.L., 'The Problem of the Definition of the "Self" in Self-Determination', (1993), *NURP* No.13; UNESCO *International Meeting of Experts on Further Study of the Concept of the Rights of Peoples*, (1989), UN Doc.E/CN.4/Sub.2/1992/6, for details of studies into the sociological aspects of a 'people'.

216 See for example, the Human Rights Committee's *Lovelace v Canada Case*, (1981), discussed in Bayefsky, A.F., 'The HRC and the Case of Linda Lovelace', (1982), 20 Can.YIL, 244. See also the *Ominyak and the Lubikon Lake Band v Canada*, discussed in McGoldrick, D., 'Canadian Indians, Cultural Rights and the Human-Rights Committee', (1991), 40 *ICLQ*, 658. See also GA Resns 2672-C (XXV) and 3089-D (1973), confirming "...the peoples of Palestine..." as bearers of the right to self-determination.

217 Simma, supra n.11, 62.

218 Rosas, A., 'Internal Self-Determination', in Tomuschat, supra n.50, 225, at 228. The Canadian Supreme Court Decision, supra n.206, paragraph 124, notes that "It is clear that a 'people' may include only a portion of the population of an existing State [and that]...reference to 'people' does not necessarily mean the entirety of a State's population. To restrict the definition [thus] would render the granting of a right of self-determination largely duplicative, given the parrallel emphasis within the majority of the source documents on the need to protect the territorial integrity of States and would frustrate its remedial purpose".

219 Michalska, supra n.38, 74.

220 Tomuschat, supra n.53, 16.

221 Lim, supra n.215, 7. See also Franck, supra n.16, 52-6.

222 Pomerance, supra n.17, 71.

223 Mullerson, supra n.12, 74.

224 Supra n.34, 98.

225 Ibid, 108-9.

226 On the USSR, see Lukic, R. and Lynch, A., *Europe From the Balkans to the Urals: The Disintegration of Yugoslavia and the Soviet Union,* (1996), SIPRI; Eastwood, supra n.18, 320; Gray, supra n.171. On Yugoslavia, see chapter 4, section 4.3.4.

227 The "...ladder of measures..." includes a series of responses, from collective disapproval to exclusion from Commonwealth meetings, sanctions and expulsion. Crawshaw, S., *Commonwealth to Enforce Rights-Code*, (1995), 13th November,

Independent. Rwanda and Nigeria later faced economic sanctions and the threat of expulsion from the Commonwealth because of the civil war raging in the former and certain human rights abuses occurring in the latter. See Carvel, J., *EU Halts Aid for Rwanda*, (1995), 27th April, *Guardian*; Black, I., *Nigeria Faces New Action on Abuses*, (1996), 24th April, *Guardian*.

228 See Koskenniemi, supra n.104, 269, on the 'Balladur-Plan.'

229 See Helsinki Document, supra n.58, *Chapter III* on *Early Warning, Conflict Prevention and Crisis Management*.

230 Carothers, T., 'Empirical Perspectives on the Emerging Norm of Democracy in International Law', (1992), 86 *ASIL*, 261.

231 Osterland, supra n.94, 692.

232 *Continental-Shelf Case*, [1969] ICJ Rep, 3, at 43.

233 See chapter 4, sections 4.4.6. and 4.5.15.

234 See chapter 5, section 5.16.

235 Gray, supra n.171, 477.

236 Malanczuk, P., *Akehurst's Modern Introduction to International Law,* (1997), Routledge, 340.

237 Cassese, supra n.2., 347.

238 Barsch, R., 'Indigenous Peoples in the 1990s: From Object to Subject of International Law?', (1994), 7 *HarvHRJ*, 33; Hannum, H., 'New Developments in Indigenous Rights', (1988), 28 *VJIL*, 585; Berger, J. and Hunt, P., 'Towards the International Protection of Indigenous Peoples', (1994), 12 *NQHR*, 125; Kingsbury, B., 'Self-Determination and Indigenous Peoples', (1992), 86 *ASIL*, 383; Berman, H.R. et al, 'Indigenous Peoples and Self-Determination', (1993), 87 *ASIL*, 190.

239 McCorquodale, supra n.47, 857. Koskenniemi, supra n.104, at 261 n.71, and Mullerson, supra n.12, at 83, cite estimates of 8,000 distinct languages and cultures.

240 Gassama, I.J., 'World Order in the Post-Cold War Era', (1994), *Brooklyn JIL*, 255, at 282-4.

241 See Gray, supra n.171, 495 and Hanneman, A.J., 'Independence and Group Rights in the Baltics', (1995), 35 *Virg JIL*, 485, for the 'China-doll' problems of self-determination claims in the dissolution of the USSR. See also Osterland, supra n.94, 700, on the problems of Hungarian minorities in Slovakia.

242 The Commission's approach thus differs greatly from the "...minimalist, cautious and uncontroversial approach..." of the Human Rights Committee. McGoldrick, supra n.38, 249.

243 Franck, supra n.16, 57-62.

244 Supra n.17, 64.

8 Yugoslavia and Changing Threats to International Peace and Security

"To prevent war, one must analyse the war phenomenon".
Detter, I., *The Law of War*, (1987), CUP, at 5.

"No situation that has confronted the UN has been more violent, deep-seated, and complex than that which arose from the civil war in Yugoslavia in 1991".
Howard, M., 'The Historical Development of The UN's Role in International Security', in Roberts, A. and Kingsbury, B., *United Nations Divided World*, (1993), Clarendon, at 78.

8.1 Introduction

Chapter 2 described the factual events behind the dissolution of Yugoslavia. The following two chapters argues that Yugoslavia's dissolution cannot be described as *sui generis* and that it offers wider lessons on the changing nature of threats to international peace and security. If international law is to play a constructive role in meeting these new threats, the problem of intra-State conflicts, including self-determination conflicts, needs to be 'promoted' to the top of the international agenda.[1] This chapter highlights the ways in which force has been regulated *between* States and show how some aspects of this may be filtering into conflicts *within* States. It will be argued that the incremental development of legal rules preventing the use of force in inter-State relations has largely succeeded in reducing the number of inter-State conflicts to the status of anomalies in the current international environment. Nevertheless, the corresponding growth in intra-State conflicts and the specific practical problems surrounding such conflicts continue to pose threats to peace and currently lack any coherent international legal regulation. Yugoslavia's dissolution evidences the challenges posed by intra-State conflicts and the existing legal ambiguities and lacunae which prevent an adequate response from international law. This chapter focuses on the need for international law to develop so as to address the legal lacunae relating to the use of force in intra-State conflicts whilst chapter 9 focuses on the need to redress the lacunae in respect of peaceful settlement procedures in intra-State disputes. Clearly, a detailed analysis of these issues would be outside the limited scope of this work and these chapters seek merely to raise issues which may be developed furthers by others in the field.

8.2 The Extent of War in International Relations

Considerable evidence suggests that war has existed for as long as man has been capable of organising himself into fighting units capable of mobilisation against an enemy force.[2] History confirms that force has been the primary method of resolving disputes between, and within, States. This is especially true of the period before the Peace of Westphalia.[3] War has been shown to have been a persistent feature in Yugoslavia's history but the SFRY's war-torn history is certainly not unique. Numerous historical battles indicate the universal nature of armed conflict and one need only mention the ancient Persian wars,[4] the Peloppenisian war,[5] the Byzantine Empire wars,[6] the numerous battles within the Kingdoms of England, Ireland, Scotland and Wales,[7] and the other major European conflicts throughout history[8] to see this.

The reasons for the historical reliance on force are related to the nature of international relations during those periods and the international society within which these relations were conducted. Undeveloped societies tend not to have institutional mechanisms for resolving disputes and tend to rely on self-help, including forcible reprisals to redress what are seen as 'criminal' actions committed by one societal actor against another.[9] *Within* States, the formation of sovereign authorities and the development of complex governmental systems allowed dispute resolution mechanisms to be created which required self-help to be abandoned as a dispute resolution procedure. *Between* States, however, the absence of such central authority prevented similar developments and war persisted as the major means of redressing inter-State disagreements.

Another factor relating to the gradual abandonment of self-help is the degree of societal interaction. Societies with little interaction between their actors tend to be more willing to resort to conflict than those where actors are joined by bilateral or multilateral agreements, diplomatic relations or economic interests. Whilst war thus retained primary importance during early periods of international relations as States became increasingly interconnected through trade, communication, politics and other features of the developing international environment their willingness to jeopardise those connections by resorting to war tended to diminish. The fact that changing societal conditions impact on the way in which disputes are resolved and also affect the nature of disputes within that society remains relevant to contemporary international relations and will form the basis of the argument in favour of expanding international law's concern with intra-State conflicts.

Having noted the constant presence of conflict in international relations, it should also be noted that the regulation of warfare has almost as long a history as war itself, despite Clausewitz's statement that "...[t]o introduce the principle of moderation to the theory of war would always lead to logical absurdity".[10] From Sun Tzu through to the ancient Greeks, the Israelites, the Mahabharata, the Manu tribes and the Romans, evidence of limited warfare exists.[11] Many such limits were clearly not 'legal' in the Austinian sense and originated for purely selfish reasons. Since conquest of territory was a prime reasons for warfare, it was clearly preferable for conquerors to inherit lands which were not devastated and populations which were alive and capable of working.[12] Despite the political and selfish motivations behind such military limitations, one cannot deny the conclusion that such limitations reduced the levels of destruction and killing that would otherwise have occurred.

One obvious criticism of developing further constraints on the manner in which conflict can legitimately be conducted is that those new limitations often serve the interests of a small number of powerful States and are adopted for political and selfish reasons which are couched in rhetorical humanitarian terms. Treaties prohibiting the acquisition of nuclear weapons represent a prime example, since they entrench the military superiority of a handful of States which currently possess such weapons. Nevertheless, such treaties clearly prevent the widespread ownership of weapons of mass destruction and reduce the likelihood of them being used. States, and more specifically the governmental representatives thereof, are not inherently benevolent actors and require convincing that restrictions upon their sovereignty are justified. It is virtually impossible to remove political and selfish considerations from this balancing act but what must be ensured is that, once agreed upon, such legal limitations must not continue to be used to serve the interests of the few at the expense of the many.

Egoism has also proven to be an important factor in restraining the manner in which warfare has been conducted. Many historical leaders sought to maintain their decorum and reputation for honour even whilst engaged in conflict and their armies were often ordered to reflect this in their behaviour on the battlefield. Organisation of armed forces into structured military units also created pressure to adhere to certain behavioral expectations. A professional pride in dignified and controlled wartime behaviour can be traced back to the age of chivalry and the knights of the Middle Ages and it is an intrinsic element of all modern armed forces.[13] As international humanitarian law (IHL) progressed both *quantitatively* and *qualitatively*, the requirement of professionalism and organisation of armed forces seeking its protection represented an important factor.[14] Religion also played a part in moderating wartime conduct.[15] In addition to these extra-legal factors, the emergence of a framework for international relations based on the notion of *jus gentium*[16] provided a *legal* basis for regulating armed conflict. Essentially, international law has developed a three-pronged manner in which to do this - the *jus in bello* limited the legitimate *conduct* in war, the *jus ad bellum* progressively limited the legality of the *resort* to war and the development of a system of pacific dispute settlement attempted to replace the historical resort to 'self-help' with a more developed, and less violent, system of dispute resolution. To adequately discuss the manner in which such developments could be repeated in relation to intra-State conflicts would require much more time than is possible in this short book. Nevertheless, despite the enormity of these topics, it is necessary to provide a few brief examples of the manner in which these developments occurred in inter-State relations and to show how Yugoslavia highlights the need for an extension of these principles to intra-State conflicts. Only after having convinced the reader of the *need* for an extension of the principles will it be possible to galvanise the political support necessary to actually begin *discussing* the manner of doing so. In this sense, these chapters are intended to pose more questions than they provide concrete answers for.

The *jus in bello* and *jus ad bellum* will be discussed in the remainder of this chapter and the development of peaceful settlement procedures will be dealt with in chapter 9.

8.3 Changing Threats to International Peace and Security

Despite developments in the *jus gentium* and the evolution of an increasingly interdependent society of nations,[17] the twentieth century has not been free from conflict. Even a cursory glimpse at events since the ratification of the *UN Charter* shows that conflict persists as a phenomenon. Since 1945, "...over 100 major conflicts around the world have left some 20 million dead..."[18] and it has been said that "...[t]he only constant in the 20th century has been violence".[19] Nevertheless, a change in the nature of conflict has occurred.

Where inter-State conflicts occur, vital national interests are perceived to be at stake and the inter-dependence of the modern international system has reduced the number of issues which are perceived as justifying such conflict. States are now joined by a complex web of legal, political and economic agreements which are all capable of creating disagreements as to their interpretation, prolongation or replacement. However, individual disagreements are unlikely to cause States to contemplate war against each other because this would mean the severing of all other ties between those States and the proliferation of multiple interests between States means that one grievance is often forsaken in order to reap the political, economic or military rewards from other areas. In essence, a doctrine of *realpolitik* ensures that ultimatums which may result in recourse to force are rare in modern inter-State relations. This is not to deny that inter-State conflicts continue as a threat to international peace and security but the likelihood of such conflict in the post-Charter world has been greatly reduced.[20] Although some criticise a "...balance-sheet..."[21] approach, the relative infrequency of inter-State conflict when compared to previous times provides a yardstick of the UN's successes.[22] Furthermore, the *need* to resort to conflict has been reduced at the same time that the *price* of doing so has been raised, by the developing system of pacific dispute settlement.[23] Whilst inter-State conflict is by no means extinct, therefore, it represents an anomaly in the post-Charter world.[24] The same cannot be said, however, for intra-State conflicts.

Relations between sub-State groups and domestic authorities are different to those between States and the *realpolitik* of inter-State relations is often lacking. Grievances of sub-State groups receive far less international attention than inter-State grievances and international dispute settlement mechanisms are lacking. Whilst legal systems within States are clearly far more developed than those between States, this is of little relevance if the grievance arises because of dissatisfaction with existing State structures or organisation. Where this occurs there is no 'independent' third party within the State to address the grievance because existing State institutions and legal procedures will almost certainly be deemed by the sub-State group to be tainted with governmental influence. Reliance on 'self help' arises in such situations, often in the form of peaceful political protest but increasingly including resort to force. Popular demonstrations are often greeted with a stern governmental response which can encourage retaliation from sub-State groups who begin 'terrorist' activities. The use of JNA troops and republican police to quell demonstrations within Yugoslavia during its latter years illustrates this point perfectly. Despite the obvious merits of the non-intervention bias in international law, concretised in *Article 2(7)* of the Charter, an approach which leaves intra-State conflicts to be resolved by the sovereign State involved ignores the fact that the State is *part of the problem*. It is difficult to imagine any other situation in which one party to a dispute enjoys a virtual monopoly in controlling the framework within which that dispute will be resolved.

Traditionally, civil wars were deemed within the domestic jurisdiction of individual States.[25] Nevertheless, contemporary intra-State conflicts often have an international impact beyond their borders and they may disrupt the world order in a number of ways.[26] Security is threatened when States suffer unrest and the possibility of other States being dragged into conflict can rarely be excluded.[27] Yugoslavia's conflict threatened to involve neighbouring States such as Turkey, Greece, Albania and Russia. Economically, intra-State conflicts disrupt the economy of the afflicted State and threaten international trade. Third States often encounter financial burdens by virtue of a loss in trade with the warring State and the costs of accommodating refugees.[28] By January 1992, the number of refugees from the short Croatian conflict had reached 600,000 and the Kosovo conflict added a further 1 million to that.[29] International institutions may also lose credibility if they are perceived as unable to prevent or contain conflicts.[30] Anything which could lead to conflict *within* States is, therefore, capable of having an *international* impact because of the inter-dependence of contemporary international relations. This realisation is made worse when one considers the wide range of issues which can provoke intra-State conflict and it is increasingly common to hear references to the "...non-military sources of instability in the economic, social, humanitarian and ecological fields [which] have become threats to international peace and security".[31]

It is incontrovertible that the vast bulk of contemporary conflicts occur *within* States rather than *between* them and that many such conflicts result from political disagreements regarding a State's internal constitutional structure.[32] Chapter 7 described how the existing international approach allows these disagreements to degenerate into armed conflict. The following section examines whether the methods employed in controlling inter-State conflict have been duplicated in respect to intra-State conflicts and highlights some specific factual and legal problems evidenced in the Yugoslav case study.

8.4 The Yugoslav Wars and the Need for a Coherent International Response to Intra-State Conflicts

The Yugoslav conflicts evidence a number of features which make intra-State conflicts especially challenging from an international legal perspective. The nature of the forces involved in the conflicts, the behaviour of those forces and the uncertainties surrounding the relevance of law which is clearly applicable in inter-State conflicts lead us to conclude that the time is ripe for a new approach. Again, discussion is limited to the Yugoslav conflict but much of what is said is equally applicable to other intra-State conflicts.

8.4.1 *Armed Forces Involved in the Yugoslav Wars*[33]

An unusual feature in the Yugoslav case study was the number of armed forces involved in the various conflicts. Tito's policy of Total National Defence (TND) resulted in territorially based mini-armies throughout Yugoslavia with arms caches in the hands of locally organised Territorial Defence Forces (TDF's).[34] When the various republics declared themselves independent, TND allowed each republic to have at least some military capability. Thus, in addition to the JNA, whose role in the break-up has already been considered,[35] forces engaged in combat in former Yugoslavia include the Yugoslav Army (YA), the Yugoslav Peoples Army (YPA), the Bosnian Serb Army (BSA), the Krajina Serb Army (SKA), the Croatian Army (HV), the Croatian Defence Council (HVO), the Bosnian Army (BiH) and numerous TDF's.

Further problems were caused because these territorially orientated forces were "…doctrinally, tactically, operationally, and emotionally wedded to operating in their local areas".[36] Sub-State conflicts often set ethnic or territorial groups against one another and when people perceive themselves to be fighting for their homelands, their nation or in pursuit of self-determination their conduct may become over-zealous. Many TDF's displayed "…domestic brinkmanship…"[37] in their operations, even to the point of disobeying direct military orders. Even the JNA's command-and-control structures were adversely affected by the refusal of Croats and Muslims to fight against their own ethnic groups.[38] The situation was made worse because numerous mercenaries, paramilitary and irregular forces joined these fledgling armies as combatants, whose rapid formation meant that their command-and-control structures were woefully below the standards demanded of most national armed forces. A UN Commission of Experts (UN-COE) was created to find evidence of breaches of the laws of war in the former Yugoslavia and to report to the International Criminal Tribunal for Yugoslavia (ICTY).[39] The UN-COE's reports described the widespread use of irregular forces in all the conflicts arising from Yugoslavia's dissolution and identify at least 83 different paramilitary groupings and 45 other special forces, including mercenary groups.[40] These forces were either government organised troops outside regular armed forces command structures or mercenaries from outside Yugoslavia. Mercenaries were "…supplied and often trained by the respective Governments that they served. […] As these units operated independently and outside the apparent chain of command, their order of battle is not known".[41] Some of these groups, such as Arkan's Tigers and the White Eagles, became infamous for committing atrocities but the behaviour of all of these groups was far from exemplary.

Yugoslavs were easily recruited to irregular groups as a result of a combination of propaganda and a self-perpetuating desire for retribution. The UN-COE described how these groups were "…fuelled by the wide circulation of stories of atrocities committed by all sides. Serbs, for instance, were shown pictures allegedly depicting the Mujahedin forces holding the severed heads of Serb soldiers. All sides view themselves as victims, not as perpetrators, thereby creating a desire for revenge and providing justification for their own deeds".

The situation is clearly different from inter-State conflicts where clear command-and-control structures exist and where political and military leaders are answerable for their forces' conduct. Yugoslavia shows how intra-State conflicts generate numerous groups of combatants, rapidly recruited from civilian populations, without clear command-structures and often no idea who their leaders were. The blurring of command-and-control issues "...may well be intended by some of the parties to provide a shield of plausible deniability...".[42] It also creates difficulties in distinguishing civilian populations from combatants, however.

Much of the *jus in bello* developed from the controlled wartime conduct of professional armed forces, reinforced by political leaders who endorse the notion of controlled warfare. Yugoslavia is unusual because of the TND policy but evidences the general principle that such control is often lacking in internal conflicts. This had a direct impact on the conduct of these forces during combat.

8.4.2 *Conduct of the Various Forces*

The fanatical loyalties for which sub-State groups fight, the ill-disciplined organisation of numerous fighting forces and the improbability of a domestic political compromise without international coercion[43] affect the conduct of sub-State combatants. Whereas regular armies have internal legal systems to prevent and punish undisciplined wartime conduct, sub-State forces generally do not and, whereas army operations cease when political leaders order so, sub-State groups fighting to revenge family deaths or the destruction of their home are likely to continue fighting. A self-perpetuating cycle of violence is caused where "...each side sees only its own victimisation, and not what their side has done to others".[44] This section contains merely a few examples of the barbarity which epitomised the Yugoslav wars, particularly the Bosnian conflict.

Non-combatants. Certain groups, such as women, children and the infirm, have historically been exempted from conflict and have been treated with greater compassion by conquerors.[45] The *Geneva Convention on the Treatment of Wounded 1864* began a series of treaties prohibiting attacks on medical personnel and buildings, prisoners-of-war, the wounded and those rendered *hors de combat* by "...sickness, wounds, detention or other cause...".[46] The fourth Geneva Convention *Relative to the Protection of Civilian Persons in Time of War* broke new ground in focusing on treatment of civilian populations in the aftermath of World War II. Civilian populations were granted protection from violence, threats, insult, public curiosity, physical or moral coercion, physical suffering, murder, torture, medical or scientific experiments, pillage, unlimited interment and unnecessary restrictions on religious, intellectual or physical activities.[47]

Changes in the nature of warfare and growth in intra-State conflicts and guerrilla warfare blurred traditional distinctions between combatants and civilians and prompted the adoption of two Additional Protocols (AP's) to the Geneva Conventions in 1977.[48] API dealt with international conflicts but expanded that concept to include "...armed conflicts in which peoples are fighting against colonial domination and alien occupation and against racist regimes in the exercise of their right of self-determination...".[49] *Article 96(3)* allowed such groups to declare their intention to apply the Protocol against the State party to the conflict, even though they could not ratify the Protocol. For these purposes, "...liberation movements were put on the very same footing as States".[50] *Article 44(3)* took account of guerrilla warfare in extending the status of combatant from regular armed forces[51] to persons whom "...owing to the nature of the hostilities..." were unable to distinguish themselves from civilian population whilst engaged in, or preparing for, an attack, providing they carried arms openly during attacks or whilst visible to the adversary when preparing for an attack.

APII covered civilians in non-international conflicts. Until common *Article 3* appeared in the 1949 Geneva Conventions, intra-State insurgent groups were required to be recognised as legitimate belligerents before IHL applied. States rarely accorded such status to 'terrorist groups'.[52] *Article 3*, however, merely required non-combatants to be "...treated humanely..." although violence, torture, hostage-taking, summary executions and outrages upon personal dignity were specifically prohibited. A Commission of Experts report criticised Article 3 as "...so general and incomplete that [it] cannot be regarded as an adequate guide for the conduct of belligerents in such conflicts...".[53] APII *Article 1* required insurgents to be "...organised...under responsible command, exercise such control over a part of [the signatory State's] territory as to enable them to carry out sustained and concentrated military operations and to implement this Protocol".[54] It prohibits orders that 'no quarter' shall be given, rape, hostage-taking, terrorism and pillage (*Article 4*), prohibits attacks on medical units, transport and personnel (*Articles 9-12*), and guarantees civilians "...general protection against the dangers arising from military operations..." including freedom from direct attack, acts intended to spread terror and acts aimed at the destruction of objects indispensable to civilian population survival (*Articles 13-14*). The displacement of civilian populations is prohibited unless for the security of those populations or for imperative military reasons (*Article 17*). Although APII was designed primarily to protect civilian victims of intra-State conflict, it caused concern amongst many States who feared that recognising rights of intra-State insurgents would legitimise 'terrorist' groups and hinder their capacity to quell internal rebellions. Nevertheless, the concerns of the International Red Cross (ICRC) that increasing numbers of conflicts were falling outside existing IHL prompted many States, including Yugoslavia, to ratify both Protocols.[55]

The crucial distinction between combatant and non-combatant was blurred in the composition of Yugoslavia's various armed forces as a result of the rapid expansion in the numerous TDF and other armed forces from former civilians. Numerous breaches of the rules on non-combatants have also been documented. Civilians on all sides have been raped,[56] executed,[57] taken hostage,[58] and been the object of indiscriminate attacks.[59] Atrocities have been committed by all ethnic groups involved in the Yugoslav wars, either to encourage populations to move from certain areas under the policy of 'ethnic cleansing' or to revenge atrocities committed by other ethnic groups.[60] These and other acts evidence the growing need for international law to respond to changes in the manner in which intra-State conflicts are now commonly fought. Armed forces often fail to fulfill the criteria of a self-determination conflict because API *Article 96(3)* includes only the anti-colonial, anti-occupation and anti-apartheid manifestations of self-determination, these being the predominant motives underpinning self-determination claims at the time the AP's were adopted. APII is also inadequate in the sense that *Article 3* is extremely vague and many sub-State forces do not comply with the definition of organised insurgents contained in *Article 1*. The New World Order offers a new period of international relations in which a reassessment of the nature of intra-State conflicts and the rules regarding non-combatants therein could prove invaluable.

Military necessity and proportionality. Proportionality has a history pre-dating its crystallisation into an international legal norm by many centuries.[61] It was introduced in treaty form for the first time under the 1868 *St. Petersburg Declaration*[62] which prohibited acts that "...uselessly aggravate the suffering of disabled men, or render their death inevitable...". Section II of the *1907 Hague Regulations* prohibited "...unnecessary suffering..."

caused by weapons or methods of war and *Article 51(5)(b)* of APII prohibits "…an attack which may be expected to cause incidental loss of civilian life, injury to civilians, damage to civilian objects, or a combination thereof, which would be excessive in relation to the concrete and direct military advantage anticipated".[63] Proportionality is also accepted as an element of many well established rules of customary law, such as the law of reprisals.[64] When the Badinter Commission required implementation of non-forcible reprisals against any State refusing to cooperate in the succession negotiations to be "…in accordance with international law…"[65] one of these requirements would be proportionality. Forcible reprisals were prohibited by the UN Charter but the right of self defence, which retains legality, still requires "…observance of the criteria of the necessity and proportionality of the measures taken…".[66]

Although a well-established rule in inter-State conflicts, the status of proportionality in intra-State conflicts is unclear. Yugoslavia provides numerous examples where a breach of this rule would apply in inter-State cases. Summary executions were a common occurrence and part of the policy of 'ethnic cleansing'.[67] Such executions were conducted against unarmed combatants and civilian populations, in breach of aforementioned rules on non-combatants.[68] Use of non-military buildings, such as hospitals and places of religious worship, for launching armed attacks may have compromised their protected status but the response to such actions was often greatly disproportionate. If intra-State conflicts are to be controlled and to move away from the 'total war' scenario they currently represent, discussions should begin on ensuring that the rules of proportionality are applied by all sides to such conflicts.

Spatial limitations. Spatial limitations on the legitimate theatre of war are founded on the prohibition on intervention into countries declaring themselves neutral in respect of a particular conflict.[69] This principle has been gradually extended to areas *within* States. Different types of spatial limitations have developed, including Non Defended Localities (NDL's),[70] demilitarised zones[71] and neutralised zones.[72] Medical units,[73] places of worship and sites of cultural objects[74] are also prohibited military targets.

One common factor between the various spatial prohibitions is that they must be non-military in character and refrain from conducting hostilities.[75] Although the safe-areas in Bosnia were never described as aspects of IHL, they clearly aimed at limiting the theatre of war. Security

Council resolutions relating to the safe-areas required them to be "...free from any armed attack or any other hostile act..." which clearly indicates the possibility of applying concepts developed in respect of inter-State conflicts to contemporary intra-State conflicts. When only 7,500 UN troops were deployed to protect these areas, however, the organisation was politically unable to demand the disarming of local populations that had fought to protect themselves until this point and militarily unable to guarantee their safety.[76] Allegations were commonly made that hostilities were conducted from safe-areas, hospitals and places of worship.[77] Again, this indicates the importance of securing respect for rules aimed at minimising the inherent destruction of any conflict from all parties thereto, whether State-controlled or poorly-organised sub-State groups. Attacks upon the safe-areas are well-documented[78] and highlight the problems which can occur when IHL is abused by all sides. Equally, mass destruction of important cultural sites occurred, including the destruction of the Mostar bridge and many religious, educational and cultural buildings.[79] Developments in this area are necessary not only in order to minimise the financial costs of repairing States in the aftermath of conflict but also to ensure that places of tremendous historical, artistic, cultural, religious and medical value are shielded from the devastation which engulfs any theatre of war.

Weapons. Historical evidence shows that weapons deemed "...hateful to God..."[80] because of their indiscriminate modes of operation were prohibited. Cross-bows and red-hot shots were amongst the first weapons to feature on this list. Lightweight explosives, dum-dum bullets, balloon-warfare, asphyxiating gases, poison-based weapons, environmental-modification weaponry, biological and chemical weapons subsequently became treaty-based prohibitions.[81]

The use of land-mines in conflict is still not prohibited, despite recent treaty developments in this area which have limited the types of mine which may be used by States having agreed to such limitations. The use of land-mines in Bosnia highlights the dubious legality surrounding the ways in which they may be used, even if they are of a type which remains legally permissable.[82] The location of land-mines must be charted and registered by the forces laying them to allow their removal once hostilities cease. Land-mine use in Bosnia, however, was uncharted and indiscriminate, with only 50% of mined areas capable of being properly identified and many of these surrounding civilian populated areas. Again, it has been suggested that this was intentional and designed to terrorise civilian populations in pursuit of 'ethnic cleansing' of areas.[83] Land-mines are indiscriminate since they make no distinction between combatants and civilians[84] and remain potent threats even after hostilities have ceased. Where sub-State conflicts have divided communities, the visible scars left with those who have lost limbs or lives make reconciliation difficult. Finally, of course, the existence of treaty developments in this area offers little comfort in many instances where the warring parties are sub-State groups who, not being sovereign States, could not ratify such treaties.

Applicability of International Humanitarian Law. The applicability and scope of IHL have traditionally depended upon the nature of the conflict in question - i.e. whether the conflict is international or non-international. In relation to the Yugoslav case study these difficult factual and legal questions were addressed by the ICTY and the Commission of Experts created to assist the Tribunal without any real consistency of response.[85]

The UN-COE noted that Yugoslavia's dissolution originated as a civil conflict before changing into international conflict with the recognition of the successor States.[86] Nevertheless, in relation to conflicts in Bosnia and Croatia, it is submitted that the UN-COE policy was over-simplistic in "...applying the law applicable in *international* armed conflicts to the *entirety* of the armed conflicts in the territory of the former Yugoslavia".[87] The COE acknowledged that many areas in Bosnia involved only locally based groups and were clearly non-international.[88] In an interlocutory appeal challenging the jurisdiction of the ICTY to try the Dusko Tadic case,[89] the Appeals Chamber found it unnecessary to rule on the status of the Bosnian conflict, since it could prosecute criminal breaches of IHL in international and non-international conflicts.[90] The Trial Chamber concluded that the Yugoslav conflict(s) were of mixed character and that, in the Tadic case, the alleged acts were committed during non-international conflict. The FRY was deemed to have insufficient control over Bosnian-Serb forces to hold it responsible for acts committed by Tadic. Presiding Judge Kirk-McDonald strongly dissented, arguing that the agency test was wrongly applied and that the conflict remained international in character.[91] The UN's International Court of Justice (ICJ) refused to consider the nature of the conflict during the admissibility stage of the *Genocide Case* because determinations of fact and law are reserved for the merits stage.[92] State practice within the General Assembly and the Security Council offer little help, with resolutions of the former appearing to deem the Bosnian conflict international and the latter reflecting a civil conflict.[93]

The status of the conflict has traditionally been crucial to determining the applicable law. Whereas some IHL applies to both internal and international conflicts,[94] most depends on such categorisation. The COE's approach led it to conclude that the parties were only bound by the 1949 Geneva Conventions and API, which Yugoslavia had ratified and bound the successor States as a question of succession, the *Genocide Convention 1948* which bound under succession rules, customary law and *jus cogens*, and customary law prohibiting crimes against humanity.[95] Common *Article 3* and APII were inapplicable. The policy of the Appeals Chamber blurs traditional distinctions between international and non-international conflicts and represents "...a fundamental change in the liability of an individual for war crimes. He is now held to be liable for serious breaches of an extensive body of IHL committed during non-international armed conflict".[96] The Trial Chamber, however, maintained distinctions between IHL in non-international conflicts. *Article 2* of the Statute, allowing prosecution of violations against "...persons or property protected under the provisions of the relevant Geneva Conventions..."[97] was deemed unsatisfied since these Conventions pre-suppose the existence of an international conflict.[98]

Clearly, the situation regarding IHL in intra-State conflicts is ambiguous.[99] Suggestions have been made to abolish the distinction between IHL in international and non-international conflicts and, although States have resisted such proposals, the AP's clearly narrow these distinctions.[100] The effects on international society of intra-State conflicts are increasingly comparable to those from inter-State conflicts and the levels of barbarity in the former are often worse. It is submitted that Yugoslavia represents merely one, albeit extreme, example of this phenomenon and highlights the need for debate on how to address changing threats to international peace and security.

8.4.3 *Legal Ambiguities in Intra-State Conflicts*

In addition to legal ambiguities surrounding the applicability of IHL, Yugoslavia shows other ambiguities regarding the use of force in intra-State conflicts. Whereas *Article 2(4)* of the Charter clearly prohibits force in inter-State relations,[101] intra-State conflicts have generally been deemed within a

State's domestic jurisdiction, rendering international involvement incompatible with *Article 2(7)*. Nevertheless, Security Council actions under *Chapter VII* to "…maintain or restore international peace and security…"[102] remain legitimate incursions into domestic jurisdiction. Such actions require the Council to determine "…the existence of any threat to the peace, breach of the peace, or act of aggression…". Yugoslavia evidences the Council's growing willingness to categorise civil conflicts as threats to international peace and security.[103] Many intra-State conflicts are deemed to possess "…a clear international dimension…"[104] justifying international action. In relation to the initial Yugoslav conflict and the later conflict in Bosnia, however, no finding of an act of aggression nor any breach of the peace was made and the Council categorised these situations explicitly as threats to international peace and security.[105] The OSCE's Conflict Prevention Centre also discussed the Yugoslav crisis under its mandate to considered "…unusual military activities…" without classifying it as an international conflict.[106] References were made to the 'illegal' use of force by federal forces during the early stages of the conflict and the ECCY's statement of principles spoke of a prohibition on the "..unilateral change of borders by force…" without limiting this to international borders.[107] These statements create confusion about the legality of force in intra-State conflicts and the origins of any suggested prohibition thereon.

Some writers have suggested that self-determination conflicts such as in the SFRY have become a contemporary variant on the 'just war' and that norms on intra-State force have been affected by this.[108] UN declarations from as far back as 1960 have emphasised the prohibition on the use of force against groups seeking to implement self-determination in the colonial context[109] and subsequent declarations have affirmed the ability of all peoples forcibly deprived of self-determination to "…struggle to that end and to seek and receive support…".[110] This has been suggested to be the equivalent of a right of self-defence for self-determination groups.[111] API, *Article 1(4)* extended IHL protection to peoples engaged in armed conflict to implement their right to self-determination when "…fighting against colonial domination and alien occupation and against racist regimes…". Whilst many of these developments were intrinsically linked with the decolonisation, freedom from alien occupation and anti-apartheid aspects of self-determination, contemporary self-determination claimants are still described as possessing a "…legal license to use force…"[112] if forcibly deprived of their 'right'. International law's current approach creates a dangerous legal lacunae in the use of force. The problem with 'just war' theories is that one party rarely has a monopoly on the 'justness' surrounding the issues leading to conflict. Whereas universal condemnation of colonialism, apartheid and alien occupation may make assessments of the 'just' cause possible, contemporary self-determination claims involving calls for greater political participation within existing State structures are much more difficult to assess.[113] Accordingly, 'just war' theories are to be avoided wherever possible.

Chapter 7 has already suggested a way of redressing the current legal lacunae. Self-determination claims must normally be implemented within existing State borders and if domestic constitutional structures deviate from the requirements of *legitimate governance* the *dissolution doctrine* may come into effect. Instead of having a legal lacuna surrounding the use of force in intra-State conflicts, the *dissolution doctrine* prohibits forcible denial of self-determination whilst also prohibiting use of force by sub-State groups, except in extreme cases. The creation of a mechanism to help implement self-determination in specific cases would resolve problems of identifying the 'just' party and prevent recourse to force. More will be said on this in chapter 9.

A final legal question is posed by the issue of an arms embargo in the Yugoslav case study.[114] Although the embargo was adopted in respect of Yugoslavia as a whole, and with the consent of the SFRY's Federal Presidency, other intra-State conflicts have had arms embargoes imposed on them, sometimes against the will of government authorities.[115] In Rwanda, an embargo was imposed to prevent an escalation of civil conflict[116] and the embargo placed on Yugoslavia was maintained for the same reason against Bosnia, which sought to challenge its legality. The Rwandan arms embargo was suspended when the Security Council considered Rwanda to be in danger of attack from Zaire, whereas the Council remained reluctant to acknowledge any threat of inter-State attack in Bosnia's case and the ICJ sidestepped the issue when this was challenged.[117] The possibility of implementing an arms embargo against a sovereign government in order to prevent it purchasing arms to use in a civil conflict is one which clearly runs counter to traditional conceptions of State sovereignty. Nevertheless, despite some continuing confusion in the legal status of intra-State conflicts, it is possible to identify a greater willingness to categorise them as threats to international peace and security and to react in a more interventionist fashion, even against governmental authorities, in response to such threats.

Such developments would move international law towards the de-legitimisation of force in intra-State conflicts which is entirely consistent with the *dissolution doctrine*.[118]

8.5 Conclusions

Inter-State conflicts cannot yet be confined to the history books but progressive development of the *jus ad bellum* and *jus in bello* have, together with the interdependent nature of modern international relations, greatly reduced the potency of such threats. As external threats evaporate, however, internal threats are 'promoted' and intra-State situations are clearly responsible for the bulk of twentieth-century conflict.

Whilst Yugoslavia represents an extreme example of how intra-State conflicts may threaten international peace and security, this does not render it *sui generis*. Indeed, "...inter-ethnic and self-determination struggles among hostile regions of existing States...are a likely paradigm of the dawning era. We can reasonably anticipate more Yugoslavias".[119] Yugoslavia evidences principles of general application to intra-State conflicts, from the way in which they arise and are conducted to the international legal responses to such conflicts. Yugoslavia shows "...the degrees of bestiality which individuals... [and] ethnic groups can demonstrate when resorting to force to resolve problems arising from their mutual relations".[120] The level of victimisation in sub-State conflicts is enormous[121] and is exacerbated by the way in which forces are composed and operations conducted.

Developments in the *jus in bello* and *jus ad bellum* have always occurred alongside changes in the nature of warfare. Technological advances led to new treaties prohibiting certain types of weapons, protection of civilian populations followed the increasing stature of human rights in international law and atrocities during World War II and the Geneva Convention AP's reflected the growth in guerrilla warfare and self-determination conflicts. It is submitted that the time is ripe, and the need apparent, for further 'promoting' the problem of intra-State conflicts. Contemporary international lawyers will inevitably recognise the erosion of State sovereignty which such suggestions imply. Nevertheless, with an historic appreciation of the development of *jus in bello* and *jus ad bellum*, it is possible to see that each step taken by international law in relation to inter-State conflicts also involved the sacrifice of a degree of sovereignty. Each subsequent treaty represented a continuing erosion of sovereignty and provoked considerable academic discussion until a new treaty was ratified and was 'promoted' to the top of the political and academic agenda in its place. The appropriate question to be asked is not whether the developments suggested represent an erosion of sovereignty but whether that erosion is justified in light of the potential benefits to result from their adoption.

As mentioned at the outset, this chapter was intended more to pose questions than to provide answers. It was submitted that it would be more relevant to posit the usefulness of extending the scope of international law to cover intra-State conflicts and to eradicate existing legal lacunae in this respect than to delve into the details of ensuring the adherence to rules of proportionality, spatial limitations and so on. Hopefully a convincing case has been made, following on from what was said in chapter 7, for expanding international legal regulation of intra-State conflicts. In some respects, the Yugoslav case offers some interesting possible way of doing this. The narrowing of distinctions between IHL's applicability in international and non-international conflicts by the ICTY Appeals Chamber may encourage development of the *jus in bello* vis-à-vis intra-State conflicts. The imposition of arms embargoes against States encountering civil conflict and oblique references to the illegality of force in such conflicts may lead to developments in the *jus ad bellum*. The following chapter will now discuss the potential for developing the third element of regulating conflict - the peaceful settlement of disputes.

Notes

1 See chapter 3, section 3.5. on 'problem-promotion'.

2 Best, G., *War and Law Since 1945*, (1997), OUP, 14.

3 Green, L.C., *Essays on the Modern Laws of War*, (1984), Transnational Publications, 15, notes that "Until after the Thirty Years War, 1618-1648, the natural condition among the European powers tended to be one of war rather than peace...".

4 The Persian Wars ran from -490 BC to -449 BC . See Grun, B., *The Timetables of History: Third Edition*, (1991), Softback Publications, 12.

5 The War between Athens and Sparta ran from -431 BC to -404 BC. Ibid, 14.

6 See chapter 2, section 2.2.3. and ibid, 46-116.

7 See generally, Gardiner, J. and Wenborn, N. (eds.), *The History Today Companion to British History*, (1995), C&B.

8 See Grun, supra n.4, for a comprehensive account of the numerous battles during the 11th-19th centuries.

9 Stein, P., *The Development of Dispute Settlement*, (1984), Butterworths, 4.

10 Cited in Howard, M. (ed.), *Restraints on War: Studies in the Limitation of Armed Conflict*, (1979), OUP, 1.

11 Green, supra n.3, 14-20; Detter, I., *The Law of War*, (1987), CUP, 121. Cf. Best, supra n.2, 1.

12 Best, ibid, 25.

13 Howard, supra n.10, 3-4.

14 See, for example, *Additional Protocol II 1977, Article 1*, discussed in section 8.3.2.

15 Detter, supra n.11, 121; Green, supra n.3, 21. Cf. Best, supra n.2, 15.

16 Translated literally, the law of nations.

17 See chapter 3.

18 Boutros-Ghali, B., 'An Agenda for Peace: Preventive Diplomacy, Peacemaking and Peace-Keeping', reprinted in Roberts, A. and Kingsbury, B. (eds.), *United Nations Divided World*, (1993), Clarendon, 470, paragraph 14.

19 Brogan, P., *World Conflicts - Why and Where they qre Happening: Second Edition*, (1992), Bloomsbury, vii.

20 Brogan, ibid, 621-5, lists post-1945 inter-State conflicts and their estimated death-tolls. The Indo-China wars between Vietnam, Laos and Cambodia (1946-54; 1960-73; 1970-75) have an estimated death-toll of nearly 3 million; the Korean war (1950-53) killed 1.5 million; the Suez crisis (1956) had 10,000 deaths; the border-wars between India-China (1962), India-Pakistan (1965; 1971) and USSR-China (1969) had cumulative totals of 37,000; the wars of the Middle East (1947-49; 1967; 1968-70; 1973; 1982) killed an estimated 128,000; the Ogaden war between Somalia and Ethiopia (1977-78) killed a further 9,000; the invasion of Cambodia by Vietnam (1978-79) and China (1979) another 170,000; the Tanzania-Uganda war (1978-79) another 4,000; the Iran-Iraq war (1979-88) 60,000; the Falklands war (1982) 1,000; the Armenia-Ajerbaijan conflict (1988-) 2,000 and the Gulf War (1990-91) over 100,000.

21 Roberts, A. and Kingsbury, B., 'The UN's Role in International Society Since 1945', supra n.18, 1, at 15.

22 Cf. Howard, supra n.10, 80, who considers that the UN "...has not succeeded in its primary task".

23 See chapter 9, sections 9.2-9.3.

24 Parsons, A., 'The UN and the National Interests of States', supra n.18, 104, at 118.

25 Borchard, E., 'Can Civil Wars be Brought Under the Control of International Law?', (1938), 32 *AJIL*, 538.

26 See Midlarsky, M.I. (ed.), *The Internationalization of Communal Strife*, (1992), Routledge; Rupesinghe, K. (ed.), *Conflict Transformation*, (1995), Macmillan.

27 See Gasser, H, 'International Non-International Armed Conflicts: Case Studies of Afghanistan, Kampuchea and Lebanon', (1982), 31 *AULRev*, 911.

28 Boutros-Ghali, supra n.18, paragraph 13. There are currently "...17 million refugees, 20 million displaced persons and massive migrations of peoples within and beyond national borders".

29 *Report of the UN-Secretary General Pursuant to Paragraph 3 of SC Resn.713 (1991)*, UN Doc S/23169. Halperin M.H. and Scheffer, D.J., *Self-Determination in the New World Order*, (1992), Carnegie, at 1, cite estimates of over 2.5 million refugees or internally-displaced persons within the first year of the Yugoslav conflict. See also Watt, N. and Capella, P., *Perilous Return for One Million Forced Out of Kosovo*, (1999), 4th June, *Guardian*.

30 See chapter 4, section 4.1.

31 *New Risks for Stability and Security*, Security Council Summit Declaration, February 1st 1992, paragraph 4. See chapter 3, section 3.5. on 'inter-mestic' issues.

32 Urquhart, B., 'The UN and International Security After the Cold War', in Roberts, supra n.18, 100. Since 1945, civil wars have occurred in Greece (1945-49); China (1946-49); Colombia (1946-57); Cuba (1954-59); Rwanda (1959); Congo (1960-65); North Yemen (1962-69); Sudan (1963-72); Chad (1965 onwards); Nigeria (1967-70); Pakistan (1971); Uganda (1971-79); Burundi (1972); Cyprus (1974); Ethiopia (1974-91); Iraq (1974); Lebanon (1975 onwards); Angola (1975-6); Afghanistan (1978 onwards); Cambodia (1978 onwards); El Salvador (1979-92); Uganda (1979); Mozambique (1981 onwards); Sudan (1983 onwards); South Yemen (1986); Somalia (1988 onwards); Burundi (1988); Liberia (1989 onwards); Yugoslavia (1991 onwards); Chechnya (1991-2) and Georgia (1991-3). Ethnic insurrections short of civil war have occurred in Burma (1948 onwards); Malaya (1948-60); Indonesia (1950; 1953-60;1966; 1975 onwards); the Philippines (1950-60; 1969; 1974 onwards); Kenya (1952-6); Hungary (1956); Guatemala (1961 onwards); Iraq (1961-70; 1991); the Dominican Republic (1965); Namibia (1965-89); Uganda (1966); Northern Ireland (1969 onwards); Jordan (1970); Sri-Lanka (1971; 1983 onwards); Chile (1973); Pakistan (1973-77); Cambodia (1975-78); Argentina (1976-82); Angola (1976 onwards); Turkey (1977-79); Nicaragua (1978-79; 1981-90); Iran (1978); Syria (1982); Peru (1983 onwards) and; India (1984 onwards). Although accurate figures are difficult to assess in such conflicts, Brogan, supra n.19, 622-30, assesses the total death-toll at around 13 million.

33 See generally Helsinki Watch, *War Crimes in Bosnia-Hercegovina*, (1992), HRWP, 32-8.

34 *Final Report of the UN Commission of Experts Established Pursuant to SC Resn. 780 (1992) Annex III - The Military Structure, Strategy and Tactics of the Warring Factions*, UN Doc. S/1994/674/Add.2, paragraph 14.

35 See chapter 2, section 2.6.4.

36 *UN-COE Final Report, Annex VI.B - The Battle of Sarajevo and the Law of Armed Conflict,* UN Doc. S/1994/674/Add.2, paragraph 18.

37 Id, paragraph 22.

38 Id. See also *UN-COE Final Report, Annex III*, supra n.34, paragraphs 20 and 110-28.

39 See *UN-COE Final Report,* UN Doc. S/1994/674/Add.2, paragraphs 1-4.

40 *UN-COE Final Report, Annex III*, supra n.34, paragraph 24.

41 Ibid, paragraph 26.

42 Ibid, paragraph 42. See also *Report on the OSCE Conference on Politico-Military Aspects of Security*, (1997), OSCE.

43 See chapter 2, section 2.6.2.; chapter 7, section 7.5.

44 *UN-COE Final Report, Annex IIIA*, supra n.34, paragraph 319.

45 McCoubrey, H., *International Humanitarian Law: The Regulation of Armed Conflicts,* (1990), Dartmouth, 80; Green, supra n.3, 20-21.

46 *Geneva Convention for the Amelioration of the Conditions of the Wounded and Sick in Armed Forces in the Field 1949, Article 3(1)*, reprinted in Weston, B.H., Falk, R.A. and D'Amato, A. (eds.), *Basic Documents in International Law and World Order: Second Edition*, (1990), West, 170. See generally Pictet, J.S., *The Geneva Conventions of 1949: A Commentary*, (1960), ICRC. See also *Hague Convention for Adapting to Maritime Warfare the Principles of the 1864 Geneva Convention; Geneva Convention on the Wounded and Sick 1906; Hague Convention IV Respecting the Laws and Customs on Land 1907.*

47 Ibid, *Articles 13-33.*

48 Roberts, A. and Guelff, G. (eds.) *Documents on the Laws of War: Second Edition*, (1989), Clarendon, 387; Best, supra n.2, 415. See also Purcell, H., *Revolutionary War: Guerilla Warfare and Terrorism in Our Time*, (1980), Hamilton; Suter, K., *An International Law of Guerrilla Warfare,* (1984), London.

49 *Geneva Protocol Relating to the Protection of Victims of International Armed Conflicts, Article 1(4)*, reprinted in Weston, op cit, 230.

50 Detter, supra n.11, 45; See also Jennings R. and Watts, A., *Oppenheim's International Law*, (1992), Longmans, 167.

51 See *Article 43(1).*

52 In reality, States often agree to apply APII whilst denying any legal obligation to do so.

53 Roberts, supra n.18, 448. See also Turns, D., 'War-Crimes in Non-International Armed Conflict', (1995), 7 *ASICL*, 804, at 816-8.

54 Effectively, this required "...an alternative 'governmental' authority in a significant portion of the territory of the State which is itself willing to undertake the appropriate quasi-governmental obligations". McCoubrey, supra n.45, 172.

55 Weston, supra n.46, 912-3.

56 UNGA Resn. 48/143 (1993); COE Final Report, Annex IX.B, *Rape Pilot-Study*, paragraphs 7-9; Nunez, K., 'Rape and Ethnic Warfare', (1993), 5(1) *IJRL*, 111; Chinkin, C., 'Rape and Sexual Abuse of Women in International Law', (1994), 5 *EJIL*, 326; Bassiouni, C. and McCormick, M., 'Sexual Violence: An Invisible

Weapon of War in the Former Yugoslavia', (1996), *IHRLI* Occasional Paper No.1.

57 Helsinki Watch Report, supra n.33, 50-62; *Amnesty International Report on the Conflicts in the Former Yugoslavia*, (1993); *UN Human Rights Commission Special-Rapporteur Final Report on the Situation on Human Rights in the Territory of the Former Yugoslavia*, (1995), UNDPI, E/CN.4/1996/9; Ortakovski, V., 'Violation of IHL in the Armed Conflicts in Croatia and Bosnia-Hercegovina', in Biserko, S., (ed.), *Yugoslavia: Collapse, War and War Crimes*, (1993), BCAWA, 245.

58 Ibid, 89-91.

59 Ibid, 104-12; *UN Commission on Human Rights Special Session Report on the Situation in Former Yugoslavia*, (1995), Doc.E/CN.4/1996/57.

60 Ibid, 63-88.

61 Green, supra n.3, 19.

62 *Declaration Renouncing the Use, in Time of War, of Explosive Projectiles Under 400 Grammes Weight*, reprinted in Weston, supra n. 46, 128.

63 For a consideration of proportionality in relation to the first Additional Protocol, see Fenrick, W., 'The Rule of Proportionality and Protocol I in Conventional Warfare', (1982), *MilLRev*, 91.

64 See the *Naulilaa Case (Portugal v. Germany)*, 2 RIAA (1928), 1012, at 1026. See also *The Caroline Case*, (1841), 29 Brit & For.St. Papers 1137-1138.

65 *Opinion 12*, chapter 6, section 6.9.2.

66 *Nicaragua v. USA*, [1986], ICJ Rep. 14, paragraph 194. For discussion of the practical problems in assessing proportionality, see Best, supra n.2, 203, 278-80 and 323-30.

67 Helsinki Watch Report, supra n.33, 1-88.

68 Ibid, 50-63.

69 See *Hague Conventions IV* and *XIII*, (1907), supra n.46.

70 *1907 Hague Regulations, Article 25.*

71 API, *Article 60(3).*

72 GC IV, *Article 15.*

73 GC I, *Article 19*; API, *Article 12.*

74 API, *Article 53*; APII *Article 16*. See also *1907 Hague Regulations, Article 27; Hague Convention for the Protection of Cultural Property in the Event of Armed Conflict 1954*

75 See, for example, *Hague Convention 1954, Article 4.*

76 See *UN Secretary-General Report on Safe-Areas*, UN Doc.S/1994/555.

77 See Owen, at 106.

78 On the sieges of Sarajevo, Prijedor, Mostar and Medak, see *UN-COE Final Report, Annex III*, supra n.33.

79 See *Bosnian State Commission for Gathering Facts on War-Crimes: Bulletins 2-5*, (1992), bosnet (1994), July 11th.

80 Green, supra n.3, 21.

81 Best, supra n.2, 23-7 for discussion of the various treaties prohibiting these weapons.

82 See *ICRC Report on Anti-Personnel Mines: Friend or Foe?* (1996), ICRC; Cahill, K.M. (ed.), *Clearing the Fields: Solutions to the Global Land-Mines Crisis*, (1995), NY Publications.

83 Information kindly provided by UN Mine Action Centre, Marshall Tito Barracks, Sarajevo. See also Godrej, D., 'Trail of Terror', (1997), *NI*, September, 8-9.

84 Red Cross statistics from Namibia show civilians to be involved in 88% of mine-explosions. Similar studies in Mozambique and Georgia during 1994-5 showed civilian casualties of 68% and 80%. See *Red Crescent*, Issue 2, (1997), ICRC; Asia-Watch, 'Land-Mines in Cambodia: The Coward's War', (1991), PHR; Canderay, G.C., 'Anti-Personnel Mines', (1993), Int Rev. Red Cross, 273.

85 See Meron, T., 'International Criminalization of Internal Atrocities', (1995), 89 *AJIL*, 554; Gray, C., 'Bosnia-Herzegovina: Civil War or Inter-State Conflict? Characterization and Consequences', (1996) 47 *BYIL*, 155; Jakovljevic, B., 'Agreements for the Implementation of International Humanitarian Law in the Armed Conflicts in Former Yugoslavia', in Biserko, supra n.57, 161; Sahovic, M., 'International Humanitarian Law in the Yugoslav War', in Biserko, ibid, 141; Nier, C.L., 'The Yugoslav Civil War: An Analysis of the Applicability of the Laws of War Governing Non-International Armed Conflicts in the Modern World', (1992), 10(2), *DJIL*, 303.

86 *UN-COE Final Report Report, Annex I, paragraph 306*, cites Badinter Commission *Opinions 2-5* and 11 as authority for this.

87 Ibid, paragraph 43.

88 Id, paragraph 13.

89 *Decision on the Defence Motion for Interlocutory Appeal on Jurisdiction*, reprinted in, (1996), 35 *ILM*, 32. See also Rowe, P., 'The International Criminal Tribunal for Yugoslavia: The Decision of the Appeals Chamber on the Interlocutory Appeal on Jurisdiction in the Tadic Case', (1996), 45 *ICLQ*, 691.

90 *Tadic Case*, ibid, paragraphs 71-145.

91 Judge Kirk-McDonald, at paragraphs 5-33, called attempts to distinguish between the JNA and Bosnian-Serb forces "...a legal fiction..."

92 *Genocide Case (Bosnia v Yugoslavia): Jurisdiction and Admissibility*, [1996], ICJ Rep, paragraph 26.

93 Gray, supra n.84, 156-79.

94 Examples include prohibitions on starvation and destruction of cultural property.

95 Supra n.87, paragraph 42. See also *Genocide Case*, supra n.92, paragraph 31.

96 Rowe, supra n.89, 699.

97 Paragraph 578.

98 GCIV, *Article 4*.

99 Provost, R., 'Problems of Indeterminacy and Characterization in the Application of Humanitarian Law', in Sellers, M. (ed.), *The New World Order: Sovereignty, Human-Rights and the Self-Determination of* Peoples, (1996), Berg, 177. Cf. Sahovic, supra n.8.5, 144-7.

100 Gasser, supra n.27, 912.

101 Self-defence under *Article 51* remains an exception.

102 *Article 39*.

103 For other examples, see Franck, T.M., *Fairness in International Law and Institutions*, (1995), Clarendon, 224; White, N.D., *Keeping the Peace: The United Nations and the Maintenance of International Peace and Security: Second Edition*, (1997), MUP, 44.

104 UN Under-Secretary for Peacekeeping, Marrack Goulding, *The Changing Role of the United Nations in Conflict Resolution and Peacekeeping*, cited in Morphet, S., 'UN Peacekeeping and Election-Monitoring', supra n.18, 184. See also Vasques, J.A. et al (eds.), *Beyond Confrontation: Learning Conflict-Resolution in the Post-Cold War World*, (1995), MichUP.

105 See UNSC Resns. 713 and 757, chapter 4, section 4.5. Resn. 713 categorized "...the *continuation* of the situation [in the SFRY]..." as a threat to international peace and security. Note, however, UN Doc.S/PV 3009, in which the SFRY authorities expressly consented to the Security Council's consideration of the conflict.

106 Weller, M., 'The International Response to the Dissolution of the SFRY', (1992), 86 *AJIL*, 569, at 572. See also chapter 4, section 4.4.2.

107 Chapter 4, section 4.2. and 4.3.6.

108 Detter, at 81-3. Pomerance, M., *Self-Determination in Law and Practice*, (1982), Nijhoff, 61; Chadwick, E., *Self-Determination, Terrorism and the International Humanitarian Law of Armed Conflict*, Nijhoff; Von-Elbe,D., 'Evolution of the Concept of the Just War in International Law', (1939), 33 *AJIL*, 669; Walzer, M., *Just and Unjust Wars*, (1977), NY Publications.

109 GA 1514 (XV) (1960), *Article 4*

110 *GA Resn 3314 (XXIX) (1974) Resolution on the Definition of Aggression*. In the Nicaragua Case, [1986], ICJ Rep, at 103, the ICJ held this Declaration to reflect customary law. See also Singh, N., 'The UN and the Development of International Law', in Roberts, supra n.18, 384, at 399; Cassese, A., *Self-Determination of Peoples*, (1995), CUP, chapter 6.

111 Cf. Shaw, M.N., *International Law*, (1997), CUP, 796-7.

112 Cassese, supra n.109, 324; Detter, supra n.11, 83.

113 Wilenski, P., 'The Structure of the UN in the Post-Cold War Period' in Roberts, supra n.18, 439; Best, supra n.2, 377.

114 See chapter 4, section 4.5.2.

115 Gray, supra n.84, 194.

116 UNSC Resns. 918 and 997 (1994).

117 Supra n.92.

118 See Damrosch, L.F. (ed.), *Enforcing Restraint: Intervention in Internal Conflicts*, (1994), FRC Press; Zartman, W. (ed.), *Elusive Peace: Negotiating An End to Civil Wars*, (1995), Brookings.

119 Farer, T.J. and Gaer, F., 'The UN and Human-Rights: At the End of the Beginning', in Roberts, supra n.18, 240, at 290.

120 Sahovic, supra n.85, 143.

121 *UN-COE Final Report, Annex III*, supra n.34, 310.

9 Yugoslavia and the Peaceful Settlement of Disputes

"The abolition of war can only be achieved if a substitute for war is found."
Webster, C.K. and Herbert, S., *The League of Nations in Theory and Practice*, (1933), Allen-Unwin, at 119.

9.1 Introduction

Chapter 8 argued that a fundamental change has occurred in the predominant threats to international peace and security and that international laws which have largely contained threats to peace from inter-State conflicts must now turn their attention to intra-State conflicts. This chapter argues that peaceful methods of dispute settlement must also be developed for intra-State conflicts.

9.2 Peaceful Settlement of Disputes in Inter-State Relations

Disputes are an inevitable feature of any society and the manner in which they are resolved is inherently related to the nature of that society. Primitive societies tend not to possess impartial institutional dispute resolution mechanisms and rely on self-help.[1] They also tend to have few established 'laws' and actors within these systems are allowed to choose whether to settle disputes peacefully or forcefully, based on subjective interpretations of the 'correct' conclusion in each instance. Resort to conflict in such societies is endemic. War "...consists of deliberate, controlled and purposeful acts of force combined and harmonised *to attain what are ultimately political objectives* [emphasis added]".[2] The existence of conflict is, therefore, at least partially predicated on the absence of other means by which political objectives can be pursued. The development of dispute resolution mechanisms in the society of States provides an interesting example of how such procedures are required to progress beyond the primitive society scenario.

The rise of nation States in sixteenth-century Europe followed by the *Treaty of Westphalia* in 1648 represented the first move towards the contemporary State-based international relations system, although 'inter-national' relations predated the existence of sovereign States.[3] As transport, communications and trade increasingly pierced States borders, the need for a system to regulate these relations became apparent. The early international system was primitive because, unlike domestic societies, there existed no sovereign authority to impose order, no legislature to create universally applicable laws, no international police force to punish unlawful conduct and no obvious way of penalising societal actors. States were sovereign entities and their conduct could not be controlled, nor could they be compelled to resolve disputes with other States peacefully. In the absence of a sovereign international authority, the system was based on consent and reciprocity, leading writers such as Austin to argue against the classification of this society as a 'legal' system. Nevertheless, this rudimentary framework of international relations enabled the development of codes of behavioral conduct which, although not binding, became the accepted basis upon which political and economic links were established and maintained. Adherence to those codes, albeit consensual, gradually eroded the initial differences in State practice which had limited 'legal' development and an expanding body of 'rules' of State behaviour developed. It is self perpetuating - once States begin to act less heterogeneously, common assumptions arise as to the manner and content of future codes of conduct.

As described in the previous chapter, the increasing level of social interaction and the proliferation of mutual interests between States led to a decline in the resort to war when disagreements arose over those interests. Whilst the post-Westphalian international system remained scarred with conflict,[4] a growing body of State practice leaned towards a cost-benefit analysis of war and sought to remedy disputes peacefully.

The absence of international mechanisms for resolving inter-State disputes compelled States to organise their own procedures. Reluctance to cede control of the dispute-resolution process to third parties and the limited content of objective 'legal' rules led many States to rely primarily on negotiation and diplomacy, which remain key aspects of contemporary dispute settlement.[5] States often sought to prevent disputes arising by inserting clauses into treaties which provided for negotiation in the event of any disagreement regarding their interpretation or implementation. The 1866 *Treaty of Bayonne* between France and Spain is merely one example of this common practice.[6] As the scope of established codes of conduct expanded, however, it became easier to identify legal rules which were more suitable to impartial third party adjudication. The 1794 *Jay Treaty* and the 1814 *Treaty of Ghent* are early examples of this.[7] Fears of losing control over the manner in which a dispute was resolved, however, meant that third party mechanisms were often rejected in favour of resolving the problem between the parties *inter se*, by political rather than legal means. Suspicions of bias also lessened the likelihood of submitting disputes for third party resolution. In a society where most actors enjoy some degree of relations with each other, suspicion arises that any third party may have closer links with one of the disputing parties or a hidden political agenda which will affect the impartiality of their decision. Equally, doubts existed about the possibility for impartial third party resolution by tribunals, arbitration commissions or other institutional dispute-resolution mechanisms, since the disputing parties chose representatives to compose these and these people were likely to reflect the position of the State appointing them. An example of this may be seen from an incident in 1898, following which two commissions of inquiry were created to report on the sinking of an American battleship shortly before the American-Spanish civil war. America, which created the first commission, considered the sinking of the ship to be retaliation from Spain for America's support of Cuba in its attempts to gain independence from the Spanish Empire. Spain, having created a second commission out of fear that the 'American' commission would be biased, denied responsibility for the sinking. Unsurprisingly, each commission endorsed the findings of the State which created it and a peaceful settlement was no closer because of these incompatible conclusions.[8]

The pattern of early dispute resolution mechanisms was generally *ad hoc* rather than permanent because no international institutions existed to host permanent dispute-resolution organs. Nevertheless, some exceptions existed even in the absence of international institutions. The Canadian-American International Joint Commission, created in 1909, enjoyed permanent status and a wide-ranging mandate to resolve disputes between those two States.[9] Another feature of developments in international dispute-resolution mechanisms is that they were generally regional and, since European and American inter-State relations were more developed than elsewhere in the world, largely originated from these areas. Other regions had not achieved sufficient consensus on acceptable codes of conduct for inter-State relations and remained diametrically opposed to their neighbours positions on vital policy issues which ironically prevented the creation of dispute resolution procedures where they were needed most. An important feature of domestic legal systems is that they operate in areas where the disputing parties are unable to reach agreement *inter se*. The early post-Westphalian international system lacked the ability to compel peaceful resolution of disputes, however. Unless States had already created dispute-resolution mechanisms when disagreements arose it became increasingly unlikely that they would agree on a suitable settlement procedure. Where vital interests are perceived to be involved the willingness to resort to force is greatest and hence the need for peaceful settlement procedures is greatest. These remain precisely the areas which States are least likely to submit to third party assessment, however.[10] Nevertheless, these regional developments proved important in showing the benefits of avoiding inter-State conflict and thereby made attempts to develop universal mechanisms more justifiable.

Inter-State relations grew quantitatively and qualitatively throughout the eighteenth and nineteenth centuries and the expansion of Europe's various colonial empires increased the influence of European-based developments on the international system as a whole. Despite understandable contemporary distaste of the colonial era, it helped create a wider international *consensus ad idem* on appropriate inter-State behaviour which facilitated further development of international dispute-resolution mechanisms. Whilst the scope of international law remained limited and many established codes of inter-State conduct "...showed more relationship to agreements than laws..."[11] some international norms began to show a move away from a purely consensual system of international regulation. The rule requiring a State to abide by its word under international agreements - *pacta sunt servanda*[12] - cannot have been based entirely on consent.[13]

Towards the end of the nineteenth-century, a Hague Peace Conference was held which made progress on development of dispute-resolution mechanisms using impartial third parties. Following the failure of the American-Spanish commissions of inquiry, Russia suggested that inter-State disputes required the production of one authoritative report assessing questions of liability, rather than allowing States to create their own commissions which produced conflicting assessments. The 1899 *Hague Convention on the Peaceful Settlement of International Disputes* therefore created a permanent international commission, the first of its kind, to perform such a function. In order to assuage the fears of many States that the commission would be nothing more than an institutionalised version of the dominant powers of the period, it was decided that certain disputes would be removed from the commission's competence. Thus, it could consider only factual, rather than legal, issues and could not consider issues involving a State's "...honour [or] essential interests...". Furthermore, neither the use of the commission, nor the implementation of its findings were compulsory.[14]

The benefit of the commission soon became apparent when it was asked to inquire into an incident where a fleet of Russian warships had fired upon British civilian fishing boats, believing them to be part of the Japanese fleet, with whom Russia was at war. The 1904 *Dogger Bank Inquiry* took two months to report that, whilst the Russian Admiral in charge of the fleet had been genuinely mistaken as to the identity of the British ships, fault could only be deemed to lie with the Russian fleet. The report formed the basis for a friendly settlement between Britain and Russia, the latter of which paid compensation for its wrongful actions.[15] Despite the limits of its mandate, the commission clearly provided a positive impetus with its impartial report which rescued a faltering diplomatic process. The success of this incident prompted many States to follow the example set by the 1899 *Hague Convention* and America concluded 48 bilateral treaties - which came to be known as the *Bryan Treaties* - creating permanent commissions of inquiry under each.[16]

The 1899 Convention also created a Permanent Court of Arbitration (PCA).[17] The Convention established a list of arbitrators and an institutional framework which still exists, although it has been used most sparingly.[18] The PCA is, however, still thought by some to have a valid role to play in international dispute resolution and, in 1992, new Optional Arbitration Rules were adopted with the aim of making the PCA more acceptable to States.[19]

The successes of the first Hague Convention prompted the adoption of the 1907 *Hague Convention for the Peaceful Settlement of Disputes*, which continued the trend of internationalising and institutionalising dispute settlement procedure. One of the problems experienced by the Dogger Bank commission was the time taken in creating its rules of procedure, which naturally delayed the commission's substantive work. The 1907 Convention, therefore, expanded on the rudimentary framework of the 1899 Convention to prevent this happening again. It also continued the trend of resolving disputes on the basis of international 'legal' rules rather than solely by equitable principles.[20] *Article 37* stated that "International arbitration has for its object the settlement of disputes between States by judges of their own choice and on the basis of the respect for *law*. [emphasis added]".[21]

As the twentieth century began, the States of the world were still far from having abandoned the use of war as a means of pursuing their individual political agendas, whether relating to territorial expansion or territorial independence of an area within a State.[22] Domestic political turmoil was increasingly becoming an issue facing many States.[23] European global dominance remained "...an unshakeable fact..."[24] and many States were influenced into concluding bilateral treaties with other nations to ensure their disputes were resolved without force. The First World War emphasised that States remained willing to resort to force when they felt their vital interests to be threatened. The devastating human and economic costs encountered during 1914-1918, however, offered equally compelling evidence that wars often cost more than they achieve. The horrors of the Great War galvanised support for creating the first international institution to maintain international peace and security and, albeit in a tragic sense, succeeded in creating the League of Nations.

The League did not abolish war as a means of resolving disputes but required its member States to refrain from resorting to force until three months after a peaceful resolution process had been attempted. The Council of the League could be invited to produce a report on the situation or States could refer the dispute to arbitration or judicial settlement.[25] The creation of a *Permanent Court of International Justice* (PCIJ)[26] continued the trend towards legal, as opposed to political, resolution mechanisms and permanent internationally-created institutional mechanisms rather than *ad hoc* organs created by the disputing parties. Nevertheless, international law's approach has generally aimed at widening rather than narrowing the available options of peaceful settlement. This is not only politically sensible, with States dubious about the impartiality of third party organs, but also ensures due respect for the sovereignty of States to choose their preferred settlement procedure. Accordingly, the PCIJ was merely an additional settlement procedure, with States entitled to create their own organs or refer to another international mechanism if preferred.[27] Equally, the PCIJ required States to indicate their consent to issues being heard in the PCIJ by ratifying the *Protocol of Signature of the Statute of the PCIJ* and the *Optional Clause* thereto, to "...declare that they recognise as compulsory *ipso facto* and without special agreement, in relation to any other Member or State without accepting the same obligation, the jurisdiction of the Court...".[28] This is not compulsory jurisdiction in the sense of domestic courts, since consent is required and could be revoked, given for a specific time-period or made conditional on other States accepting the PCIJ's jurisdiction. Desire to encourage widespread use of the court, however, meant that even States outside the League could refer disputes on an *ad hoc* basis. Despite some obvious concessions to State's historical desire to maintain control of settlement procedures, the PCIJ represented a tremendous development in international dispute resolution.

An Advisory Committee's report formed the basis of the 1920 *Statute of the Permanent Court of Justice*, although certain of the committee's propositions were rejected. One such proposition was that the PCIJ be given jurisdiction over "...*all disputes of any kind* which may be submitted to it...[emphasis added]".[29] States remained protective of their domestic jurisdiction, particularly in political affairs, and were unwilling to accept this. *Article 36* of the Statute, therefore limited itself to areas which have now become traditionally accepted as the classic definition of a legal dispute. They included, "...(a) The interpretation of a Treaty; (b) Any question of international law; (c) The existence of any fact which, if established, would constitute a breach of an international obligation; (d) The nature or extent of the reparation to be made for the breach of an international obligation".

The structure of the PCIJ was different from any institution which preceded it, both in terms of its extensive multilateral application and in terms of the procedures used within it. The selection of judges was an issue of great controversy. In most bilateral dispute-resolution procedures, the members of the legal tribunal were chosen by the parties to the dispute and generally included equal representation of both parties with, perhaps, an independent President.[30] The PCA operated along similar lines, but the PCIJ's judges were elected by the League's political institutions, namely the Assembly and Council,[31] albeit from a list of nominees recommended by States represented in the PCA.[32] The intention was to indicate the impartiality of the court. The Advisory Committee's report recommended a provision for disputing parties to select one member of the court's panel, to avoid deviating completely from past practice and to allow the court to "...shape the form of the judgment to avoid...wounding national susceptibilities...".[33] A State-appointed judge nevertheless was required to fulfill the requirements of membership of the PCIJ in *Article 1* of the Statute which obliged them to be "...independent judges, elected regardless of their nationality...". Furthermore, State-appointed judges would still only represent a minority in the court's nine-man quorum.[34]

The move towards law-based settlement procedures was evident from *Article 38* of the Statute, which specified that the sources of law that the court should apply included "...(1) International conventions, whether general or particular, establishing rules expressly recognised by the contesting States; (2) International custom, as evidence of a general practice accepted as law; (3) The general principles of law recognised by civilised nations; (4) Subject to *Article 59*,[35] judicial decisions and the teachings of the most highly qualified publicists of the various nations, as subsidiary means for the determination of rules of law". Again, however, due attention was paid to State sovereignty and *Article 38* did not prejudice the ability of the parties to agree to have the court decide a case *ex aequo et bono*[36] if they so wished.

The submission of disputes for judicial consideration and judgment was "...a striking idea in the development of international justice..."[37] and the reputation of international 'law' grew alongside that of the court as cases came before it. During the first few years of its existence, the court considered such varied questions as the procedural requirements for the election of a delegate to the International Labour Conference;[38] the competence of the International Labour Organisation (ILO);[39] the competence of one State to challenge conferment of nationality to individuals in another State;[40] obligations under a peace treaty guaranteeing autonomy to a territory;[41] the legality of a decision to prevent a ship passing through an international waterway;[42] the status of settlers in Poland;[43] the delimitation of post-war frontiers and borders;[44] and the interpretation of post-World War One peace treaties.[45] Again, initial international legal developments spur further developments and a growing body of case-law helped to clarify the expanding scope of international norms.[46] In this sense the work of the PCIJ was of great benefit to future international legal progress and the League's 'failure' to prevent World War Two should not distract from its revolutionary contribution to the law of peace.

Just as World War One provoked the development of international institutions to maintain peace and security, World War Two led to the creation of the United Nations.[47] *Article 2(4)* of the *UN Charter*, prohibiting the use of force in international relations, is well known but the Charter clearly recognises the need to pre-empt any temptation to resort to force by placing the duty to settle international disputes peacefully before the prohibition on force.[48] An entire section of the Charter is devoted to the peaceful settlement of international disputes (PSID).[49]

The creation of an international legal obligation to settle disputes peacefully was a major development. Again, States were given discretion in the manner in which this obligation was fulfilled and *Article 33*, which summarises most of the PSID approaches pursued in the pre-Charter years, allows States to choose from "...negotiation, inquiry, mediation, conciliation, arbitration, judicial settlement, resort to regional agencies or arrangements, or other peaceful methods of their own choice".[50]

As with the League, the UN's political organs were given a prominent role in PSID by the Charter[51] but the prominent legal organ was the International Court of Justice (ICJ), which replaced the PCIJ. The *Statute of the International Court of Justice* borrowed heavily from the earlier PCIJ Statute.[52] Again, utilisation of the court was intended to be as wide as possible, all UN members were parties to the *ICJ Statute* which was annexed to the Charter and non-members could refer cases upon conditions decided by the General Assembly, after a recommendation of the Security Council.[53] The PCIJ's jurisdictional competence, contained in *Article 36* of its Statute, was repeated verbatim in *Article 36(2)* of the ICJ's Statute and the sources of international law to be used by the courts were identical.[54] The ICJ was also authorised to provide Advisory Opinions on "...any legal question..."[55] referred by authorised UN organs. The General Assembly[56] and Security Council[57] were specifically granted authorisation and the Assembly was entitled to authorise other UN organs to seek the court's advice.[58] Advisory Opinions have been given on a variety of questions from a variety of organs, including the UN's Educational, Scientific and Cultural Organisation (UNESCO),[59] Economic And Social Council (ECOSOC),[60] Inter-Governmental Maritime Consultative Organisation (IMCO),[61] and recently at the initiative of the World Health Organisation (WHO).[62]

The Charter also provided a role for regional agencies in dispute resolution. *Article 33* specifically endorsed "...resort to regional agencies..."[63] in seeking peaceful resolution of inter-State conflicts and again the aim is clearly to widen the scope of mechanisms available to States. The Cold War limited the UN's effectiveness as a universal organisation and resort to regional agencies such as the Organisation of African Unity (OAU), Organisation of American States (OAS), Arab League, NATO, and

European Communities (EC) was common.[64] Regional dispute-resolution mechanisms remain a vital source of PSID procedures, since States often feel more comfortable within organisations that are less diverse in membership and more like themselves than the UN.

Having briefly noted the manner in which the international system developed mechanisms to address inter-State disputes, the next section highlights some identifiable trends and argues that similar developments must now be made in respect of intra-State conflicts.

9.3 Trends

Attempts to remove force from inter-State relations have been three-fold. First the *jus in bello* regulated wartime conduct at a time when force remained a legitimate way of resolving disputes. Second, the *jus ad bellum* prohibited resort to force. Third, alternative peaceful methods of resolving disputes developed. These developments overlap considerably and took centuries to evolve. Evolution is a never-ending process and incremental developments in each area were never intended to be the final word. International law can only progress as quickly as States allow and developments have understandably focused on the pressing problems of different time periods. Early *jus in bello* developments concentrated on the protection of Prisoners-of-War, who were the most obvious victims of historical conflicts. From the 1864 *Geneva Convention* through later conventions of 1899, 1906, 1907 and 1949, international law expanded *qualitatively*, by affording greater protection to P-O-W's, and *quantitatively*, by including civilians within international humanitarian law's scope. Similar evolution may be seen in the *jus ad bellum*, which for a long time accepted the unconditional use of force before developing to the position under the League of Nations, which allowed conflict only after a given time period and prior attempts to resolve a dispute peacefully, and then developing further to the post-Charter position, which prohibited recourse to inter-State armed conflict. PSID has also expanded *quantitatively*, in the number of mechanisms available, and *qualitatively*, in the jurisdiction of those mechanisms. Matters which affect States 'honour' or 'essential interests' are most likely to rupture international peace and are, accordingly, no longer outside PSID processes *per se*.[65]

The evolution of the current international system has taken many centuries. The absence of a sovereign authority in the international system comparable with a domestic scenario means that new developments cannot simply be imposed but require an element of consent. Such consent is often forthcoming only when States perceive a restriction on their sovereignty to yield greater long-term advantages. Many legal developments have been accepted with "...a mixture of self-interest...and selective humanitarianism".[66] States moved away from the total-war scenario because it entailed the risk of annihilation. Other developments have required States to be convinced that they were in their interest. The role of the International Red Cross (ICRC) in securing the adoption of the 1949 *Geneva Conventions* provides a classic example of this. Both World Wars helped to create the necessary *consensus ad idem* for major international legal developments. Modern global communications may also create pressure for legal development. An example of this may be seen from the highly-publicised Vietnam war. Despite the extensive use of napalm in World War Two, the relative lack of reporting on this issue and the unavailability of television pictures meant that prohibition of such weapons was not at the top of the international agenda after this war. However, the use of similar weapons in Vietnam received tremendous media attention and the way in which it was brought into the lives of millions of people through television ensured that States felt under sufficient public pressure to focus upon it in later international conferences and to adopt the 1981 *UN Convention on Certain Conventional Weapons* dealing, amongst other things, with napalm.[67]

The creation of a *consensus ad idem* is easier among like-minded nations and the influence of American and European States on the international system has been enormous. Regional practices which successfully avoid conflict create pressure to develop similar universal practices. Lieber's Code, for example, was named after the German writer who codified the battle-conduct of American troops during the American civil war. The Code included many elements which are now fundamental to international humanitarian law (IHL), such as military necessity, controls on armed retaliation against enemy attack, protection of cultural property, prohibition of pillage, proportionality, illegality of certain weapons and treatment of prisoners of war. Similar codes were later adopted by Prussia, the Netherlands, France, Russia, Argentina, Great Britain and Spain before it developed into part of the universal *jus in bello*. The signatories of the 1868 *St. Petersburg Declaration*, which was the first treaty-based codification of the proportionality rule,[68] were primarily European,[69] as were the instigators of the Hague Conferences of 1899 and 1907, which led to subsequent universal developments.[70] The 1928 *Treaty for the Renunciation of War as an Instrument of National Policy*, originating as an American-French initiative, was the first multilateral instrument to renounce war as an instrument of national policy.[71] The League of Nations was the brain-child of America's President Woodrow Wilson and the UN originated from the predominantly European wartime alliance of World War Two. The evolution of PSID procedures from regional to universal mechanisms has been discussed already in this chapter. It is clear, therefore, that powerful regional groupings can be most influential in encouraging universal international legal developments.

International institutions, both universal and regional, have also assisted the development of international law. They create a multilateral forum within which States may develop new procedures for maintaining peace or propose adaptation of existing norms to contemporary problems. Those institutions have the capability to ensure that dispute-resolution procedures are impartial and thereby encourage faith in such processes which facilitates the creation of permanent peaceful settlement mechanisms. The creation of a permanent court for the prosecution of war crimes is an example of this, following as it did the creation of *ad hoc* tribunals for Yugoslavia and Rwanda. These settlement mechanisms are capable of moving dispute resolution away from the purely political sphere and into the 'legal' sphere. Increasing access to dispute resolution mechanisms de-legitimises self-help and provides a growing body of jurisprudence to further develop the *jus gentium*. International law and States' domestic jurisdiction are intrinsically related and a historical perspective evidences a diminution of the latter as the former expands. As the PCIJ itself has noted, the scope of domestic jurisdiction is "...essentially a relative question; it depends upon the development of international relations".[72] International institutions have progressively "...poked a tentative finger through the dyke of domestic jurisdiction..."[73] and, although universal and regional organs generally include reserve-domain clauses,[74] these have not provided significant stumbling blocks to further international developments.

Incrementalism has been matched by innovation within international institutions. The development of peace-keeping forces under the *UN Charter*,[75] the involvement of the organisation in election monitoring and the development of multi-party democracy,[76] and humanitarian intervention[77] are all innovative concepts which arrived through creative interpretation of the Charter rather than revision thereof and have no obvious constitutional legitimacy.[78] This suggests that it is the *political will* which is most important in such innovation, rather than any explicit constitutional authority.

The peaceful settlement of disputes currently represents one of the fundamental pillars of international relations.[79] Its development from a political aspiration to an international legal reality is reflective of how many such norms have developed.[80] A case will now be made for developing a similar approach to intra-State conflicts.

9.4 The Need for Peaceful-Resolution Mechanisms in Intra-State Conflicts

International legal developments have always responded to immediate priorities of the time periods within which they evolved. It is submitted that changing international problems require a reassessment of what are the immediate priorities of the post-Cold War world. The bulk of force in the international system now exists within States rather than between them.[81] International law must turn its attention to intra-State conflicts, notably those involving claims to self-determination where the threat of territorial fragmentation is greatest, and 'promote' them to the top of the agenda if it is to address the primary threats to peace and security.[82] Whereas the *jus in bello* and, arguably, the *jus ad bellum* have expanded to cover intra-State conflicts, little progress has been made in respect of the peaceful-settlement of disputes.

Chapter 7 made a number of suggestions regarding the role of peaceful dispute resolution in self-determination conflicts. It was suggested that an approach which leaves the resolution of such claims solely as questions of domestic jurisdiction is likely to encourage, rather than prevent, a degeneration into civil conflict. Resolution of inter-State disputes was greatly improved when third party dispute resolution mechanisms were created and resort to 'self-help' was de-legitimised. Impartial legal organs ensure help to alleviate any imbalance of power between the disputing parties, such as exist in intra-State conflicts, and ensure a greater consistency in the manner such disputes are resolved. As discussed above, growing jurisprudence can help to clarify acceptable codes of conduct and generate binding international norms.

Clearly, these suggestions would affect the current balance between domestic jurisdiction and issues of international concern. Every new legal development has done this to some extent, however, and this cannot be sufficient justification for rejecting further developments. The primary cause for PSID developments has been that States considered them to be in their interests. The challenge is to convince States that similar developments in intra-State conflicts are entirely in their interests, despite apparently involving a shrinking of their domestic jurisdiction. Yugoslavia shows how unresolved intra-State conflicts can result in horrific civil conflicts which cause enormous loss of life, extensive human rights abuses, ethnic cleansing and the destruction of cultural and historical property.[83] Such conflicts divide populations and can divide States if secessionist claims are allowed to arise. In neither case is State sovereignty respected and the approach suggested here aims at preserving such sovereignty rather than allowing it to be destroyed.

Inter-State PSID mechanisms developed incrementally from regional to universal approaches. They also developed from voluntary procedures into a binding international norm requiring the pacific settlement of disputes. They further developed from a situation in which *ad hoc* settlement mechanisms represented the only viable option into the contemporary situation, where a wide range of permanent international settlement mechanisms exist alongside the remaining possibility of creating *ad hoc* organs for specific disputes. Extending the scope of international law to incorporate intra-State conflicts may require similar developments and Yugoslavia's dissolution may be argued to offer some evidence that a European approach may be developing in this direction.

The Badinter Commission was intended to assist in the peaceful resolution of an intra-State constitutional crisis and, although the EC's delayed intervention changed the commission's role, it still played an important part as a legal organ in a conflict which was, for much of its working-life, an internal one. Greater benefits would have arrived, however, if the commission had been involved before force had been used by the SFRY and sub-State parties. Another *ad hoc* dispute-resolution mechanism involved in the Yugoslav crises was the Brcko arbitral tribunal, which was created to rule on the status of an area in independent Bosnia and decide whether it should be allocated to Bosnian-Muslims or Bosnian-Serbs. Equally, however, the Brcko tribunal was created only after conflict had arisen and the Bosnian communities had been divided militarily, geographically and psychologically by the most brutal post-Cold War conflict of its kind. Both of these organs represent instances where international dispute-resolution mechanisms have been used in an intra-State scenario, however.

Other evidence exists to suggest an emerging norm to settle disputes peacefully, whether within or between States. The EC has followed its role in Yugoslavia with missions to Israel and Algeria, seeking to assist political settlements to conflicts within recognised States. The UN also appears increasingly willing to intervene in intra-State conflicts which it considers pose a threat to international peace and security and El Salvador, Haiti, Croatia, Bosnia, Macedonia, Cambodia, Mozambique, Angola, Iraq, Somalia and Serbia have all witnessed UN intervention to various degrees in recent years. Some have suggested that involvement in internal conflicts will expand to become "...the principal preoccupation of the UN in the field of peace, security and humanitarian considerations".[84]

Whilst intervention in internal affairs is increasingly common, however, the examples cited above indicate that it is generally once conflict has arisen that it takes place. Whilst preferable to no intervention, this is unsatisfactory in that chances for a peaceful settlement are greatly diminished once lives have been lost by both disputing parties. States become more determined not to appease 'terrorist' actions and sub-State groups more determined to achieve independence or overthrow the existing government. It is unlikely that any international dispute-resolution mechanism could provide instant solutions to long-standing conflicts such as Northern Ireland, Israel-Palestine or Somalia but this is not an argument against the notion of intra-State mechanisms, merely one which recognises the importance of early international involvement. Intra-State conflicts are identical to inter-State conflicts in that they are more easily prevented than terminated. Of course, States will naturally be most reluctant to seek international involvement in 'internal' issues. If no armed conflict exists, States will argue that the issue is of no concern to the international community. If conflict has begun, States will be unwilling to lose complete control of the way in which it is resolved. Currently, the international community is unwilling to countenance intervention in the absence of consent by the relevant State or the presence of factors such as large refugee numbers, extensive human-rights violations or fears over other States becoming involved, which translate internal conflicts into international problems. Rejection of EC mediation offers by India in respect of the Kashmir problem provide recent confirmation of this. The most viable way of beginning a new approach appears to be making the process voluntary and it is in this respect that European States bear a responsibility to accept international involvement in their own internal conflicts before expecting other States to do so. African States were initially very reluctant to resort to judicial settlement of disputes, but use of the ICJ by other States legitimised the process of judicial settlement as much as the ICJ itself and greater recourse to the court by African States followed.[85] A willingness to accept the involvement of the international community would indicate that States were confident their actions were beyond reproach and the sub-State's demands were unreasonable or unsubstantiated. Earlier international involvement is necessary if the proliferation of internal conflicts is to be halted and, to be accepted, such involvement must be disassociated from situations which inevitably involve armed conflict. The role of organs such as the OSCE's High Commissioner on National Minorities (HCNM) and Conflict Prevention Centre (CPC) may prove crucial in this process.[86]

Standard-setting is a vital pre-cursor to legal development, both regional and universal.[87] Most developed States, and certainly EU Members and America, could adopt the approach suggested here with absolutely no fear of territorial fragmentation. It is scarcely plausible that separatists in northern-Italy, Scotland or Texas, who have very little domestic support for secessionist claims, would receive greater support by the international community. Of course, one may cite the Northern Ireland example as a more difficult example but, again, this is asking the new preemptive approach to redress a long-standing problem in an area divided by conflict which was at least partially caused by the failings of the more traditional approach. A self-determination commission, however, would help eradicate fears of the inherent destructiveness of self-determination and the loss of sovereignty inherent in accepting international involvement in intra-State affairs. The limited scope of this book prevent discussion of the practicalities behind the creation of such an organ but political will remains the key factor and not constitutional intricacies. Even at UN level, *Article 29* of the Charter allows the Security Council to create "...such subsidiary organs as it deems necessary for the performance of its functions." With the primary function being the preservation of international peace and security, and the nature of threats to that peace having changed, the creation of a similar organ is no less constitutional than the development of peace-keeping forces.

Institutional innovations have been seen in the creation of the Fact-Finding Commission created under API to establish whether alleged grave breaches[88] or other serious violations of the law of armed conflict had occurred[89] the International War Crimes Tribunals for Rwanda and Yugoslavia and the Truth Commission in South Africa. Whilst these are vital to increase the legitimacy of international intervention, they remain post-conflict, rather than pre-conflict, organs and can offer less to prevent conflict than the approach suggested here.[90] Whether the Yugoslav conflict will provoke the development of new international mechanisms for dispute resolution in the same way as they developed following both World Wars remains to be seen.

A final benefit of the suggested approach, less important from a philosophical viewpoint but tremendously important in encouraging States to accept the approach, is that earlier international intervention would not only reduce the likelihood of intra-State conflicts becoming threats to international peace, but would be more efficient from a financial perspective. It is instructive to note that the UN's annual expenses, including peacekeeping and emergency operations, could have been covered by the cost of two days of the Gulf War 'Desert Storm' operation.[91] The financial costs of the Yugoslav conflicts have run into billions and are likely to continue growing. Having refrained from providing substantial economic support at a time when Yugoslavia's crumbling economy was providing an explosive backdrop to the rise of nationalism in that State, the international community is now faced with spending which dwarf whatever sums may have been required to stabilise the SFRY's economy. The costs of the ECCY and ICFY, the financing of the ECMM, WEU, CSCE, NATO, UNPROFOR, I-FOR, S-FOR and K-FOR missions, the provision of humanitarian assistance, the creation of the ICTY, the costs of de-mining areas, the massive redevelopment projects underway and the loss of trade with all Yugoslav republics for various periods during the crisis indicates that, even without mentioning the human costs of the various conflicts, the purely financial costs of Yugoslavia's dissolution were incredible and largely unnecessary.

9.5 Conclusions

This chapter builds on chapter 8 and highlights the way in which inter-State conflict has been reduced in, if not removed from, the contemporary international system. A three-fold approach saw 'total' wars progressively controlled by the *jus in bello*, progressively prohibited by the *jus ad bellum* and provided alternatives means to using force to resolve disputes by developing pacific dispute resolution mechanisms. The interdependency of the current international system prevents the effects of intra-State conflicts being isolated within a State's borders. The proliferation of intra-State conflicts means that these pose the chief threat to international peace and security. Currently, international law adopts a restrictive approach to such conflicts and intervenes, if at all, only once conflict has begun. It should not be surprising that, in such circumstances, international involvement often fails to prevent the continuation of these conflicts. This approach must be adapted if more success is to be had. International institutions cannot safeguard new peace and security threats by maintaining an approach which is rooted in an earlier time of international relations. The problem of intra-State conflicts have 'promoted' themselves as the major threats to international peace and new approaches must be 'promoted' to deal with them. This is easier to aspire to than to achieve. The historical absence of a sovereign authority capable of imposing legal developments remains largely reflective of the contemporary international system. The existence of numerous international institutions, the greater levels of interdependence and the strength of economic leverage in encouraging States to adapt existing modes of conduct only partially redress this situation but they make it possible nevertheless. Ultimately, political will remains the key pre-requisite to international legal development. Academics share responsibility for developing arguments in favour of new developments, however, and to generate such political will. This is a lengthy and arduous task which took many centuries in respect of inter-State conflicts and may take many more for intra-State conflicts. Beginning such a process almost inevitably sets aspirational standards apart from existing practice. Academic debate must, however, push beyond existing practice if existing standards are to be exceeded.[92]

Notes

1 Merrills, J.G., *International Dispute Settlement: Second Edition*, (1991), Grotius, 1; Stein, P., *Legal Institutions: The Development of Dispute Settlement*, (1984), Butterworths, 220.

2 Howard, M., 'Temperamenta Belli: Can War be Controlled?', in Howard, M. (ed.), *Restraints on War*, (1979), OUP, 1, at 3. See also Howard, M., *The Causes of War*, (1983), OUP.

3 Shaw, M.N., *International Law*, (1997), CUP, 12-16. See chapter 3, section 3.4. for further references to the development of the international system.

4 Following the Peace of Westphalia, colonial expansion and the forceful protection of issues perceived as vital national interests created many conflicts. France's Empire was extended across America, from Quebec to the Mississippi River (1679); France and Spain went to war (1683); the Roman Empire began battle with France (1688); the Russo-Turkish War saw Peter the Great pitted against the Turks (1695), who had themselves been successful in battles for territory in the Balkan region (1690); the British fought against France in its American territories (1759); Russia increases its territories in the Crimea (1771); Britain intensifies its colonial struggle in Africa and India (1779), before losing its control over America (1777-1783); Napoleon renews France's quest for dominance in the international community with attacks against Austria, Sardinia, Prussia, Egypt, Italy and the Holy Roman Empire (1792-1799) before meeting defeat at the Battle of Waterloo (1815). See Grun, B., *The Timetables of History*, (1991), Softback Publications, 105-85.

5 For further details on negotiation and consultation, see Merrills, supra n.1, 1-26.

6 For details of the *Lake Lanoux* dispute, see 24 ILR, 101; Merills, supra n.1, 8; Shaw, supra n.3, 541-2.

7 Merrills, supra n.1, 80-81.

8 Merrills, supra n.1, 44.

9 Ibid, at 9. The Commission was composed of an equal number of representatives from both countries and was competent to deal with disputes relating *inter alia* to territorial questions, industrial development and pollution.

10 For example, the legality of the use of force by States is obviously a vital question in international law, yet has been considered only once by the ICJ, in the *Nicaragua Case*, [1986], ICJ Rep. 14, and only in relation to certain aspects. Even then, this was unintended as far as America was concerned.

11 See Fockema Andreae, J.P., *An Important Chapter from the History of Legal Interpretation: The Jurisdiction of the First Permanent Court of International Justice, 1922-1940*, (1948), Sitjhoff, 10.

12 This is now reflected in the *Vienna Convention on the Law of Treaties* (1969), *Article 26*.

13 Shaw, supra n.3, 41; Shearer, I.A., *Starke's International Law*, (1994), Butterworths, 22.

14 See the *Hague Convention 1899, Articles 9-14*.

15 Merrills, supra n.1, 44-47.

16 Shaw, supra n.3, 636.

17 It is common to note that the PCA was "...neither permanent nor a court". Shearer, supra n.13, 443.

18 Since 1945, only 11 cases have been submitted to the PCA or conducted with the co-operation of the Courts International Bureau. Two international Conciliation Commissions and one international Commission of Inquiry have also been created using members of the PCA as members. For full details, see *Permanent Court of Arbitration, Annual Report 1992.*

19 The 1992 Rules were based upon the Rules of the UN Commission on International Trade Law (UNCITRAL). For further details of the changes in procedure, see generally Redfern, A. and Hunter, M., *Law and Practice of International Commercial Arbitration: Second Edition*, (1991), S&M.

20 Equity, nevertheless, plays a continuing role in contemporary international law. See Shaw, supra n.3, 82-6, for examples.

21 Cf. Wehberg, H., *The Problem of an International Court of Justice*, (1918), Clarendon, 46-53, who laments the PCA's failure to remedy the historical predominance of equitable considerations in arbitral tribunals. Writing in 1918, he proposed the creation of a truly judicial body more akin to a domestic legal tribunal. Although falling short in many respects, the PCIJ was soon to be created, in an attempt to fill the institutional void identified in the above work.

22 For examples, see Grun, supra n.185-225.

23 Grenville, J.A.S. (ed.), *The Collins History of the World in the Twentieth Century*, (1994), 15-67, provides case-studies of Germany, France, Italy, Britain, America, Russia and the Austrian Empire to show the proliferation of internal social tensions facing those States, as well as the international threats to their positions in the world.

24 Id, 7.

25 *Article 12.*

26 The PCIJ was independent of the League of Nations, although naturally, the latter played an extremely important role in respect of the former. See Webster, C.K. and Herbert, S., *The League of Nations in Theory and Practice*, (1933), Allen and Unwin, chapter 8.

27 *Article 14*. Fachiri, A., *The PCIJ: Its Constitution, Procedure and Work*, (1925), OUP, 240.

28 *ICJ Statute, Article 36.*

29 Fachiri, supra n.27, 6-13 and 289. Other changes included the addition of English as an official language of the Court, when French was originally the only proposition (*Article 37* of the Jurists proposals), and to increase the number of nominations capable of being put forward by each State from 2 to 4 (*Article 5*).

30 See Merrills, supra n.1, 8-9, 45, 80-108.

31 *ICJ Statute, Article 4.*

32 For details, see Fachiri, supra n.27, 1-31.

33 Ibid, 47. For details, see *Draft Scheme for the Establishment of the PCIJ, Mentioned in Article 14 of the Covenant of the League of Nations, Presented to*

the Council of the League by the Advisory Committee of Jurists, Article 28, quoted ibid, 293, and *Article 31* of the *Statute of the Court*, ibid, 247.

34 *Article 25*. See also *Article 4* of the *Rules of the Court*, quoted ibid, 262.

35 *Article 59* provides that the Court's decisions have no binding force other than between the parties to the current dispute.

36 Translated literally, this means 'according to what is good in equity and good conscience'. Parry, C. and Grant, J.P. (eds.) *Encyclopaedic Dictionary of International Law*, (1986), Oceana, 96.

37 Fachiri, supra n.27, 6.

38 *Designation of the Dutch Workers' Delegate to the 3rd Session of the International Labour Conference*, [1922], PCIJ Series A, 23. Ibid, 126-134 for details.

39 *Position of the ILO in Regard to Agriculture*, [1922], PCIJ Rep., Series B, 86. Ibid, 134-44.

40 *Tunis And Morocco Nationality Decrees Case,* [1923], PCIJ Rep., Series B, No. 4, 23. Ibid, 144-56.

41 *Status of Eastern Carelia*, [1923], PCIJ Series B, 27. Ibid, 156-64.

42 *SS Wimbledon Case*, [1923], PCIJ Series A, 25. Ibid, 164-74. This case is described as "...a landmark in the history of legal proceedings...", since it was the first case to be submitted to the PCIJ under the compulsory-jurisdiction clause, rather than as an Advisory Opinion from the Council of the League.

43 *German Settlers in Poland*, [1923], PCIJ Series A, 36. Ibid, 175-90.

44 *Delimitation of the Polish-Czechoslovakian Frontier*, [1923], PCIJ Series B, 48. Ibid, 198-202.

45 *Interpretation of the Neuilly Peace Treaty*, [1924], PCIJ Series A, 4. Ibid, 216-8.

46 Wehberg, supra n.21, 7; Schermers, H.G. and Blokker, N.M. (eds.), *International Institutional Law*, (1995), Nijhoff, 441. Whilst many of the cases mentioned are Advisory Opinions, requested by the League's political institutions rather than States, this is not true of all of them. Furthermore, the participation of Members, even within those Advisory Opinions, and their apparent acceptance of the judicial procedure created by the PCIJ were truly remarkable developments in State practice. For analysis of PCIJ jurisprudence, see Webster, supra n.26, 159-79.

47 For reference material, see chapter 4, section 4.5.

48 *UN Charter, Articles 1(1)* and *2(3).*

49 *Chapter VI, Articles 33-8.*

50 This formula is repeated in the *Friendly Relations Declaration*, GA Resn. 2625 (XXV), (1970).

51 See *League of Nations Covenant, Article 15* for the role of the League's Council and Assembly in PSID; *UN Charter*, *Articles 24*, *34*, *36* and *38* cover the Security Council's role and *Articles 10-12* cover the General Assembly's role in PSID. Whilst the Security Council has primary responsibility for ensuring international peace and security, the excessive use of the Permanent Members' veto during the Cold War led the General Assembly to adopt the *Uniting for Peace Resolution, GA Resn. 377(V)*, (1950), which asserted the Assembly's right,

assuming stalemate in the Council, to make "...appropriate recommendations... for collective measures, including in the case of a breach of the peace or act of aggression the use of armed force when necessary, to maintain or restore international peace and security". See Dixon, M. and McCorquodale, R. (eds.), *Cases and Materials on International Law*, (1995), Blackstones, 590. In the *Certain Expenses Case*, [1962], ICJ Rep., 151, the ICJ stated that the Security Council's primary role did not prevent the Assembly making recommendations regarding a dispute unless the Council was "...taking some kind of action...". For suggestions that the General Assembly may have blurred the division of powers during its role in the Yugoslav conflict, see Gray, C., 'Bosnia-Hercegovina: Civil War or Inter-State Conflict? Characterization and Consequences', (1996), 47 *BYIL*, 155, at 180-2.

52 *UN Charter, Article 92.* See, Hudson, M.O., 'The Succession of the International Court of Justice to the Permanent Court of International Justice', (1957), 51 *AJIL*, 569.

53 *ICJ Statute, Article 3(3).*

54 Ibid, *Article 38.*

55 Ibid, *Article 65.*

56 *Admissions Case*, [1947-8], ICJ Rep., 57; *Reparations Case*, [1949], ICJ Rep., 174; *Certain Expenses Case*, [1962], ICJ Rep., 151; and *Western Sahara Case*, [1975], ICJ Rep., 12, are a few examples.

57 *Namibia (South-West Africa) Case*, [1971], ICJ Rep., 16.

58 *UN Charter, Article 96.*

59 *Judgements of the ILO Administrative Tribunal Upon Complaints Against UNESCO*, [1956], ICJ Rep., 77.

60 *Privileges and Immunities of the UN Case*, [1989], ICJ Rep., 9.

61 *Maritime Safety-Committee Constitution Case*, [1960], ICJ Rep., 160.

62 *Legality of the Threat or Use of Nuclear Weapons*, [1996], ICJ Rep., 1.

63 See also *Article 52.*

64 Parsons, A., *The UN and the National Interests of States*, in Roberts, A. and Kingsbury, B. (eds.), *United Nations, Divided World*, (1993), Clarendon, 111. See also chapter 3, section 3.3.1.

65 Note that the new CSCE Court on Conciliation and Arbitration limits the court's competence to issues which do not involve questions of "...territorial integrity, national defence, title to sovereignty over land teritory or competing claims with regard to jurisdiciotn over other areas...". See *Statute of the CSCE Court on Conciliation and Arbitration, Article 26(2)*, (1993), 4 *EJIL*, 24.

66 Best, G., *War and Law Since 1945*, (1997), OUP, 294.

67 Ibid, 296-7. See Roberts, A. and Guelff, G. (eds.), *Documents on the Laws of War: Second Edition*, (1989), Clarendon, 396, for text of the *1981 Convention.*

68 See chapter 8, section 8.4.2.

69 Weston, B.H., Falk, R.A. and D'Amato, A. (eds.), *Basic Documents in International Law and World Order: Second Edition*, (1990), West, 899, list the signatories to the 1868 Convention as Austria-Hungary; Baden; Bavaria; Belgium; Brazil; Denmark; France; Great Britain; Greece; Italy; Netherlands;

Persia; Portugal; Prussia and the North German Confederation; Russia; Sweden-Norway; Switzerland; Turkey and Wurtemberg.

70 The *1907 Convention Respecting the Laws and Customs of War on Land*, thus gained the signature of States as diverse as Bolivia, Brazil, China, Cuba, Dominican Republic, El Salvador, Ethiopia, Fiji, Finland, Guatemala, Haiti, Nicaragua, Panama and Thailand. See Weston, ibid, 899.

71 The *Pact of Paris* or *Kellog-Briand Pact* takes its more commonly known title from the surnames of the American and French Foreign Ministers who initially concluded the agreement and the place of its signing.

72 *Tunis and Morocco Nationality Decrees Case*, supra n.40.

73 Best, supra n.66, 58.

74 Schermers, supra n.46, 143 for examples.

75 Howard, M., 'The Historical Development of the UN's Role in International Security', in Roberts, supra n.64, 77, notes that peace-keeping forces "...were not even envisaged in the Charter...[but]...simply grew in response to numerous crises within and between States: in Israel and neighbouring States (since 1948); in India and Pakistan (since 1949); in West Irian (1962-1963); in the Congo (1960-1964); in Yemen (1963-1964); and in Cyprus (since 1964)". To this list, one might add the deployment of peace-keeping troops in Macedonia as a pre-conflict 'trip-wire' force. See chapter 4, section 4.5.5.

76 Roberts, A. and Kingsbury, B., 'The UN's Role in International Society Since 1945', in Roberts, supra n.64, 1, at 51. See Boutros-Ghali, B., *Agenda for Peace*, paragraphs 9 and 81-2 for discussion of the UN's expanding role in the development of democracy. For a historical account of the development of the UN role in election-monitoring, including the role played in Yugoslavia, see Morphet, S.M., 'UN Peacekeeping and Election-Monitoring', in Roberts, ibid, 183; Beigbeder, Y., *International Monitoring of Plebiscites, Referenda and National Elections: Self-Determination and Transition to Democracy*, Nijhoff.

77 See Rodley, N.S. (ed.), *To Loose the Bands of Wickedness: International Intervention in Defence of Human Rights*, (1992), Brasseys; Ramsbotham, O. and Woodhouse, T., *Humanitarian Intervention in Contemporary Conflicts: A Reconceptualisation*, (1996), Polity; Lewer, N., *Something Must Be Done: Towards an Ethical Framework for Humanitarian Intervention*, (1993), BUP.

78 The 'creation' of the UN's peace-keeping capacity was unsuccessfully challenged by Russia and France in the *Certain Expenses UN Case*, [1962], ICJ Rep., 151. Similarly, involvement in election-monitoring has no constitutional basis within the Charter and, in respect of the admission of Russia to the Security Council in place of the defunct USSR, the content of the Charter was explicitly rejected without amendment or revision to *Article 23* thereof. On this latter question, see Roberts, supra n.64, 42.

79 Cassesse, A., *International Law in a Divided World*, (1986), Clarendon, 125-65.

80 See chapter 7, section 7.2. for a similar analysis of self-determination.

81 See chapter 8, section 8.3.

82 Farer, T.J. and Gaer, F., 'The UN and Human-Rights: At the End of the Beginning', in Roberts, supra n.64, 240, state that "...[i]t is increasingly clear

that international peace and security requires the international community to take proactive measures including providing a forum where aggrieved communities can seek third party assistance in peaceful settlement and/or redress of grievances". Cf. Parsons, supra n.64, 121, who states that there are intrinsic dangers in such interventionist trends.

83 See chapter 8, section 8.4.2.

84 Parsons, supra n.64, 118. See id for discussion of SC Resn. 687 (1991) against Iraq - "...the most stringent and intrusive cease-fire provisions imposed on any State since the treaty of Versailles...".

85 See Akinrinade, S. and Sesay, A. (eds.), *Africa in the Post-Cold War International System*, (1998), Pinter.

86 See chapter 4, section 4.4.

87 Roberts, supra n.64, at 48.

88 For the definition of grave breaches, see *Articles 11* and *85(3)-(5)* of the *AP I 1977*.

89 Green, L.C., *Essays on the Modern Laws of War*, (1984), Transnational Publications, 274.

90 See Bassiouni, C., 'The Penal Characteristics of Conventional International Criminal Law', (1983), 15 *CWRJIL*, 32, for discussion of the importance of institutional jurisprudence in spurring growth in international criminal law.

91 Urquhart, B., 'A Double Standard', (1992), *NYBR*, 9th April, 42. The estimated costs of Desert Storm were around a billion dollars a day. Grenville, J.A.S., *Collins History of the World in the Twentieth Century*, (1994), Harper-Collins, 925, cites estimates that the total cost of the Gulf War was in the region of $60 billion. This estimate does not include the loss of trade with Iraq suffered by many exporters, the cost of repairing the infrastructure of the affected areas where fighting occurred, nor the numerous aid and development programmes which are involved in the aftermath of such a conflict.

92 Singh, N., 'The UN and Development of International Law', in Roberts, supra n.64, 384, at 418, makes the same point, whilst noting that aspirational standards must not be set to high as to "...flaw their efficacy".

10 Conclusions

> "War is not inevitable, peace is not inevitable and human survival is not inevitable. Whether we kill each other or help each other depends on us." Ferencz, B.B., *New Legal Foundations for Global Survival*, (1994), Oceana, at 355.

The primary purpose of this book was to investigate Yugoslavia's dissolution and the role of the Badinter Commission in the international community's attempts to restore peace in the region. Having discussed Yugoslavia's turbulent history, it was suggested that blaming the SFRY's dissolution on irrepressible ethnic hatreds amongst the Yugoslav communities ignores the possibility that similar events could occur in other States.[1] Nevertheless, the vast bulk of media reporting during the time of the crisis referred in some way to the 'senselessness' and 'irrationality' of the behaviour of the Yugoslavs and, in doing so, failed to communicate the message that the SFRY's chief problems were economic and political rather than some historical pre-destiny. This clouds the real issues behind the conflict and creates a feeling, which must have influenced public and political responses to the conflict, that this was a *sui generis* example of an artificial State's dissolution in the post-Communist world amidst incomprehensible tribal behaviour which could not seriously be expected to occur in western Europe. Furthermore, it can only have assisted nationalists within Yugoslavia who were attempting to divide communities with reference to long-standing ethnic hatreds and historical injustices perpetuated by the other ethnic groups. The internal political problems which befell Yugoslavia were doubly disruptive because Tito had only recently died and the SFRY's declining importance on the world stage resulted in it receiving less economic and political attention at the very time it needed it most. The reasons for the relative lack of concentration on Yugoslavia's crumbling political system are open to interpretation. Those people adopting a 'tribal ethnic hatreds' understanding of the brewing conflict presumably saw little value in intervening, since these were not considered political problems and presumably those involved would eventually come to see sense and desist from fighting. Those governments considering an increased focus on internal domestic affairs to be the main political and financial priorities in the post-Cold War world would equally have limited their involvement. Neither of these assessments proved accurate, however, and when conflict escalated the major international institutions and their member States were compelled to focus on Yugoslavia, both politically and economically. The outbreak of fighting prompted a series of diplomatic and economic measures from the EC which, although possible of exerting great influence if used pre-emptively, failed to yield results in the hostile environment which had hitherto developed in the Balkans. The EC's lack of independent military capacity and inexperience in assuming control of situations such as those it faced in Yugoslavia highlighted the UN's folly in delaying its involvement in the conflict. Nevertheless the UN *per se* cannot be blamed, since it is merely an institution directed in its policy by its member States and it is clear that financial concerns amongst those States, combined with the arrears of certain important members, played an important role in postponing UN intervention. It will be interesting to note future developments in the EU's Common Foreign and Security Policy pillar given the difficulties shown during Yugoslavia's dissolution surrounding the organisation's military inadequacies and the ability of political pressure from a few member States to dictate it's foreign policy agenda. Equally interesting will be whether the UN continues to adopt a cautious approach to intervention in civil strife given its experiences with having delegated initial control of the Yugoslav conflict to the EC.

The reasons behind the apparent reluctance to instigate institutional involvement in the brewing Yugoslav conflict may be explained in different ways and from different perspectives. The international lawyer may claim it is in deference to the notion of State sovereignty and the traditional lack of legitimacy for interference in civil conflicts. The international relations student may claim it is a reaction to the uncertainties surrounding the post-Cold War period and that the world's most powerful States were unwilling to jeopardise improvements in East-West relations in the absence of a unified desire to intervene. The politics student may claim that the primary reasons were financially motivated and that, in addition to the desire to spend the 'peace dividend' domestically, politicians were aware that expenditure which prevents conflict arising was unlikely to invoke much media interest and hence unlikely to win votes. Subsequent involvement in existing high-profile conflicts, however, offer the possibility of media exposure, political kudos and potential contracts for domestic industry to assist in the reconstruction of areas which have been devastated by war.

It is clear that the prevailing international environment impacted on Yugoslavia's fortunes,[2] but the real question is how much of an impact the dissolution of Yugoslavia will have on international politics and law. This wider question has permeated each of the chapters in this book and this brief conclusion seeks to draw together some of the suggestions which have been put forward and to address potential criticisms thereof.

At the outset of this work a methodological approach was suggested which challenged international lawyers, international relations students and students of politics alike to avoid feeling constrained from suggesting progressive developments to existing legal and political lacunae where existing State practice is equivocal.[3] The current state of flux in the New World Order will increase the instances in which a choice must be made between a progressive solution to those lacunae, which is nevertheless lacking full support in State practice, and a retrogressive approach which is equally unsupported by modern State practice but prefers to cling to traditional conceptions of the 'proper' role of international law without suggesting how international law may react to the new international environment. This writer chose the former approach, preferring to make proposals which sometimes venture ahead of existing State practice whilst making a case for practice to develop in this direction. It was noted that research which spans the disciplines of politics, international relations and international law almost certainly involves subjective value judgements in terms of the materials used and the very *interpretation* of State practice. The reader may disagree with the hypotheses adopted, the materials selected, the conclusions reached or the suggestions made for future developments but the same reader should be aware that his alternative beliefs will be as equally founded on qualitative research assumptions, interpretative materials and subjective hypotheses as those he has rejected.

Having recapitulated some of the criticisms of policy towards the dissolution of Yugoslavia it remains to reiterate the major suggestions made throughout this book for future developments in international law.

Clearly, one of the primary messages conveyed herein has been that intra-State conflicts currently present the most immediate and compelling of threats to international peace and security. What has been suggested is an extension of the principles which have developed to prevent inter-State conflicts to these new sources of international disruption. As international law currently stands in relation to intra-State conflicts the *jus in bello* is inadequate. The *jus ad bellum* is difficult to assess given the legal difficulties surrounding civil conflicts which, although traditionally matters of domestic jurisdiction, are now increasingly likely to be categorised by the UN as threats to international peace and security or claimed by sub-State groups to be legitimate self-determination struggles in opposition to the forcible denial of this right. Equally, the development of peaceful dispute-resolution procedures for intra-State conflicts has remained limited. Nevertheless, the Yugoslav case-study offers some tentative evidence that State practice may be moving in the suggested direction. The narrowing of the distinctions between liability for war crimes in inter-State and intra-State conflicts by the ICTY Appeals Chamber may provoke developments in the *jus in bello*.[4] The references to the 'illegality' of JNA force against the Yugoslav republics during the early stages of the conflict and the imposition of an arms embargo against the SFRY may indicate developments in the *jus ad bellum*.[5] Finally, the creation of *ad hoc* organs such as the Badinter Commission, the Brcko Tribunal and the ICTY may provide some indication of a growing willingness to create dispute-resolution mechanisms for intra-State conflicts, albeit in a post-conflict situation.

The Badinter Commission, which has remained a primary focus of this work, may be seen as a prime example of how such mechanisms may be developed. The commission was created by the EC, thus perpetuating the strong influence of western European States on international law. It was an *ad hoc* organ which was created in response to a high-profile conflict and it provided only advisory opinions which were not considered binding by the EC's political organs and representatives for which they were intended. These are classic features of the incremental manner in which inter-State dispute-resolution procedures have developed and may herald similar developments in civil conflicts.[6] The commission's jurisprudence has also been suggested to offer new insights into the development of a number of important international legal doctrines. Self-determination appears to have been treated as a principle with various manifestations, not all of which have yet been fully explored in State practice. The denial of political representation and participation within existing SFRY structures was found to precipitate the dissolution of that State, whilst the recognition of successor States was made conditional upon provision of those same criteria and the principle of *uti possidetis juris* was extended to internal borders.[7] In short, the commission offers some interesting and thought-provoking possibilities for expanding international intervention in intra-State conflicts.

Another consistent criticism of policy in the Balkans conflicts has been that the timing of international intervention must be improved and a preference for more pre-emptive intervention has been expressed. Earlier intervention not only provides greater hope for successfully defusing potential conflict situations but also offers greater long-term protection to State sovereignty and reduces human and financial costs. Conflicts arising from political divisions within States are clearly more difficult to resolve once such political division is joined by military opposition, yet international intervention still appears likely to be delayed until violence has erupted.

A number of potential criticisms must be addressed at this stage, however, in relation to calls for greater and earlier international intervention. Critical readers may argue that existing international institutions have shown themselves to be capable of domination by a handful of powerful States and are often specifically designed to allow that. This would allow any extension of international institutional competencies, and any expansion of international legal doctrines, to be abused for the political aims of those powerful States rather than impartially applied by the institutions of which they are members. Clearly, this writer acknowledges the need to ensure that international law, as any law, is impartially applied and this must be read as inherent in each of the suggestions made.

The critic will argue that extensions to international law's remit are unjustified given the potential for abuse. The point is however that, in the absence of extending international law in the manner suggested, the issues surrounding intra-State conflicts - such as the legality of force by governmental and sub-State forces and the outcome of self-determination claims - still incite tremendous political interest from the same powerful States and it is naïve in the extreme to think that they would not become involved in the resolution of such issues if they felt themselves to have a national interest therein.

In the absence of acknowledging the legitimate interest of international legal actors such as the UN and other regional agencies, however, such involvement is unconstrained and not subject to any doctrinal foundation nor subject to public scrutiny. Compare, for example, the numerous criticisms which have been written regarding the failings of the EC and UN in the Yugoslav conflict with the relative absence of academic writing surrounding the actions of individual States in the same conflict.

A starker example is provided by the USA's extensive involvement in South America during the Cold War years. First, criticism of the USA's activities was more difficult by virtue of the fact that those activities were clandestine and information was not in the public arena, unlike the reported resolutions on Yugoslavia from the UN and EC. This is not to underestimate the extent of clandestine discussions which take place between the representatives of States acting within those international institutions prior to the publication of these resolutions but merely to highlight the difference that the eventual production of a public resolution against which subsequent actions by those institutions can be evaluated is a notable improvement. Second, since it is virtually impossible for any single State to dictate the entire policy of an international institution there is an inherent mitigation against intervention designed to benefit that State, which would not be the case if the international community as a whole were excluded from the process. It is inconceivable to think that the USA would have been able to convince the Organisation of American States or the United Nations to sanction its activities in South America whereas, left as a question of individual foreign policy, these constraints are removed. Third, even accepting the control exerted by certain States within their respective international institutions, this is usually confined to merely one organ of those institutions and is often countered by other organs of the same institution. The permanent members of the UN Security Council, therefore, are able to veto any resolution from that organ but are incapable of preventing the General Assembly, which is much more balanced in its global representation and political parity, from adopting resolutions on the same issue. Equally, the dominance of France, Germany, Italy, UK and Spain within the EC's Commission and Council of Ministers is not matched within the European Parliament. It is true that the General Assembly and European Parliament possess law-making powers far weaker than either the Security Council or the EC's Council of Ministers. Nevertheless, these organs are capable of bringing to the public awareness their disagreement with the policies adopted in those other organs which critics would accuse of being subject to political abuse by powerful member States. Divergent policies within the UN were thus clear from comparing General Assembly resolutions on the issue of lifting the arms embargo against Bosnia with the Security Council's refusal to adopt a similar resolution. Equally, the European Parliament's resolutions expressing its desire for Kosovo and Vojvodina to be accorded an active role in the ECCY contrasted starkly with the exclusion of those areas at the decision of the EC's foreign ministers. Weak as these powers may be, they introduce a level of transparency which facilitates critical discussion that would not be possible if intervention had been undertaken by individual States outside international institutional structures.

The practical realities are that State sovereignty is often used as a shield behind which governmental authorities unaccountably repress their own populations. This shield is upheld from a rhetorical perspective by all States, jealous to ensure non-intervention in their own affairs, whilst at the same time it is capable of being regularly, and unaccountably, pierced by powerful States that benefit from the reluctance to extend the legitimate competencies of international institutions in this regard. Whilst critics are right to demand a focus on the dominance exerted by certain States within regional and universal institutions, they should not be allowed to escape the conclusion that, by maintaining their opposition to expanding the competencies of those institutions, they obliquely support the unchecked dominance of those same States outside any public arena.

A further potential criticism of the extension of international institutional competency is the identity of the particular institutions which would benefit from the erosion of State sovereignty. The suggested pre-emptive interventions into areas traditionally within a State's domestic jurisdiction are designed to ensure that intervention occurs at a stage before conflict has arisen and is relatively low-key in comparison with intervention in Yugoslavia. Measures would include the monitoring of elections, the deployment of human-rights rapporteurs and the publication of reports assessing self-determination claims by sub-State groups. Economic, diplomatic and political support would be provided to support domestic initiatives to redress domestic political unrest before it reached the stage of violently exploding onto the world's television screens. The OSCE appears to be the organisation most orientated in this direction and it is regrettable that the High Commissioner for National Minorities, Office for Democratic Institutions and Human Rights and Conflict Prevention Centre were not sufficiently operational to allow their involvement before Yugoslavia's fate was sealed by the outbreak of conflict.[8] The vast bulk of the OSCE's work takes place without media reportage and in the absence of civil conflict, unlike more widely recognised UN operations such as UNPROFOR which can do little to resolve a conflict and are resigned to merely limiting its destructiveness. The practical problem surrounding a shift away from high-profile operations is that the OSCE, and numerous other Non-Governmental Organisations engaged in conflict-prevention missions, fall way short of the financial capacity of the larger organisations such as the EC, NATO and UN. A shift in responsibility towards pre-emptive intervention cannot seriously be contemplated without a corresponding shift in resources and political support. It is in this respect that we must now turn to the question of political support for the approaches and developments suggested throughout this book. To what extent can it be said that the States of the world are ready to contemplate the erosions on their sovereignty which would inevitably flow from the adoption of the developments suggested herein?

It has already been shown how the horrors of both World Wars were instrumental in shocking the international community into developing institutional mechanisms designed to prevent such conflict recurring.[9] Whether Yugoslavia will have a similar impact in respect of intra-State conflict remains to be seen, although some tentative conclusions may be offered. On the one hand, the recent adoption of the *Statute of a Permanent International Criminal Court* is a development which was not politically feasible even in the aftermath of both World Wars but the experiences of the Yugoslav and Rwandan War-Crimes Tribunals appear to have caused States to reassess their objections to such an institution. The indictment of Milosevic before the ICTY is the first time a wartime chief of staff has been charged with crimes against humanity. The deployment of UN peace-keepers in a preventive pre-conflict capacity in Macedonia also represents a significant development.[10] The imposition of an arms embargo and the creation of safe-areas within sovereign States encountering civil conflict may also indicate a new approach to intra-State conflicts, although the impact of these is limited in the sense that the former was requested by the sovereign State in which conflict was underway and the latter received only rhetorical, as opposed to realistic, international support.[11] On the other hand, reaction to the Yugoslav conflict differs in a number of ways from post-World War developments. Yugoslavia's dissolution did not have the same human impact on other States as did the World Wars, which affected every part of the globe. Although people outside Yugoslavia were aware of events taking place there, through media communications and political discussions, the Yugoslav conflicts had little tangible effect on everyday life outside the Balkan region and States did not engage in conflict with one another as they had done during 1914-18 and 1939-45. Put simply, Yugoslavia shocked the international community but qualitatively less so than either World War. States' willingness to contemplate encroachments upon their domestic jurisdiction in respect of inter-State conflict following the World Wars was not matched by a willingness to allow dilution of their control of intra-State conflicts following Yugoslavia's dissolution, despite the prevalence of civil conflict.[12]

Given the suggested need for international legal developments and the relative lack of State support for such developments, what can be done? It has been stated on numerous occasions throughout this book that legal developments, of any kind, are not brought into existence solely by wishing for them. It has also been stated that the academic bears a moral responsibility to suggest way to best redress existing legal and political lacunae, rather than simply accepting them as historical and contemporary truisms. In this sense, this final paragraph is the most important in the book.

If States are currently reluctant to authorise the pro-active international law approach suggested throughout this work, the academic must seek to generate public awareness that these developments are in the best interests of the international community and of individual States themselves. Although States are the primary legal actors in the international system, they have no true decision-making capacity of their own and it is political leaders who decide issues on their behalf. Political leaders are, in turn, answerable to public opinion and academics must play a role in shaping public opinion to redress existing legal deficiencies.[13] If this book can convince one reader of the need for a new approach to redress these deficiencies and, in turn, inspire that reader to convince others of this message, the effort will certainly have been worth it.

Notes

1 See chapter 2, section 2.7.
2 See chapter 3.
3 See chapter 1 generally.
4 See chapter 8, section 8.4.2.
5 See chapter 4, sections 4.2, 4.3.3, 4.4.2 and 4.5.5.
6 See chapter 9, section 9.3.
7 See chapter 5, sections 5.7.7, 5.9.1, 5.9.2 and chapter 7, sections 7.4 and 7.5.
8 See chapter 4, section 4.4.3 and 4.4.4.
9 See chapter 9, section 9.3.

10 See chapter 4, section 4.5.5.
11 See chapter 4, sections 4.5.2 and 4.5.6.
12 See chapter 8, section 8.3.
13 See chapter 1, section 1.3.

Bibliography

Books

Allot, P., Carty, T., Koskenniemi, M., Warbrick, C., *Theory and International Law: An Introduction*, (1991), BIICL/ILG.

Allot, P., *Eunomia: A New Order for a New World*, (1990), OUP.

Alrdich, G.H., *The Jurisprudence of the Iran-US Claims Tribunal*, (1996), Clarendon.

Anderson, M., *Frontiers*, (1996), Polity.

Avanessian, A.B., *The Iran-US Claims Tribunal in Action*, (1993), G&T.

Bailey, S., *The General Assembly of the United Nations: A Study of Procedure and Practice*, (1960), Clarendon.

Beetham, D. (ed.), *Defining and Measuring Democracy*, (1994), SAGE.

Beetham, D., *The Legitimation of Power*, (1991), Macmillan.

Beigbeder, Y., *International Monitoring of Plebiscites, Referenda and National Elections: Self-Determination and Transition to Democracy*, (1998), CUP.

Bermann, G.A., Goebel, R.J., Davey, W.J. and Fox, E.M, *Cases and Materials on European Community Law*, (1993), West.

Best, G., *War and Law Since 1945*, (1997), OUP.

Bethlehem, D. and Weller, M. (eds.), *The Yugoslav Crisis in International Law: General Issues, Part I*, (1997), CUP.

Biserko, S., (ed.), *Yugoslavia: Collapse, War and War Crimes*, (1993), BCAWA.

Blix, H., *Sovereignty, Aggression and Neutrality*, (1970), A&W.

Blum, Y., *Eroding the United Nations Charter*, (1993), Nijhoff.

Bordon, A. (ed.), *Breakdown, War and Reconstruction in Yugoslavia*, (1992), IWPR.

Borowiec, A., *Yugoslavia after Tito*, (1977), Praeger.

Bourantonis, D. and Evriviades, M. (eds.), *A United Nations for the Twenty-First Century*, (1996), Kluwer.

Brands, H.W., *The Devil We Knew: The Cold War*, (1993), OUP.

Brook, S., *Claws of the Crab: Georgia and Armenia in Crisis*, (1992), Picador.

Buchan, D., *Europe: The Strange Superpower*, (1993), Dartmouth.

Buchanan, A., *Secession: The Morality of Political Divorce from Fort Sumter to Lithuania and Quebec*, (1991), Westview.

Buchheit, L.C., *Secession: The Legitimacy of Self-Determination*, (1978), YUP.

Burg, S.L., *Conflict and Cohesion in Socialist Yugoslavia: Political Decision-Making Since 1966*, (1983), PUP.

Cahill, K.M. (ed.), *Clearing the Fields: Solutions to the Global Land-Mines Crisis*, (1995), NY Publications.

Carlsson, I. (ed.), *Our Global Neighbourhood: The Report of the Commission on Global Governance*, (1995), OUP.

Carr, E.H., *What is History?*, (1961), Macmillan.

Cassese, A., *Self-Determination of Peoples - A Legal Reappraisal*, (1995), CUP.

Cassese, A., *International Law in a Divided World*, (1986), Clarendon.

Chadwick, E., *Self-Determination, Terrorism and the International Humanitarian Law of Armed Conflict*, (1992), Nijhoff.

Chomsky, N., *Deterring Democracy*, (1991), Verso.

Chowdhuri, R.N., *International Mandates and Trusteeship System: A Comparative Study*, (1955), Stevens.

Claude, R.P. and Weston, B.H., *Human Rights in a World Community*, (1989), Princeton.

Cohen, L.J., *Broken Bonds*, (1993), Westview.

Connors, D. (ed.), *The True Cost of Conflict*, (1995), Saferworld.

Crawford, J., *Democracy in International Law*, (1994), CUP.

Crawford, J., *The Creation of Statehood in International Law*, (1979), OUP.

Creswell, J.W., *Research Design - Qualitative and Quantitative Approaches*, (1994), SAGE.

Curtis, M., *The Great Deception*, (1998), Pluto.

Damrosch, L.F. (ed.), *Enforcing Restraint: Intervention in Internal Conflicts*, (1994), FRC Press.

Darby, H.C., *A Short History of Yugoslavia from Early Times to 1966*, (1966), CUP.

Denitch, B., *Ethnic Nationalism: The Tragic Death of Yugoslavia*, (1994), MinUP.

Denitch, B. (ed.), *Legitimation of Regimes: International Frameworks for Analysis*, (1979), SAGE.

Detter, I., *International Legal Order*, (1994), Dartmouth.

Detter, I., *The Law of War*, (1987), CUP.

Dickson, B., *Introduction to French Law*, (1994), Pitmans.

Dixon, M. and McCorquodale, R. (eds.), *Cases and Materials on International Law*, (1995), Blackstones.

Donia, R.J., and Fine, V.A., *Bosnia-Hercegovina: A Tradition Betrayed*, (1994), Hurst.

Dragnich, A.N., *The First Yugoslavia: Search for a Viable Political System*, (1983), Hoover.

Dugard, J., *Recognition and the United Nations*, (1987), Grotius.

Dyker, D.A., *Yugoslavia: Socialism, Development and Debt*, (1990), Routledge.

Edwards, D., *Free to Be Human*, (1998), Green Books Ltd.

Edwards, S. (ed.), *European World Yearbook*, (1993), EWY.

Evans, J. (ed.), *Bias in Human Reasoning: Causes and Consequences*, (1990), Lawrence-Erlbaum.

Fachiri, A., *The Permanent Court of International Justice: Its Constitution, Procedure and Work*, (1925), OUP.

Feilchenfeld, E.H., *Public Debts and State Succession*, (1931), Macmillan.

Ferencz, B.B., *New Legal Foundations for Global Survival*, (1994), Oceana.

Ferencz, B.B. (ed.), *World Security for the 21st Century*, (1991), Oceana.

Fink-Hafner, D. and Robbins, J.R. (eds.), *Making a New Nation: The Formation of Slovenia*, (1997), Dartmouth.

Fleming, D.F., *The Cold War and its Origins*, (1961), Doubleday.

Forsythe, D.P., *Human Rights and Peace: International and National Dimensions*, (1993), NUP.

Franck, T.M., *Fairness in International Law and Institutions*, (1995), Clarendon.

Franck, T.M., *The Power of Legitimacy among Nations*, (1990), OUP.

Fry, C.B. and Ranjitsinhji, K. (eds.), *Key Book of the League of Nations*, (1923), H&S.

Gardiner, J. and Wenborn, N. (eds.), *The History Today Companion to British History*, (1995), C&B.

Gayim, E., *The Principle of Self-Determination: A Study of its Historical and Contemporary Legal Evolution*, (1990), NIHR.

Giddens, A., *The Consequences of Modernity*, (1990), Polity.

Glenny, M., *The Fall of Yugoslavia*, (1993), Penguin.

Gow, J., *Legitimacy and the Military: The Yugoslav Crisis*, (1992), Pinter.

Green, L.C., *Essays on the Modern Laws of War*, (1984), Transnational Publications.

Grenville, J.A.S., *The Collins History of the World in the Twentieth Century*, (1994), Collins.

Grun, B., *The Timetables of History*, (1991), Softback Publications.

Gutman, R., *A Witness to Genocide*, (1993), Macmillan.

Hall, D., *Mandates, Dependencies and Trusteeships*, (1948), OUP.

Halperin M.H. and Scheffer, D.J., *Self-Determination in the New World Order*, (1992), Carnegie.

Hampson, F., *Incitement and the Media: Responsibility of and for the Media in the Conflicts in the Former Yugoslavia*, (1992), EUP.

Hannum, H., *Autonomy, Sovereignty and Self-Determination: The Accommodation of Conflicting Rights*, (1990), PenUP.

Harris, D.J., *Cases and Materials on International Law*, (1997), S&M.

Henkins, L. and Hargrove, J.L., *Human Rights: An Agenda for the Next Century*, (1994), ASIL.

Herman, E.S. and Chomsky, N., *Manufacturing Consent: The Political Economy of the Mass Media*, (1998), Pantheon.

Higgins, R., *Problems and Process: International Law and How We Use It*, (1994), Clarendon.

Holder, W.E. and Brennan, G.A. (eds.), *The International Legal System*, (1972), Butterworths.

Holtzman, H.M. and Neuhaus, J.E. (eds.), *UNCITRAL Model Law on International Commercial Arbitration*, (1989), Kluwer.

Horsman, M. and Marshall, A., *After the Nation-State*, (1994), Harper-Collins.

Howard, M. (ed.), *The Causes of War and other Essays*, (1983), Temple-Smith.

Howard, M. (ed.), *Restraints on War: Studies in the Limitation of Armed Conflict*, (1979), OUP.

Hulsman, J.C., *A Paradigm for the New World Order*, (1997), Macmillan.

Hunter, B. (ed.), *The Statesman's Yearbook*, (1992-3), Macmillan.

Ignatieff, M., *The Warrior's Honor - Ethnic War and Modern Conscience*, (1998), C&W.

Jeffer, J., *Shockwaves: Eastern Europe after the Revolution*, (1992), Southend.

Jennings R. and Watts, A., *Oppenheim's International Law: Volume I*, (1992), Longmans.

Jennings, I., *The Approach to Self-Government*, (1956), CUP.

Joffe, P., *Sovereign Injustice: Forcible Inclusion of the James-Bay Crees and Cree Territory into a Sovereign Quebec*, (1995), Grand Council of the Crees Publication.

Karaosmanoglu, A.L., *Crisis in the Balkans*, (1993), UNIDR.

Kazancigil, A. (ed.), *Rethinking Democracy*, (1991).

Kennedy, P., *Preparing for the Twenty-First Century*, (1993), Harper-Collins.

Khan, R., *The Iran-United States Claims Tribunal*, (1990), Nijhoff.

Knight, D.B. and Davies, M. (eds.), *Self-Determination: An Interdisciplinary Annotated Bibliography*, (1987), Garland.

Koskenniemi, M., *From Apology to Utopia - The Structure of International Legal Argument*, (1989), Finnish Lawyers.

Kuhn, T. S., *The Structure of Scientific Revolutions*, (1970), Chicago.

Lambrinidis, J.S., *The Structure, Function and Law of a Free-Trade Area*, (1965), Stevens.

Lasok, K.P.E., *The European Court of Justice: Practice and Procedure*, (1984), Nijhoff.

Lee, E., *Dictionary of Arbitration Law and Practice*, (1986), Mansfield.

Leurdijk, D., *The UN and NATO in The Former Yugoslavia*, (1994), NIIR.

Levinson, L.L. (ed.), *Bartlett's Unfamiliar Quotations*, (1972), Allen and Unwin.

Lewer, N., *Something Must be Done: Towards an Ethical Framework for Humanitarian Intervention*, (1993), BUP.

Lorenz, J.P.P., *The UN after the Cold War*, (1997), S&W.

Lowe, V. and Warbrick, W. (eds.), *The United Nations and the Principles of International Law*, (1994), Routledge.

Luard, E., *The United Nations: What it is and What it Does*, (1994), Macmillan.

Lukic, R. and Lynch, A., *Europe from the Balkans to the Urals: The Disintegration of Yugoslavia and the Soviet Union*, (1996), OUP.

Lutz, E.L., Hannum, H. and Burke, K.J. (eds.), *New Directions in Human Rights*, (1989), PenUP.

Lydall, H., *Yugoslavia in Crisis*, (1989), Clarendon.

Lyons, G.M. and Mastanduno, M., *Beyond Westphalia? State Sovereignty and International Intervention*, (1995), JHUP.

MacDonald, R.St.J. and Johnston, D.M. (eds.), *The Structure and Process of International Law*, (1983), Nijhoff.

Mahoney, K.E. and Mahoney, P. (eds.), *Human Rights in the 21st Century: A Global Challenge*, (1993), Nijhoff

Malanczuk, P., *Akehurst's Modern Introduction to International Law*, (1997), Routledge.

Malcolm, N., *A Short History of Kosovo*, (1998), Macmillan.

Malcolm, N., *A Short History of Bosnia*, (1994), Macmillan.

Mallaby, S., *After Apartheid*, (1992), Faber.

Mapp, W., *The Iran-US Claims Tribunal: The First 10 Years*, (1993), MUP.

Mayall, J., *Nationalism and International Society*, (1990), CUP.

McCoubrey, H., *International Humanitarian Law: The Regulation of Armed Conflicts*, (1990), Dartmouth.

McFarlane, B., *Yugoslavia: Politics, Economy and Society*, (1988), Pinter.

McGoldrick, D., *International Relations Law of the EU*, (1997), Longmans.

McGoldrick, D., *Documents on the Human Dimension of the OSCE*, (1995), OSCE Publications.

McGoldrick, D., *The Human Rights Committee: Its Role in the Development of the ICCPR*, (1991), Clarendon.

Mercer, D. (ed.), *Chronicle of the Second World War*, (1994), Chronicles.

Merrills, J.G., *The Development of International Law by the European Court of Human Rights*, (1993), MUP.

Merrills, J.G., *International Dispute Settlement*, (1991), Grotius.

Midlarsky, M.I. (ed.), *The Internationalisation of Communal Strife*, (1992), Routledge.

Milazzo, M.J., *The Chetnik Movement and Yugoslav Resistance*, (1975), JHUP.

Miller, R.F., *Tito As Political Leader and External Factors in Yugoslav Political Development*, (1977), AUP.

Moore, J.B., *International Adjudication:- Volume One*, (1929), OUP.

Morris, V. and Scharf, M., *An Insider's Guide to the ICTY*, (1996), Transnational Publications.

Muller, S., and Mijs, W., *The Flame Rekindled - New Hopes for International Arbitration*, (1993), Leiden.

Mullerson, R., *International Law, Rights and Politics: Developments in Eastern Europe and the CIS*, (1994), Routledge.

Musgrave, T.D., *Self-Determination and National Minorities*, (1997), OUP.

Nowak, M., *UN Covenant on Civil and Political Rights: Commentary*, (1993), Engel.

O'Connell, D.P., *State Succession in Municipal and International Law*, (1967), CUP.

Osborn, P.G., *Concise Law Dictionary*, (1947), S&M.

Owen, D., *Balkan Odyssey*, (1995), Victor-Gollancz.

Parry, C. and Grant, J.P. (eds.), *Encyclopaedic Dictionary of International Law*, (1986), Oceana.

Patil, A.V., *The UN in World Affairs 1946-1990: A Complete Record and Case-Histories of the Security Council's Veto*, (1992), Mansell.

Pavlowich, S.K., *The Improbable Survivor: Yugoslavia and its Problems 1918-1988*, (1988), Hurst.

Phillips, A. (ed.), *Minorities in the Balkans*, (1989), MRG.

Phillips, A. and Rosas, A. (eds.), *The UN Minority-Rights Declaration*, (1993), Turku.

Pictet, J.S., *The Geneva Conventions of 1949: A Commentary*, (1960), ICRC.

Pomerance, M., *Self-Determination in Law and Practice*, (1982), Nijhoff.

Purcell, H., *Revolutionary War: Guerilla Warfare and Terrorism in our Time*, (1980), Hamilton.

Ramcharan, B.G. (ed.), *The International Conference on the Former Yugoslavia Official Papers*, (1997), Kluwer.

Ramcharan, B.G., *The International Law and Practice of Early-Warning and Preventive Diplomacy*, (1991) Nijhoff.

Ramet, P. (ed.), *Yugoslavia in The 1980s*, (1985), Westview.

Ramsbotham, O. and Woodhouse, T., *Humanitarian Intervention in Contemporary Conflicts: A Reconceptualisation*, (1996), Polity.

Rasmussen, H., *On Law and Policy in the European Court of Justice: A Comparative Study in Judicial Policy-making*, (1986), Nijhoff.

Redfern, A., and Hunter, M., *Law and Practice of International Commercial Arbitration*, (1991), S&M.

Remington, R.A., *The Warsaw Pact - Case Studies in Communist Conflict Resolution*, (1971), Clarendon.

Renner, M., *Budgeting for Disarmament*, (1995), WIP.

Riley, G. (ed.), *Values, Objectivity and the Social Sciences*, (1974), Addison-Wesley.

Roberts, A. and Guelff, G. (eds.), *Documents on The Laws of War*, (1989), Clarendon.

Roberts, A. and Kingsbury, B. (eds.), *United Nations, Divided World*, (1993), Clarendon.

Rodley, N.S. (ed.), *To Loose The Bands of Wickedness: International Intervention in Defence of Human Rights*, (1992), Brasseys.

Rosenne, S., *The World Court: What it is and How it Works*, (1994), Nijhoff.

Rosenne, S., *Practice and Methods of International Law*, (1984), Oceana.

Rowe, P.J. (ed.), *The Gulf War 1990-91 in International and English Law*, (1993), Routledge.

Rubinstein, A.Z., *Yugoslavia and the Non-Aligned World*, (1970), PUP.

Rupesinghe, K. (ed.), *Conflict Transformation*, (1995), Macmillan.

Rusinow, D. (ed.), *Yugoslavia: A Fractured Federalism*, (1988), Wilson.

Schachter, O. and Joyner, C.C. (eds.), *United Nations Legal Order*, (1995), CUP.

Schermers, H.G. and Blokker, N.M. (eds.), *International Institutional Law - Unity Within Diversity*, (1995), Nijhoff.

Schwarzenberger, G., *The League of Nations and World Order*, (1936), Constable.

Sellers, M. (ed.), *The New World Order: Sovereignty, Human Rights and The Self-Determination of Peoples*, (1996), OIP.

Shaw, M.N., *International Law*, (1997), CUP.

Shearer, I.A., *Starke's International Law*, (1994), Butterworths.

Shihata, I.F.I., *The European Bank for Reconstruction and Development: A Comparative Analysis of the Constituent Agreement*, (1990), Routledge.

Silber, L. and Little, A., *The Death of Yugoslavia*, (1995), Penguin.

Simma, B., *The Charter of the United Nations: A Commentary*, (1994), OUP.

Simmie, J. and Dekleva, J. (eds.) *Yugoslavia in Turmoil: After Self-Management*, (1991), Pinter.

Simmonds, N.E., *Central Issues in Jurisprudence: Justice, Law and Rights*, (1986), S&M.

Simpson, J.L. and Fox, H., *International Arbitration: Law and Practice*, (1959), Stevens.

Singleton, F., and Carter, B., *The Economy of Yugoslavia*, (1982), Croom-Helm.

Smith, J., *The Cold War: 1945-1991*, (1997), OUP.

Sohn, L.B., *The Future of Dispute Settlement*, (1986), OUP.

Stankovic, S., *The End of an Era: Yugoslavia's Dilemmas*, (1981), Hoover.

Stein, P., *The Development of Dispute Settlement*, (1984), Butterworths.

Suter, K., *An International Law of Guerrilla Warfare*, (1984), London.

Thompson, M., *A Paper House: The Ending of Yugoslavia*, (1992), Pantheon.

Tillotson, J., *EC Law: Text, Cases and Materials*, (1994), Cavendish.

Tomuschat, C. (ed.), *Modern Law of Self-Determination*, (1993), Nijhoff.

Trifunovska, S. (ed.), *Yugoslavia Through Documents: From its Creation to its*

Dissolution, (1994), Nijhoff.

Twining, W. (ed.), *Issues of Self-Determination*, (1991), AbUP.

Vasques, J.A. et al (eds.), *Beyond Confrontation: Learning Conflict-Resolution in the Post-Cold War World*, (1995), MichUP.

Walker, M., *The Cold War*, (1993), Fourth-Estate.

Walters, F.P., *A History of the League of Nations*, (1960), RIIA .

Walzer, M., *Just and Unjust Wars*, (1977), NY Publications.

Weatherill, S., *Cases and Materials on EC Law*, (1998), CUP.

Weiss, T.G., Coate, R.A. and Forsythe D.P., *The UN and Changing World Politics*, (1997), CUP.

West, R.W., *Tito and the Rise and Fall of Yugoslavia*, (1994), Sinclair-Stevenson

Westlake, J., *Chapters on the Principles of International Law*, (1984), Grotius.

Weston, B.H., Falk, R.A. and D'Amato, A. (eds.), *Basic Documents in International Law and World Order*, (1990), West.

White, N.D., *Keeping The Peace: The United Nations and the Maintenance of International Peace and Security*, (1997), MUP.

White, N.D., *The Law of International Organisations*, (1996), MUP.

Wilson, D., *Tito's Yugoslavia*, (1979), CUP.

Woodward, S., *Balkan Tragedy*, (1995), Brookings.

Zartman, W. (ed.), *Elusive Peace: Negotiating an end to Civil Wars*, (1995), Brookings.

Articles

Allot, P., 'Reconstituting Humanity - New International Law', (1992), 3 *EJIL*, 219.

Allot, P., 'New International Law', in Allot et al, *Theory and International Law: An Introduction*, (1991), *BIICL/ILG*, 107.

Anderson, K., 'Illiberal Tolerance and the Fall of Yugoslavia', (1993), 33 *VJIL*, 385.

Badinter, R., 'Final Report', in Engel, N.P. (ed.), *Universality of Human Rights in a Pluralistic World*, (1990), CEP, 168.

Bagwell, B., 'Yugoslav Constitutional Questions: Self-Determination and Secession of Member Republics', (1991), *GAJICL*, 489.

Barsch, R., 'Indigenous Peoples in the 1990s: From Object to Subject of International Law?', (1994), 7 *HarvHRJ*, 33.

Bassiouni, C. and McCormick, M., 'Sexual Violence: An Invisible Weapon of War in the Former Yugoslavia', (1996), *IHRLI* Occasional Paper No.1.

Bayefsky, A.F., 'The HRC and the Case of Linda Lovelace', (1982), 20 *Can.YIL*,

244.
Bengoetxea, J., 'Nationalism and Self-Determination', in Twining, W. (ed.), *Issues of Self-Determination*, (1991), AbUP. 133.
Bennet-Jones, O., 'Macedonia and The UN', (1994), *www.writenet.co.*
Benvenisti, E., 'The Israeli-Palestinian Declaration of Principles: A Framework for Future Settlement', (1993), 4 *EJIL*, 542.
Berger, J. and Hunt, P., 'Towards the International Protection of Indigenous Peoples', (1994), 12 *NQHR*, 125.
Berman, H.R. et al, 'Indigenous Peoples and Self-Determination', (1993) 87 *ASIL*, 190.
Berthoud, P., 'The United Nations Development Programme, Framework and Procedures', (1970), 4 *JWTL*, 155.
Bicanic, I., 'Fractured Economy', in Rusinow, D. (ed.), *Yugoslavia: A Fractured Federalism*, (1988), Wilson, 126.
Bieber, R., 'EC Recognition of Eastern European States: A New Perspective for International Law?', (1992), 86 *ASIL*, 374.
Binder, G., 'The Case for Self-Determination', (1993), 29 *Stan.JIL*, 223.
Bindman, G., 'The New South Africa: A Revolution in the Making', 13th May (1994), *NLJ*, 648.
Blum, Y., 'Russia Takes Over USSR's Seat at the UN', (1992), 3 *EJIL*, 254.
Blum, Y., 'UN Membership of the "New" Yugoslavia: Continuity or Break?', (1992), 86 *AJIL*, 830.
Bohr, S., 'Sanctions by the UN Security Council and the EC', (1993), 1 *EJIL*, 35.
Borchard, E., 'Can Civil Wars be Brought Under the Control of International Law?', (1938), 32 *AJIL*, 538.
Boutros-Ghali, B., 'Democracy: A Newly Recognised Imperative', (1995), 1 *Global Governance*, 3.
Boutros-Ghali, B., 'Great Expectations: The UN at 50', (1995), 20 *MULRev*, 1.
Brilmayer, L., 'Secession and Self-Determination', (1991), 16 *YJIL*, 177.
Broms, B., 'Subjects: Entitlement in the International Legal System', in MacDonald, R.St.J. and Johnston, D.M. (eds.), *The Structure and Process of International Law*, (1983), Nijhoff, 383.
Brownlie, I., 'The Reality and Efficacy of International Law', (1981), 52 *BYIL*, 1.
Bruckner, P., 'The EC and the UN', (1990), 1 *EJIL*, 174.
Burkett, J. and Skegro, B., 'Are Economic Fractures Widening?', in Rusinow, D. (ed.), *Yugoslavia: A Fractured Federalism*, (1988), Wilson.
Campbell, A.I.L., 'The Attitudes and Practices of the Specialised Agencies and the UN Organs and the Interpreting of their Basic Constitutions', (1986), 2 *JRev*, 177.
Canderay, G.C., 'Anti-Personnel Mines', (1993), *Int Rev. Red Cross*, 273.
Carothers, T., 'Empirical Perspectives on the Emerging Norm of Democracy in International Law', (1992), 86 *ASIL*, 261.

Carty, A., 'Why Theory: The Implications for International Law Teaching', in Allot et al, *Theory and International Law: An Introduction*, (1991), BIICL/ILG, 75.

Cass, D.Z., 'Rethinking Self-Determination: A Critical Analysis of Current International Law Theories', (1992), 18 *Syracuse JICL*.

Cassese, A., 'The Fundamental Principles Governing International Relations', in Cassese, A. (ed.), *International Law in a Divided World*, (1986), CUP, 320.

Cassese, A., 'Political Self-Determination: Old Concepts and New Developments', in Aan den Rijn, A. (ed.), *UN Law and Fundamental Rights*, (1979), Sijthoff, 137.

Chan, J.M.M., 'The Right to Nationality as a Human Right', (1991), 12 *HRLJ*, 1.

Chinkin, C.M., 'The East Timor Case', (1996), 45 *ICLQ*, 712.

Chinkin, C.M., 'Rape and Sexual Abuse of Women in International Law', (1994), 5 *EJIL*, 326.

Chinkin, C.M. and Sadurska, R., 'Learning About International Law Through Dispute Resolution', (1991), 40 *ICLQ*, 529.

Closa, C., 'The Concept of Citizenship in the Treaty on European Union', (1992), *CMLRev*, 137.

Codevilla, A.M., 'NATO Today: Curing Self-Inflicted Wounds', (1982), *IEDSS*.

Cohen, P.J., 'Ending The War and Securing Peace in Former Yugoslavia', (1994), 6 *PILRev*, 19.

Condorelli, L., 'En Attendent la Cour de Conciliation et D'arbitrage de la CSCE: Quelques Remarques sur le Droit Applicable', in Dominicé, C., Patry, R. and Reymond, C. (eds.), *Études de Droit International en L'Honneur de Pierre Lalive*, (1993), RCADI, 457.

Conlon, P., 'Legal Problems at the Centre of UN Sanctions', (1996), *NordJIL*, 73.

Craven, M.C.R., 'The European Community Arbitration Commission on Yugoslavia', (1995), 66 *BYIL*, 333.

Crawford, J., 'Review of Self-Determination of Peoples: A Legal Reappraisal', (1996), 90 *AJIL*, 331.

De-George, R.T., 'The Myth of the Right of Collective Self-Determination', in Twining, W. (ed.), *Issues of Self-Determination*, (1991), AbUP.

Dehousse, R., 'The International Practice of the EC: European Political Cooperation in 1991', (1993), 4 *EJIL*, 141.

Dunnett, D.R.R., 'The European Bank for Reconstruction and Development: A Legal Survey', (1991), *CMLRev*, 571.

Eastwood, L.S., 'Secession: State Practice and International Law after the Dissolution of Yugoslavia', (1993), 3 *Duke JCIL*, 299.

Espiell, H.G.G., 'Self-Determination and *Jus Cogens*', in Cassese, A. (ed.), *UN Law, Fundamental Rights*, (1979), Clarendon, 167.

Fenrick, W., 'The Rule of Proportionality and Protocol I in Conventional Warfare', (1982), *MilLRev*, 91.

Figa-Talamance, N., 'The Role of NATO in the Peace Agreement for Bosnia-Hercegovina', (1996), 2 *EJIL*, 164.

Fox, G.H., 'Self-Determination in the Post-Cold War Era: A New Internal Focus?', (1995), 16 *Mich.JIL*, 733.

Fox, G.H., 'The Right to Political Participation in International Law', (1992), 86 *ASIL*, 249.

Fox, G.H., 'States and the Undertaking to Arbitrate', (1988), 37 *ICLQ*, 1.

Franck, T.M., 'Democracy as a Human Right', in Henkin, L. and Hargrove, L. (eds.), *Human Rights: An Agenda for the Next Century*, (1994), *ASIL*, 73.

Franck, T.M., 'The Emerging Right to Democratic Governance', (1992) 86 *AJIL*, 46.

Franck, T.M., 'International Law after the Cold War', (1990), 84 *ASIL*, 156.

Franck, T.M. and Nolte, G., 'The Good Offices Function of the UN Secretary-General', in Roberts, A. and Kingsbury, B. (eds.), *United Nations, Divided World*, (1993), Clarendon, 143.

Frowein, J.A., 'Self-Determination as a Limit to Obligations in International Law', in Tomuschat, C. (ed.), *Modern Law of Self-Determination*, (1993), Nijhoff, 211.

Gaeta, P., 'The Dayton Agreements and International Law', (1996), 2 *EJIL*, 147.

Gassama, I.J., 'World Order in the Post-Cold War Era',(1994), *BrooklynJIL*, 255.

Gasser, H., 'International Non-International Armed Conflicts: Case Studies of Afghanistan, Kampuchea and Lebanon', (1982), 31 *AULRev*, 911.

Georgiev, D., 'Deconstruction and Legitimacy in International Law', (1993), 4 *EJIL*, 1.

Gow, J., 'Belgrade and Bosnia: An Assessment of the Yugoslav Military', (1993), *JIRev*, 243.

Gowlland-Debbas, V., 'Security Council Enforcement and Issues of State-Responsibility', (1994), 43 *ICLQ*, 55.

Gray, C., 'Bosnia-Herzegovina: Civil War or Inter-State Conflict? Characterisation and Consequences', (1996), 47 *BYIL*, 155.

Gray, C., 'Self-Determination and the Breakup of the Soviet Union', (1992), *YEL*, 465.

Greenwood, C., 'The Prosecution of War Criminals in the Former Yugoslavia', (1994), *Bracton LJ*, 13.

Greenwood, C., 'New World Order or Old? The Invasion of Kuwait and the Rule of Law', (1992), 55 *MLRev*, 153.

Grossman, C., 'The Right to Political Participation in International Law', (1992), 86 *ASIL*, 257.

Guelke, A., 'International Legitimacy, Self-Determination and Northern Ireland', (1985), 2 *Rev Int Stud.*

Hambro, E., 'The Authority of the Advisory Opinions of the International Court of Justice', (1954), 3 *ICLQ*, 2.

Hanneman, A.J., 'Independence and Group Rights in the Baltics', (1995), 35 *Virg JIL*, 485.

Hannum, H., 'Minorities, Indigenous Peoples and Self-Determination', in Henkins, L. and Hargrove, J.L., *Human Rights: An Agenda for the Next Century*, (1994), ASIL.

Hannum, H., 'Rethinking Self-Determination', (1993), 34 *VirgJIL*, 1.

Hannum, H., 'Yugoslavia and Europe: Old Wine in New Bottles?', (1993), 3 *TLCP*, 57.

Hannum, H., 'The Limits of Sovereignty and Majority Rule: Minorities, Indigenous Peoples and the Right to Autonomy', in Lutz, E.L., Hannum, H. and Burke, K.J. (eds.), *New Directions in Human Rights*, (1989), PenUP, 5.

Hannum, H., 'New Developments in Indigenous Rights', (1988), 28 *VJIL*, 585.

Hermann, G., 'The *UNCITRAL* Model Law: Its Background, Salient Featues and Purposes', (1985), 1 *ArbInt*.

Herring, E., 'The Manufacture of Consent for the Arms Embargo on Bosnia-Hercegovina', (1995), 6 *OIRev*, 32.

Higgins, R., 'Peace and Security: Achievements and Failures', (1995), 6 *EJIL*, 445.

Higgins, R., 'Time and The Law: International Perspectives on an Old Problem', (1997), 46 *ICLQ*, 501.

Higgins, R., 'The Identity of International Law', in Cheng, B. (ed.), *International Law: Teaching and Practice*, (1982), Stevens, 37.

Hille, S., 'Mutual Recognition of Croatia and Serbia (+Montenegro)', (1995), 6 *EJIL*, 598.

Hrvatin, S.B., 'The Role of the Media in the Transition', in Fink-Hafner, D. and Robbins, J.R. (eds.), *Making a New Nation: The Formation of Slovenia*, (1997), Dartmouth, 274.

Iglar, R.F., 'The Constitutional Crisis in Yugoslavia and the International Law of Self-Determination', (1992), 15 *Boston JICL*, 213.

Isby, D.C., 'Yugoslavia 1991: Armed Forces in Conflict', (1991), *JIRev*, 394.

Jakovljevic, B., 'Agreements for the Implementation of International Humanitarian Law in the Armed Conflicts in Former Yugoslavia', in Biserko, S., (ed.), *Yugoslavia: Collapse, War and War Crimes*, (1993), BCAWA, 161.

Kahn, P.W., 'Lessons for International Law from the Gulf War', (1993), 45 *SLR*, 425.

Kimminich, O., 'A Federal Right of Self-Determination?', in Tomuschat, C. (ed.), *Modern Law of Self-Determination*, (1993), Nijhoff, 310.

Kingsbury, B., 'Claims by Non-State Groups in International Law', (1992),

Cornell JIL, 481.
Kingsbury, B., 'Self-Determination and Indigenous Peoples', (1992), 86 *ASIL*, 383.
Kirgis, F.L., 'Degrees of Self-Determination in the UN Era, (1994), 88 *AJIL* 304.
Koskenniemi, M., 'National Self-Determination Today: Problems of Legal Theory and Practice', (1994), 43 *ICLQ*, 241.
Koskenniemi, M., 'The Future of Statehood', (1991), *HILJ*, 46.
Koskenniemi, M. 'Theory: Implications for the Practitioner', in Allot, P., Carty, T., Koskenniemi, M., Warbrick, C. (eds.), *Theory and International Law: An Introduction*, (1991), *BIICL/ILG*, 3.
Kostic, B., 'FRY Position on the ECCY', (1991), 42 *RIA*, 14.
Kostunica, V., 'The Constitution and the Federal States', in Rusinow, D. (ed.), *Yugoslavia: A Fractured Federalism*, (1988), Wilson.
Krause, K.R., 'The United Nations in The Post-Cold War World: Adaptation, Transformation, Openness or Obsolescence?', (1993), 87 *ASIL*.
Kreca, M., 'Succession and the Continuity of Yugoslavia', (1992), 39 *JRMP*, 178.
Lal, D. et al, 'Foreign Aid: Who Needs It?', (1996), 16(5) *JIEA*, 35.
Lee, R.S., 'The Rwanda Tribunal', (1996), 9 *LJIL*, 225.
Lim, C.L., 'The Problem of the Definition of the "Self" in Self-Determination', (1993), *NURP* No.13.
Lyons, G.M. and Mastanduno, M., 'International Intervention, State Sovereignty and the Future of International Society', in Lyons, G.M. and Mastanduno, M., *Beyond Westphalia? State Sovereignty and International Intervention*, (1995), JHUP.
MacCormack, N., 'Is Nationalism Philosophically Credible?', in Twining, W. (ed.), *Issues of Self-Determination*, (1991), AbUP, 8.
McCorquodale, R., 'Self-Determination: A Human Rights Approach', (1994), 43 *ICLQ*, 857.
McGoldrick, D., 'Sustainable Development and Human Rights: An Integrated Concept', (1996), 45 *ICLQ*, 796.
McGoldrick, D., 'Yugoslavia - The Responses of the International Community and of International Law', (1996), 49 *CLP*, 375.
McGoldrick, D., 'The Principle of Non-Intervention: Human Rights', in Lowe, V. and Warbrick, W. (eds.), *The United Nations and the Principles of International Law*, (1994), Routledge, 85.
McGoldrick, D., 'The CSCE: From Process to Institution', in McGoldrick, D. and Jackson, B.S. (eds.), *Legal Visions of a New Europe*, (1993), LUP, 135.
McGoldrick, D., 'The Development of The CSCE after the Helsinki 1992 Conference, (1993), 42 *ICLQ*, 411.
McGoldrick, D., 'Canadian Indians, Cultural Rights and the Human-Rights Committee, (1991), 40 *ICLQ*, 658.
Meron, T., 'International Criminalisation of Internal Atrocities', (1995), 89 *AJIL*,

554.

Michalska, A., 'Rights of Peoples to Self-Determination in International Law', in Twining, W. (ed.), *Issues of Self-Determination*, (1991), AbUP, 71.

Morera, R., 'The Appointment of Arbitrators by the International Court of Arbitration', (1996), 2 *ICC/ICA Bull*, 32.

Morphet, S., 'UN Peacekeeping and Election Monitoring', in Roberts, A. and Kingsbury, B. (eds.), *United Nations, Divided World*, (1993), Clarendon, 183.

Mullerson, R., 'The Continuity and Succession of States by Reference to the Former USSR and Yugoslavia', (1993), 42 *ICLQ*, 473.

Murswieck, D., 'The Issue of a Right of Succession Reconsidered', in Tomuschat, C. (ed.), *Modern Law of Self-Determination*, (1993), Nijhoff.

Nagan, W.P., 'Rethinking Bosnia's Right of Self-Defence', (1994), 52 *ICJur*, 34.

Nier, C.L., 'The Yugoslav Civil War: An Analysis of the Applicability of the Laws of War Governing Non-International Armed Conflicts in the Modern World, (1992), 10(2), *DJIL*, 303.

Nowak, M., 'Country-Orientated Human Rights Protection by the UN Commission on Human Rights and its Sub-Commission', (1991), 36 *Neth YIL*, 39.

Nunez, K., 'Rape and Ethnic Warfare', (1993), 5(1) *IJRL*, 111.

O'Brien, J.C.O., 'The International Criminal Tribunal for Yugoslavia', (1993), 87 *AJIL*, 639.

O'Connell, D.P., 'Reflections on the State Succession Convention', (1979), 24 *ZAORV*, 725.

Ofuatey-Kodjoe, 'Self-Determination', in Schachter, O. and Joyner, C.C. (eds.), *United Nations Legal Order*, (1995), CUP, 349.

Onuf, N., 'The Constitution of International Society', (1994), 5 *EJIL*, 1.

Ortakovski, V., 'Violation of IHL in the Armed Conflicts in Croatia and Bosnia-Hercegovina', in Biserko, S., (ed.), *Yugoslavia: Collapse, War and War Crimes*, (1993), BCAWA, 245.

Osterland, H.A., 'National Self-Determination and Secession: The Slovak Model', (1993), 25 *CWRJIL*, 655.

Owen, D., 'The Limits of Enforcement', (1995), *NethILR*, 249

Parra, A.R., '*ICSID* and New Trends in International Dispute Settlement', (1993), 87 *ASIL*, 2.

Parsons, A., 'The UN and the National Interests of States', in Roberts, A. and Kingsbury, B. (eds.), *United Nations, Divided World*, (1993), Clarendon.

Paust, J., 'Democracy and Legitimacy: Is There an Emerging Duty to Ensure a Democratic Government in General and Regional Customary International Law?', (1991), 85 *ASIL*, 98.

Paust, J., 'Self-Determination: A Definitional Focus', in Alexander, Y. and

Friedlander, R.R. (eds.), *Self-Determination: National, Regional and Global Dimensions*, (1980), 13.

Pellet, A., 'L'Activité de la Commission D'Arbitrage de la Conférence Internationale pour L'Ancienne Yougoslavie', (1993), 39 *AFDDI*, 294.

Pellet, A., 'L'Activité de la Commission D'Arbitrage de la Conférence Européene pour la Paix en Yougoslavie', (1992), 38 *AFDDI*, 220.

Pellet, A., 'The Opinions of the Badinter Arbitration Committee: A Second Breath for the Self-Determination of Peoples', (1992), 3 *EJIL*, 178.

Pellet, A., 'Note sur la Commission D'Arbitrage de la Conférence Européene pour la Paix en Yougoslavie', (1991), 37 *AFDDI*, 329.

Perez de Cuellar, J., 'The Role of the UN Secretary-General', in Roberts, A. and Kingsbury, B. (eds.), *United Nations, Divided World*, (1993), Clarendon, 125.

Petrovic, D., 'International Humanitarian Assistance to the Civilian Population of Sarajevo', in Biserko, S. (ed.), *Yugoslavia: Collapse, War, War Crimes*, (1993), BCAWA, 267.

Pinto, M.C.W., 'Thoughts on The "Essence" of International Arbitration', in Muller, S., and Mijs, W., *The Flame Rekindled - New Hopes for International Arbitration*, (1993), Leiden, 46.

Plender, R., 'Rules of Procedure in the International Court and the European Court', (1992), 3 *EUZW*, 1.

Pogany, I., 'The Role of the President of the UN Security Council', (1982), 31 *ICLQ*, 231.

Pomerance, M., 'The Badinter Commission: The Use and Misuse of the International Court of Justice's Jurisprudence', (1998), 20 *MichJIL*, 31.

Pomerance, M., 'The Admission of Judges Ad Hoc in Advisory Proceedings: Some Reflections in Light of the Namibia Case', (1973), 69 *AJIL*, 446.

Provost, R., 'Problems of Indeterminacy and Characterisation in the Application of Humanitarian Law', in Sellers, M. (ed.), *The New World Order: Sovereignty, Human-Rights and the Self-Determination of Peoples*, (1996), OUP.

Ragazzi, M., 'Conference on Yugoslavia Arbitration Commission: Introductory Note', (1992), 31 *ILM*, 1488.

Rama-Montaldo, M., 'International Legal Personality and Implied Powers of International Organisations', (1970), *BYIL*, 111.

Ramcharan, B.G., 'The Bosnian Peace-Accord', (1996), 9 *LJIL*, 131.

Ramet, P., 'The Yugoslav Press in Flux', in Ramet, P. (ed.), *Yugoslavia in The 1980s*, (1985), Westview, 100.

Reisman, W.M., 'The Constitutional Crisis in the UN', (1993), 87 *AJIL*, 83.

Reisman, W.M., 'Sovereignty and Human Rights in Contemporary International Law', (1990), 84 *AJIL*, 866.

Remington, R.A., 'Foreign Policy', in Rusinow, D. (ed.), *Yugoslavia: A Fractured Federalism*, (1988), Wilson.

Remington, R.A., 'Political-Military Relations in Post-Tito Yugoslavia', in Ramet, P. (ed.), *Yugoslavia in the 1980s*, (1985), Westview.

Rich, R., 'Recognition of States: The Collapse of Yugoslavia and the USSR, (1993) 4 *EJIL*, 36.

Rogoff, M.A., 'The Obligation to Negotiate in International Law: Rules and Realities', (1994), 16 *Mich JIL*, 141.

Rosas, A., 'Internal Self-Determination', in Tomuschat, C. (ed.), *Modern Law of Self-Determination*, (1993), Nijhoff.

Rosas, A., 'Internal Conflicts and the CSCE Process', (1992), 3(2) *Helsinki Monitor*, 5

Rosenau, J.N., 'Sovereignty in a Turbulent World', in Lyons, G.M. and Mastanduno, M., *Beyond Westphalia? State Sovereignty and International Intervention*, (1995), JHUP, 191.

Rosenstock, R., 'The Declaration of Principles of International Law Concerning Friendly Relations', (1971), 65 *AJIL*, 43.

Rossanet, B., 'Protecting the Rights of Ethnic and National Communities and Minorities: The Experience of the ICFY', (1994), 2 *IJGR*, 79.

Rowe, P., 'The ICTY: The Decision of the Appeals Chamber on the Interlocutory Appeal on Jurisdiction in the Tadic Case', (1996), 45 *ICLQ*, 691.

Rusinow, D., 'Yugoslavia: Balkan Breakup?', in Forsyth, D.P., *Foreign Policy*, (1992), UNP.

Sahovic, M., 'The Former Yugoslav Federation and International Law', in McDonald, R. (ed.), *Essays in Honour of Wang Tieya*, (1994), Nijhoff, 619.

Sahovic, M., 'International Humanitarian Law in the Yugoslav War', in Biserko, S., (ed.), *Yugoslavia: Collapse, War and War Crimes*, (1993), BCAWA, 141.

Salmon, J., 'Internal Aspects of the Right to Self-Determination: Towards a Democratic Legitimacy Principle?', in Tomuschat, C. (ed.), *Modern Law of Self-Determination*, (1993), Nijhoff, 252.

Sands, P., 'International Law in the Field of Sustainable Development', (1994), 65 *BYIL*, 303.

Schachter, O., 'State Succession: The Once and Future Law', (1993), 33 *VJIL*, 253.

Scharf, M., 'Musical Chairs: The Dissolution of States and Membership in the UN', (1995), 28 *Cornell JIL*, 29.

Schreuer, C., 'The Waning of the Sovereign State: Towards a New Paradigm for International Law?', (1993), 4 *EJIL*, 447.

Schreur, C.H., 'Recommendations and the Traditional Sources of International Law', (1977), *GYIL*, 103.

Scott, C. et al, 'A Memorial for Bosnia: Framework of Legal Arguments Concerning the Lawfulness of the Maintenance of the UN Security Council's

Arms Embargo on Bosnia-Hercegovina', (1994), 16 *MichJIL*, 1.
Scott, S.V., 'International Law as Ideology: Theorising the Relationship Between International Law and International Politics', (1994), 5 *EJIL*, 313.
Senarclens, P., 'The Realist Paradigm and International Conflicts', (1991), 127 *ISSJ*, 5.
Shaw, M.N., 'The Heritage of States: The Principle of *Uti Possidetis Juris* Today', (1996), 67 *BYIL*, 77.
Shelton, D., 'Representative Democracy and Human-Rights in the Western Hemisphere', (1991), 12 *HRLJ*, 353.
Shraga, D. and Zacklin, R., 'The ICTY', (1994), 5(3) *EJIL*, 360.
Simonovcic, I., 'Socialism, Federalism and Ethnic Identity', in Rusinow, D. (ed.), *Yugoslavia: A Fractured Federalism*, (1988), Wilson.
Sinclair, I., 'The Significance of the Friendly Relations Declaration', in Lowe, V. and Warbrick, W. (eds.), *The United Nations and the Principles of International Law*, (1994), Routledge.
Smith, E.M., 'The UN: Meeting the Challenges of the Post-Cold War World', (1993), 87 *ASIL*, 268.
Stanovcic, V., 'History and Status of Ethnic Conflicts', in Rusinow, D. (ed.), *Yugoslavia: A Fractured Federalism*, (1988), Wilson, 23.
Stark, B., 'Postmodern Rhetoric, Economic Rights and an International Text', (1993), 33 *VJIL*, 433.
Steiner, H.J., 'Ideals and Counter-Ideals in the Struggle Over Autonomy Regimes for Minorities', (1991), 66 *NDLRev.*, 1539.
Stopford, M., 'The UN and the New World Disorder', (1994), 34 *VJIL*, 685.
Stromseth, J.E., 'Self-Determination, Secession and Humanitarian Intervention by the UN', (1992), 86 *ASIL*, 370.
Sveinsson, T.H., 'Activities of the Nordic Council 1990-1992', (1993), 36 *GYIL*, 495.
Szasz, P.C., 'Documents on the Yugoslav Conflict', (1992), 31 *ILM*, 1421.
Thornberry, P., 'The Principle of Self-Determination', in Lowe and Warbrick (eds.), *The UN and the Principles of International Law*, (1994), Routledge.
Thornberry, P., 'The Democratic or Internal Aspect of Self-Determination', in Tomuschat, C. (ed.), *Modern Law of Self-Determination*, (1993), Nijhoff.
Thornberry, P., 'Self-Determination, Minorities, Human Rights: A Review of International Instruments', (1989), 38 *ICLQ*, 867.
Tomuschat, C., 'Self-Determination in a Post-Colonial World', in Tomuschat, C. (ed.), *Modern Law of Self-Determination*, (1993), Nijhoff.
Tupman, W.M., 'Challenge and Disqualification of Arbitrators in International Commercial Arbitration', (1989), 38 *ICLQ*, 26.
Turk, D., 'Recognition of States: A Comment', (1993), 4 *EJIL*, 66.
Turns, D., 'War-Crimes in Non-International Armed Conflict', (1995), 7(4) *ASICL*, 804.

Urquhart, B., 'The UN and International Security After the Cold War', in Roberts, A. and Kingsbury, B. (eds.), *United Nations, Divided World*, (1993), Clarendon, 100.

Urquhart, B., 'A Double Standard', (1992), *NYBR*, 123.

Vagts, D.F., 'State Succession: The Codifiers View', (1993), 33 *VJIL*, 295.

Van Boven, T., 'Is There an Emerging Right to Good Governance?', (1995), 13(3) *NethQHR*, 304.

Vego, M., 'The Croatian Forces in Bosnia-Hercegovina', (1993), *JIRev*, 99.

Vego, M., 'Yugoslavia's Ground Forces', (1993), *JIRev*, 247.

Von-Elbe, D., 'Evolution of the Concept of the Just War in International Law', (1939), 33 *AJIL*, 669.

Warbrick, C., 'International Criminal Law', (1995), 44 *ICLQ*, 466.

Warbrick, C., 'The Principle of Sovereign Equality', in Lowe, V. and Warbrick, W. (eds.), *The United Nations and the Principles of International Law*, (1994), Routledge, 204.

Warbrick, C., 'Recognition of States', (1993), 41 *ICLQ*, 473 and 42 *ICLQ*, 432.

Warbrick, C., 'The Theory of International Law: is there an English Contribution?', in Allot, P., Carty, T., Koskenniemi, M., Warbrick, C., *Theory and International Law: An Introduction*, (1991), BIICL/ILG, 47.

Watson, J., S., 'A Realistic Jurisprudence of International Law', *YWA*, (1980), 265.

Weisburd, M., 'The Emptiness of the Concept of *Jus Cogens* as Illustrated by the War in Bosnia-Hercegovina', (1995), 17 *MichJIL*, 1.

Weissbrodt, D., 'The 44th Session of the UNHCR and the Special Session on the Situation in the Former Yugoslavia', (1993), 15 *HRQ*, 123.

Weller, M., 'The EU Within the European Security Architecture', in Koskenniemi, M. (ed.), *International Law Aspects of the European Union*, (1998), Kluwer.

Weller, M., 'The International Response to the Dissolution of the SFRY', (1992), 86 *AJIL*, 569.

Whelan, A., 'Wilsonian Self-Determination and the Versailles Settlement', (1994), 43 *ICLQ*, 99.

White, G., 'The Principle of Good Faith', in Lowe, V. and Warbrick, C. (eds.), *The UN and the Principles of International Law*, (1994), Routledge, 230.

White, N., 'The Legitimacy of NATO Action in Bosnia', (1994), *NLJ*, 649.

White, R.C.A., 'Self-Determination: Time for a Reassessment?', (1981), 28 *Neth ILR*, 225.

Williams, P.R., 'State Succession and International Financial Institutions: Political Criteria Versus Protection of Outstanding Financial Obligations', (1994), 43 *ICLQ*, 777.

Williamson, E.D. and Osborn, J.E., 'A US Perspective on Treaty Succession and Related Issues in the Wake of the Breakup of the USSR and Yugoslavia', (1993) 33 *VJIL*, 261.

Wolfrum, R., 'The International Legal System Following the Bipolar World', (1993), *ASIL*, 153.

Wood, D.P. et al, 'The Internationalisation of Domestic Law: The Shrinking Domaine Réservé', (1993), 87 *ASIL*, 553.

Yee, S., 'The New Constitution of Bosnia-Hercegovina', (1996), 2 *EJIL*, 164.

UN Documents

Resolutions and Reports Relating to the Yugoslav Conflict

Boutros-Ghali, B., Confronting New Challenges - The Secretary-General's Annual Report on the Work of the UN Organisation, (1995), UNDPI.

Boutros-Ghali, B., An Agenda for Peace - Report of the Secretary-General Pursuant to the Statement Adopted by the Summit Meeting of the Security Council on 31st January 1992.

Concept for a Peacekeeping Operation in Yugoslavia, (1991) 31 ILM, 1442.

Dayton General Framework Agreement for Peace in Bosnia-Hercegovina 1995.

Final Report of The UN Commission of Experts Established Pursuant to UNSC Resn. 780, (1992), S/1994/674.

ICTY Prosecutor's Press Releases CC/PIO/013-E (25th July 1995) and CC/PIO/026-E (16th November 1995).

London Conference: Rules of Procedure, (1992).

London Conference: Statement of Principles, (1992).

New Risks for Stability and Security, Security Council Summit Declaration, February 1st 1992.

Reports of the ICFY Steering Committee Co-Chairmen. Amongst these are Report numbers S/26260 of August 6th 1993, S/26922 of 29th December 1993, S/1994/1074 of 19th September 1994, S/1994/1124 of 3rd October 1994, S/1994/1454 of 29th December 1994 and S/1995/175 of 2nd March 1995.

Report of the UN Secretary-General on The ICFY, (1992).

Report of the UN-Secretary General Pursuant to Paragraph 3 of SC Resn.713 (1991), UN Doc S/23169.

Rome Statute of the International Criminal Court.

The United Nations and the Situation in the Former Yugoslavia, (1994), UNDPI.

The Role of The United Nations in the Former Yugoslavia, (1994), UNDPI.

UN-COE Final Report, Annex VI.B - The Battle of Sarajevo and the Law of Armed Conflict, UN Doc. S/1994/674/Add.2.

UN-COE Final Report, Annex IX.B, - Rape Pilot-Study.
UN Commission on Human Rights Special Session Report on the Situation in Former Yugoslavia, (1995), Doc.E/CN.4/1996/57.
UN General Assembly Resns. 45/150 (1990), 46/137 (1991), 47/135 (1992), 48/88 (1993), 48/143 (1993).
UN Human Development Report, (1993), UNDPI.
UN Human Rights Commission Special-Rapporteur Final Report on the Situation on Human Rights in the Territory of the Former Yugoslavia, (1995), UNDPI, E/CN.4/1996/9 and Annexes thereto, E/CN.4/1997/S-1/9:28/8-1992.
UN Secretary-General's Report on Aspects of Establishing an International Tribunal for the Prosecution of Persons Responsible for Serious Violations of International Humanitarian Law Committed in the Former Yugoslavia (1993).
UN Security Council Draft Resn. S/25997, 29th June 1993 and SC Verbatim Record S/PV.3247, 29th June.
UN Security Council Resns. 713, 724, 743, 757, 762, 769, 780, 787, 795, 802, 816, 820, 824, 836, 943 and 1031.
UN Security Council Presidential Statements S/24346, S/PRST/1994/6, S/PRST/1994/6, S/25162

Other UN Resolutions and Reports

Capotorti, F., Study on the Rights of Persons Belonging to Ethnic, Religious and Linguistic Minorities, (1979), UN Publications, Doc.E.78.XIV.1.
Cristescu, A., The Right to Self-Determination: Historical and Current Development on the Basis of UN Instruments, (1981), UN DocE/CN.4/ Sub.2/404.
Espiell, H.G.G., Study for the UN Sub-Commission on Protection of Discrimination and Protection of Minorities of the Commission of Human Rights, (1977), UN Doc. E/CN.4/Sub.2/390.
ILO Convention 169 on Indigenous Tribal Peoples in Independent Countries (1991).
UN General Assembly Resns. 1262(XI) (1958); 1514 (XV) (1960) - Declaration on the Granting of Independence to Colonial Countries and Peoples; 1541 (XV) (1960) - Declaration on Principles Relating to Non-Self-Governing Territories; 1803 (1962) - Declaration on Permanent Sovereignty Over Natural Resources; 2379 (1968); 2625 (XXV) (1970) - Friendly Relations Declaration; 2672-C (XXV) and 3089-D (1973); 31/98 (1976); 45/150 (1990) and 46/137 (1991) - Enhancing the Effectiveness of the Principle of Periodic and Genuine Elections; 47/135 (1992) - Declaration on the Rights of Persons Belonging to National or Ethnic, Religious and Linguistic Minorities.

UN Security Council Resns. 216 and 217 (1965), 221 (1966), 418 (1977) and 556 (1984).

UNESCO International Meeting of Experts on Further Study of the Concept of the Rights of Peoples, (1989), UN Doc.E/CN.4/Sub.2/1992/6.

CSCE Documents

Resolutions and Reports Relating to the Yugoslav Conflict

CPC Consultative Committee Decision, 1st July 1991.

CSCE Statement of 15th April 1992.

CSO Declaration on Bosnia 1992.

CSO Decision of 8th July 1992.

ODIHR Report on Re-Run of Serbian Presidential Election, 7th and 21st December 1997.

ODIHR Report on Republika Srpska National Assembly Elections 22nd-23rd November 1997.

ODIHR Report on Montenegro's Presidential Election of 5th and 19th October 1997.

ODIHR Report on Serbian Parliamentary Elections 21st September 1997 and Presidential Elections of 21st September and 5th October 1997.

ODIHR Report on Bosnia-Hercegovina Municipal Elections Report 13th-14th September 1997.

OSCE Report on Cooperation Among International Institutions: Experiences in Bosnia-Hercegovina, (1997).

OSCE Seminar on Cooperation Between International Institutions: Experiences in Bosnia-Hercegovina, (1997), OSCE.

Report of The CSCE Exploratory Mission to Kosovo, Vojvodina and Sandjak, 13th August 1992.

Report of The CSCE Follow-Up Human-Rights Mission to Yugoslavia: 3rd-9th May 1992.

Report of The CSCE Human-Rights Rapporteur Mission to Yugoslavia: 12th-20th December 1991 and 7th-10th January 1992.

Report of The CSCE Mission to Croatia Established Under the Human-Dimension Mechanism According to Paragraph 12 of the Moscow Document, (1992).

Other Resolutions and Reports

CSCE Budapest Summit Declaration: Towards a Genuine Partnership in a New Europe, (1994).

ODIHR Background Reports, (1997).
ODIHR Semi-Annual Report, (1998), Spring.
OSCE Seminar Within the Framework for the Common and Comprehensive Security Model for Europe for the Twenty-First Century: Regional Security and Cooperation, (1997).
Prague Document on Further Development of CSCE Institutions and Structures: Safeguarding Human-Rights, Democracy and the Rule of Law, (1992).
Report of CSCE Experts on Peaceful Settlement of Disputes, (1991).
Report of the OSCE Conference on Politico-Military Aspects of Security, (1997).
Report on the Role of the High-Commissioner on National Minorities in OSCE Conflict Prevention, (1997).
Statute of the CSCE Court on Conciliation and Arbitration, (1993).
Survey of OSCE Long-Term Missions and Other Field Activities, (1996).
Van Der Stoel, M., 'Reports of the OSCE High Commissioner on National Minorities', (1996) and (1997).

NATO Documents

Kirchberg Declaration, 1994.
Petersberg Declaration, 1992.
Solana, J., 'NATO's Role in Bosnia: Charting a New Course for the Alliance', (1993), 44 *NATO Review*, 3.

EC/EU Documents

Brioni Accord: 8th July 1991.
Council Regulations: 3567/91 (1991); 542/92 (1992); 1432/92 (1992); 3953/92 (1992).
EPC Statements: 26th March (1991); 8th May (1991); 12th June (1991); 5th July (1991); 28th August (1991); 3rd September (1991); 5th October (1991); 6th October (1991); 5th November (1991); 16th December (1991) - Guidelines on Recognition and Declaration on Yugoslavia; 7th January (1992); 15th January (1992) - recognition of Croatia and Slovenia; 6th April (1992) - recognition of Bosnia.
Joint-Statements: EC-USA-USSR 18th October (1991); EC-USA 10th March (1992).
Parliamentary Resolutions: 15th March (1991); 10th October (1991).

Non-Institutional Reports

Asia-Watch, 'Land-Mines in Cambodia: The Coward's War', (1991), PHR.
Amnesty International Report on the Conflicts in the Former Yugoslavia, (1993).
Bosnian State Commission for Gathering Facts on War-Crimes, (1992).
Helsinki Watch, 'War Crimes in Bosnia-Hercegovina', (1992).
ICRC Report, 'Anti-Personnel Mines: Friend or Foe?', (1996).
Sandoz, Y., 'View of The ICRC on the Law of Armed Conflict in a New Strategic Environment', available from http://www.icrc.ch/icrcnews/4312.htm.

Newspaper References

Black, I., 'Nigeria Faces New Action on Abuses', (1996), 24th April, *Guardian*.
Bone, J., 'UN Chief to Appeal for Reform Backing', (1997), 22nd September, *Times*.
Carvel, J., 'EU Halts Aid for Rwanda', (1995), 27th April, *Guardian*.
Castle, S., 'Arkan May Surrender to Extradition', (1999), 15th July, *Independent*.
Coleman, K., 'SAS Kills War-Crimes Suspect in Bosnian Raid', (1997), 11th July, *Guardian*.
Crawshaw, S., 'Commonwealth to Enforce Rights-Code', (1995), 13th November, *Independent*.
Dowden, R., 'Western Troops Leave Somalia', (1994), 19th March, *Guardian*.
Evans, K., 'Reasons for Intervention are the Same: Kuwait's Oil', (1994), 12th October, *Guardian*.
Fairhill, D., 'NATO-Russia Deal on Bosnia Force', (1995), 29th November, *Guardian*.
Khan, H., 'Milosevic Indicted by War Crimes Tribunal', (1999), 1st July, *bosnet*.
Kurin, M., 'Kosovo's Attempted Liberation Crushed', (1998), 14th August, *bosnet*.
Mufson, S., 'Can an Accused War Criminal Deal for Peace?', (1999), 28th May, *Herald Tribune*.
Prentice, E.A., 'One Man Opens Floodgates for Wave of Serbian Protest', (1999), 7th July, *Times*.
Putman, D., 'Cease-Fire Holds in Sri Lanka's 11-Year War', (1995), 9th January, *Guardian*.
Rugman, J., 'Kurds Find Enemy Within is Themselves', (1994), 12th June, *Sunday Times*.
Solomon, B., 'Migrants Get Hint of Power in Turin's Mini-Parliament', (1995), 5th August, *Guardian*.
Steele, J., 'Serbs Forced to Settle for Less', (1999), 4th June, *Guardian*.

Thorpe, N., 'Montenegro Hopes for Amicable Divorce', (1999), 6th July, *Guardian*.

Tran, M., 'Annan Acts to Curb UN Bureaucracy', (1997), 17th July, *Guardian*.

Trueheart, C., 'Hague Indictment Names Serb Chiefs', (1999), 28th May, *Herald Tribune*.

Walker, M., 'Massacre of the Innocent: Britain and Ireland Vow to Crush Splinter IRA', (1998), August 17th, *Times*.

Watt, N. and Capella, P., 'Perilous Return for 1 Million Forced Out of Kosovo', (1999), 4th June, *Guardian*.

Williams, D., 'S-FOR's Mandate Makes Life Uncomfortable for War-Crimes Suspects', (1997), 26th June, *bosnews*.

Miscellaneous Sources

Balkan Odyssey: CD ROM, (1995), Victor Gollancz.

Death of Yugoslavia, (1995), BBC TV Videos.

House of Commons Defence Committee Report: 'The Future of NATO', (1995), HMSO.

Justice in Cataclysm: International Law Conference, Brussels, 20th July 1996.

Index

For Product Safety Concerns and Information please contact our EU representative GPSR@taylorandfrancis.com Taylor & Francis Verlag GmbH, Kaufingerstraße 24, 80331 München, Germany

Batch number: 10726013

Printed by Printforce, the Netherlands